THE GREEN LANTERN GREEN ARROW

COLLECTION

VOLUME TWO

DENNIS O'NEIL / ELLIOT S! MAGGIN
WRITERS

NEAL ADAMS
PENCILLER

DICK GIORDANO / BERNIE WRIGHTSON
INKERS

**CORY ADAMS / JACK ADLER
TANYA AND RICHARD HORIE**
COLORISTS

JOHN COSTANZA / JOE LETTERESE
LETTERERS

GREEN LANTERN/GREEN ARROW VOLUME TWO

Published by DC Comics. Cover, introduction and compilation
copyright © 2004 DC Comics. All Rights Reserved.

Originally published in single magazine form in GREEN LANTERN 83-87,
89, FLASH 217-219, 226. Copyright © 1971, 1972, 1973, 1974, 1992,
1993, 2000 DC Comics. All Rights Reserved. All characters, their
distinctive likenesses and related elements featured in this publication
are trademarks of DC Comics. The stories, characters, and incidents
featured in this publication are entirely fictional. DC Comics does not
read or accept unsolicited submissions of ideas, stories, or artwork.

DC Comics, 1700 Broadway, New York, NY 10019
A Warner Bros. Entertainment Company
Printed in Canada. First Printing.
ISBN: 1-4012-0230-6

Cover illustration by Neal Adams.

TABLE OF
CONTENTS

INTRODUCTION BY

DICK GIORDANO

It was the sixties and the winds of change swept through our society. Some of the change was superficial: we let our hair grow longer, men especially; we dressed in a way radically different (and office dress codes have never been quite the same). But the real change was in how we thought and felt. It was the dawn of the communications age, and the massive new influx of information caused us to reexamine every aspect of our lives. No longer was the acceptance of prior values automatic; we questioned every situation that smelled of the status quo. Seemingly overnight a generation developed a social conscience. Everyone was involved in scrutinizing man's inhumanity to man and designing a course of action to curtail these immoral activities. Activists sought to lead us out of ignorance and into an era of enlightenment so that we could see, and deal with, our social ills. If we worked hard enough we could find ways to end racial discrimination, war, sexual repression, abuse of authority, drug addiction, street crime and political skulduggery. If we worked hard enough....

As is often the case, popular entertainment was at the forefront of the crusade: film, television news, drama and rock and roll music all led the charge. All felt that they had to try to show us the way. If a way existed.

Simultaneously, comics came of age.

Almost from its birth, the comic book was thought to be nothing more than escapist literature for preadolescents. Creators were interchangeable and generally were not encouraged to pursue or illuminate their personal causes in their work. Crime and espionage were about the only socially aberrant behaviors detailed in adventure comic stories, and the denouement was typically an act of violence in which the good guy subdued the bad guy, making the world a better place — until next issue, anyway. In the early sixties, Stan Lee, Steve Ditko and Jack Kirby expanded the comics tableau by adding real-world personalities with real-world personal problems to their characters and the flawed, but nevertheless pure-of-heart, hero was born.

In the mid-sixties, Denny O'Neil, Neal Adams and editor Julie Schwartz teamed up to revitalize Green Lantern. The result was a comic in which social issues that concerned the creators could be dramatized and become the basis for a series of action-adventure stories. Julie, ever the visionary, agreed with the then-radical idea and the very special, award-winning Green Lantern/Green Arrow opus began with the publication of GREEN LANTERN #76. (That's how the indicia read: the cover sported the now familiar but brand-new at the time, Green Lantern/Green Arrow logo).

And what a journey it was! I was lucky enough to be along for the ride in two ways. I was an editor at DC at the time and shared an office with Julie. In addition, I was often (but not always) the inker for the series. And my work on it still ranks as some of the most exciting work I've done in the industry. I was overjoyed to be a part (albeit a minor one) of an event — a happening. I knew the series would have an historic impact on the comics scene even before the accolades and awards started rolling in.

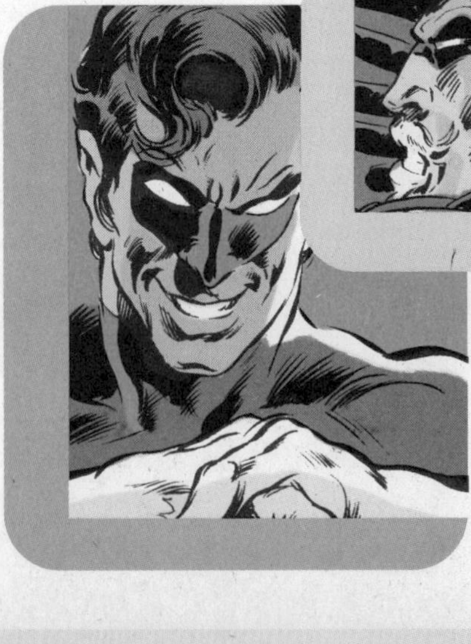

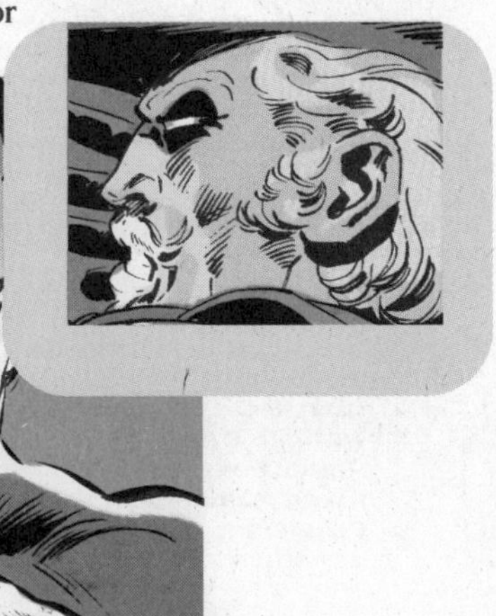

The popularity of Green Lantern/Green Arrow inspired a host of other creators to include social issues as backdrops for their stories. Management, ever mindful of the commercial value of a fresh creative approach, ordered more editors to try the "we care about important issues" approach to storytelling. Some titles worked, some didn't fare so well. But this groundbreaking series did have an effect on the way comics stories were written from that time on: sophisticated characterization, plot lines and storytelling techniques replaced the old way — a story told in a linear fashion with a two-dimensional hero involved in a simplistic Good vs. Evil struggle. The series also solidly established the creative reputations of Denny, Neal and to a degree, yours truly.

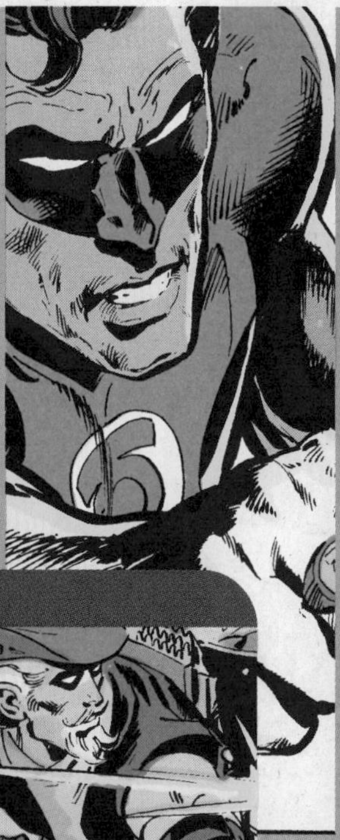

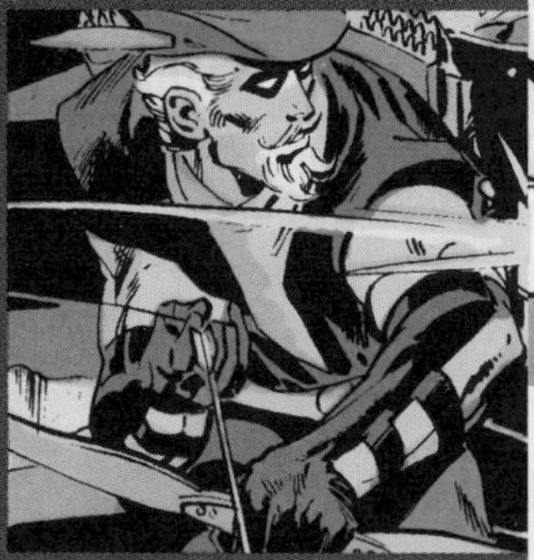

I'd like to close with some reminiscences. Most of these are personal and didn't have much impact on anything. Sort of. I was there and this is what I was thinking, doing, or saying. Real trivial stuff, trust me. In no particular order, then, I remember:

After issue #85, the first of a two-part story detailing Speedy's drug addiction, we received a letter from Mayor John V. Lindsay of New York commending our contribution in the war against drugs. The letter was published in GL/GA #86.

Julie Schwartz showing off the cover of #82 to a group of us milling in the hall. The cover depicted Green Arrow and Green Lantern being attacked by beasts that were half women, half birds. Julie admitting he hadn't yet worked out the cover copy. I turned to walk away, chanting, "The harpies are coming, the harpies are coming" (paraphrasing a popular movie of the day, *The Russians are Coming! The Russians are Coming!*). That turned out to be the cover copy. I was (am!) pleased.

Getting a giggle when I realized that heavies Sybil and Grandy in issue #83 looked an awful lot like President Richard Nixon and Vice President Spiro Agnew. Neither was popular with artist Neal Adams.

My lying in bed, real sick, with the pencil art for #84 on my desk downstairs, late, awaiting my recuperation. The doorbell rang. I could hear Sol Harrison (then DC's production manager, my close friend and a next-town neighbor) talking to my wife Marie. He left shortly and Marie came up to tell me the news. They couldn't wait for me to get better. The book was very late. They took the pages and Bernie Wrightson did a great job inking them.

But I really wanted to ink that job. Sigh.

Getting awards for inking the series. I loved the attention. And I think I mostly done good stuff. But I'm still surprised (as I was then) to see how closely I was associated with the Green Lantern/Green Arrow series when in fact I only inked about half the issues, starting with the fifth issue (#80). Even that one was co-inked with Mike Peppe, who wasn't credited.

I inked six issues.

Go figure.

Thank you and Good Afternoon.

Dick Giordano
1993

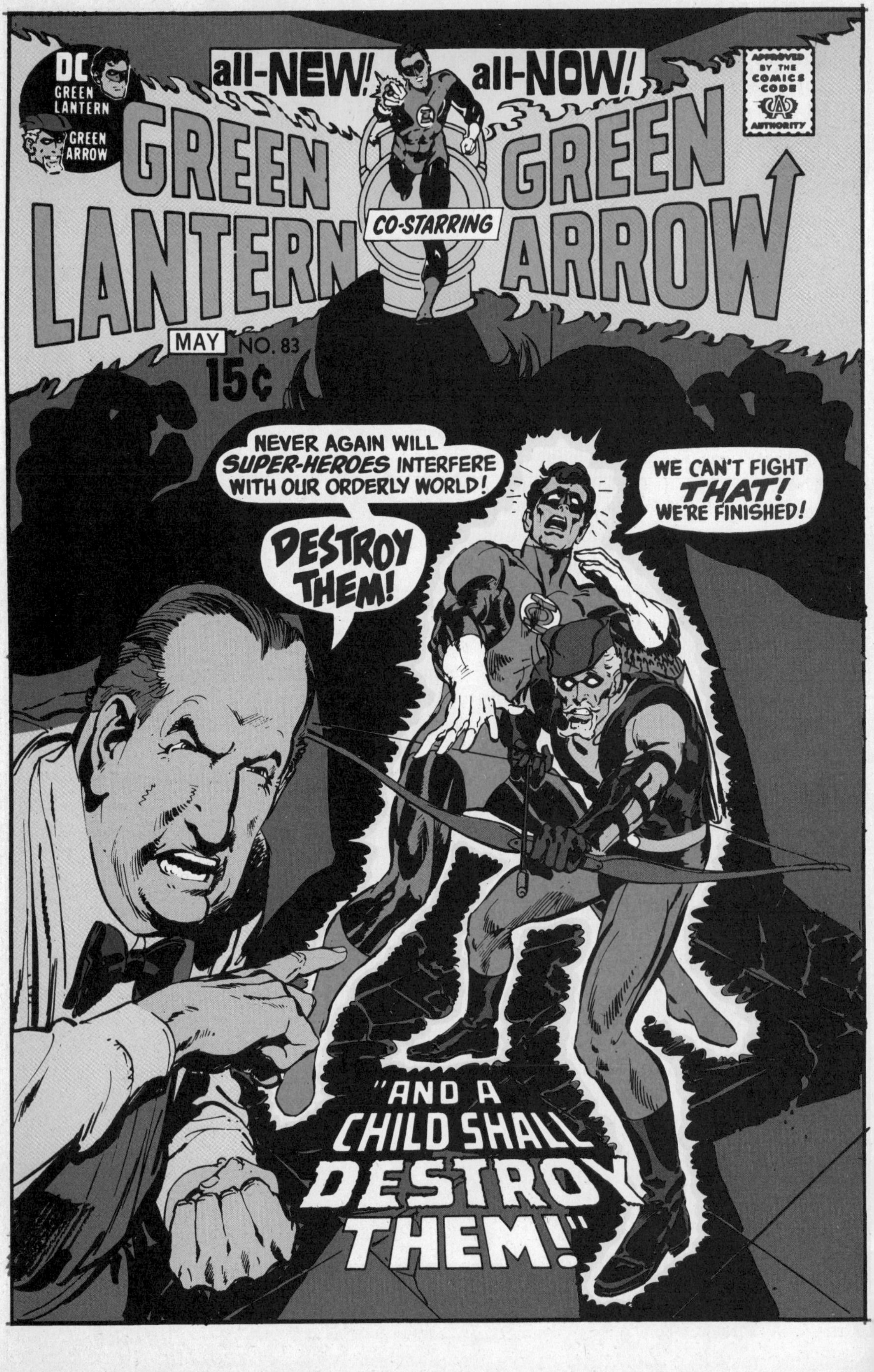
DC
GREEN LANTERN
GREEN ARROW
all-NEW! all-NOW!
APPROVED BY THE COMICS CODE AUTHORITY
GREEN LANTERN
CO-STARRING
GREEN ARROW
MAY
NO. 83
15¢
NEVER AGAIN WILL SUPER-HEROES INTERFERE WITH OUR ORDERLY WORLD!
DESTROY THEM!
WE CAN'T FIGHT THAT! WE'RE FINISHED!
"AND A CHILD SHALL DESTROY THEM!"

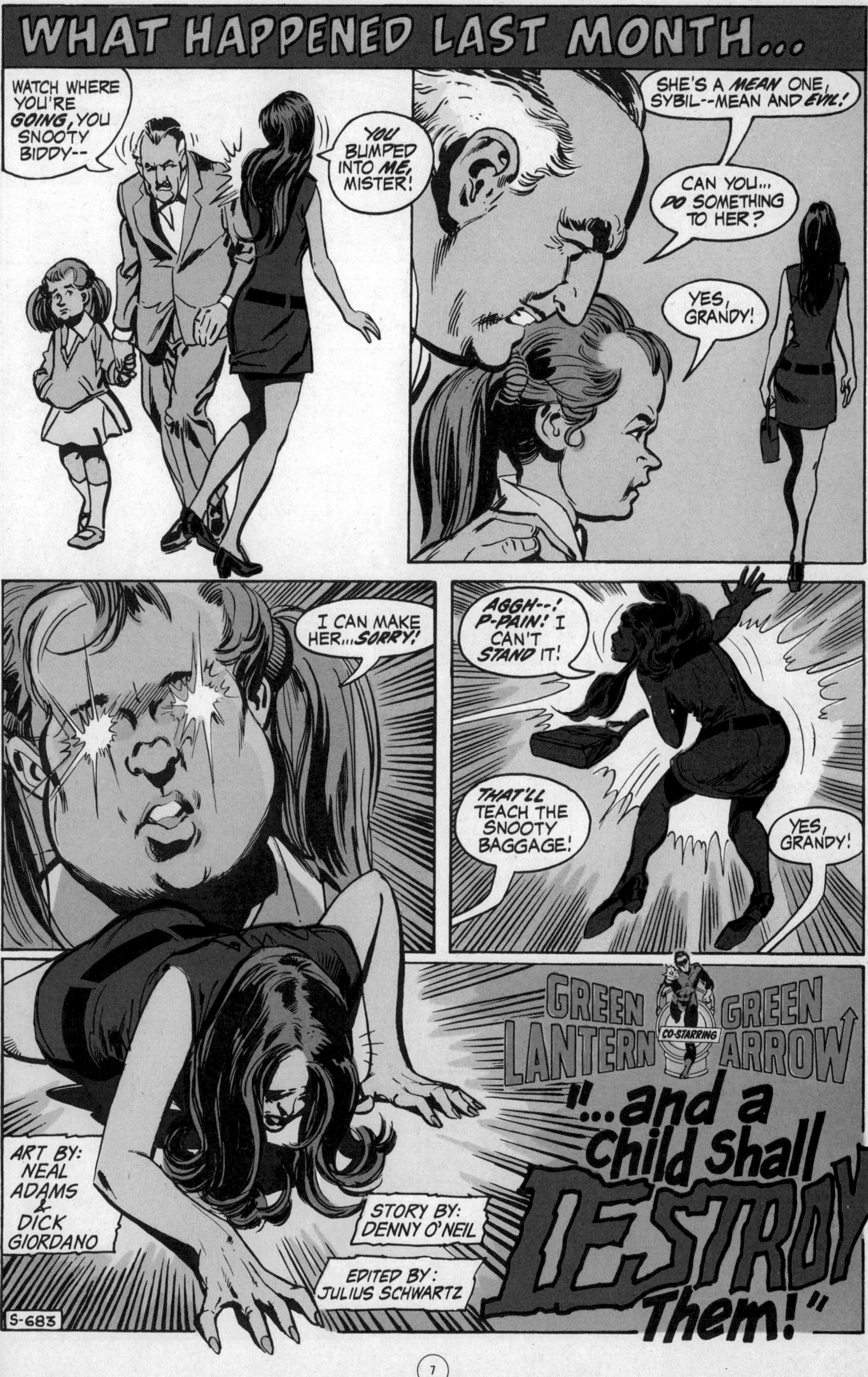

WHAT HAPPENED LAST MONTH...
WATCH WHERE YOU'RE GOING, YOU SNOOTY BIDDY--
YOU BUMPED INTO ME, MISTER!
SHE'S A MEAN ONE, SYBIL--MEAN AND EVIL!
CAN YOU... DO SOMETHING TO HER?
YES, GRANDY!
I CAN MAKE HER... SORRY!
AGGH--! P-PAIN! I CAN'T STAND IT!
THAT'LL TEACH THE SNOOTY BAGGAGE!
YES, GRANDY!
GREEN LANTERN CO-STARRING GREEN ARROW
"...and a Child Shall DESTROY Them!"
ART BY: NEAL ADAMS & DICK GIORDANO
STORY BY: DENNY O'NEIL
EDITED BY: JULIUS SCHWARTZ
S-683

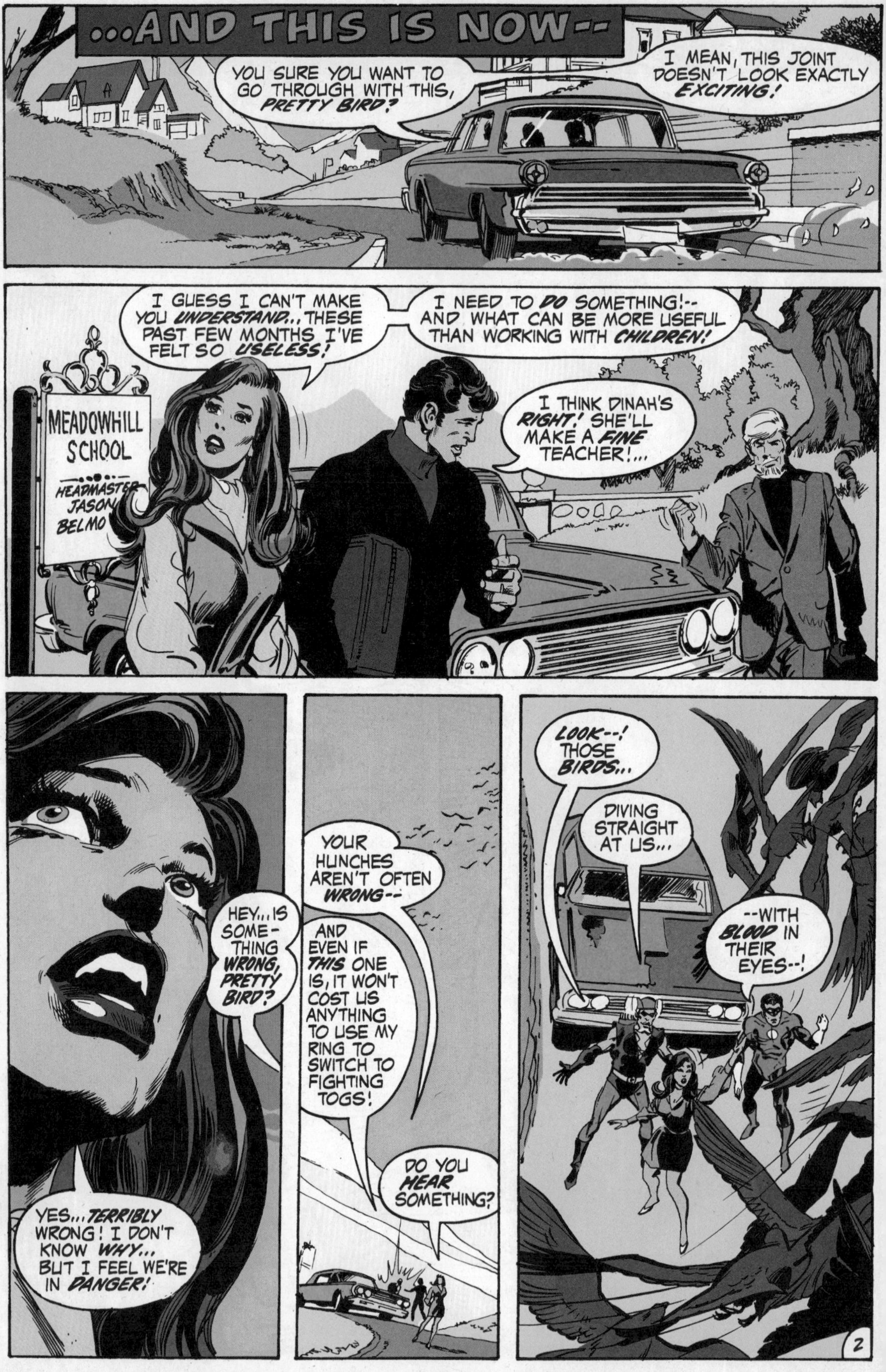
...AND THIS IS NOW--
YOU SURE YOU WANT TO GO THROUGH WITH THIS, PRETTY BIRD?
I MEAN, THIS JOINT DOESN'T LOOK EXACTLY EXCITING!
I GUESS I CAN'T MAKE YOU UNDERSTAND... THESE PAST FEW MONTHS I'VE FELT SO USELESS!
I NEED TO DO SOMETHING!-- AND WHAT CAN BE MORE USEFUL THAN WORKING WITH CHILDREN!
MEADOWHILL SCHOOL
HEADMASTER JASON BELMO
I THINK DINAH'S RIGHT! SHE'LL MAKE A FINE TEACHER!...
HEY... IS SOMETHING WRONG, PRETTY BIRD?
YES... TERRIBLY WRONG! I DON'T KNOW WHY... BUT I FEEL WE'RE IN DANGER!
YOUR HUNCHES AREN'T OFTEN WRONG--
AND EVEN IF THIS ONE IS, IT WON'T COST US ANYTHING TO USE MY RING TO SWITCH TO FIGHTING TOGS!
DO YOU HEAR SOMETHING?
LOOK--! THOSE BIRDS...
DIVING STRAIGHT AT US...
--WITH BLOOD IN THEIR EYES--!
2

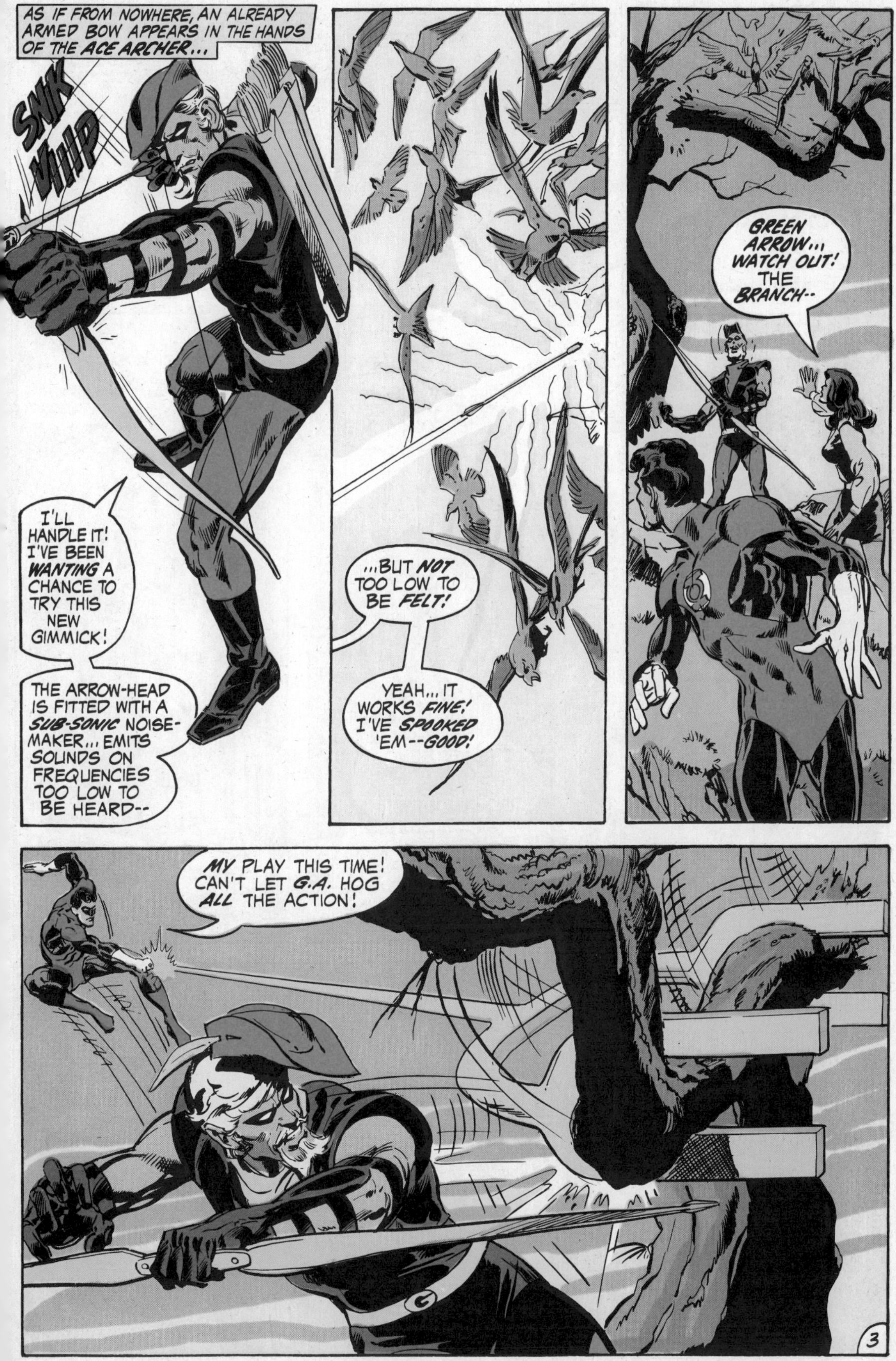
AS IF FROM NOWHERE, AN ALREADY ARMED BOW APPEARS IN THE HANDS OF THE ACE ARCHER...
SNIK
VIIIP
I'LL HANDLE IT! I'VE BEEN WANTING A CHANCE TO TRY THIS NEW GIMMICK!
THE ARROW-HEAD IS FITTED WITH A SUB-SONIC NOISE-MAKER... EMITS SOUNDS ON FREQUENCIES TOO LOW TO BE HEARD--
...BUT NOT TOO LOW TO BE FELT!
YEAH... IT WORKS FINE! I'VE SPOOKED 'EM--GOOD!
GREEN ARROW... WATCH OUT! THE BRANCH--
MY PLAY THIS TIME! CAN'T LET G.A. HOG ALL THE ACTION!
3

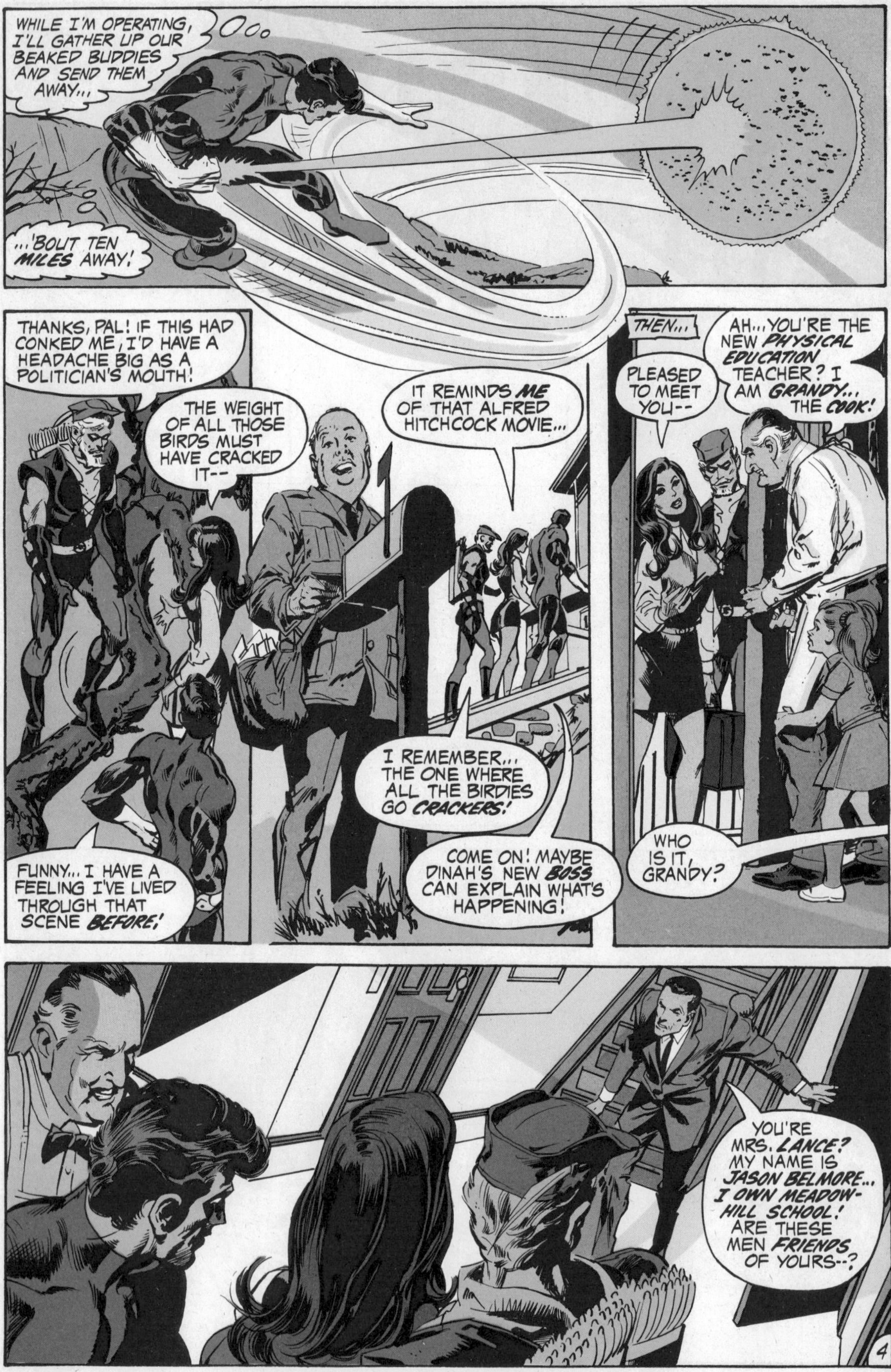
WHILE I'M OPERATING, I'LL GATHER UP OUR BEAKED BUDDIES AND SEND THEM AWAY...
...'BOUT TEN MILES AWAY!
THANKS, PAL! IF THIS HAD CONKED ME, I'D HAVE A HEADACHE BIG AS A POLITICIAN'S MOUTH!
THE WEIGHT OF ALL THOSE BIRDS MUST HAVE CRACKED IT--
FUNNY... I HAVE A FEELING I'VE LIVED THROUGH THAT SCENE BEFORE!
IT REMINDS ME OF THAT ALFRED HITCHCOCK MOVIE...
I REMEMBER... THE ONE WHERE ALL THE BIRDIES GO CRACKERS!
COME ON! MAYBE DINAH'S NEW BOSS CAN EXPLAIN WHAT'S HAPPENING!
THEN...
PLEASED TO MEET YOU--
AH... YOU'RE THE NEW PHYSICAL EDUCATION TEACHER? I AM GRANDY... THE COOK!
WHO IS IT, GRANDY?
YOU'RE MRS. LANCE? MY NAME IS JASON BELMORE... I OWN MEADOW-HILL SCHOOL! ARE THESE MEN FRIENDS OF YOURS--?
4

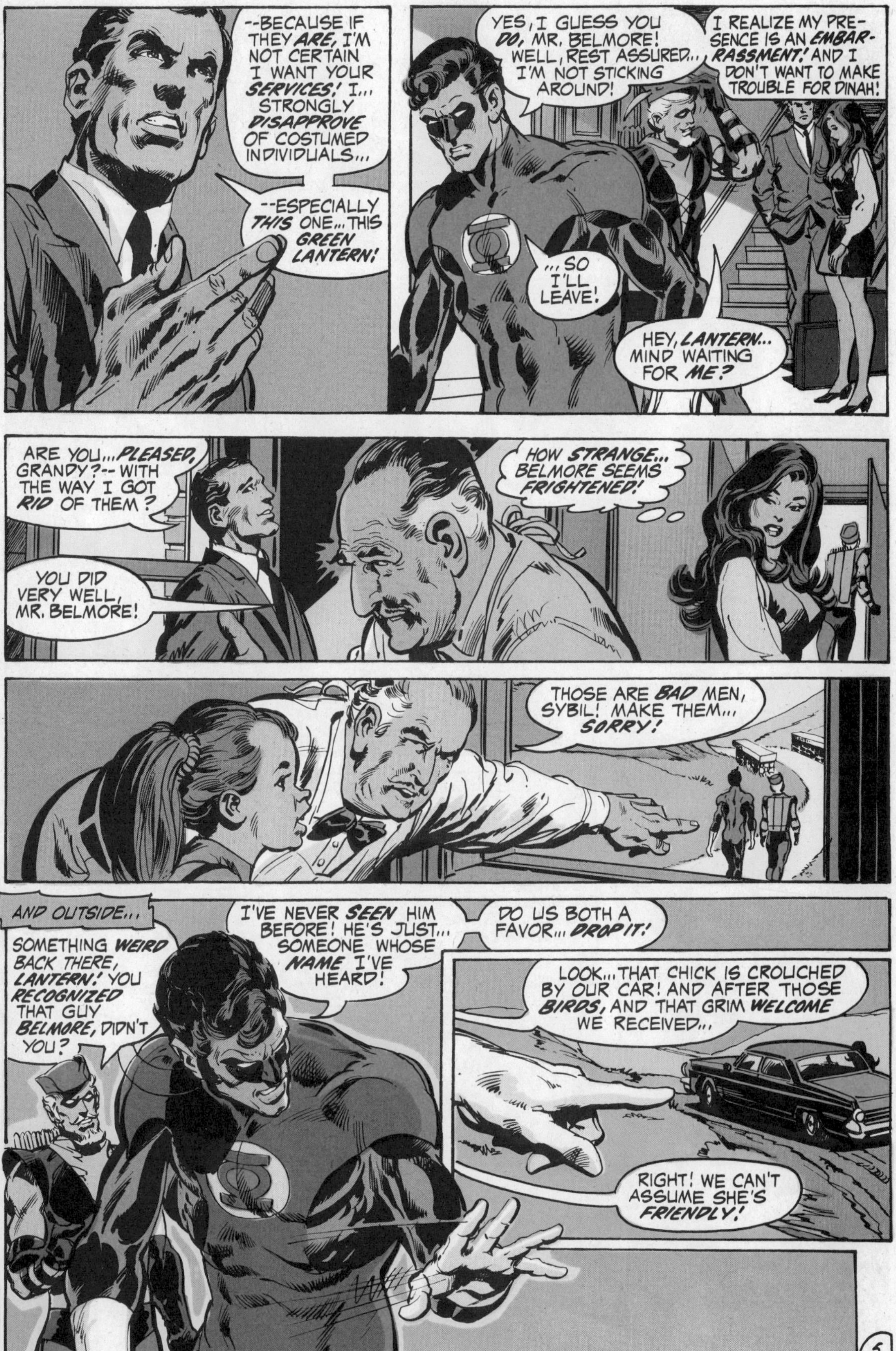
--BECAUSE IF THEY ARE, I'M NOT CERTAIN I WANT YOUR SERVICES! I... STRONGLY DISAPPROVE OF COSTUMED INDIVIDUALS...
--ESPECIALLY THIS ONE... THIS GREEN LANTERN!
YES, I GUESS YOU DO, MR. BELMORE! WELL, REST ASSURED... I'M NOT STICKING AROUND!
I REALIZE MY PRESENCE IS AN EMBARRASSMENT! AND I DON'T WANT TO MAKE TROUBLE FOR DINAH!
...SO I'LL LEAVE!
HEY, LANTERN... MIND WAITING FOR ME?
ARE YOU... PLEASED, GRANDY?-- WITH THE WAY I GOT RID OF THEM?
YOU DID VERY WELL, MR. BELMORE!
HOW STRANGE... BELMORE SEEMS FRIGHTENED!
THOSE ARE BAD MEN, SYBIL! MAKE THEM... SORRY!
AND OUTSIDE...
SOMETHING WEIRD BACK THERE, LANTERN! YOU RECOGNIZED THAT GUY BELMORE, DIDN'T YOU?
I'VE NEVER SEEN HIM BEFORE! HE'S JUST... SOMEONE WHOSE NAME I'VE HEARD!
DO US BOTH A FAVOR... DROP IT!
LOOK... THAT CHICK IS CROUCHED BY OUR CAR! AND AFTER THOSE BIRDS, AND THAT GRIM WELCOME WE RECEIVED...
RIGHT! WE CAN'T ASSUME SHE'S FRIENDLY!
5

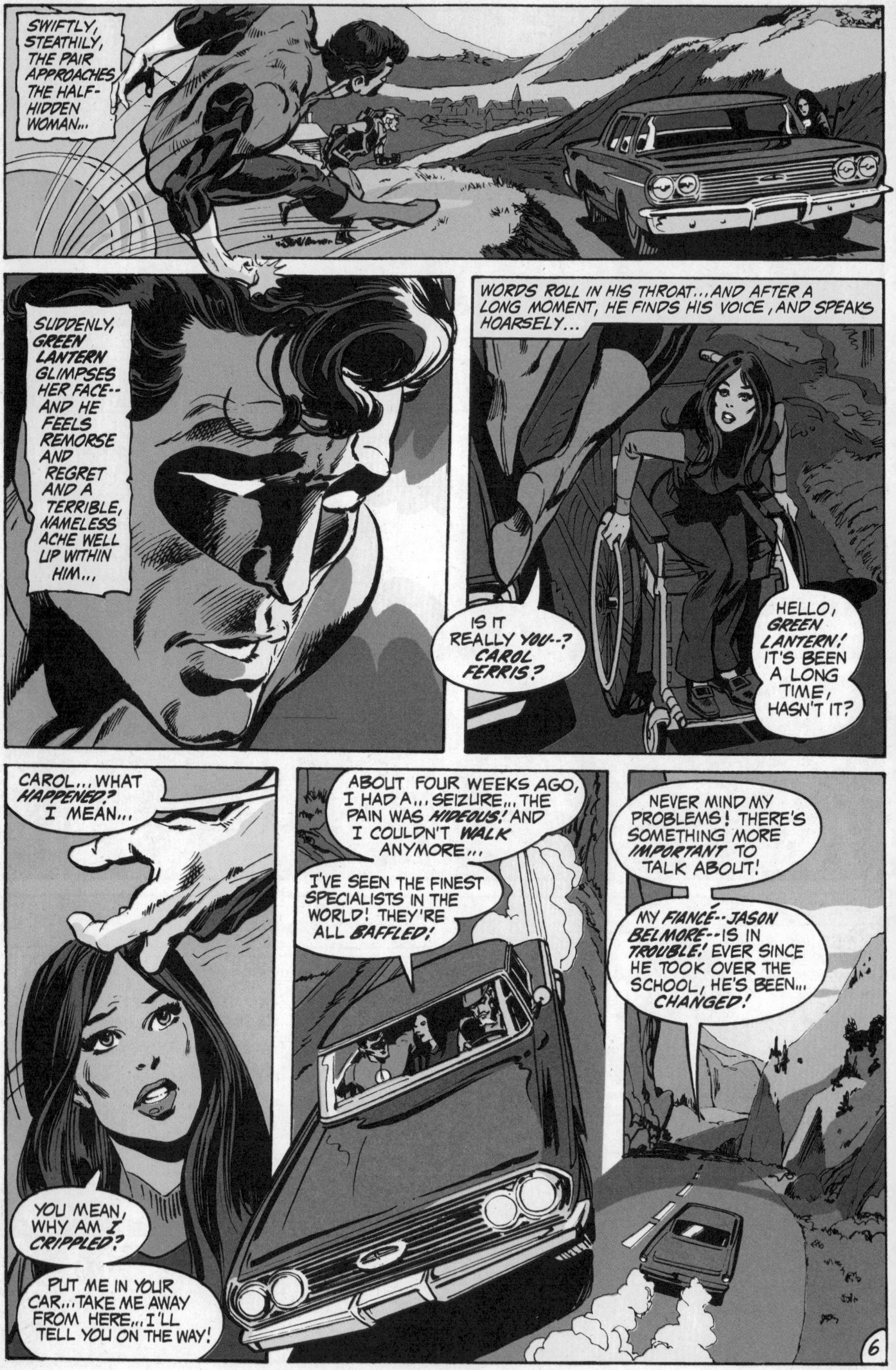
SWIFTLY, STEATHILY, THE PAIR APPROACHES THE HALF-HIDDEN WOMAN...
SUDDENLY, GREEN LANTERN GLIMPSES HER FACE-- AND HE FEELS REMORSE AND REGRET AND A TERRIBLE, NAMELESS ACHE WELL UP WITHIN HIM...
WORDS ROLL IN HIS THROAT... AND AFTER A LONG MOMENT, HE FINDS HIS VOICE, AND SPEAKS HOARSELY...
IS IT REALLY YOU--? CAROL FERRIS?
HELLO, GREEN LANTERN! IT'S BEEN A LONG TIME, HASN'T IT?
CAROL... WHAT HAPPENED? I MEAN...
YOU MEAN, WHY AM I CRIPPLED?
PUT ME IN YOUR CAR... TAKE ME AWAY FROM HERE... I'LL TELL YOU ON THE WAY!
ABOUT FOUR WEEKS AGO, I HAD A... SEIZURE... THE PAIN WAS HIDEOUS! AND I COULDN'T WALK ANYMORE...
I'VE SEEN THE FINEST SPECIALISTS IN THE WORLD! THEY'RE ALL BAFFLED!
NEVER MIND MY PROBLEMS! THERE'S SOMETHING MORE IMPORTANT TO TALK ABOUT!
MY FIANCÉ--JASON BELMORE--IS IN TROUBLE! EVER SINCE HE TOOK OVER THE SCHOOL, HE'S BEEN... CHANGED!
6

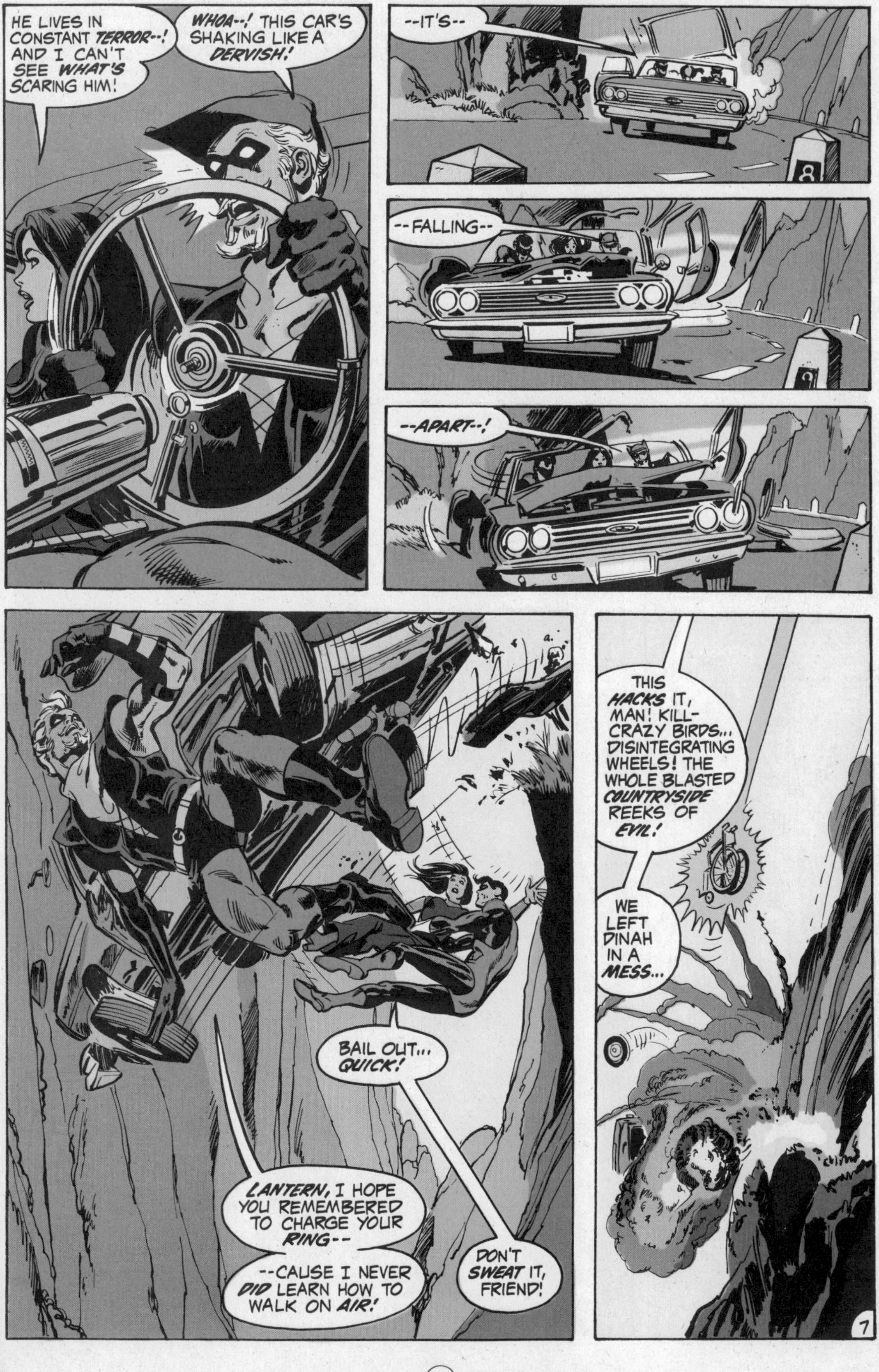
HE LIVES IN CONSTANT TERROR--! AND I CAN'T SEE WHAT'S SCARING HIM!
WHOA--! THIS CAR'S SHAKING LIKE A DERVISH!
--IT'S--
--FALLING--
--APART--!
BAIL OUT... QUICK!
LANTERN, I HOPE YOU REMEMBERED TO CHARGE YOUR RING--
--CAUSE I NEVER DID LEARN HOW TO WALK ON AIR!
DON'T SWEAT IT, FRIEND!
THIS HACKS IT, MAN! KILL-CRAZY BIRDS... DISINTEGRATING WHEELS! THE WHOLE BLASTED COUNTRYSIDE REEKS OF EVIL!
WE LEFT DINAH IN A MESS...
7

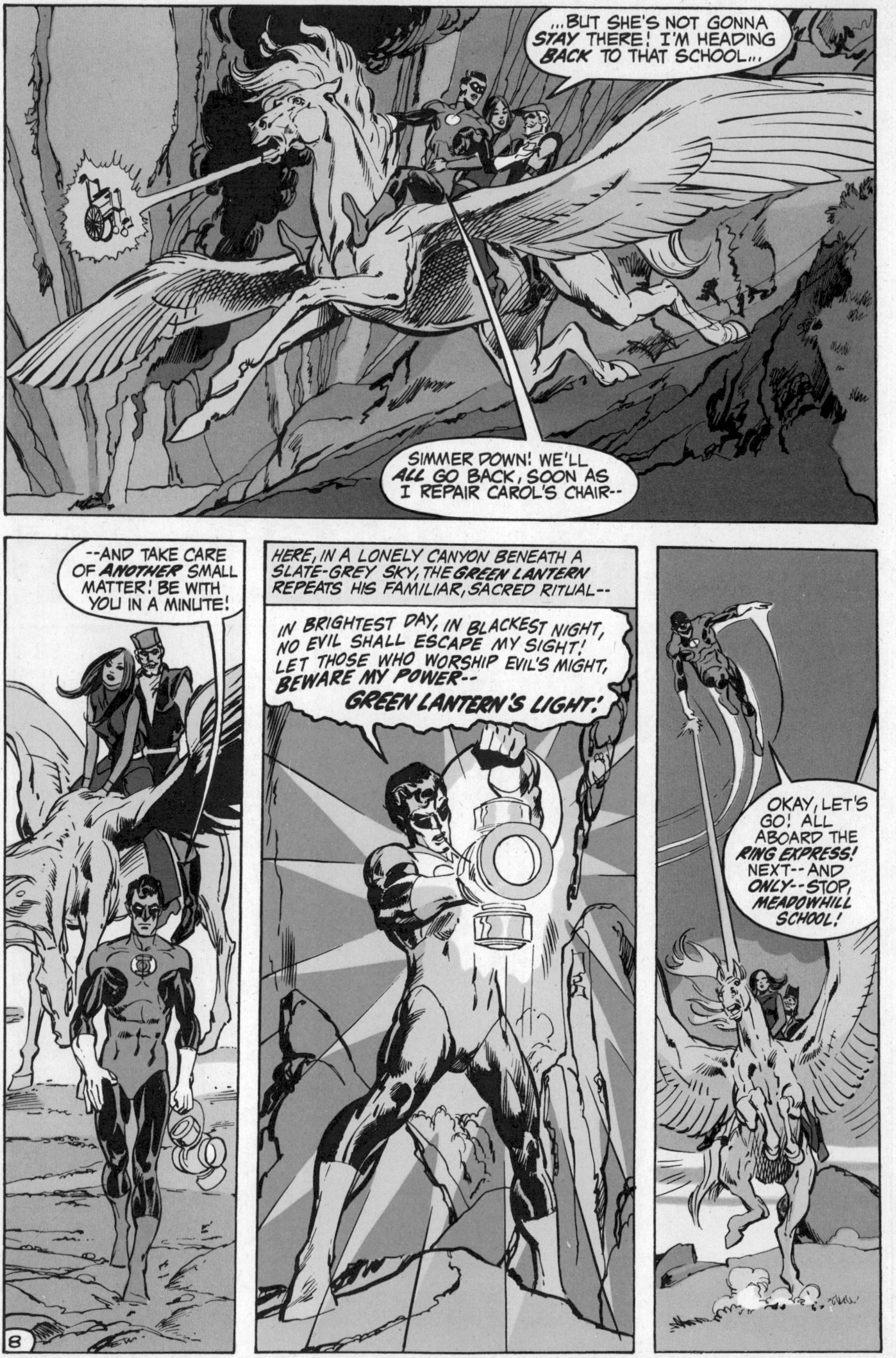
...BUT SHE'S NOT GONNA STAY THERE! I'M HEADING BACK TO THAT SCHOOL...
SIMMER DOWN! WE'LL ALL GO BACK, SOON AS I REPAIR CAROL'S CHAIR--
--AND TAKE CARE OF ANOTHER SMALL MATTER! BE WITH YOU IN A MINUTE!
8
HERE, IN A LONELY CANYON BENEATH A SLATE-GREY SKY, THE GREEN LANTERN REPEATS HIS FAMILIAR, SACRED RITUAL--
IN BRIGHTEST DAY, IN BLACKEST NIGHT, NO EVIL SHALL ESCAPE MY SIGHT! LET THOSE WHO WORSHIP EVIL'S MIGHT, BEWARE MY POWER-- GREEN LANTERN'S LIGHT!
OKAY, LET'S GO! ALL ABOARD THE RING EXPRESS! NEXT--AND ONLY--STOP, MEADOWHILL SCHOOL!

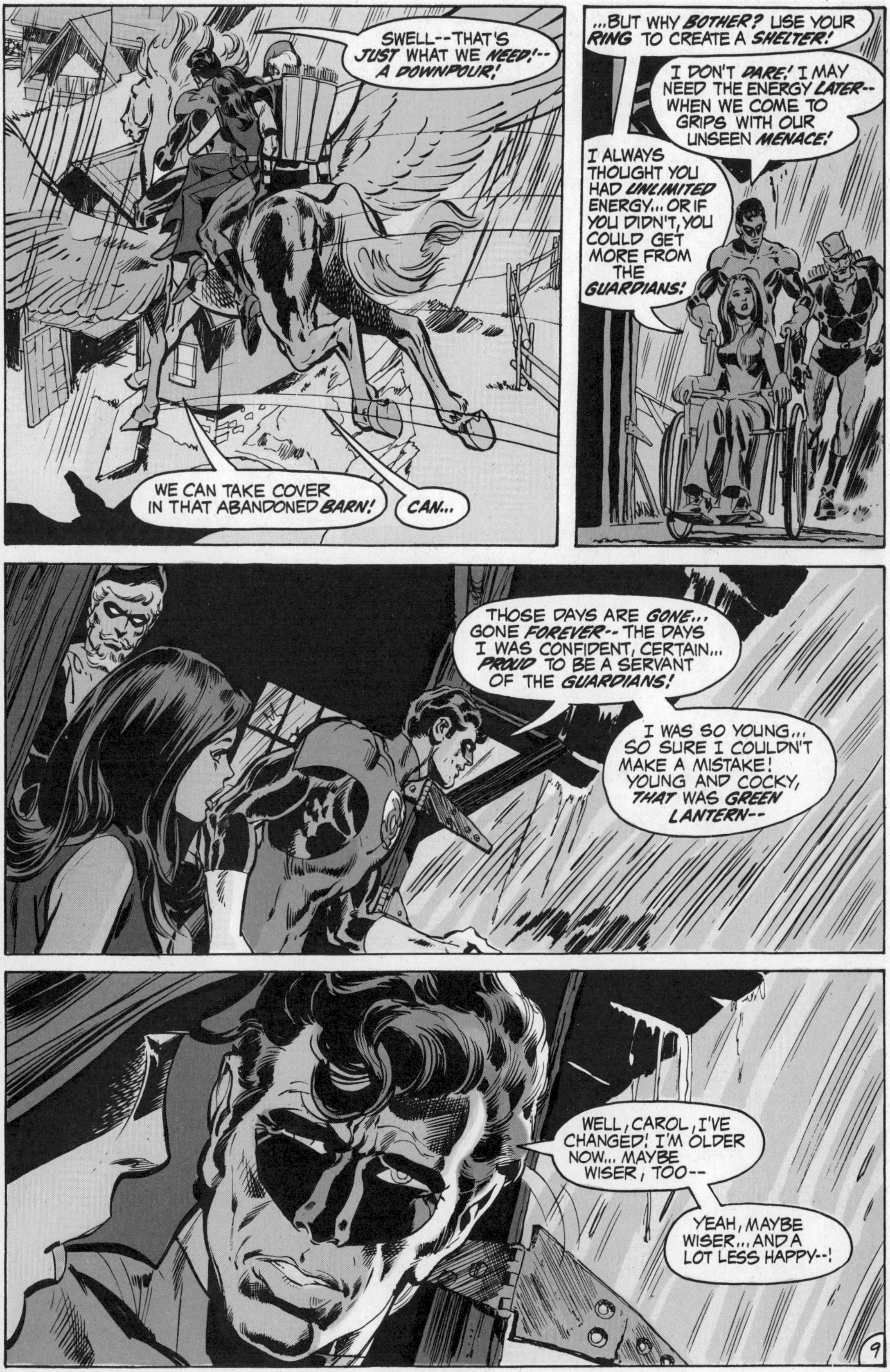
SWELL--THAT'S JUST WHAT WE NEED!-- A DOWNPOUR!
WE CAN TAKE COVER IN THAT ABANDONED BARN!
CAN...
...BUT WHY BOTHER? USE YOUR RING TO CREATE A SHELTER!
I DON'T DARE! I MAY NEED THE ENERGY LATER-- WHEN WE COME TO GRIPS WITH OUR UNSEEN MENACE!
I ALWAYS THOUGHT YOU HAD UNLIMITED ENERGY... OR IF YOU DIDN'T, YOU COULD GET MORE FROM THE GUARDIANS!
THOSE DAYS ARE GONE... GONE FOREVER-- THE DAYS I WAS CONFIDENT, CERTAIN... PROUD TO BE A SERVANT OF THE GUARDIANS!
I WAS SO YOUNG... SO SURE I COULDN'T MAKE A MISTAKE! YOUNG AND COCKY, THAT WAS GREEN LANTERN--
WELL, CAROL, I'VE CHANGED! I'M OLDER NOW... MAYBE WISER, TOO--
YEAH, MAYBE WISER... AND A LOT LESS HAPPY--!
9

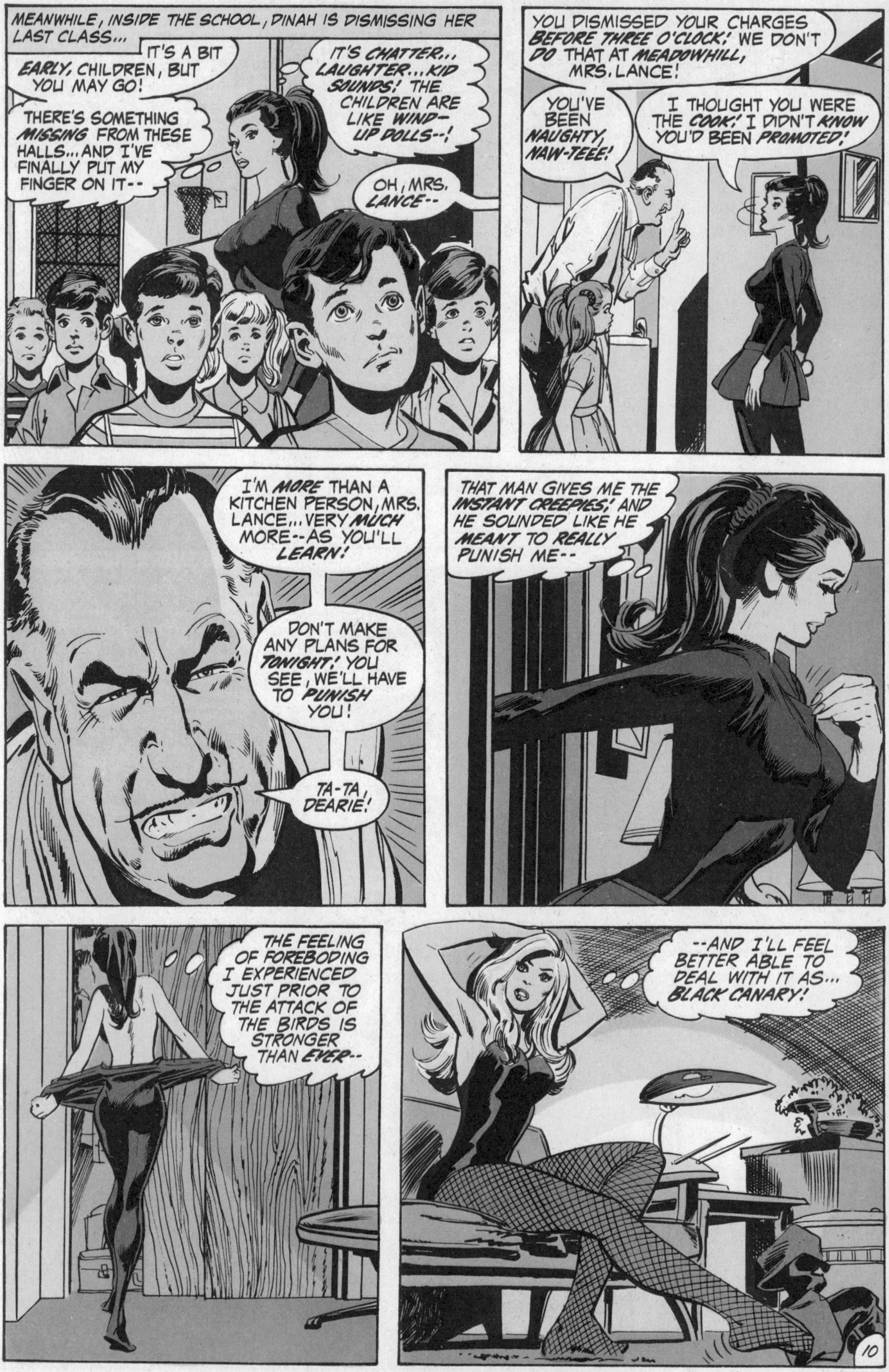

MEANWHILE, INSIDE THE SCHOOL, DINAH IS DISMISSING HER LAST CLASS...
IT'S A BIT EARLY, CHILDREN, BUT YOU MAY GO!
THERE'S SOMETHING MISSING FROM THESE HALLS... AND I'VE FINALLY PUT MY FINGER ON IT--
IT'S CHATTER... LAUGHTER... KID SOUNDS! THE CHILDREN ARE LIKE WIND-UP DOLLS--!
OH, MRS. LANCE--
YOU DISMISSED YOUR CHARGES BEFORE THREE O'CLOCK! WE DON'T DO THAT AT MEADOWHILL, MRS. LANCE!
YOU'VE BEEN NAUGHTY, NAW-TEEE!
I THOUGHT YOU WERE THE COOK! I DIDN'T KNOW YOU'D BEEN PROMOTED!
I'M MORE THAN A KITCHEN PERSON, MRS. LANCE... VERY MUCH MORE--AS YOU'LL LEARN!
DON'T MAKE ANY PLANS FOR TONIGHT! YOU SEE, WE'LL HAVE TO PUNISH YOU!
TA-TA, DEARIE!
THAT MAN GIVES ME THE INSTANT CREEPIES! AND HE SOUNDED LIKE HE MEANT TO REALLY PUNISH ME--
THE FEELING OF FOREBODING I EXPERIENCED JUST PRIOR TO THE ATTACK OF THE BIRDS IS STRONGER THAN EVER--
--AND I'LL FEEL BETTER ABLE TO DEAL WITH IT AS... BLACK CANARY!
10

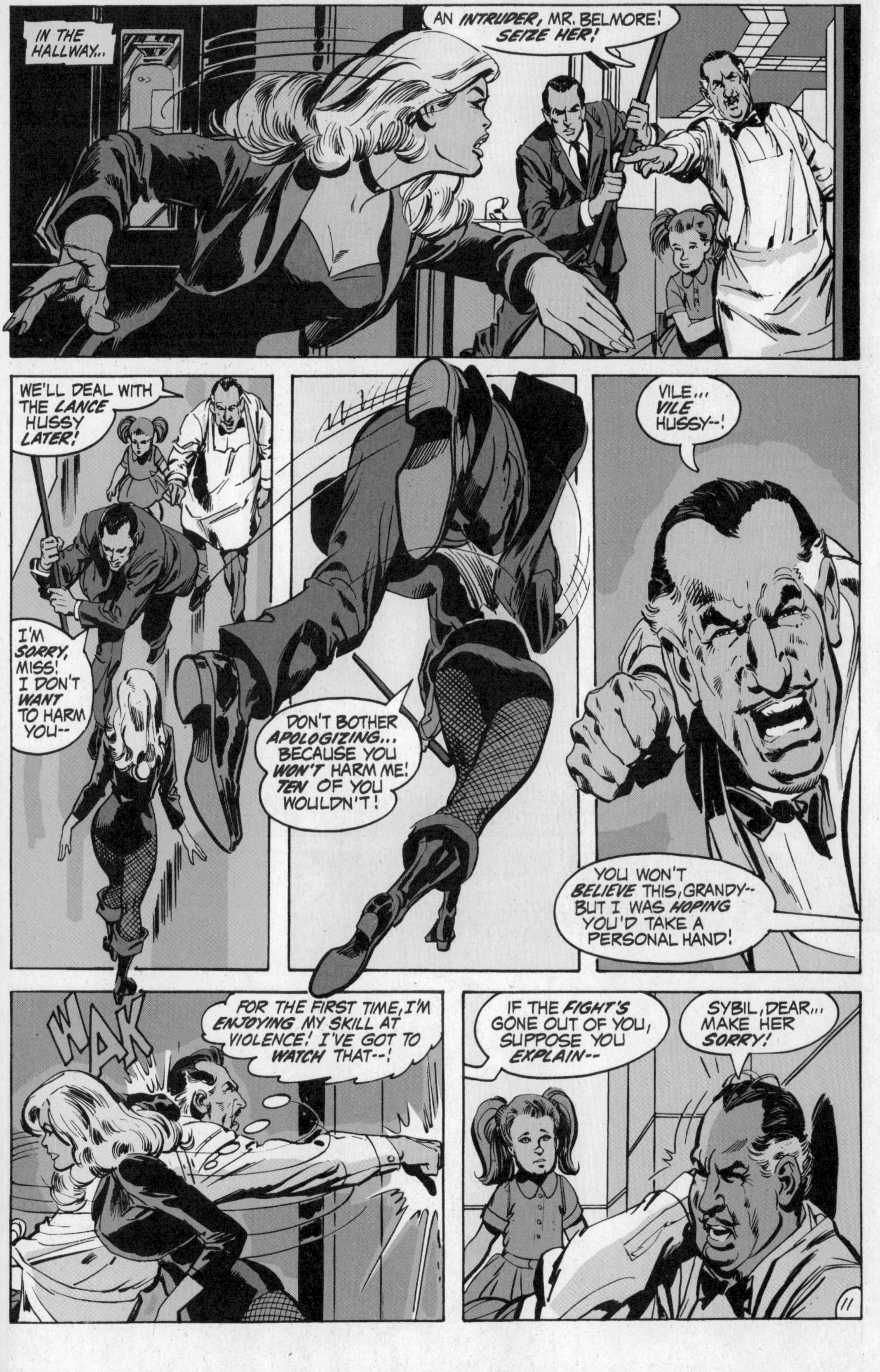
IN THE HALLWAY...
AN *INTRUDER*, MR. BELMORE! *SEIZE HER!*
WE'LL DEAL WITH THE *LANCE* HUSSY *LATER!*
I'M *SORRY,* MISS! I DON'T *WANT* TO HARM YOU--
DON'T BOTHER *APOLOGIZING...* BECAUSE YOU *WON'T* HARM ME! *TEN* OF YOU WOULDN'T!
VILE... *VILE* HUSSY--!
YOU WON'T *BELIEVE* THIS, GRANDY-- BUT I WAS *HOPING* YOU'D TAKE A PERSONAL HAND!
WAK
FOR THE FIRST TIME, I'M *ENJOYING* MY SKILL AT VIOLENCE! I'VE GOT TO *WATCH* THAT--!
IF THE *FIGHT'S* GONE OUT OF YOU, SUPPOSE YOU *EXPLAIN*--
SYBIL, DEAR... MAKE HER *SORRY!*
11

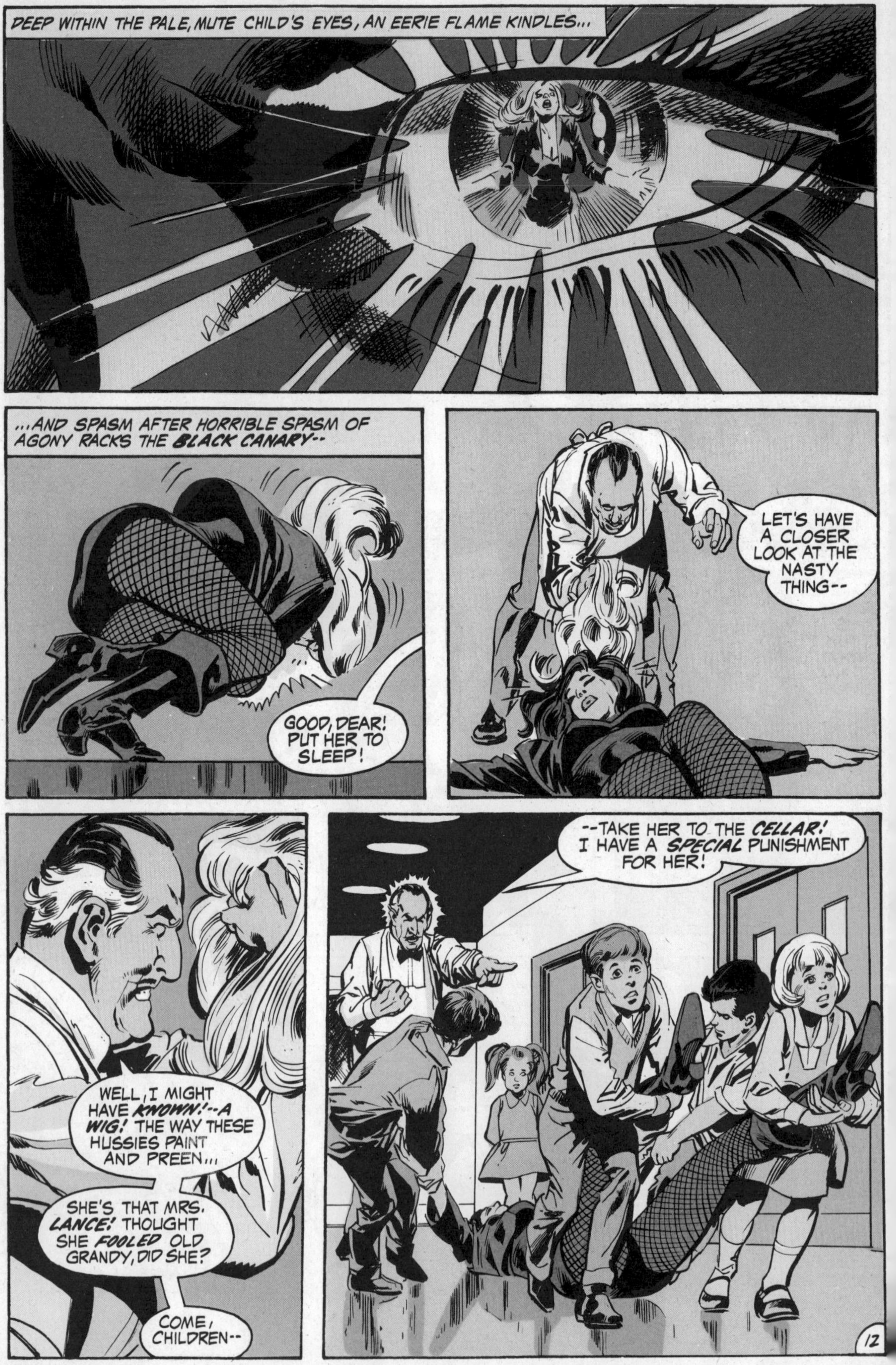
DEEP WITHIN THE PALE, MUTE CHILD'S EYES, AN EERIE FLAME KINDLES...
...AND SPASM AFTER HORRIBLE SPASM OF AGONY RACKS THE BLACK CANARY--
GOOD, DEAR! PUT HER TO SLEEP!
LET'S HAVE A CLOSER LOOK AT THE NASTY THING--
WELL, I MIGHT HAVE KNOWN!--A WIG! THE WAY THESE HUSSIES PAINT AND PREEN...
SHE'S THAT MRS. LANCE! THOUGHT SHE FOOLED OLD GRANDY, DID SHE?
COME, CHILDREN--
--TAKE HER TO THE CELLAR! I HAVE A SPECIAL PUNISHMENT FOR HER!
12

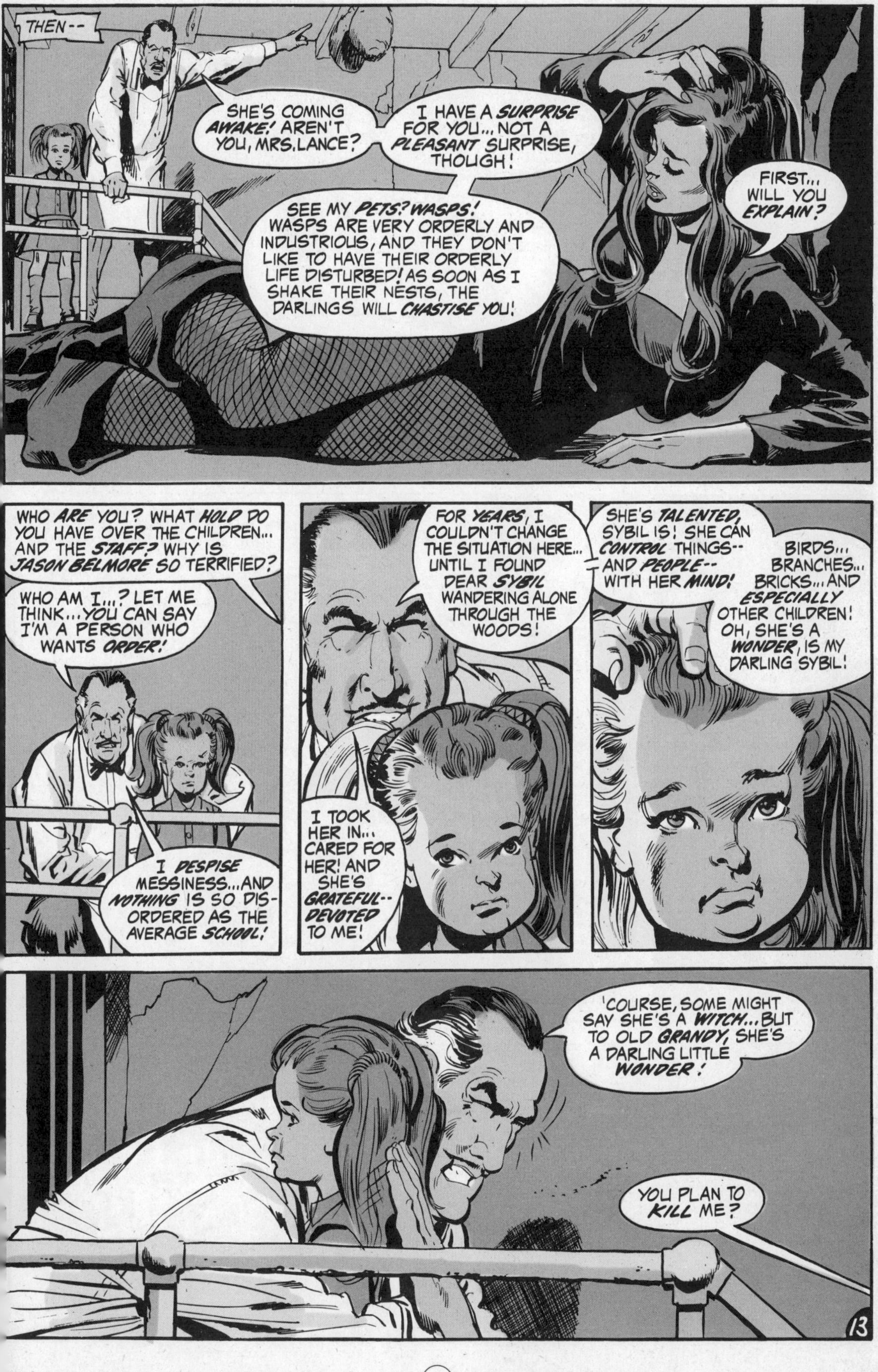
THEN--
SHE'S COMING AWAKE! AREN'T YOU, MRS. LANCE?
I HAVE A SURPRISE FOR YOU... NOT A PLEASANT SURPRISE, THOUGH!
SEE MY PETS? WASPS! WASPS ARE VERY ORDERLY AND INDUSTRIOUS, AND THEY DON'T LIKE TO HAVE THEIR ORDERLY LIFE DISTURBED! AS SOON AS I SHAKE THEIR NESTS, THE DARLINGS WILL CHASTISE YOU!
FIRST... WILL YOU EXPLAIN?
WHO ARE YOU? WHAT HOLD DO YOU HAVE OVER THE CHILDREN... AND THE STAFF? WHY IS JASON BELMORE SO TERRIFIED?
WHO AM I...? LET ME THINK... YOU CAN SAY I'M A PERSON WHO WANTS ORDER!
I DESPISE MESSINESS... AND NOTHING IS SO DISORDERED AS THE AVERAGE SCHOOL!
FOR YEARS, I COULDN'T CHANGE THE SITUATION HERE... UNTIL I FOUND DEAR SYBIL WANDERING ALONE THROUGH THE WOODS!
I TOOK HER IN... CARED FOR HER! AND SHE'S GRATEFUL-- DEVOTED TO ME!
SHE'S TALENTED, SYBIL IS! SHE CAN CONTROL THINGS-- AND PEOPLE-- WITH HER MIND!
BIRDS... BRANCHES... BRICKS... AND ESPECIALLY OTHER CHILDREN! OH, SHE'S A WONDER, IS MY DARLING SYBIL!
'COURSE, SOME MIGHT SAY SHE'S A WITCH... BUT TO OLD GRANDY, SHE'S A DARLING LITTLE WONDER!
YOU PLAN TO KILL ME?
13

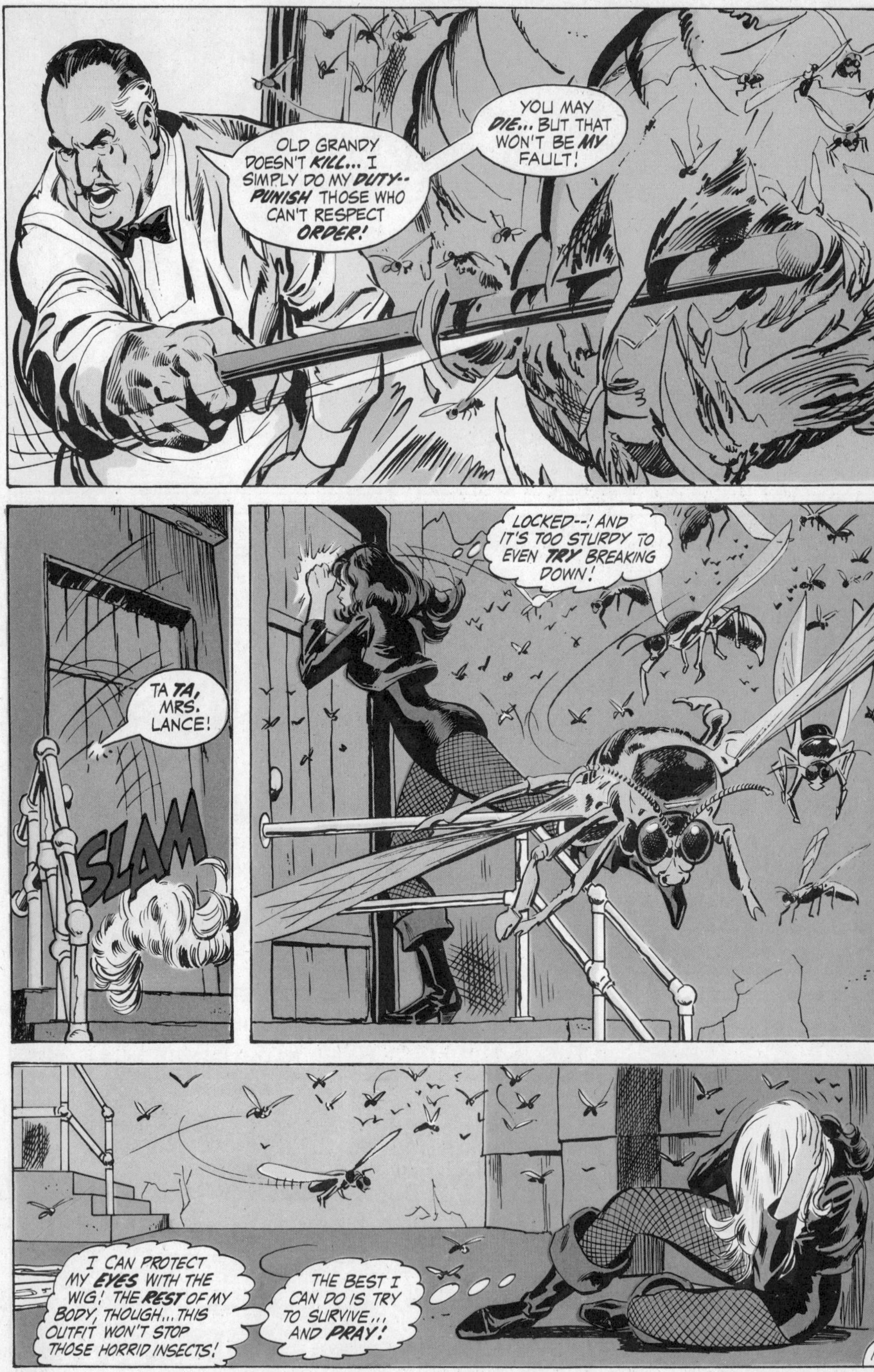
OLD GRANDY DOESN'T KILL... I SIMPLY DO MY DUTY-- PUNISH THOSE WHO CAN'T RESPECT ORDER!
YOU MAY DIE... BUT THAT WON'T BE MY FAULT!
TA TA, MRS. LANCE!
SLAM
LOCKED--! AND IT'S TOO STURDY TO EVEN TRY BREAKING DOWN!
I CAN PROTECT MY EYES WITH THE WIG! THE REST OF MY BODY, THOUGH... THIS OUTFIT WON'T STOP THOSE HORRID INSECTS!
THE BEST I CAN DO IS TRY TO SURVIVE... AND PRAY!
14

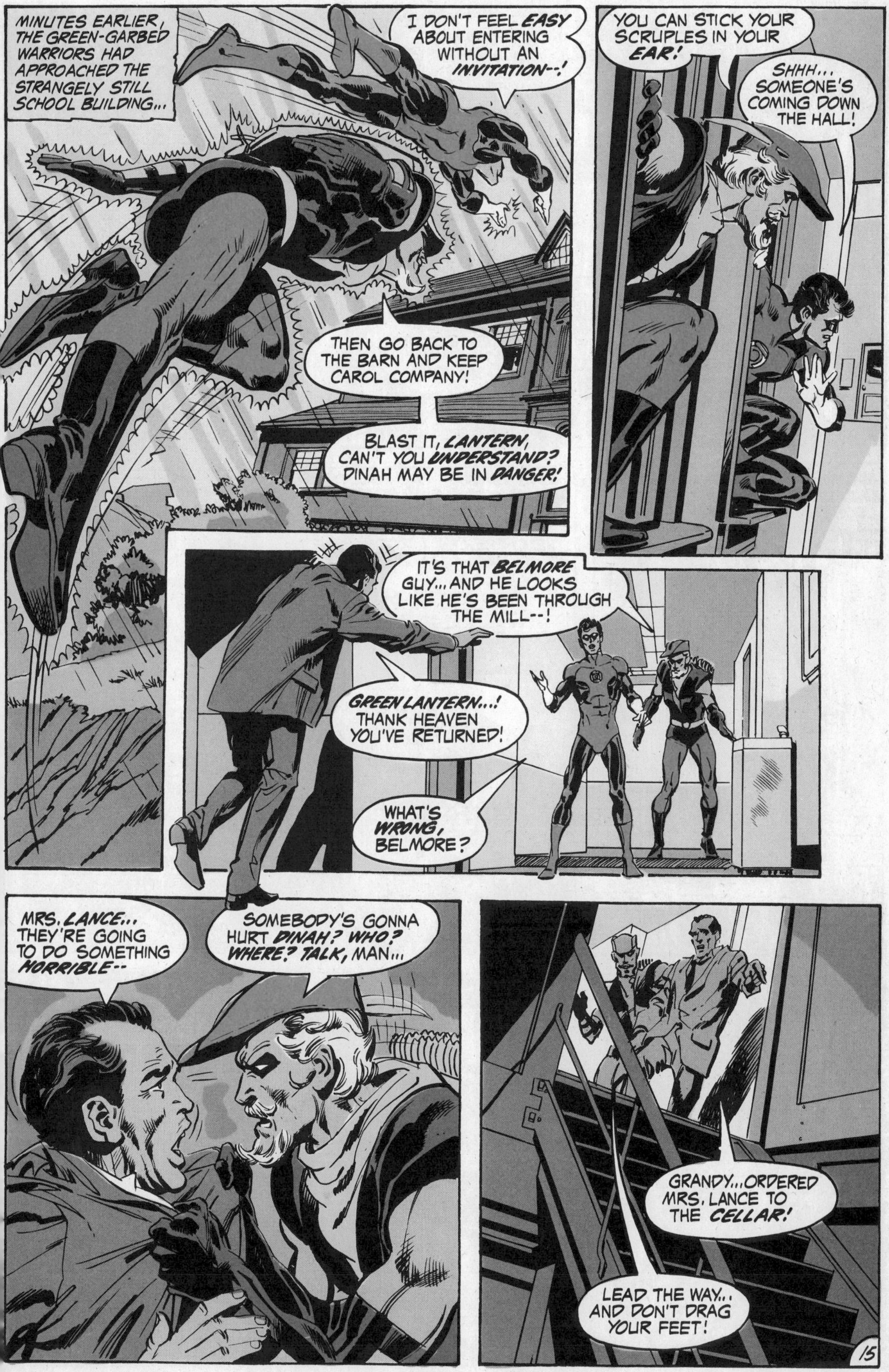
MINUTES EARLIER, THE GREEN-GARBED WARRIORS HAD APPROACHED THE STRANGELY STILL SCHOOL BUILDING...
I DON'T FEEL EASY ABOUT ENTERING WITHOUT AN INVITATION--!
THEN GO BACK TO THE BARN AND KEEP CAROL COMPANY!
BLAST IT, LANTERN, CAN'T YOU UNDERSTAND? DINAH MAY BE IN DANGER!
YOU CAN STICK YOUR SCRUPLES IN YOUR EAR!
SHHH... SOMEONE'S COMING DOWN THE HALL!
IT'S THAT BELMORE GUY... AND HE LOOKS LIKE HE'S BEEN THROUGH THE MILL--!
GREEN LANTERN...! THANK HEAVEN YOU'VE RETURNED!
WHAT'S WRONG, BELMORE?
MRS. LANCE... THEY'RE GOING TO DO SOMETHING HORRIBLE--
SOMEBODY'S GONNA HURT DINAH? WHO? WHERE? TALK, MAN...
GRANDY... ORDERED MRS. LANCE TO THE CELLAR!
LEAD THE WAY... AND DON'T DRAG YOUR FEET!
15

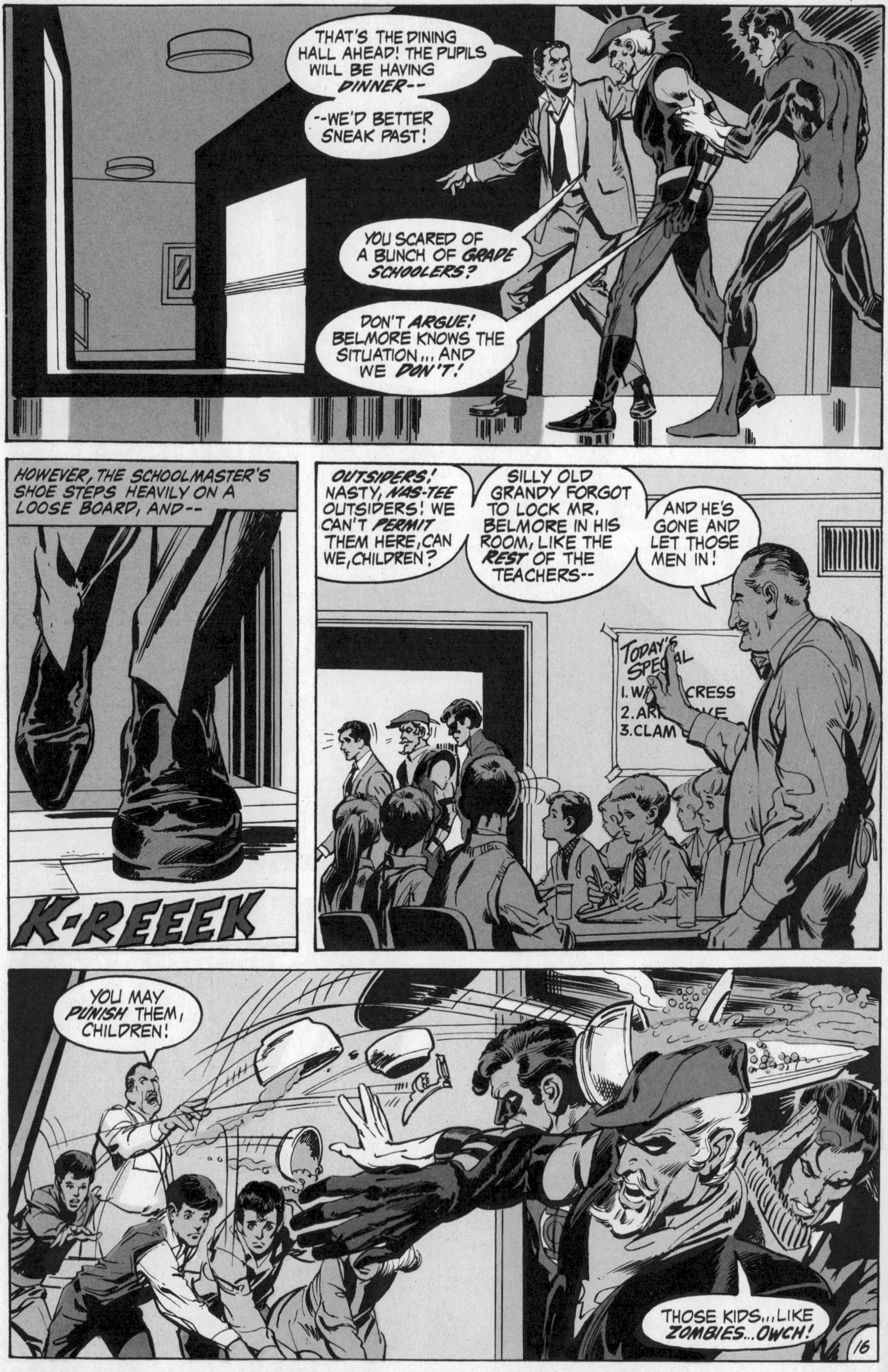

THAT'S THE DINING HALL AHEAD! THE PUPILS WILL BE HAVING DINNER--
--WE'D BETTER SNEAK PAST!
YOU SCARED OF A BUNCH OF GRADE SCHOOLERS?
DON'T ARGUE! BELMORE KNOWS THE SITUATION... AND WE DON'T!
HOWEVER, THE SCHOOLMASTER'S SHOE STEPS HEAVILY ON A LOOSE BOARD, AND--
K-REEEK
OUTSIDERS! NASTY, NAS-TEE OUTSIDERS! WE CAN'T PERMIT THEM HERE, CAN WE, CHILDREN?
SILLY OLD GRANDY FORGOT TO LOCK MR. BELMORE IN HIS ROOM, LIKE THE REST OF THE TEACHERS--
AND HE'S GONE AND LET THOSE MEN IN!
TODAY'S SPECIAL
3.CLAM
YOU MAY PUNISH THEM, CHILDREN!
THOSE KIDS... LIKE ZOMBIES... OWCH!
16

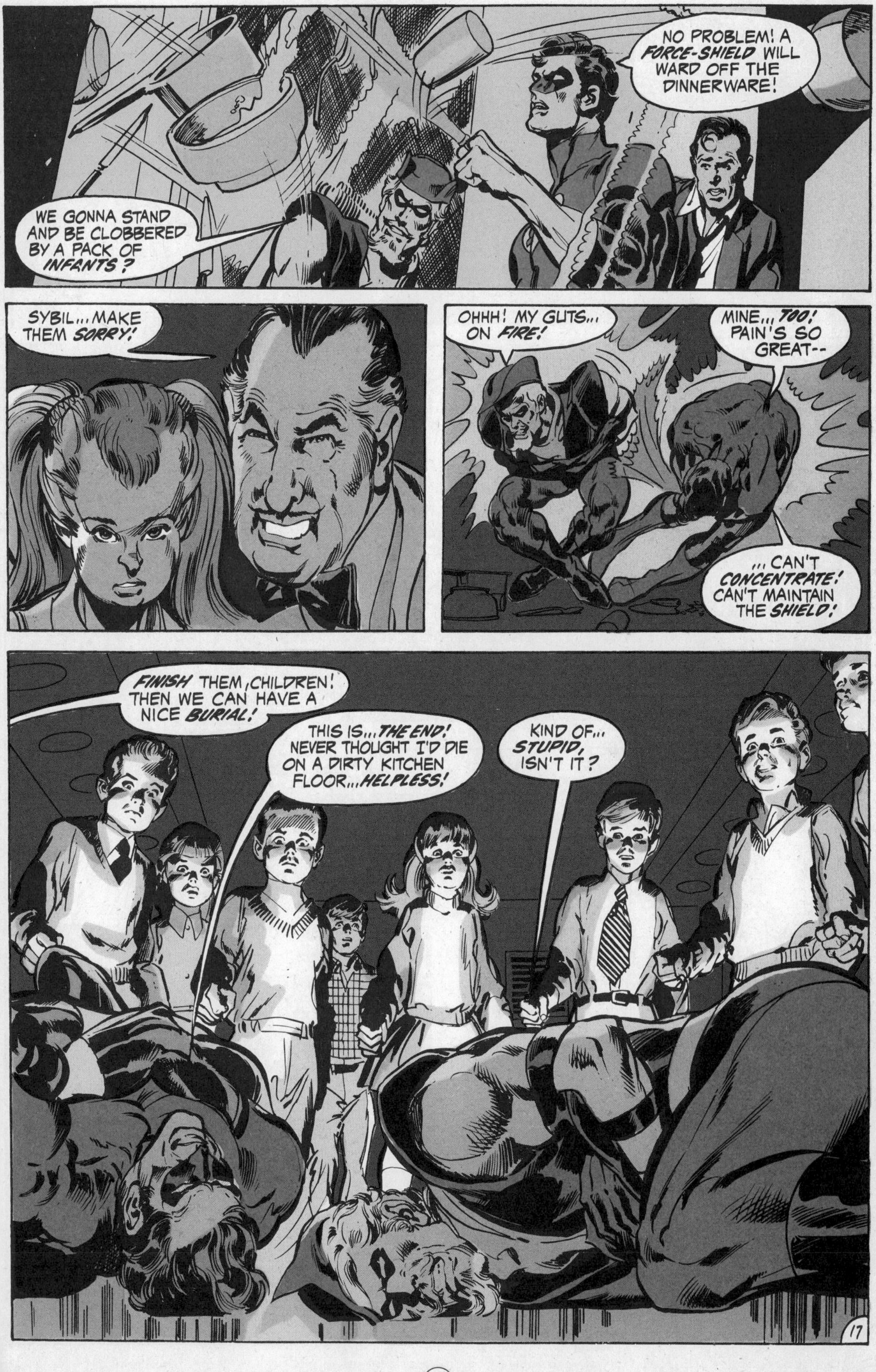
NO PROBLEM! A FORCE-SHIELD WILL WARD OFF THE DINNERWARE!
WE GONNA STAND AND BE CLOBBERED BY A PACK OF INFANTS?
SYBIL... MAKE THEM SORRY!
OHHH! MY GUTS... ON FIRE!
MINE... TOO! PAIN'S SO GREAT--
...CAN'T CONCENTRATE! CAN'T MAINTAIN THE SHIELD!
FINISH THEM, CHILDREN! THEN WE CAN HAVE A NICE BURIAL!
THIS IS... THE END! NEVER THOUGHT I'D DIE ON A DIRTY KITCHEN FLOOR... HELPLESS!
KIND OF... STUPID, ISN'T IT?
17

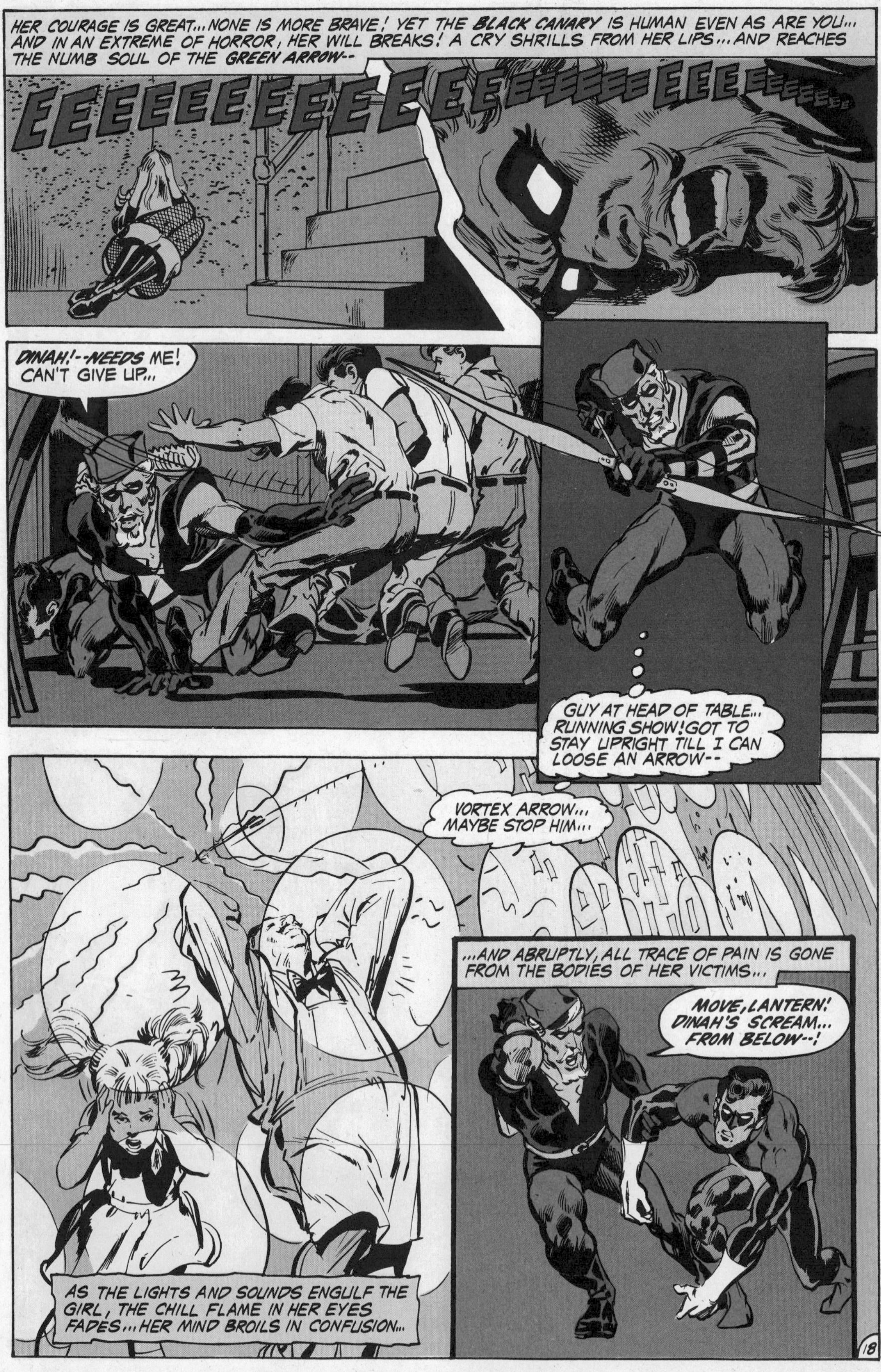
HER COURAGE IS GREAT... NONE IS MORE BRAVE! YET THE BLACK CANARY IS HUMAN EVEN AS ARE YOU... AND IN AN EXTREME OF HORROR, HER WILL BREAKS! A CRY SHRILLS FROM HER LIPS... AND REACHES THE NUMB SOUL OF THE GREEN ARROW--
EEEEEEEEEEEEEEEEEEEEEEEE
DINAH!--NEEDS ME! CAN'T GIVE UP...
GUY AT HEAD OF TABLE... RUNNING SHOW! GOT TO STAY UPRIGHT TILL I CAN LOOSE AN ARROW--
VORTEX ARROW... MAYBE STOP HIM...
AS THE LIGHTS AND SOUNDS ENGULF THE GIRL, THE CHILL FLAME IN HER EYES FADES... HER MIND BROILS IN CONFUSION...
...AND ABRUPTLY, ALL TRACE OF PAIN IS GONE FROM THE BODIES OF HER VICTIMS...
MOVE, LANTERN! DINAH'S SCREAM... FROM BELOW--!
18

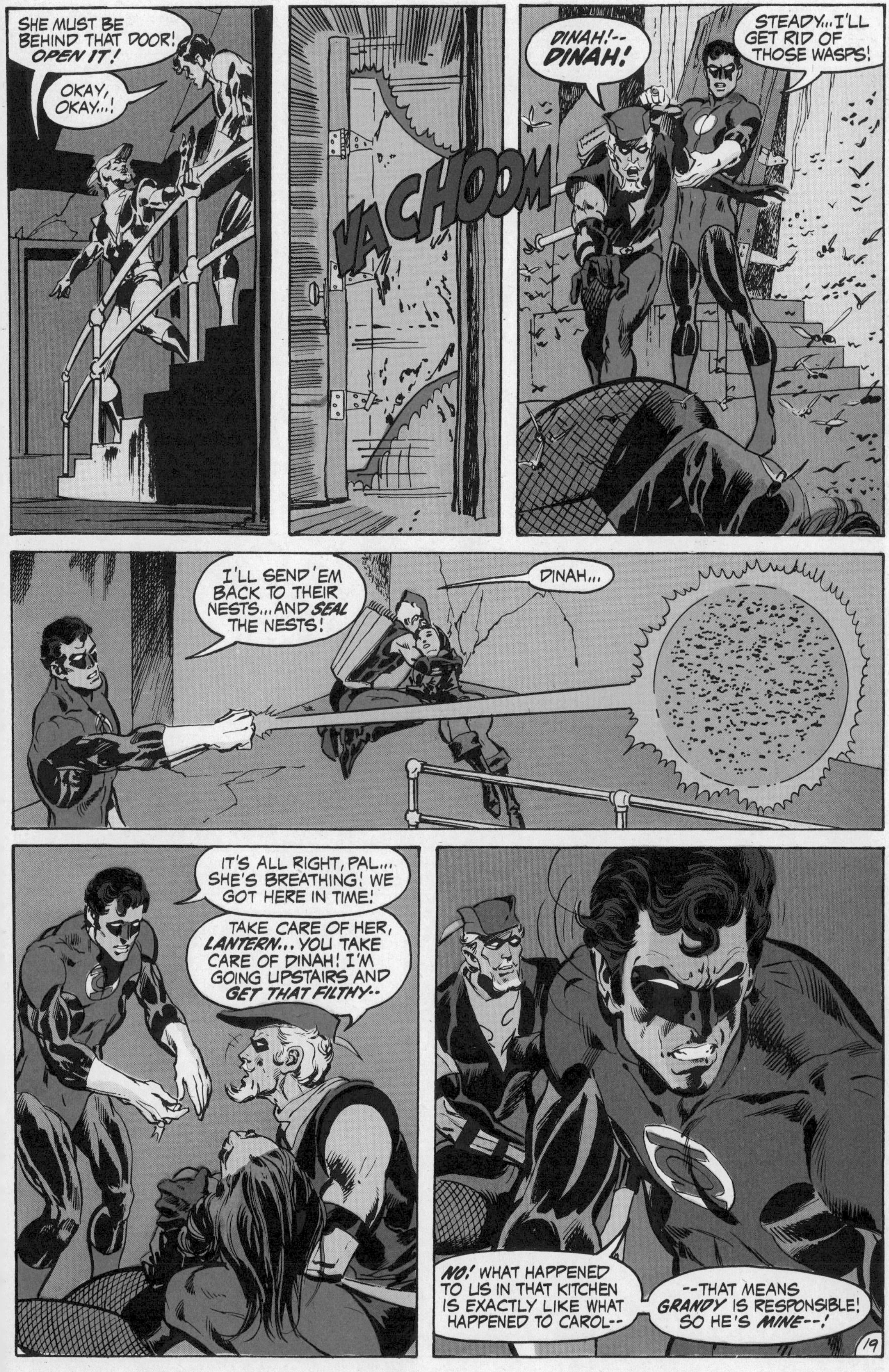
SHE MUST BE BEHIND THAT DOOR! OPEN IT!
OKAY, OKAY...!
VACHOOM
DINAH!-- DINAH!
STEADY...I'LL GET RID OF THOSE WASPS!
I'LL SEND 'EM BACK TO THEIR NESTS...AND SEAL THE NESTS!
DINAH...
IT'S ALL RIGHT, PAL... SHE'S BREATHING! WE GOT HERE IN TIME!
TAKE CARE OF HER, LANTERN... YOU TAKE CARE OF DINAH! I'M GOING UPSTAIRS AND GET THAT FILTHY--
NO! WHAT HAPPENED TO US IN THAT KITCHEN IS EXACTLY LIKE WHAT HAPPENED TO CAROL--
--THAT MEANS GRANDY IS RESPONSIBLE! SO HE'S MINE--!
19

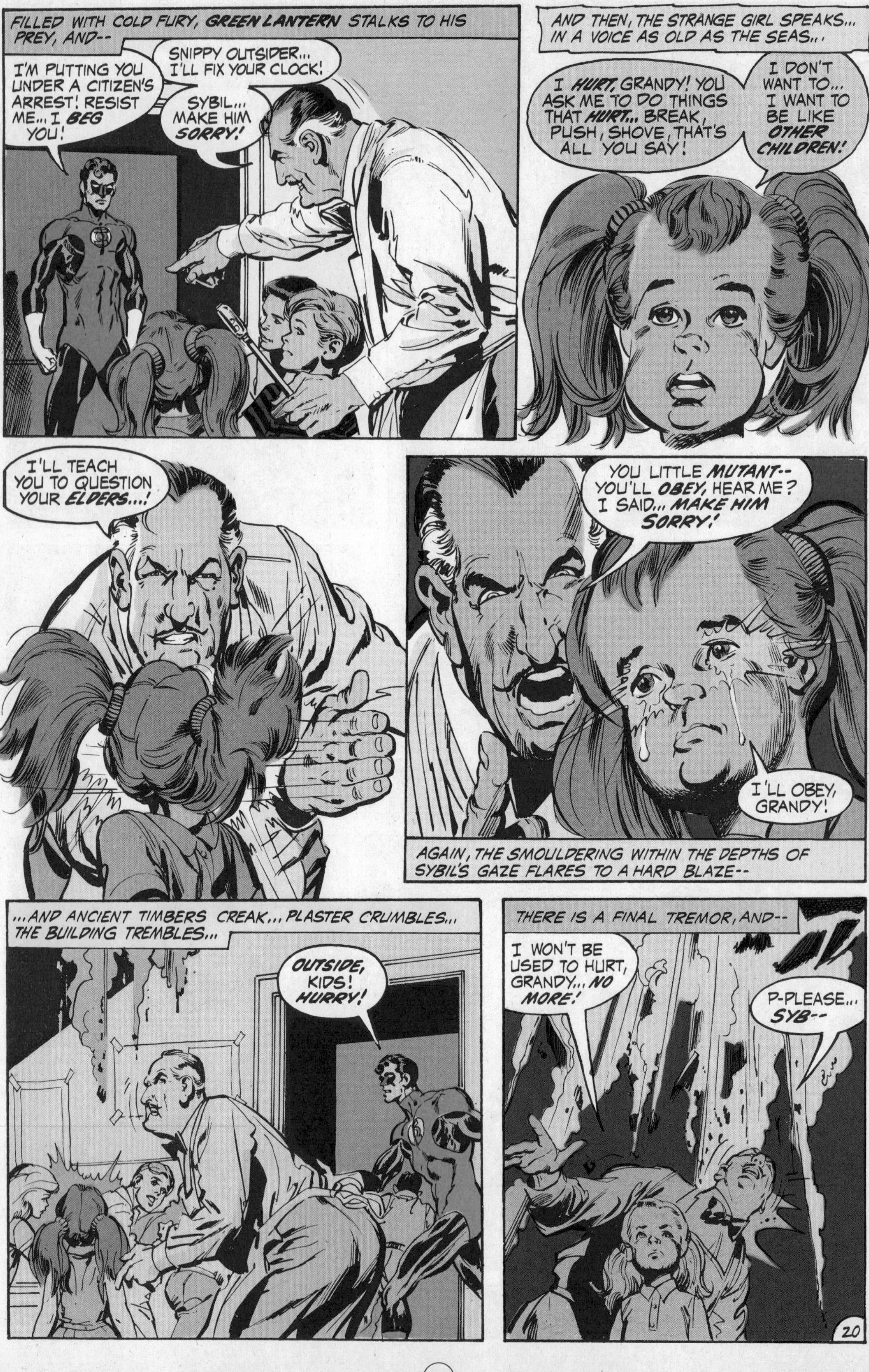
FILLED WITH COLD FURY, GREEN LANTERN STALKS TO HIS PREY, AND--
I'M PUTTING YOU UNDER A CITIZEN'S ARREST! RESIST ME... I BEG YOU!
SNIPPY OUTSIDER... I'LL FIX YOUR CLOCK!
SYBIL... MAKE HIM SORRY!
AND THEN, THE STRANGE GIRL SPEAKS... IN A VOICE AS OLD AS THE SEAS...
I HURT, GRANDY! YOU ASK ME TO DO THINGS THAT HURT... BREAK, PUSH, SHOVE, THAT'S ALL YOU SAY!
I DON'T WANT TO... I WANT TO BE LIKE OTHER CHILDREN!
I'LL TEACH YOU TO QUESTION YOUR ELDERS...!
YOU LITTLE MUTANT-- YOU'LL OBEY, HEAR ME? I SAID... MAKE HIM SORRY!
I'LL OBEY, GRANDY!
AGAIN, THE SMOULDERING WITHIN THE DEPTHS OF SYBIL'S GAZE FLARES TO A HARD BLAZE--
...AND ANCIENT TIMBERS CREAK... PLASTER CRUMBLES... THE BUILDING TREMBLES...
OUTSIDE, KIDS! HURRY!
THERE IS A FINAL TREMOR, AND--
I WON'T BE USED TO HURT, GRANDY... NO MORE!
P-PLEASE... SYB--
20

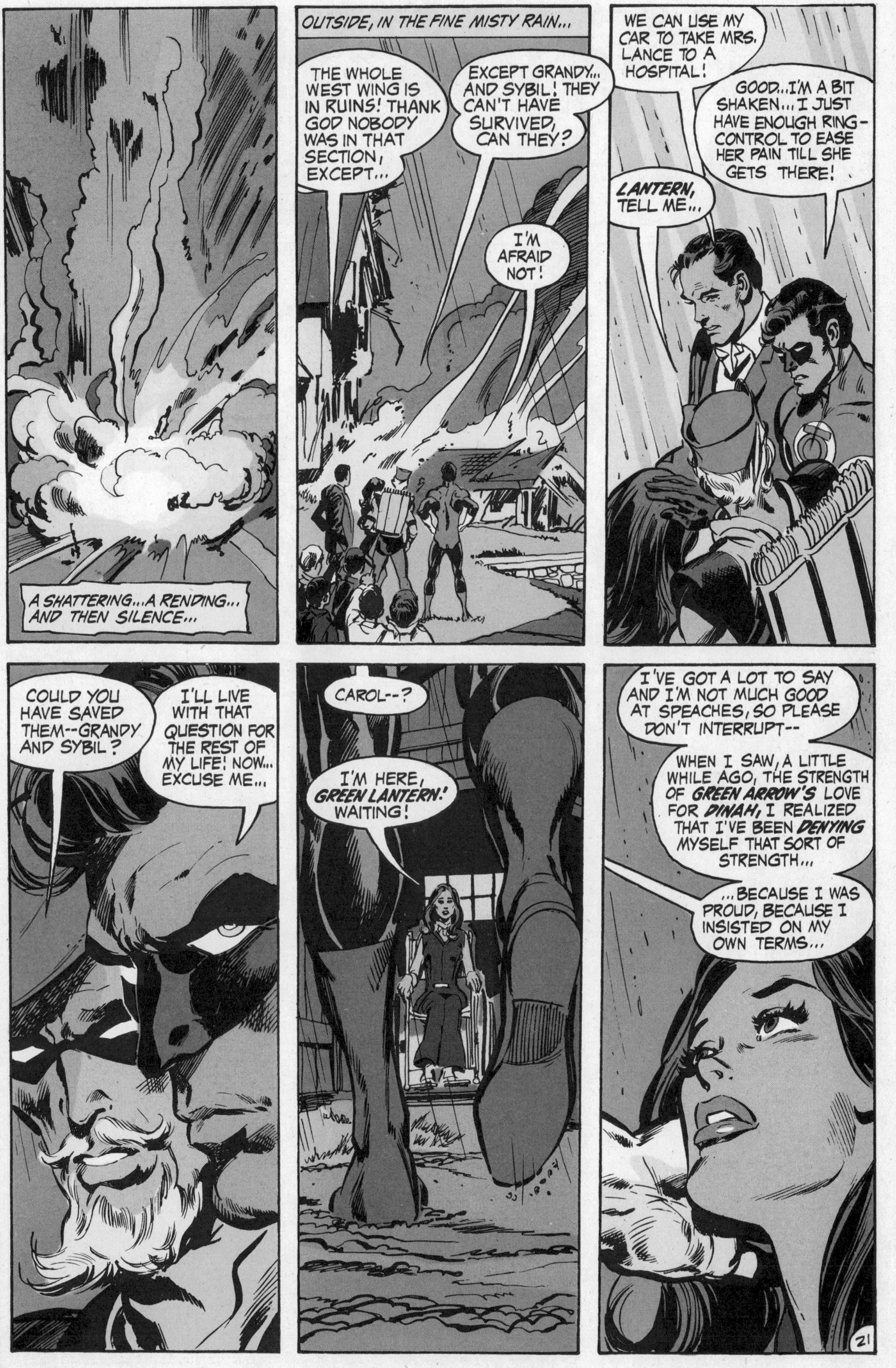
A SHATTERING...A RENDING... AND THEN SILENCE...
OUTSIDE, IN THE FINE MISTY RAIN...
THE WHOLE WEST WING IS IN RUINS! THANK GOD NOBODY WAS IN THAT SECTION, EXCEPT...
EXCEPT GRANDY... AND SYBIL! THEY CAN'T HAVE SURVIVED, CAN THEY?
I'M AFRAID NOT!
WE CAN USE MY CAR TO TAKE MRS. LANCE TO A HOSPITAL!
GOOD...I'M A BIT SHAKEN... I JUST HAVE ENOUGH RING-CONTROL TO EASE HER PAIN TILL SHE GETS THERE!
LANTERN, TELL ME...
COULD YOU HAVE SAVED THEM--GRANDY AND SYBIL?
I'LL LIVE WITH THAT QUESTION FOR THE REST OF MY LIFE! NOW... EXCUSE ME...
CAROL--?
I'M HERE, GREEN LANTERN! WAITING!
I'VE GOT A LOT TO SAY AND I'M NOT MUCH GOOD AT SPEACHES, SO PLEASE DON'T INTERRUPT--
WHEN I SAW, A LITTLE WHILE AGO, THE STRENGTH OF GREEN ARROW'S LOVE FOR DINAH, I REALIZED THAT I'VE BEEN DENYING MYSELF THAT SORT OF STRENGTH...
...BECAUSE I WAS PROUD, BECAUSE I INSISTED ON MY OWN TERMS...
21

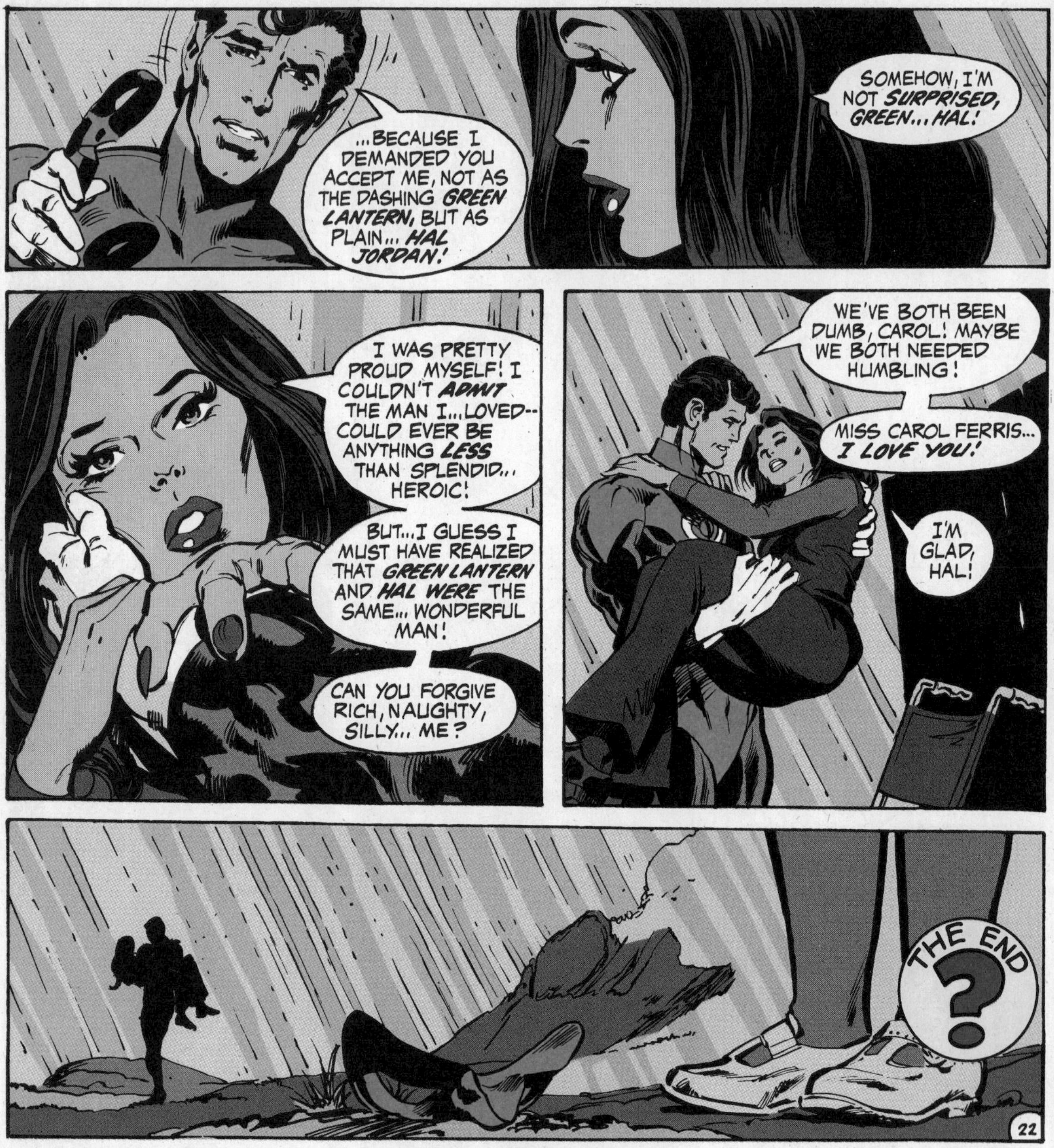
...BECAUSE I DEMANDED YOU ACCEPT ME, NOT AS THE DASHING GREEN LANTERN, BUT AS PLAIN... HAL JORDAN!
SOMEHOW, I'M NOT SURPRISED, GREEN... HAL!
I WAS PRETTY PROUD MYSELF! I COULDN'T ADMIT THE MAN I...LOVED-- COULD EVER BE ANYTHING LESS THAN SPLENDID... HEROIC!
BUT...I GUESS I MUST HAVE REALIZED THAT GREEN LANTERN AND HAL WERE THE SAME... WONDERFUL MAN!
CAN YOU FORGIVE RICH, NAUGHTY, SILLY... ME?
WE'VE BOTH BEEN DUMB, CAROL! MAYBE WE BOTH NEEDED HUMBLING!
MISS CAROL FERRIS... I LOVE YOU!
I'M GLAD, HAL!
THE END ?
22

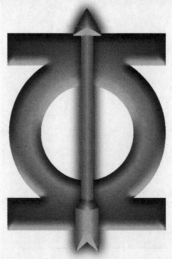

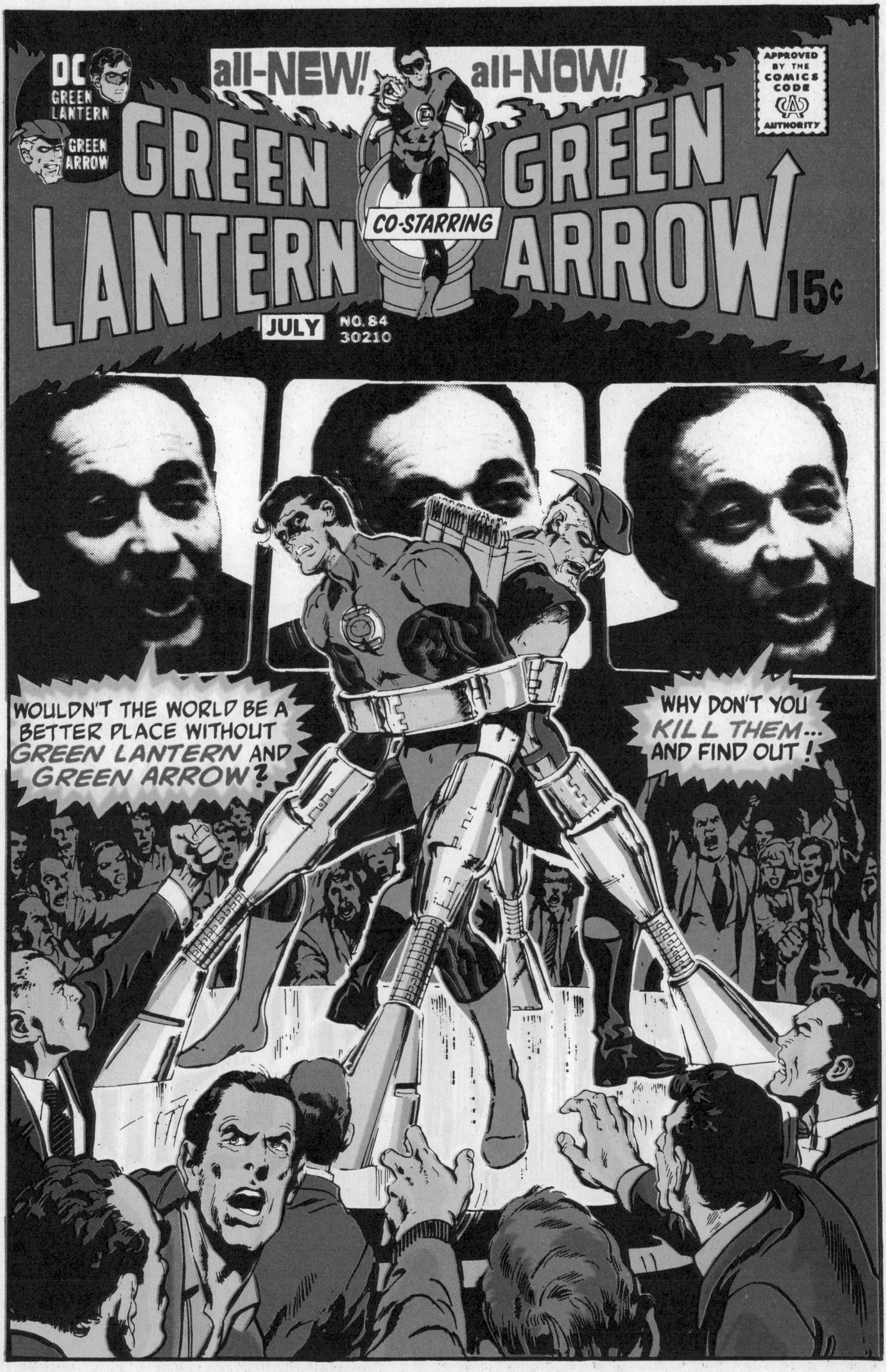
DC
GREEN LANTERN
GREEN ARROW
all-NEW! all-NOW!
APPROVED BY THE COMICS CODE AUTHORITY
GREEN LANTERN
CO-STARRING
GREEN ARROW
15¢
JULY
NO. 84
30210
WOULDN'T THE WORLD BE A BETTER PLACE WITHOUT GREEN LANTERN AND GREEN ARROW?
WHY DON'T YOU KILL THEM... AND FIND OUT!

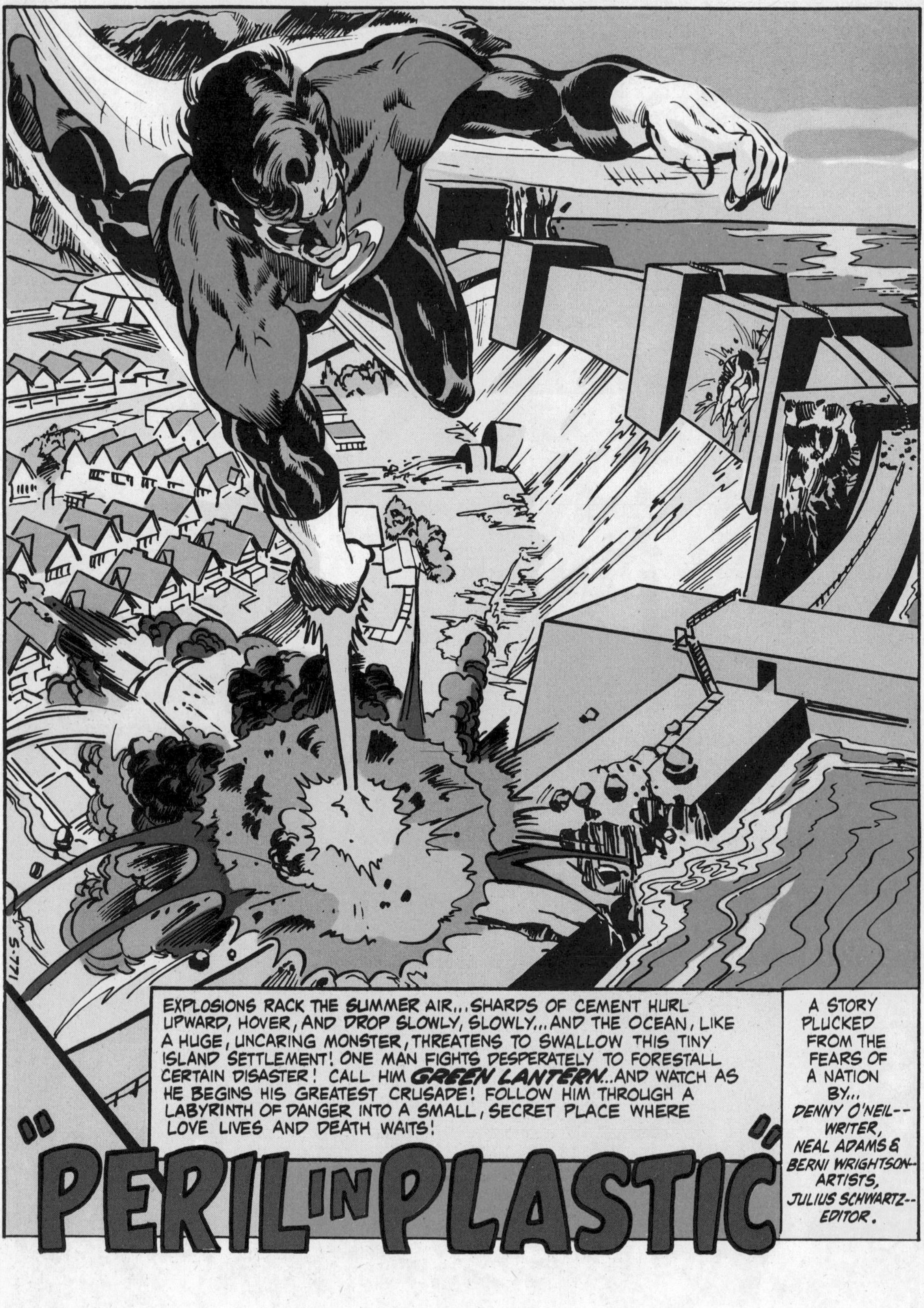

EXPLOSIONS RACK THE SUMMER AIR... SHARDS OF CEMENT HURL UPWARD, HOVER, AND DROP SLOWLY, SLOWLY... AND THE OCEAN, LIKE A HUGE, UNCARING MONSTER, THREATENS TO SWALLOW THIS TINY ISLAND SETTLEMENT! ONE MAN FIGHTS DESPERATELY TO FORESTALL CERTAIN DISASTER! CALL HIM GREEN LANTERN... AND WATCH AS HE BEGINS HIS GREATEST CRUSADE! FOLLOW HIM THROUGH A LABYRINTH OF DANGER INTO A SMALL, SECRET PLACE WHERE LOVE LIVES AND DEATH WAITS!
A STORY PLUCKED FROM THE FEARS OF A NATION BY... DENNY O'NEIL--WRITER, NEAL ADAMS & BERNI WRIGHTSON--ARTISTS, JULIUS SCHWARTZ--EDITOR.
"PERIL IN PLASTIC"

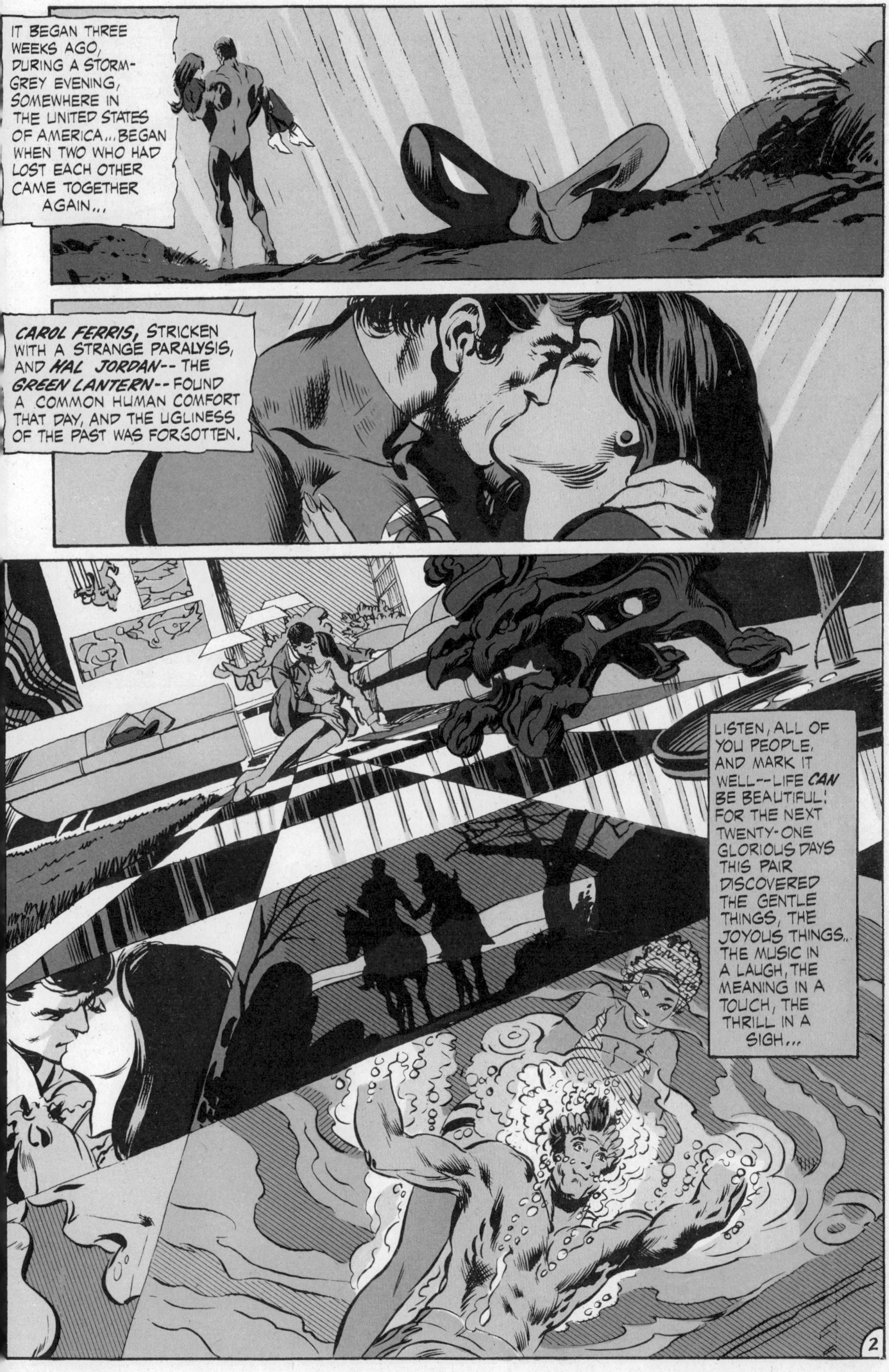
IT BEGAN THREE WEEKS AGO, DURING A STORM-GREY EVENING, SOMEWHERE IN THE UNITED STATES OF AMERICA... BEGAN WHEN TWO WHO HAD LOST EACH OTHER CAME TOGETHER AGAIN...
CAROL FERRIS, STRICKEN WITH A STRANGE PARALYSIS, AND HAL JORDAN-- THE GREEN LANTERN-- FOUND A COMMON HUMAN COMFORT THAT DAY, AND THE UGLINESS OF THE PAST WAS FORGOTTEN.
LISTEN, ALL OF YOU PEOPLE, AND MARK IT WELL--LIFE CAN BE BEAUTIFUL! FOR THE NEXT TWENTY-ONE GLORIOUS DAYS THIS PAIR DISCOVERED THE GENTLE THINGS, THE JOYOUS THINGS.. THE MUSIC IN A LAUGH, THE MEANING IN A TOUCH, THE THRILL IN A SIGH...
2

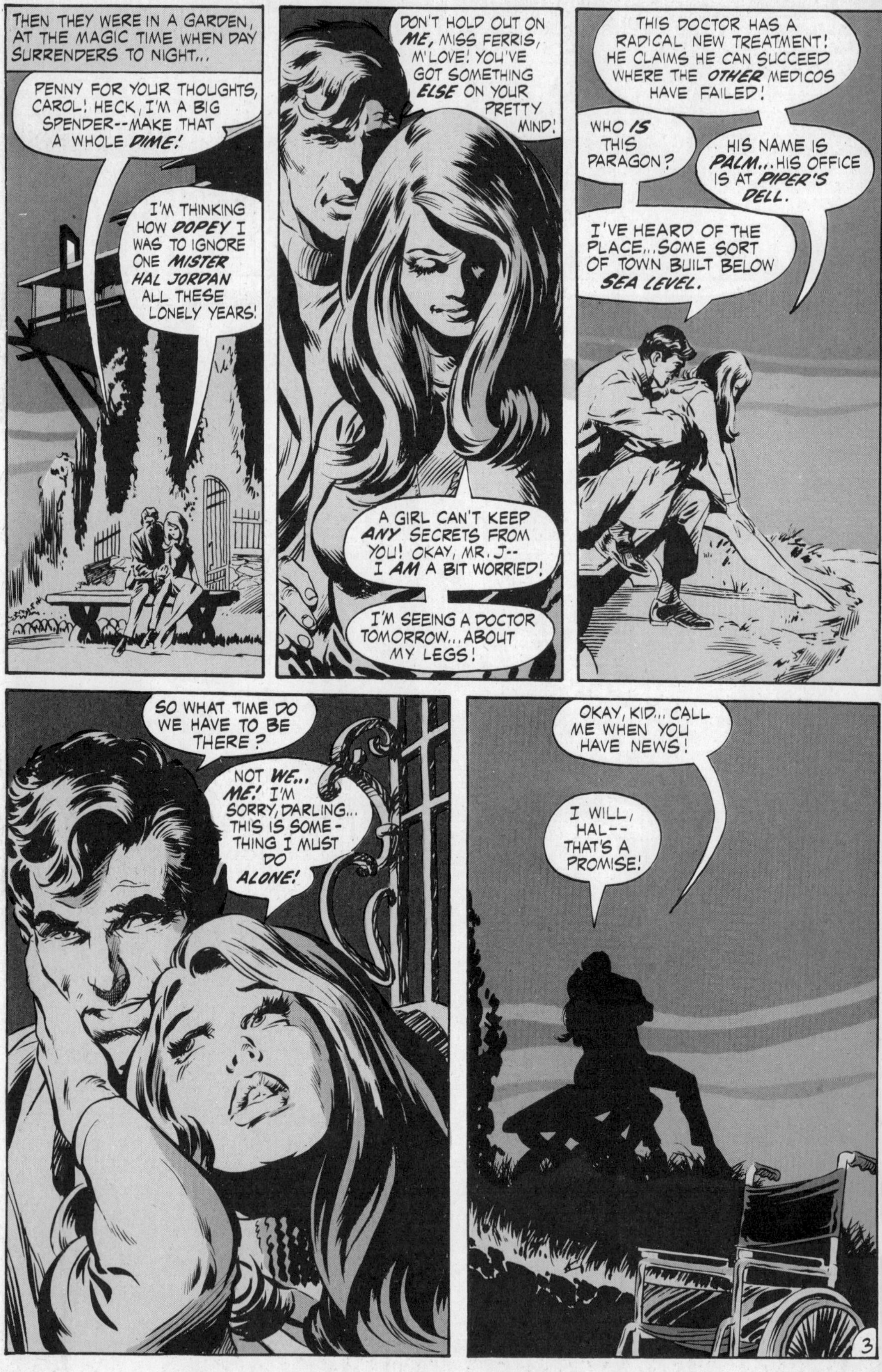
THEN THEY WERE IN A GARDEN, AT THE MAGIC TIME WHEN DAY SURRENDERS TO NIGHT...
PENNY FOR YOUR THOUGHTS, CAROL! HECK, I'M A BIG SPENDER--MAKE THAT A WHOLE DIME!
I'M THINKING HOW DOPEY I WAS TO IGNORE ONE MISTER HAL JORDAN ALL THESE LONELY YEARS!
DON'T HOLD OUT ON ME, MISS FERRIS, M'LOVE! YOU'VE GOT SOMETHING ELSE ON YOUR PRETTY MIND!
A GIRL CAN'T KEEP ANY SECRETS FROM YOU! OKAY, MR. J-- I AM A BIT WORRIED!
I'M SEEING A DOCTOR TOMORROW... ABOUT MY LEGS!
THIS DOCTOR HAS A RADICAL NEW TREATMENT! HE CLAIMS HE CAN SUCCEED WHERE THE OTHER MEDICOS HAVE FAILED!
WHO IS THIS PARAGON?
HIS NAME IS PALM... HIS OFFICE IS AT PIPER'S DELL.
I'VE HEARD OF THE PLACE... SOME SORT OF TOWN BUILT BELOW SEA LEVEL.
SO WHAT TIME DO WE HAVE TO BE THERE?
NOT WE... ME! I'M SORRY, DARLING... THIS IS SOME-THING I MUST DO ALONE!
OKAY, KID... CALL ME WHEN YOU HAVE NEWS!
I WILL, HAL-- THAT'S A PROMISE!
3

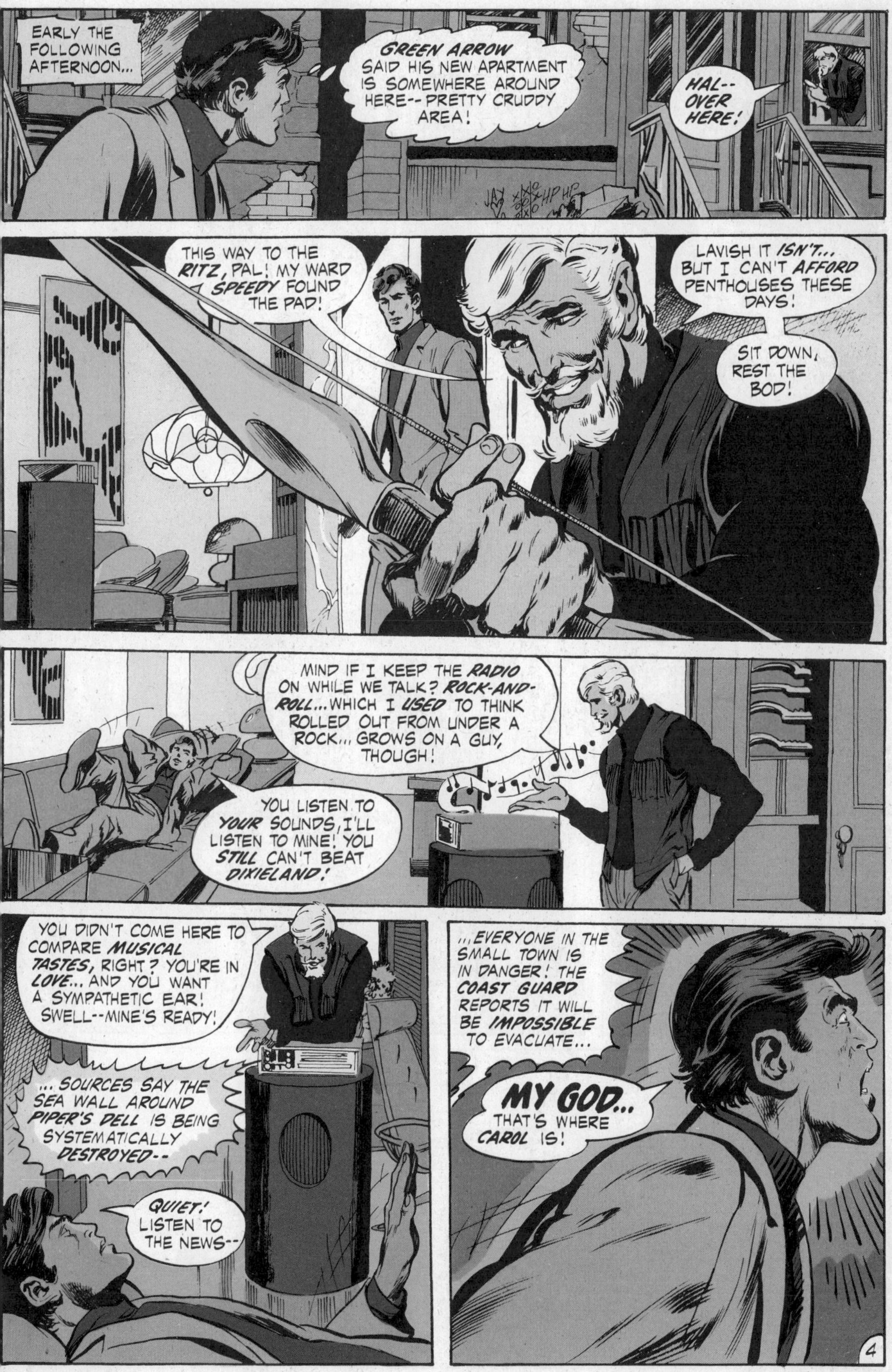
EARLY THE FOLLOWING AFTERNOON...
GREEN ARROW SAID HIS NEW APARTMENT IS SOMEWHERE AROUND HERE--PRETTY CRUDDY AREA!
HAL--OVER HERE!
THIS WAY TO THE RITZ, PAL! MY WARD SPEEDY FOUND THE PAD!
LAVISH IT ISN'T... BUT I CAN'T AFFORD PENTHOUSES THESE DAYS!
SIT DOWN, REST THE BOD!
MIND IF I KEEP THE RADIO ON WHILE WE TALK? ROCK-AND-ROLL...WHICH I USED TO THINK ROLLED OUT FROM UNDER A ROCK... GROWS ON A GUY, THOUGH!
YOU LISTEN TO YOUR SOUNDS, I'LL LISTEN TO MINE! YOU STILL CAN'T BEAT DIXIELAND!
YOU DIDN'T COME HERE TO COMPARE MUSICAL TASTES, RIGHT? YOU'RE IN LOVE... AND YOU WANT A SYMPATHETIC EAR! SWELL--MINE'S READY!
...SOURCES SAY THE SEA WALL AROUND PIPER'S DELL IS BEING SYSTEMATICALLY DESTROYED--
QUIET! LISTEN TO THE NEWS--
...EVERYONE IN THE SMALL TOWN IS IN DANGER! THE COAST GUARD REPORTS IT WILL BE IMPOSSIBLE TO EVACUATE...
MY GOD... THAT'S WHERE CAROL IS!
4

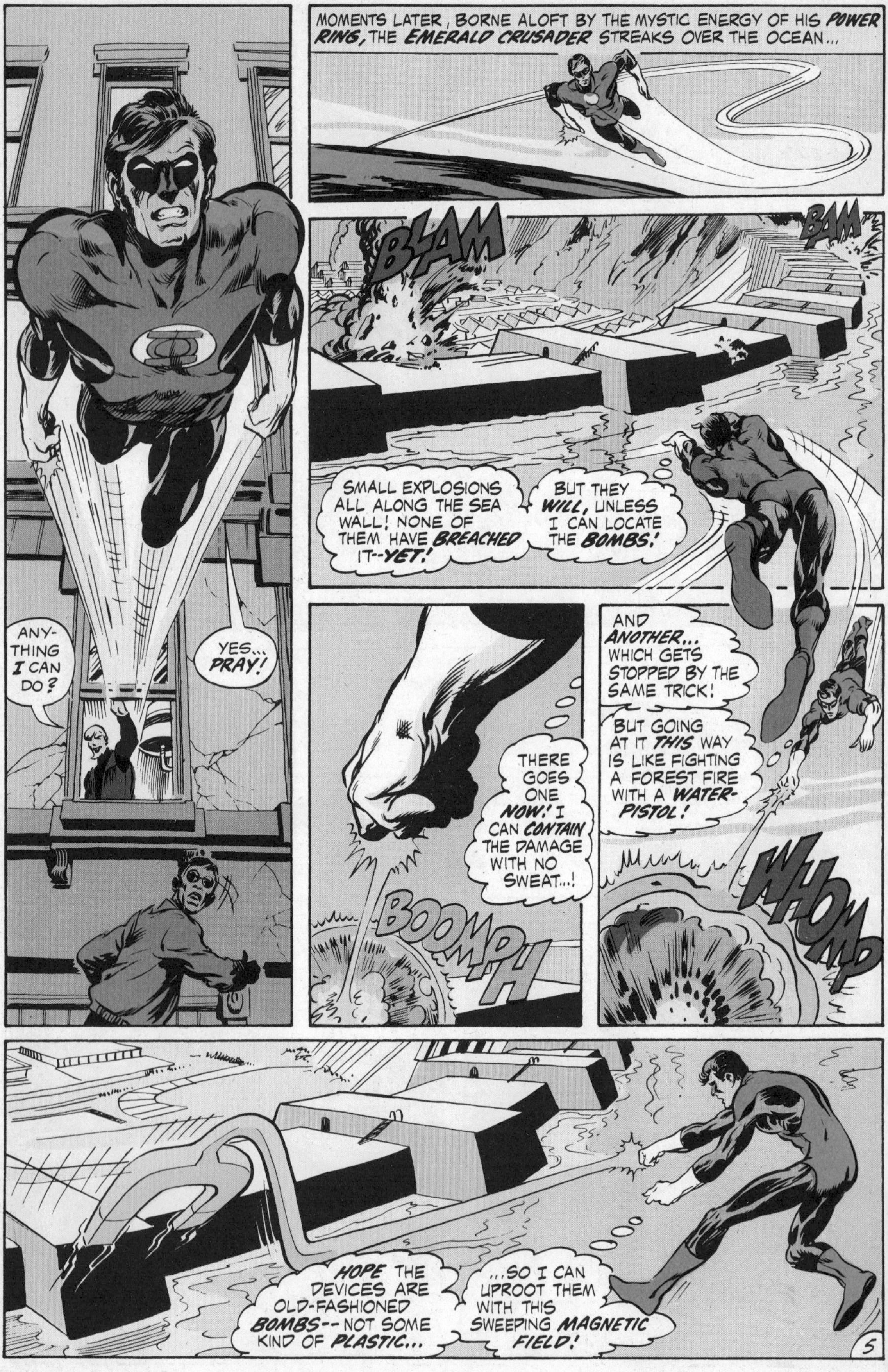
ANY-THING I CAN DO?
YES... PRAY!
MOMENTS LATER, BORNE ALOFT BY THE MYSTIC ENERGY OF HIS POWER RING, THE EMERALD CRUSADER STREAKS OVER THE OCEAN...
BLAM
BAM
SMALL EXPLOSIONS ALL ALONG THE SEA WALL! NONE OF THEM HAVE BREACHED IT--YET!
BUT THEY WILL, UNLESS I CAN LOCATE THE BOMBS!
THERE GOES ONE NOW! I CAN CONTAIN THE DAMAGE WITH NO SWEAT...!
BOOMPH
AND ANOTHER... WHICH GETS STOPPED BY THE SAME TRICK!
BUT GOING AT IT THIS WAY IS LIKE FIGHTING A FOREST FIRE WITH A WATER-PISTOL!
WHOMP
HOPE THE DEVICES ARE OLD-FASHIONED BOMBS-- NOT SOME KIND OF PLASTIC...
...SO I CAN UPROOT THEM WITH THIS SWEEPING MAGNETIC FIELD!
5

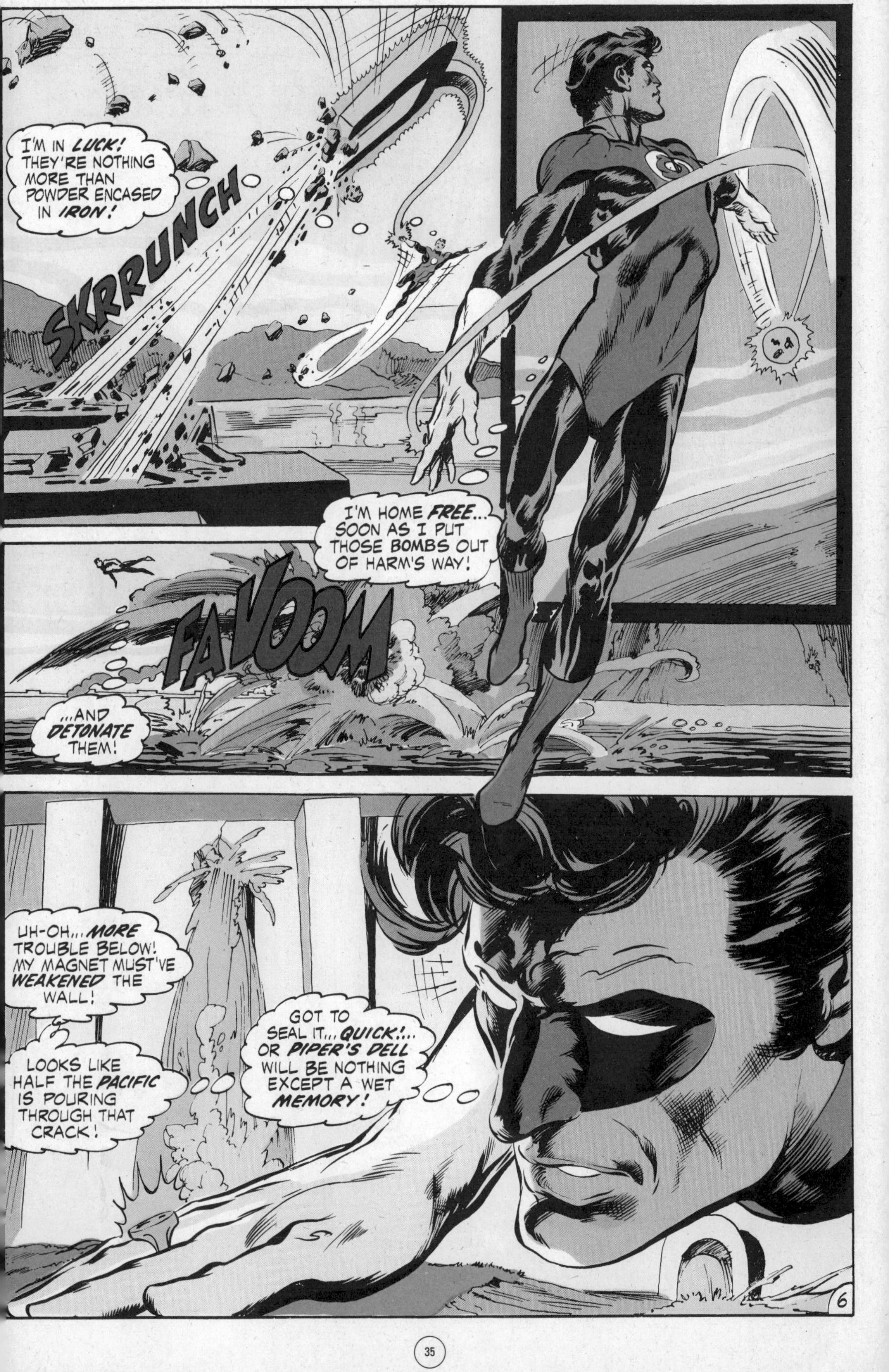
I'M IN LUCK! THEY'RE NOTHING MORE THAN POWDER ENCASED IN IRON!
SKRRUNCH
I'M HOME FREE... SOON AS I PUT THOSE BOMBS OUT OF HARM'S WAY!
FAVOOM
...AND DETONATE THEM!
UH-OH... MORE TROUBLE BELOW! MY MAGNET MUST'VE WEAKENED THE WALL!
LOOKS LIKE HALF THE PACIFIC IS POURING THROUGH THAT CRACK!
GOT TO SEAL IT... QUICK!... OR PIPER'S DELL WILL BE NOTHING EXCEPT A WET MEMORY!
6

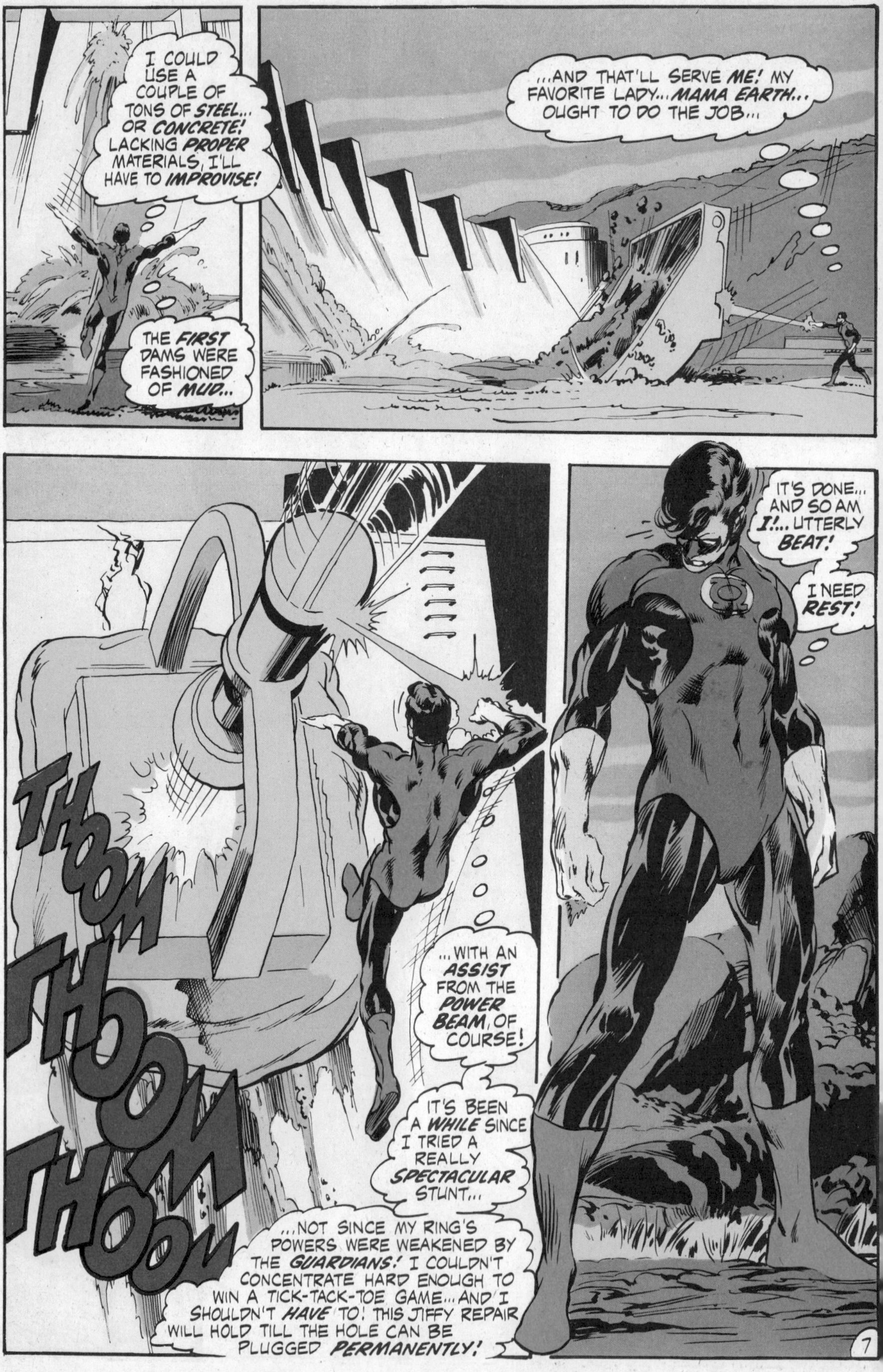
I COULD USE A COUPLE OF TONS OF STEEL... OR CONCRETE! LACKING PROPER MATERIALS, I'LL HAVE TO IMPROVISE!
THE FIRST DAMS WERE FASHIONED OF MUD...
...AND THAT'LL SERVE ME! MY FAVORITE LADY... MAMA EARTH... OUGHT TO DO THE JOB...
THOOM THOOM THOOM THOOM
...WITH AN ASSIST FROM THE POWER BEAM, OF COURSE!
IT'S BEEN A WHILE SINCE I TRIED A REALLY SPECTACULAR STUNT...
...NOT SINCE MY RING'S POWERS WERE WEAKENED BY THE GUARDIANS! I COULDN'T CONCENTRATE HARD ENOUGH TO WIN A TICK-TACK-TOE GAME... AND I SHOULDN'T HAVE TO! THIS JIFFY REPAIR WILL HOLD TILL THE HOLE CAN BE PLUGGED PERMANENTLY!
IT'S DONE... AND SO AM I!... UTTERLY BEAT!
I NEED REST!
7

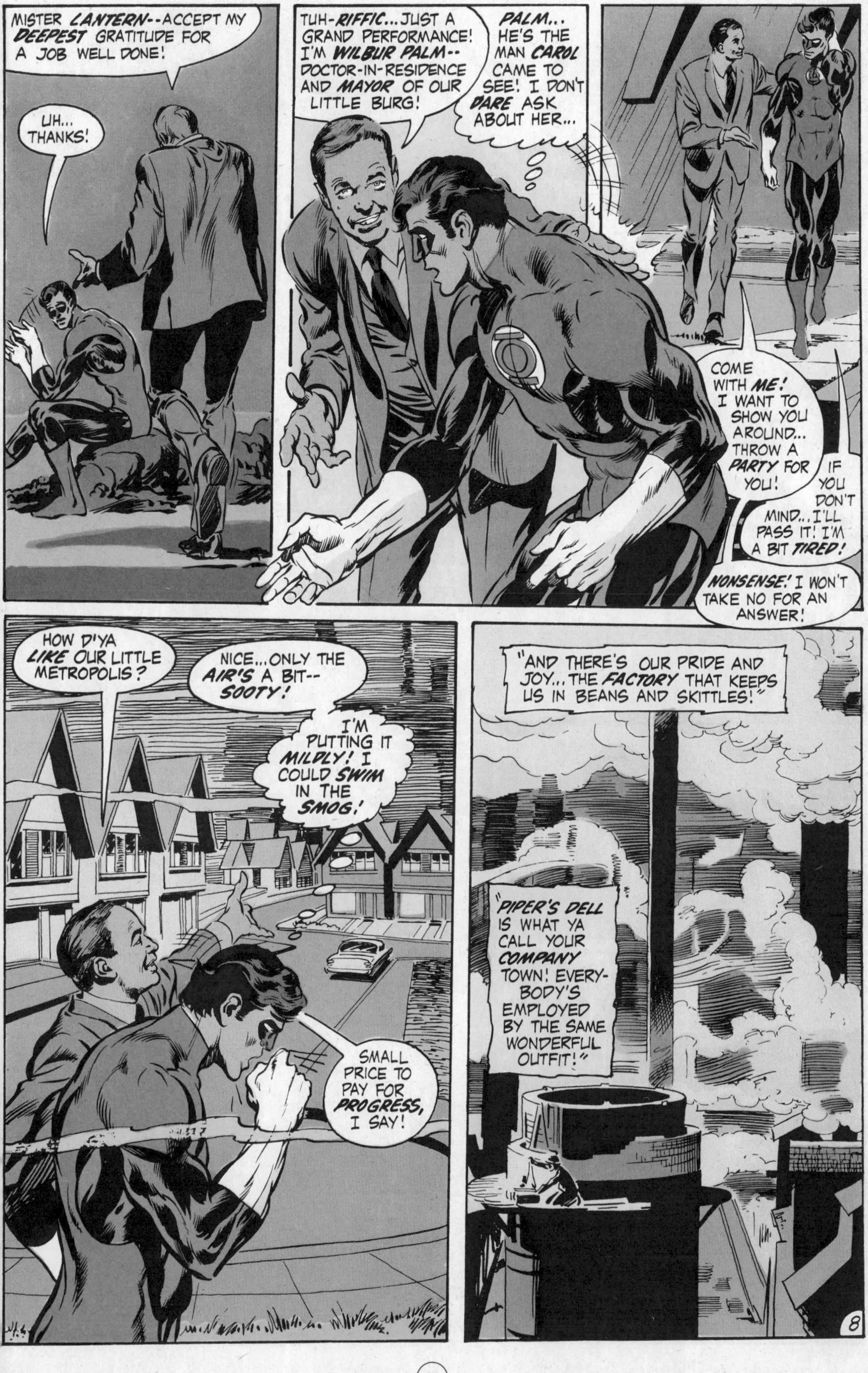
MISTER LANTERN--ACCEPT MY DEEPEST GRATITUDE FOR A JOB WELL DONE!
UH... THANKS!
TUH-RIFFIC... JUST A GRAND PERFORMANCE! I'M WILBUR PALM-- DOCTOR-IN-RESIDENCE AND MAYOR OF OUR LITTLE BURG!
PALM... HE'S THE MAN CAROL CAME TO SEE! I DON'T DARE ASK ABOUT HER...
COME WITH ME! I WANT TO SHOW YOU AROUND... THROW A PARTY FOR YOU!
IF YOU DON'T MIND... I'LL PASS IT! I'M A BIT TIRED!
NONSENSE! I WON'T TAKE NO FOR AN ANSWER!
HOW D'YA LIKE OUR LITTLE METROPOLIS?
NICE... ONLY THE AIR'S A BIT-- SOOTY!
I'M PUTTING IT MILDLY! I COULD SWIM IN THE SMOG!
SMALL PRICE TO PAY FOR PROGRESS, I SAY!
"AND THERE'S OUR PRIDE AND JOY... THE FACTORY THAT KEEPS US IN BEANS AND SKITTLES!"
"PIPER'S DELL IS WHAT YA CALL YOUR COMPANY TOWN! EVERY-BODY'S EMPLOYED BY THE SAME WONDERFUL OUTFIT!"
8

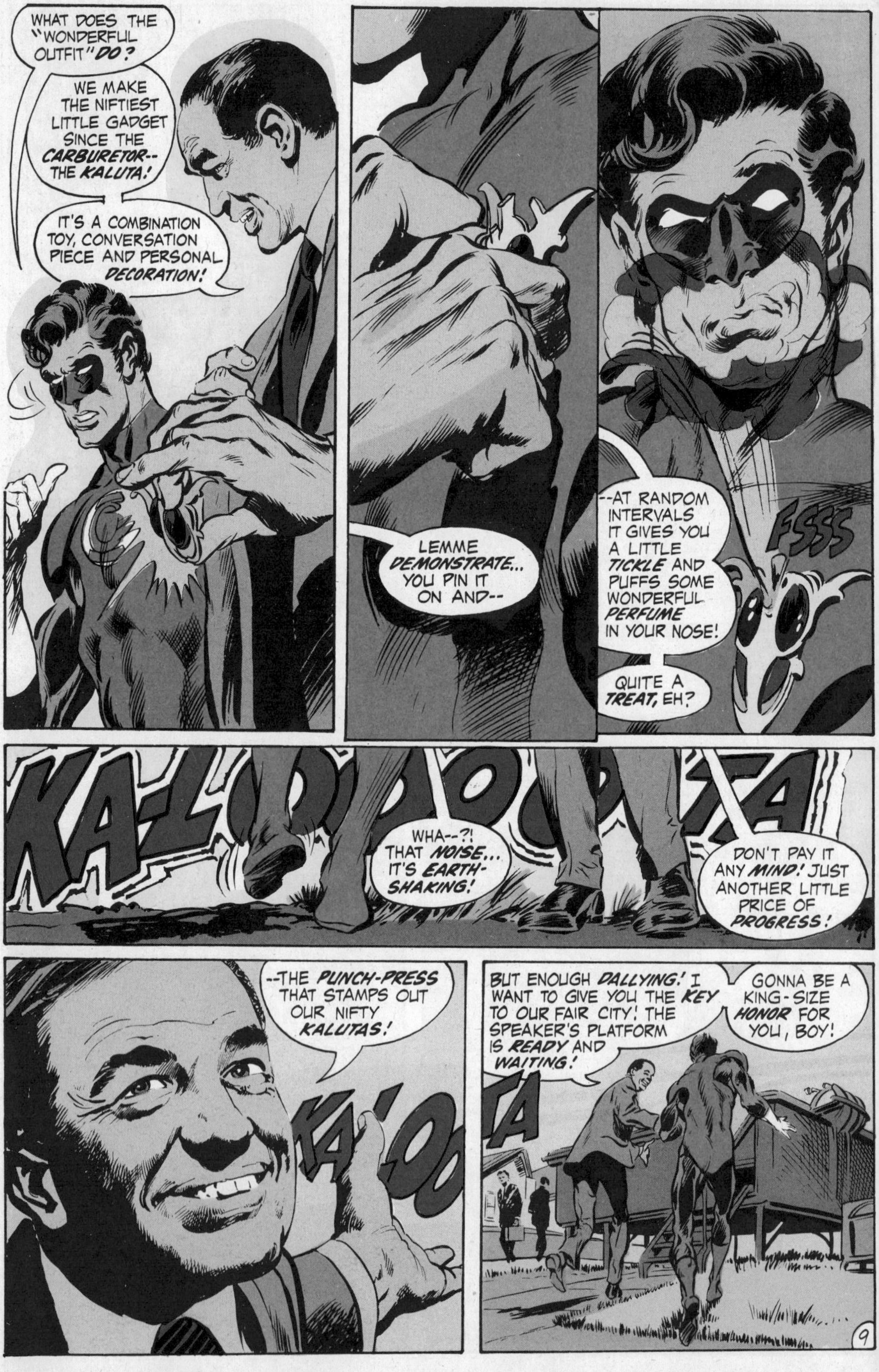
WHAT DOES THE "WONDERFUL OUTFIT" DO?
WE MAKE THE NIFTIEST LITTLE GADGET SINCE THE CARBURETOR-- THE KALUTA!
IT'S A COMBINATION TOY, CONVERSATION PIECE AND PERSONAL DECORATION!
LEMME DEMONSTRATE... YOU PIN IT ON AND--
--AT RANDOM INTERVALS IT GIVES YOU A LITTLE TICKLE AND PUFFS SOME WONDERFUL PERFUME IN YOUR NOSE!
FSSS
QUITE A TREAT, EH?
KA-LOOOOOOTA
WHA--?! THAT NOISE... IT'S EARTH-SHAKING!
DON'T PAY IT ANY MIND! JUST ANOTHER LITTLE PRICE OF PROGRESS!
--THE PUNCH-PRESS THAT STAMPS OUT OUR NIFTY KALUTAS!
KA'OO
BUT ENOUGH DALLYING! I WANT TO GIVE YOU THE KEY TO OUR FAIR CITY! THE SPEAKER'S PLATFORM IS READY AND WAITING!
TA
GONNA BE A KING-SIZE HONOR FOR YOU, BOY!
9

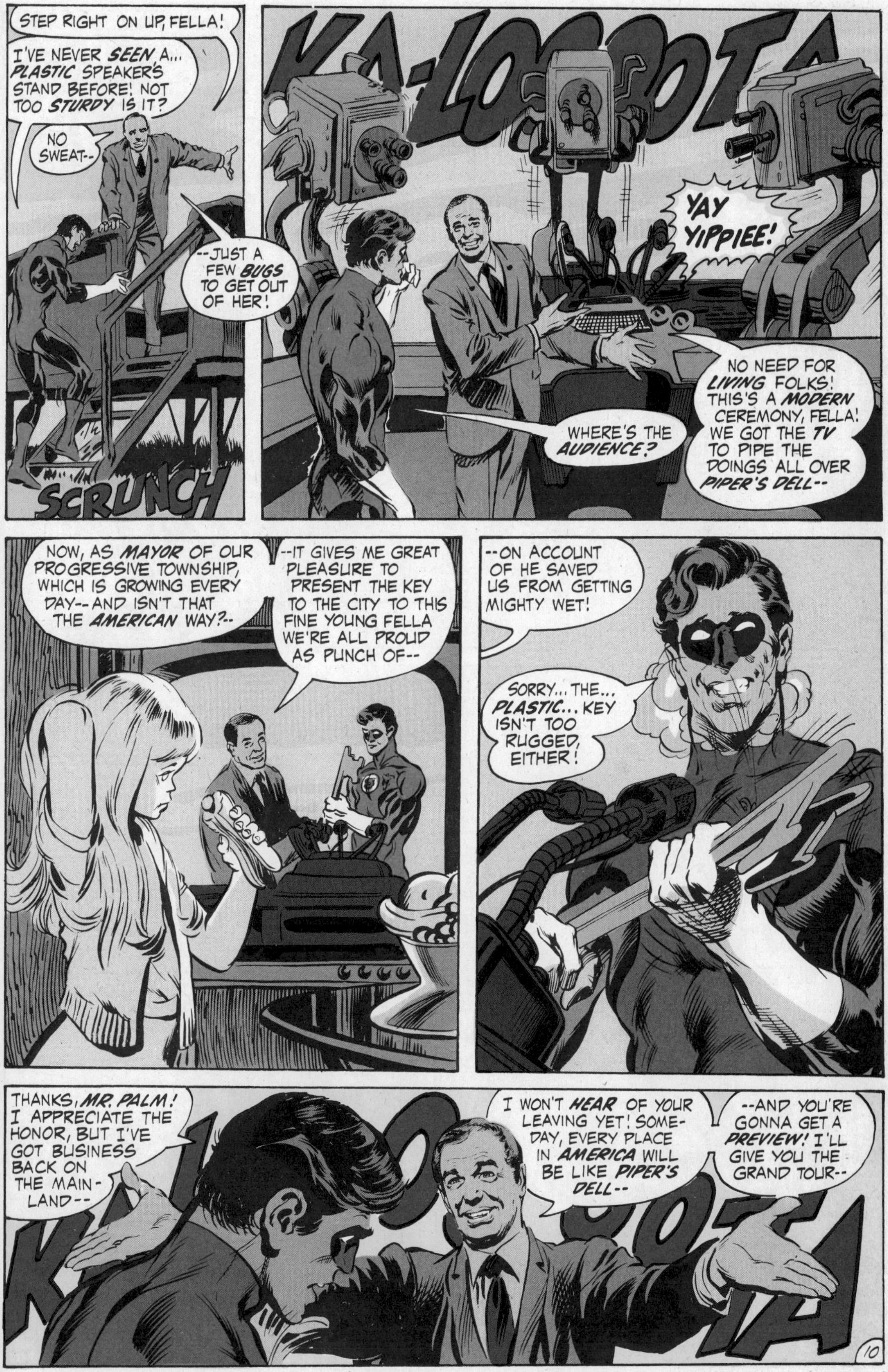

STEP RIGHT ON UP, FELLA!
I'VE NEVER SEEN A... PLASTIC SPEAKER'S STAND BEFORE! NOT TOO STURDY IS IT?
NO SWEAT--
--JUST A FEW BUGS TO GET OUT OF HER!
SCRUNCH
KA-LOOOOTA
YAY YIPPIEE!
WHERE'S THE AUDIENCE?
NO NEED FOR LIVING FOLKS! THIS'S A MODERN CEREMONY, FELLA! WE GOT THE TV TO PIPE THE DOINGS ALL OVER PIPER'S DELL--
NOW, AS MAYOR OF OUR PROGRESSIVE TOWNSHIP, WHICH IS GROWING EVERY DAY-- AND ISN'T THAT THE AMERICAN WAY?--
--IT GIVES ME GREAT PLEASURE TO PRESENT THE KEY TO THE CITY TO THIS FINE YOUNG FELLA WE'RE ALL PROUD AS PUNCH OF--
--ON ACCOUNT OF HE SAVED US FROM GETTING MIGHTY WET!
SORRY... THE... PLASTIC... KEY ISN'T TOO RUGGED, EITHER!
THANKS, MR. PALM! I APPRECIATE THE HONOR, BUT I'VE GOT BUSINESS BACK ON THE MAIN-LAND--
I WON'T HEAR OF YOUR LEAVING YET! SOME-DAY, EVERY PLACE IN AMERICA WILL BE LIKE PIPER'S DELL--
--AND YOU'RE GONNA GET A PREVIEW! I'LL GIVE YOU THE GRAND TOUR--
10

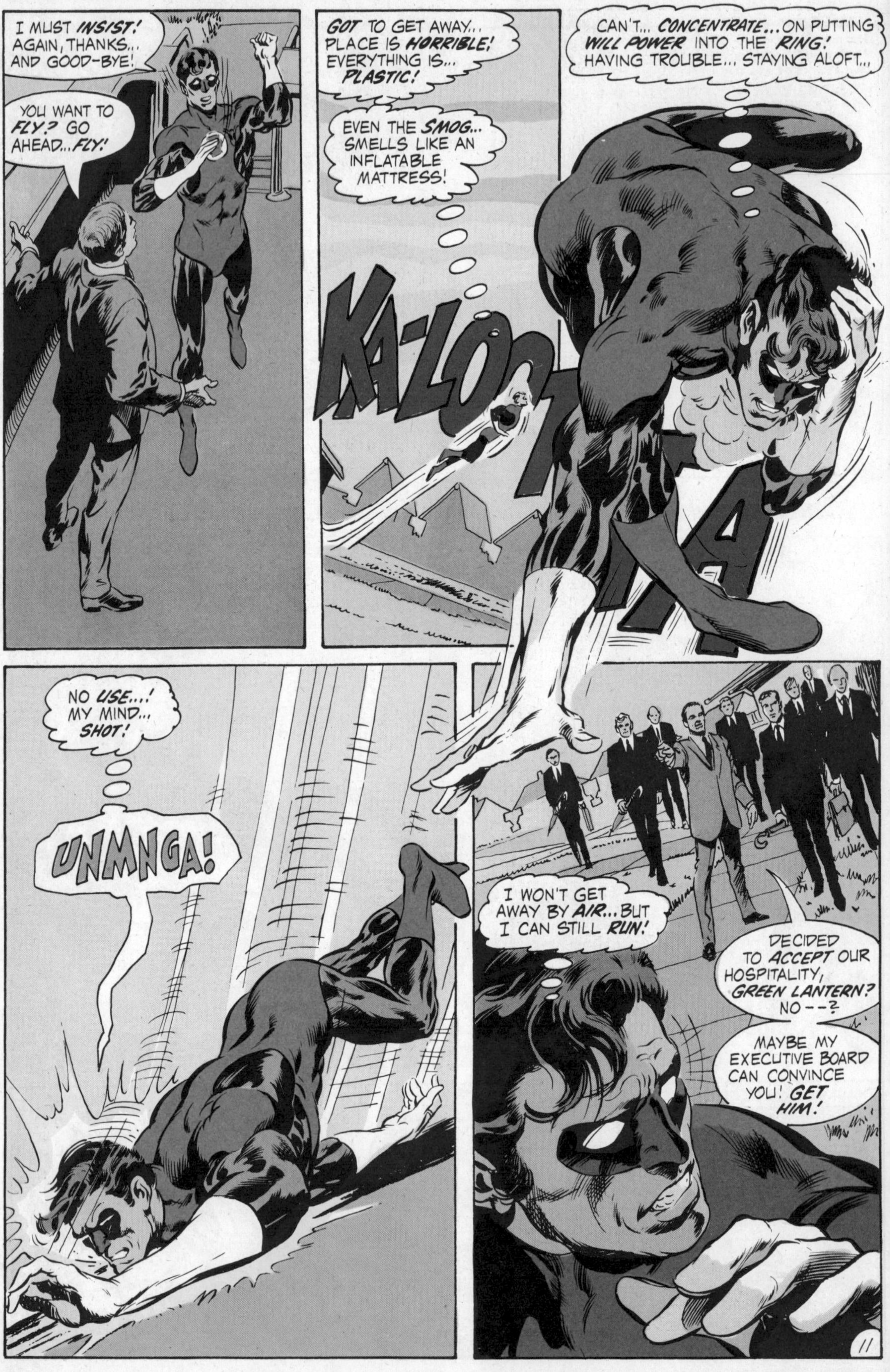
I MUST INSIST! AGAIN, THANKS... AND GOOD-BYE!
YOU WANT TO FLY? GO AHEAD...FLY!
GOT TO GET AWAY... PLACE IS HORRIBLE! EVERYTHING IS... PLASTIC!
EVEN THE SMOG... SMELLS LIKE AN INFLATABLE MATTRESS!
KA-LOOTTA
CAN'T... CONCENTRATE... ON PUTTING WILL POWER INTO THE RING! HAVING TROUBLE... STAYING ALOFT...
NO USE...! MY MIND... SHOT!
UNMNGA!
I WON'T GET AWAY BY AIR... BUT I CAN STILL RUN!
DECIDED TO ACCEPT OUR HOSPITALITY, GREEN LANTERN? NO--?
MAYBE MY EXECUTIVE BOARD CAN CONVINCE YOU! GET HIM!
11

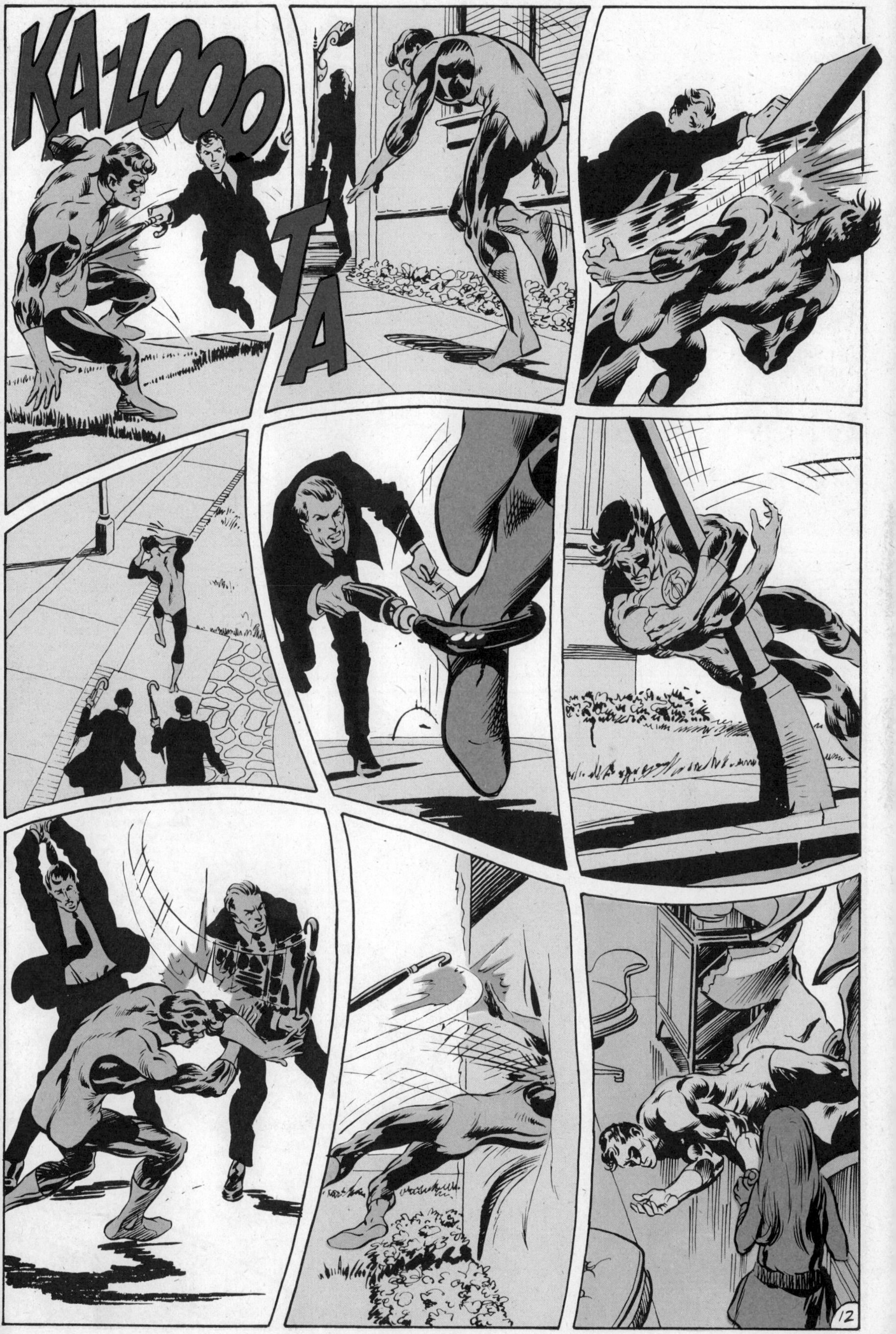
KA-LOOO
TA
12

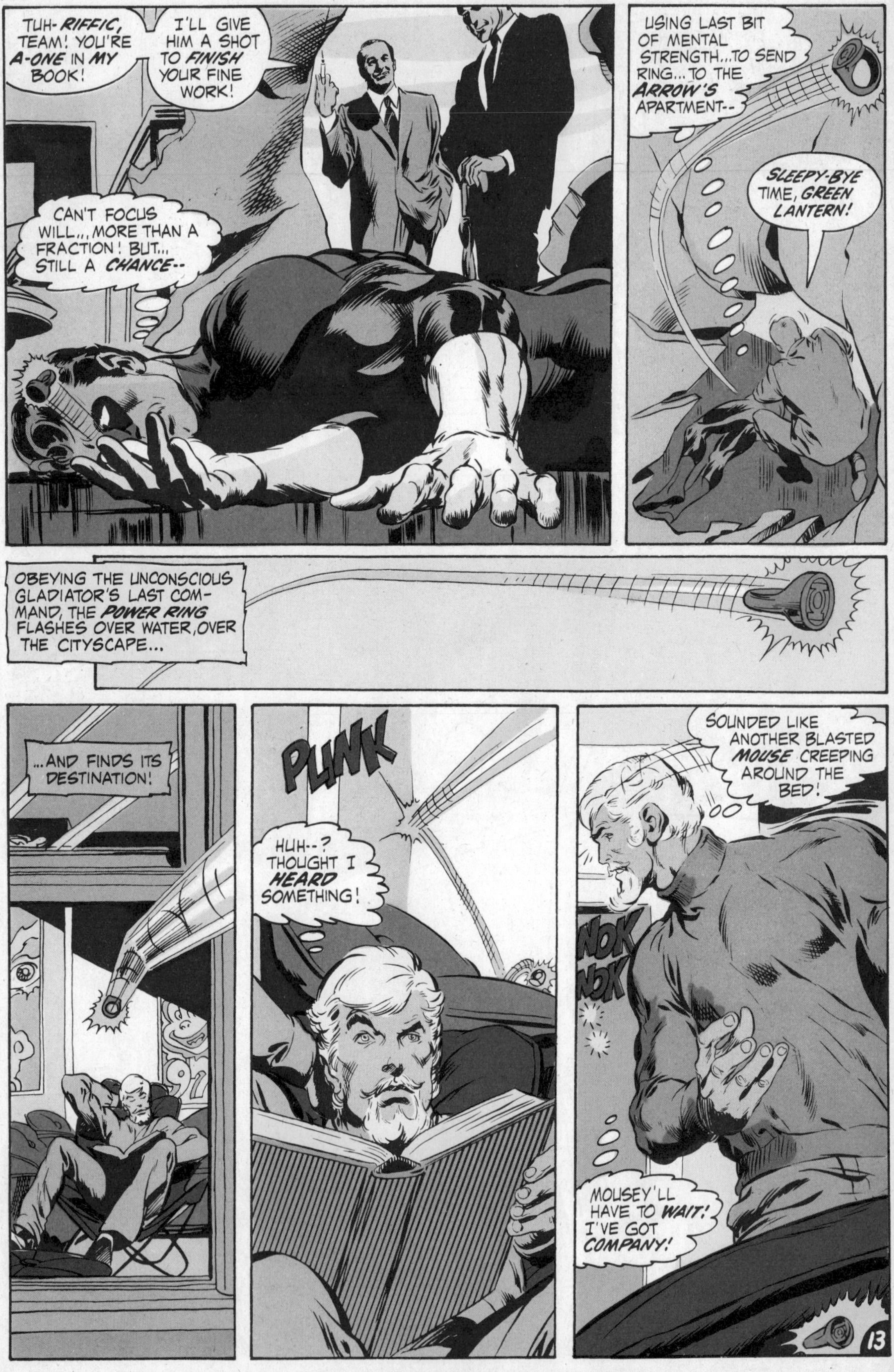
TUH-RIFFIC, TEAM! YOU'RE A-ONE IN MY BOOK!
I'LL GIVE HIM A SHOT TO FINISH YOUR FINE WORK!
CAN'T FOCUS WILL... MORE THAN A FRACTION! BUT... STILL A CHANCE--
USING LAST BIT OF MENTAL STRENGTH... TO SEND RING... TO THE ARROW'S APARTMENT--
SLEEPY-BYE TIME, GREEN LANTERN!
OBEYING THE UNCONSCIOUS GLADIATOR'S LAST COMMAND, THE POWER RING FLASHES OVER WATER, OVER THE CITYSCAPE...
...AND FINDS ITS DESTINATION!
PLINK
HUH--? THOUGHT I HEARD SOMETHING!
SOUNDED LIKE ANOTHER BLASTED MOUSE CREEPING AROUND THE BED!
NOK NOK
MOUSEY'LL HAVE TO WAIT! I'VE GOT COMPANY!
13

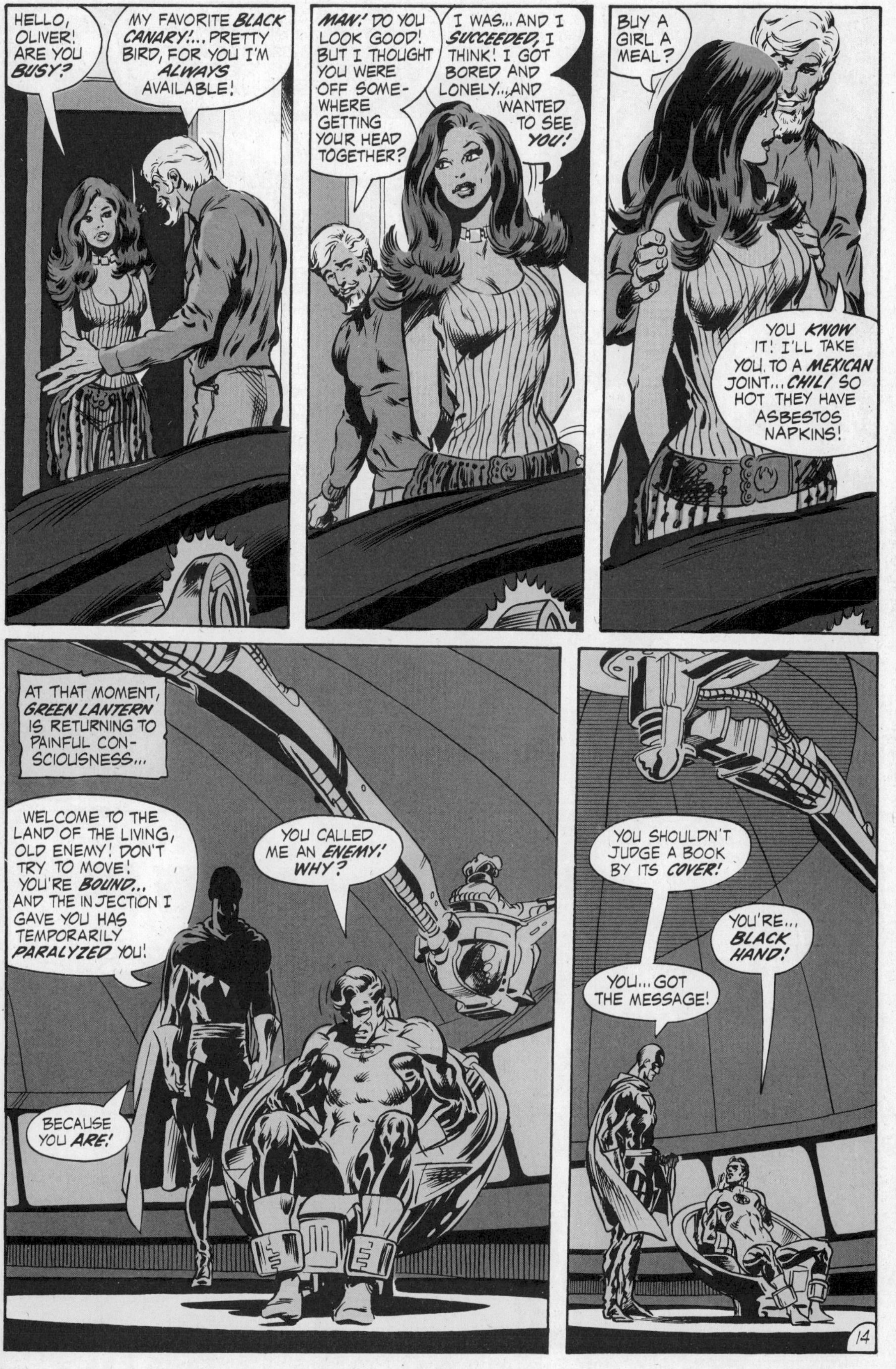

HELLO, OLIVER! ARE YOU BUSY?
MY FAVORITE BLACK CANARY!... PRETTY BIRD, FOR YOU I'M ALWAYS AVAILABLE!
MAN! DO YOU LOOK GOOD! BUT I THOUGHT YOU WERE OFF SOMEWHERE GETTING YOUR HEAD TOGETHER?
I WAS... AND I SUCCEEDED, I THINK! I GOT BORED AND LONELY... AND WANTED TO SEE YOU!
BUY A GIRL A MEAL?
YOU KNOW IT! I'LL TAKE YOU TO A MEXICAN JOINT... CHILI SO HOT THEY HAVE ASBESTOS NAPKINS!
AT THAT MOMENT, GREEN LANTERN IS RETURNING TO PAINFUL CONSCIOUSNESS...
WELCOME TO THE LAND OF THE LIVING, OLD ENEMY! DON'T TRY TO MOVE! YOU'RE BOUND... AND THE INJECTION I GAVE YOU HAS TEMPORARILY PARALYZED YOU!
YOU CALLED ME AN ENEMY! WHY?
BECAUSE YOU ARE!
YOU SHOULDN'T JUDGE A BOOK BY ITS COVER!
YOU'RE... BLACK HAND!
YOU... GOT THE MESSAGE!
14

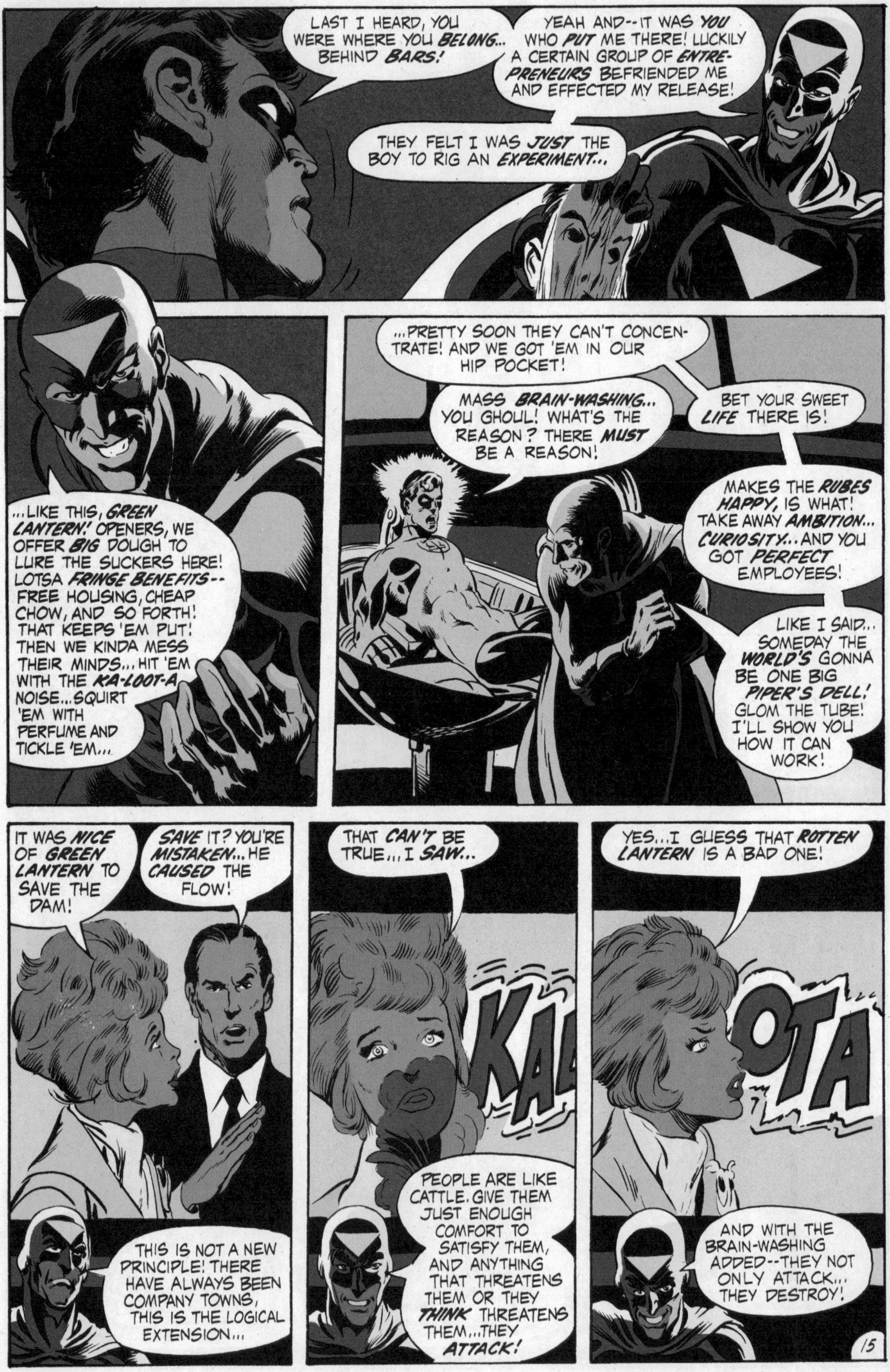

LAST I HEARD, YOU WERE WHERE YOU BELONG... BEHIND BARS!
YEAH AND--IT WAS YOU WHO PUT ME THERE! LUCKILY A CERTAIN GROUP OF ENTRE-PRENEURS BEFRIENDED ME AND EFFECTED MY RELEASE!
THEY FELT I WAS JUST THE BOY TO RIG AN EXPERIMENT...
...LIKE THIS, GREEN LANTERN! OPENERS, WE OFFER BIG DOUGH TO LURE THE SUCKERS HERE! LOTSA FRINGE BENEFITS--FREE HOUSING, CHEAP CHOW, AND SO FORTH! THAT KEEPS 'EM PUT! THEN WE KINDA MESS THEIR MINDS... HIT 'EM WITH THE KA-LOOT-A NOISE...SQUIRT 'EM WITH PERFUME AND TICKLE 'EM...
...PRETTY SOON THEY CAN'T CONCEN-TRATE! AND WE GOT 'EM IN OUR HIP POCKET!
MASS BRAIN-WASHING... YOU GHOUL! WHAT'S THE REASON? THERE MUST BE A REASON!
BET YOUR SWEET LIFE THERE IS!
MAKES THE RUBES HAPPY, IS WHAT! TAKE AWAY AMBITION... CURIOSITY...AND YOU GOT PERFECT EMPLOYEES!
LIKE I SAID... SOMEDAY THE WORLD'S GONNA BE ONE BIG PIPER'S DELL! GLOM THE TUBE! I'LL SHOW YOU HOW IT CAN WORK!
IT WAS NICE OF GREEN LANTERN TO SAVE THE DAM!
SAVE IT? YOU'RE MISTAKEN... HE CAUSED THE FLOW!
THIS IS NOT A NEW PRINCIPLE! THERE HAVE ALWAYS BEEN COMPANY TOWNS, THIS IS THE LOGICAL EXTENSION...
THAT CAN'T BE TRUE... I SAW...
KA
PEOPLE ARE LIKE CATTLE. GIVE THEM JUST ENOUGH COMFORT TO SATISFY THEM, AND ANYTHING THAT THREATENS THEM OR THEY THINK THREATENS THEM... THEY ATTACK!
YES... I GUESS THAT ROTTEN LANTERN IS A BAD ONE!
OTA
AND WITH THE BRAIN-WASHING ADDED--THEY NOT ONLY ATTACK... THEY DESTROY!
15

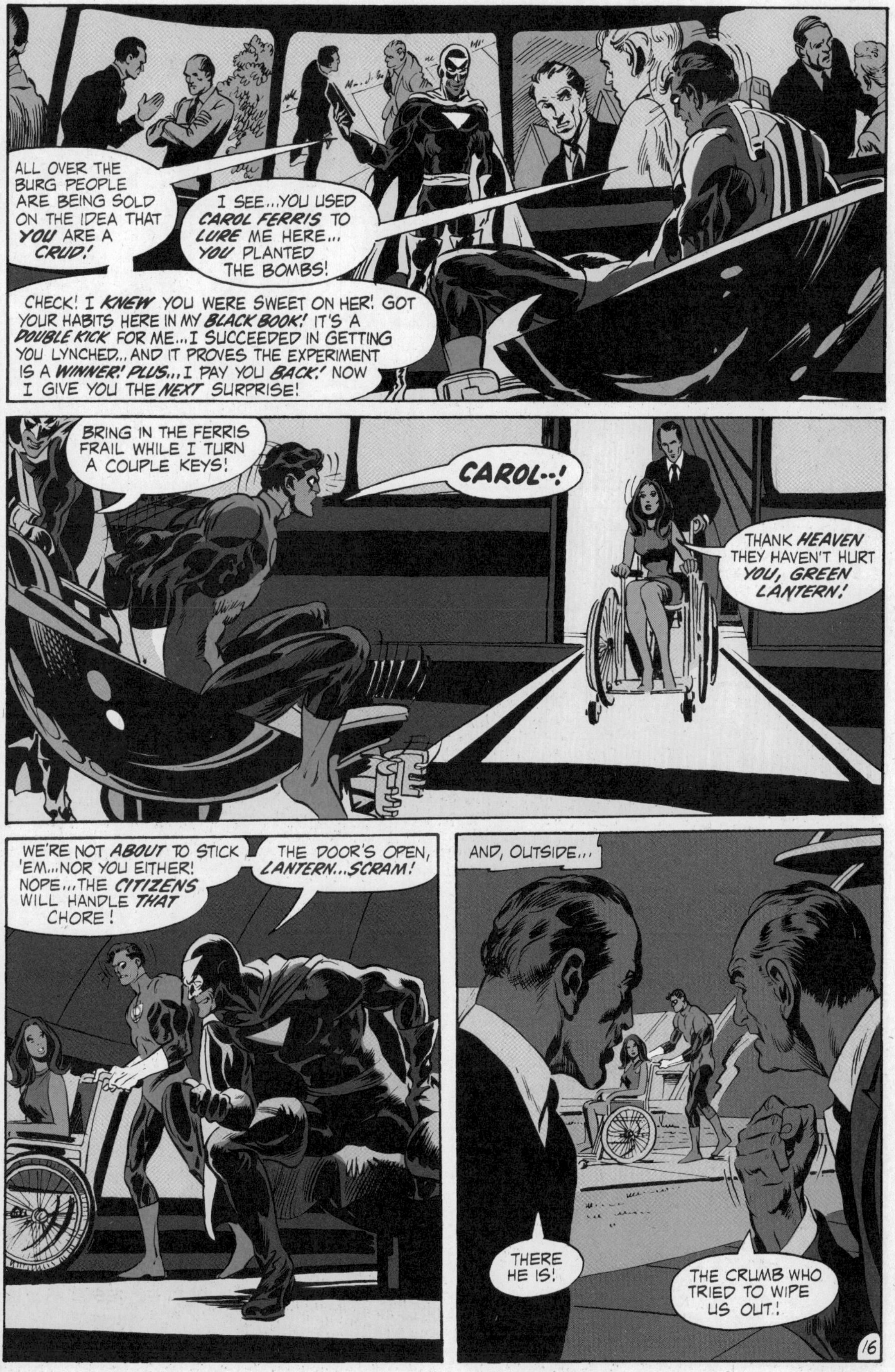

ALL OVER THE BURG PEOPLE ARE BEING SOLD ON THE IDEA THAT YOU ARE A CRUD!
I SEE...YOU USED CAROL FERRIS TO LURE ME HERE... YOU PLANTED THE BOMBS!
CHECK! I KNEW YOU WERE SWEET ON HER! GOT YOUR HABITS HERE IN MY BLACK BOOK! IT'S A DOUBLE KICK FOR ME...I SUCCEEDED IN GETTING YOU LYNCHED... AND IT PROVES THE EXPERIMENT IS A WINNER! PLUS... I PAY YOU BACK! NOW I GIVE YOU THE NEXT SURPRISE!
BRING IN THE FERRIS FRAIL WHILE I TURN A COUPLE KEYS!
CAROL--!
THANK HEAVEN THEY HAVEN'T HURT YOU, GREEN LANTERN!
WE'RE NOT ABOUT TO STICK 'EM...NOR YOU EITHER! NOPE...THE CITIZENS WILL HANDLE THAT CHORE!
THE DOOR'S OPEN, LANTERN...SCRAM!
AND, OUTSIDE...
THERE HE IS!
THE CRUMB WHO TRIED TO WIPE US OUT!
16

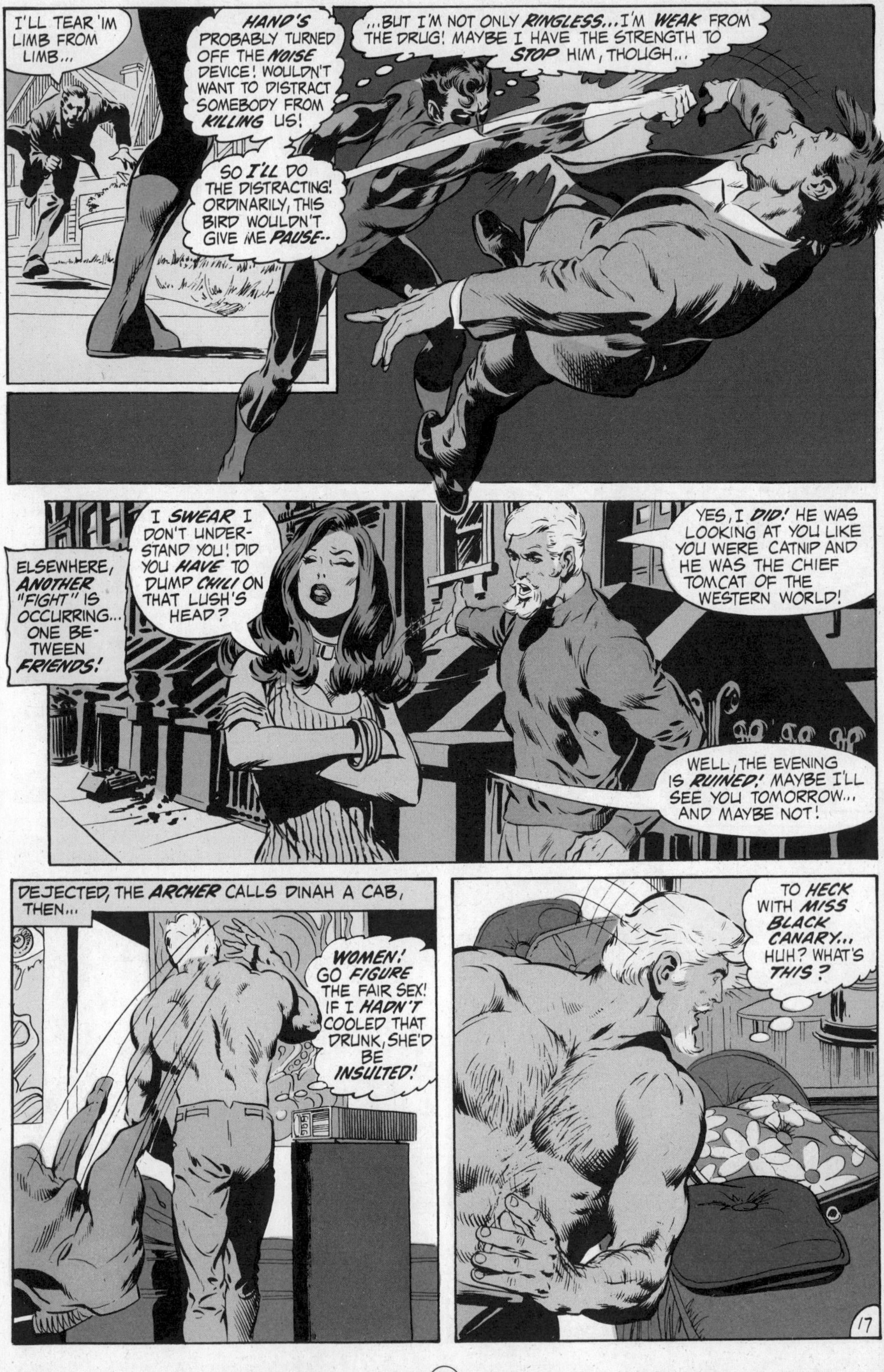

I'LL TEAR 'IM LIMB FROM LIMB...
HAND'S PROBABLY TURNED OFF THE NOISE DEVICE! WOULDN'T WANT TO DISTRACT SOMEBODY FROM KILLING US!
...BUT I'M NOT ONLY RINGLESS...I'M WEAK FROM THE DRUG! MAYBE I HAVE THE STRENGTH TO STOP HIM, THOUGH...
SO I'LL DO THE DISTRACTING! ORDINARILY, THIS BIRD WOULDN'T GIVE ME PAUSE..
ELSEWHERE, ANOTHER "FIGHT" IS OCCURRING... ONE BETWEEN FRIENDS!
I SWEAR I DON'T UNDERSTAND YOU! DID YOU HAVE TO DUMP CHILI ON THAT LUSH'S HEAD?
YES, I DID! HE WAS LOOKING AT YOU LIKE YOU WERE CATNIP AND HE WAS THE CHIEF TOMCAT OF THE WESTERN WORLD!
WELL, THE EVENING IS RUINED! MAYBE I'LL SEE YOU TOMORROW... AND MAYBE NOT!
DEJECTED, THE ARCHER CALLS DINAH A CAB, THEN...
WOMEN! GO FIGURE THE FAIR SEX! IF I HADN'T COOLED THAT DRUNK, SHE'D BE INSULTED!
TO HECK WITH MISS BLACK CANARY... HUH? WHAT'S THIS?
17

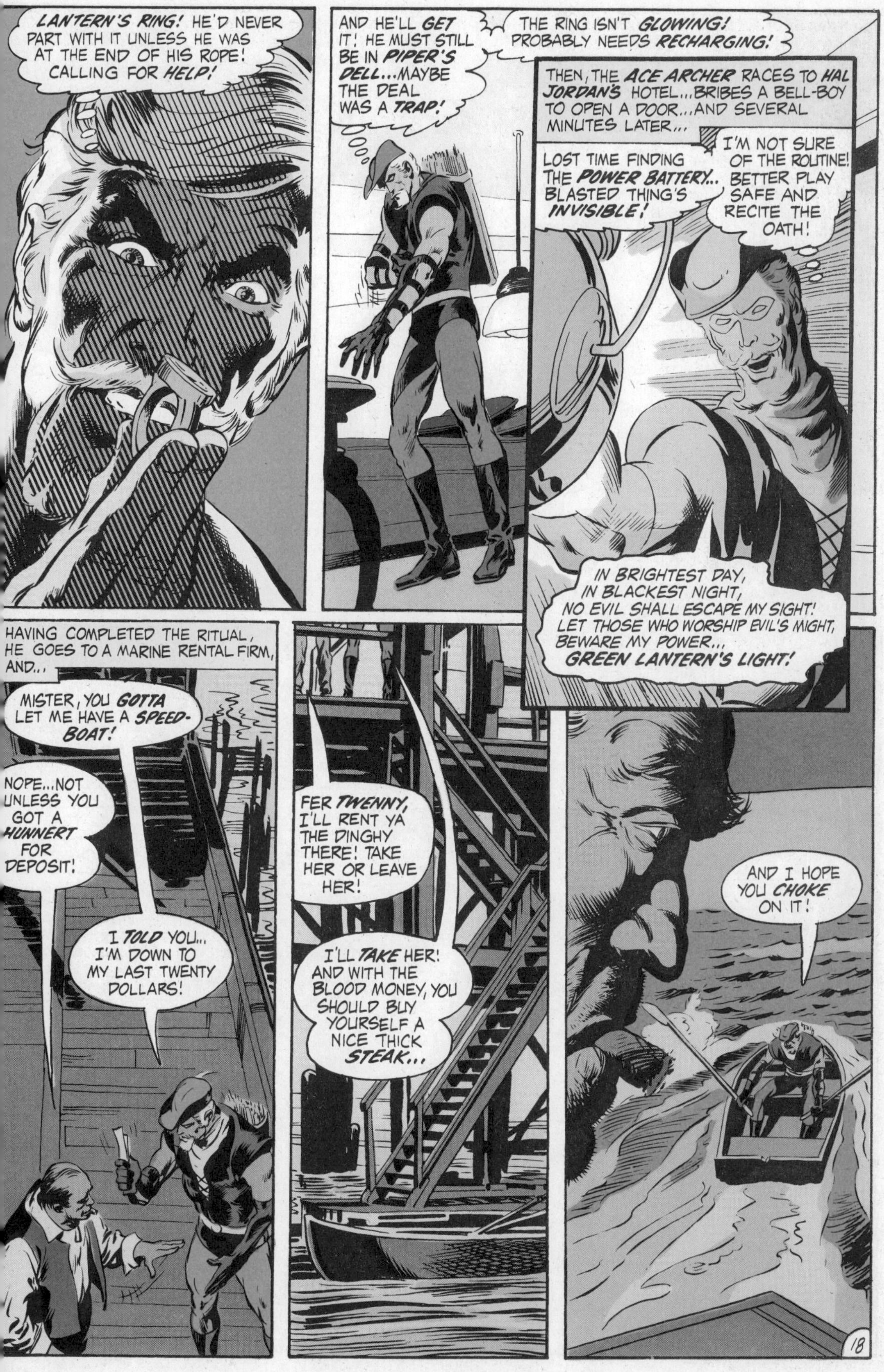
LANTERN'S RING! HE'D NEVER PART WITH IT UNLESS HE WAS AT THE END OF HIS ROPE! CALLING FOR HELP!
AND HE'LL GET IT! HE MUST STILL BE IN PIPER'S DELL...MAYBE THE DEAL WAS A TRAP!
THE RING ISN'T GLOWING! PROBABLY NEEDS RECHARGING!
THEN, THE ACE ARCHER RACES TO HAL JORDAN'S HOTEL...BRIBES A BELL-BOY TO OPEN A DOOR...AND SEVERAL MINUTES LATER...
LOST TIME FINDING THE POWER BATTERY... BLASTED THING'S INVISIBLE!
I'M NOT SURE OF THE ROUTINE! BETTER PLAY SAFE AND RECITE THE OATH!
IN BRIGHTEST DAY, IN BLACKEST NIGHT, NO EVIL SHALL ESCAPE MY SIGHT! LET THOSE WHO WORSHIP EVIL'S MIGHT, BEWARE MY POWER... GREEN LANTERN'S LIGHT!
HAVING COMPLETED THE RITUAL, HE GOES TO A MARINE RENTAL FIRM, AND...
MISTER, YOU GOTTA LET ME HAVE A SPEED-BOAT!
NOPE...NOT UNLESS YOU GOT A HUNNERT FOR DEPOSIT!
I TOLD YOU... I'M DOWN TO MY LAST TWENTY DOLLARS!
FER TWENNY, I'LL RENT YA THE DINGHY THERE! TAKE HER OR LEAVE HER!
I'LL TAKE HER! AND WITH THE BLOOD MONEY, YOU SHOULD BUY YOURSELF A NICE THICK STEAK...
AND I HOPE YOU CHOKE ON IT!
18

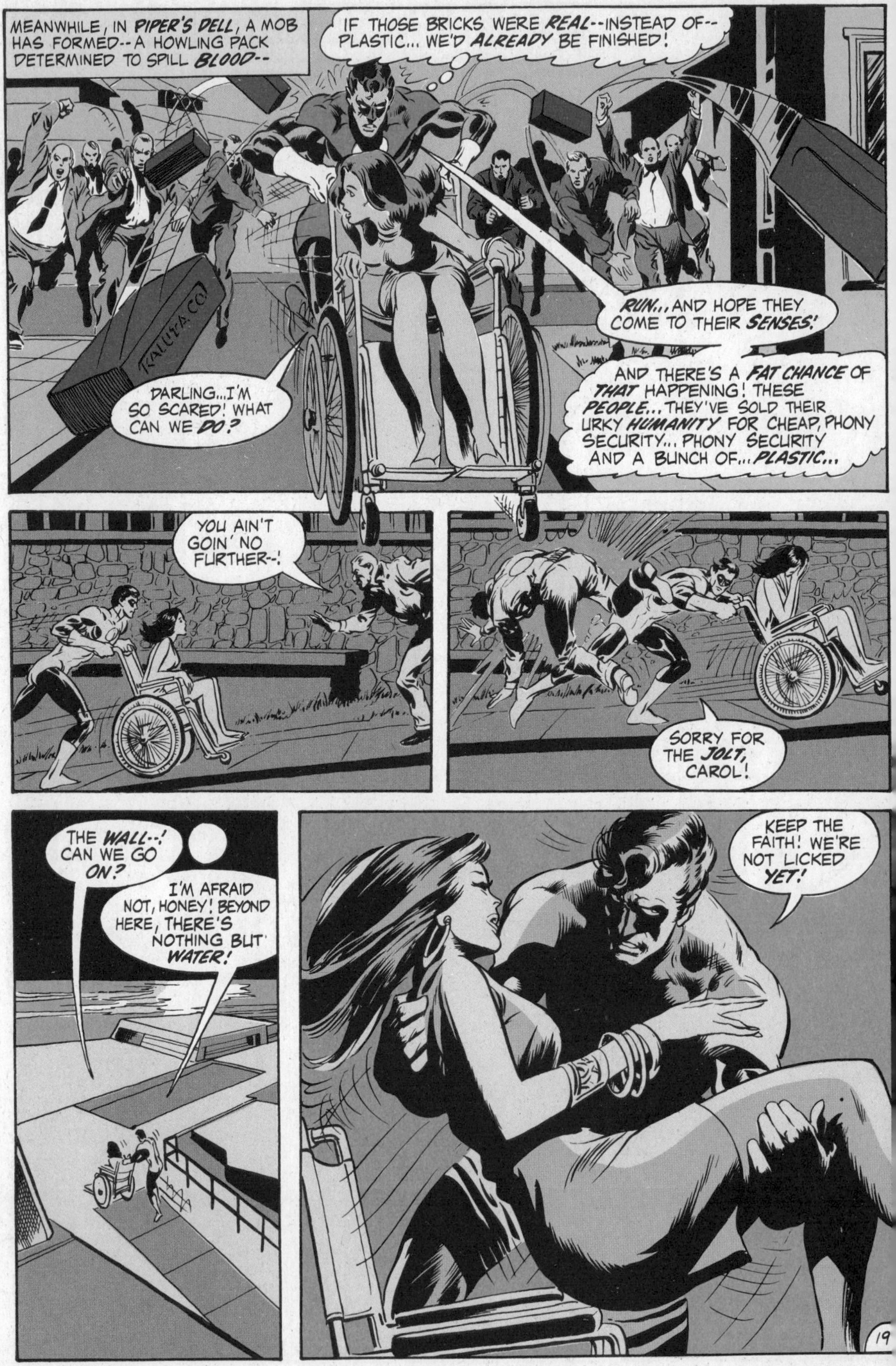

MEANWHILE, IN PIPER'S DELL, A MOB HAS FORMED--A HOWLING PACK DETERMINED TO SPILL BLOOD--
IF THOSE BRICKS WERE REAL--INSTEAD OF--PLASTIC... WE'D ALREADY BE FINISHED!
KALUTA CO.
DARLING...I'M SO SCARED! WHAT CAN WE DO?
RUN... AND HOPE THEY COME TO THEIR SENSES!
AND THERE'S A FAT CHANCE OF THAT HAPPENING! THESE PEOPLE... THEY'VE SOLD THEIR URKY HUMANITY FOR CHEAP, PHONY SECURITY... PHONY SECURITY AND A BUNCH OF... PLASTIC...
YOU AIN'T GOIN' NO FURTHER--!
SORRY FOR THE JOLT, CAROL!
THE WALL--! CAN WE GO ON?
I'M AFRAID NOT, HONEY! BEYOND HERE, THERE'S NOTHING BUT WATER!
KEEP THE FAITH! WE'RE NOT LICKED YET!
19

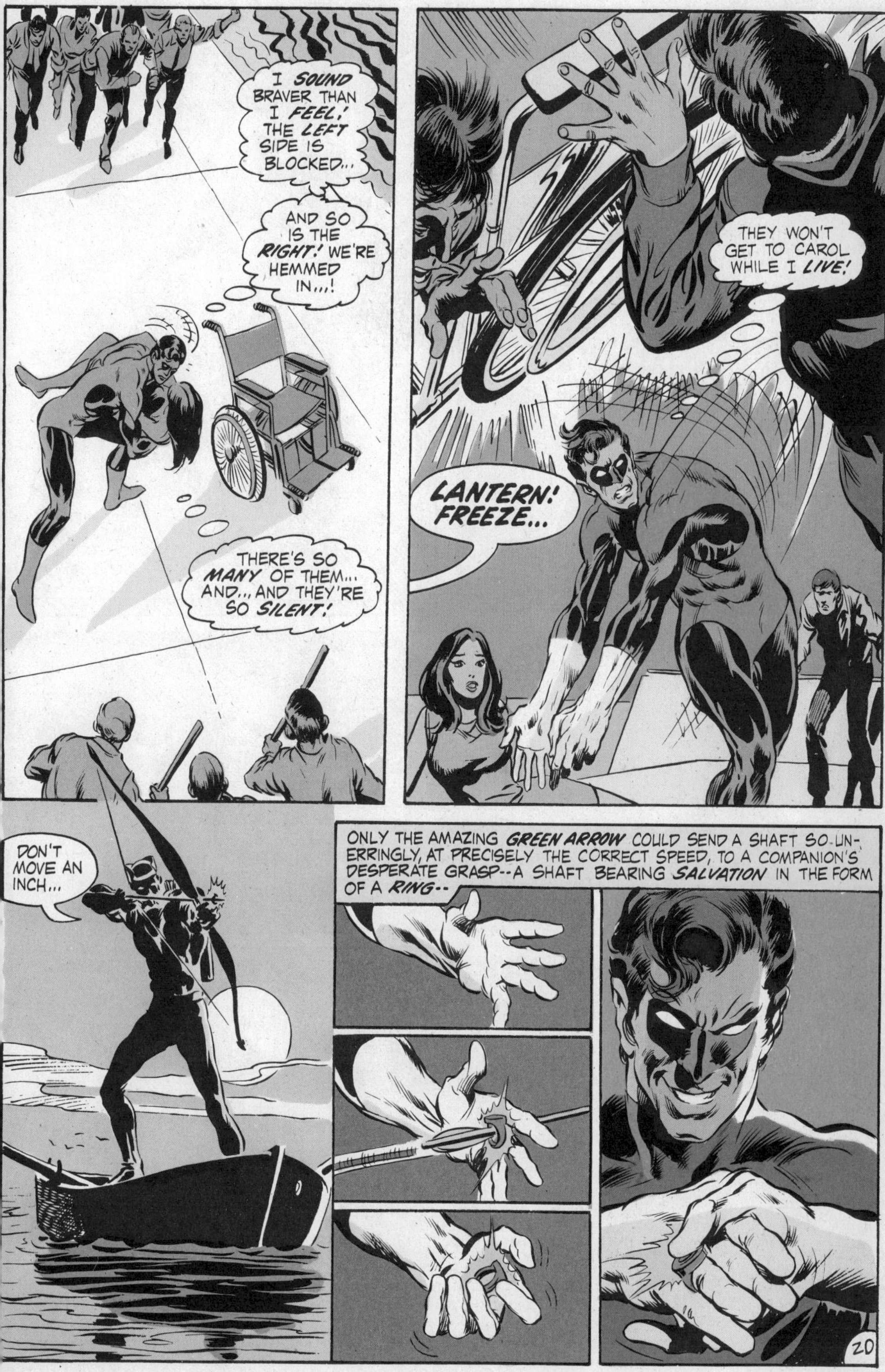
I SOUND BRAVER THAN I FEEL! THE LEFT SIDE IS BLOCKED...
AND SO IS THE RIGHT! WE'RE HEMMED IN...!
THERE'S SO MANY OF THEM... AND... AND THEY'RE SO SILENT!
THEY WON'T GET TO CAROL WHILE I LIVE!
LANTERN! FREEZE...
DON'T MOVE AN INCH...
ONLY THE AMAZING GREEN ARROW COULD SEND A SHAFT SO UN-ERRINGLY, AT PRECISELY THE CORRECT SPEED, TO A COMPANION'S DESPERATE GRASP--A SHAFT BEARING SALVATION IN THE FORM OF A RING--
20

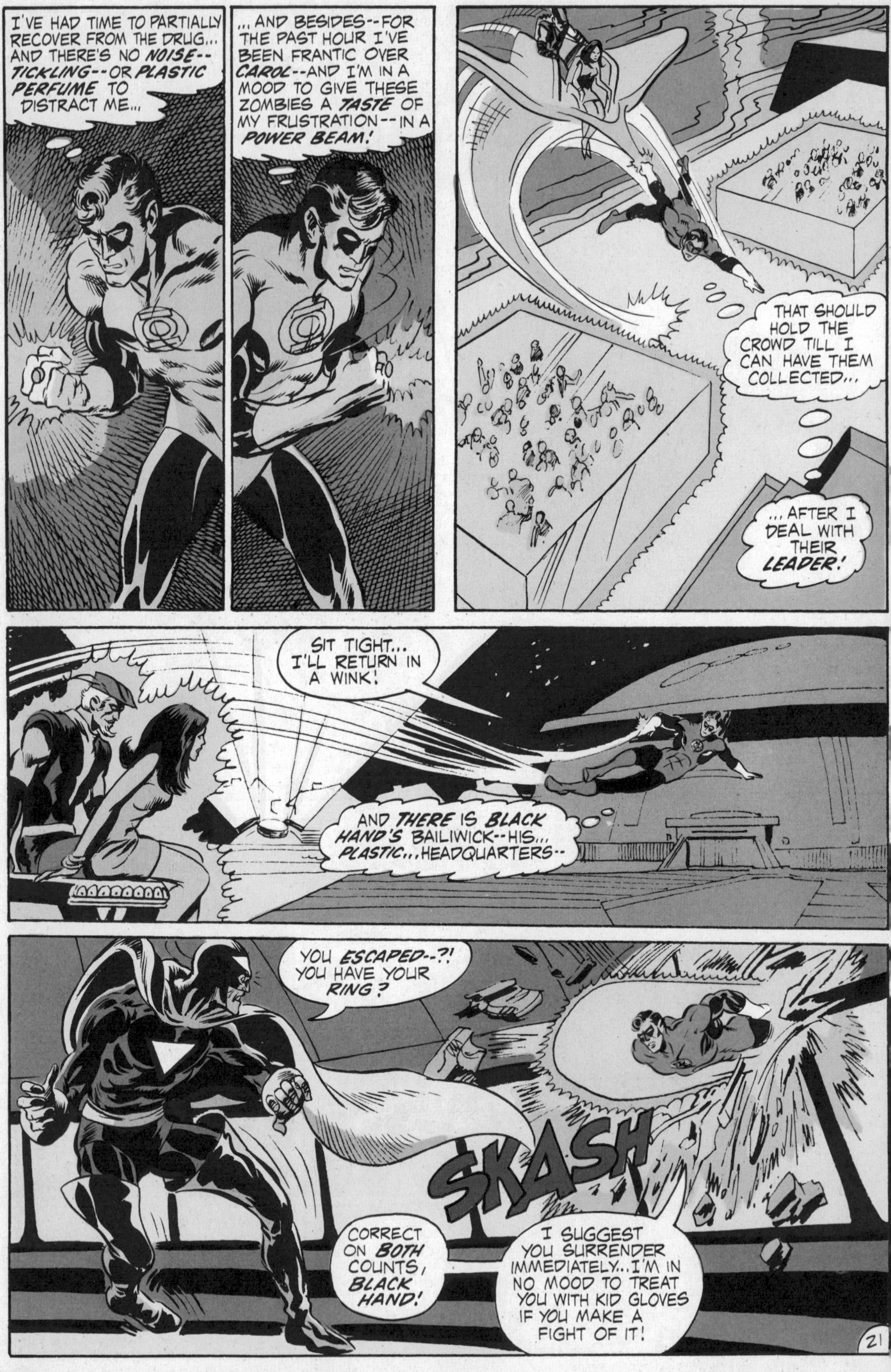
I'VE HAD TIME TO PARTIALLY RECOVER FROM THE DRUG... AND THERE'S NO NOISE-- TICKLING--OR PLASTIC PERFUME TO DISTRACT ME...
...AND BESIDES--FOR THE PAST HOUR I'VE BEEN FRANTIC OVER CAROL--AND I'M IN A MOOD TO GIVE THESE ZOMBIES A TASTE OF MY FRUSTRATION--IN A POWER BEAM!
THAT SHOULD HOLD THE CROWD TILL I CAN HAVE THEM COLLECTED...
...AFTER I DEAL WITH THEIR LEADER!
SIT TIGHT... I'LL RETURN IN A WINK!
AND THERE IS BLACK HAND'S BAILIWICK--HIS... PLASTIC... HEADQUARTERS--
YOU ESCAPED--?! YOU HAVE YOUR RING?
SKASH
CORRECT ON BOTH COUNTS, BLACK HAND!
I SUGGEST YOU SURRENDER IMMEDIATELY...I'M IN NO MOOD TO TREAT YOU WITH KID GLOVES IF YOU MAKE A FIGHT OF IT!
21

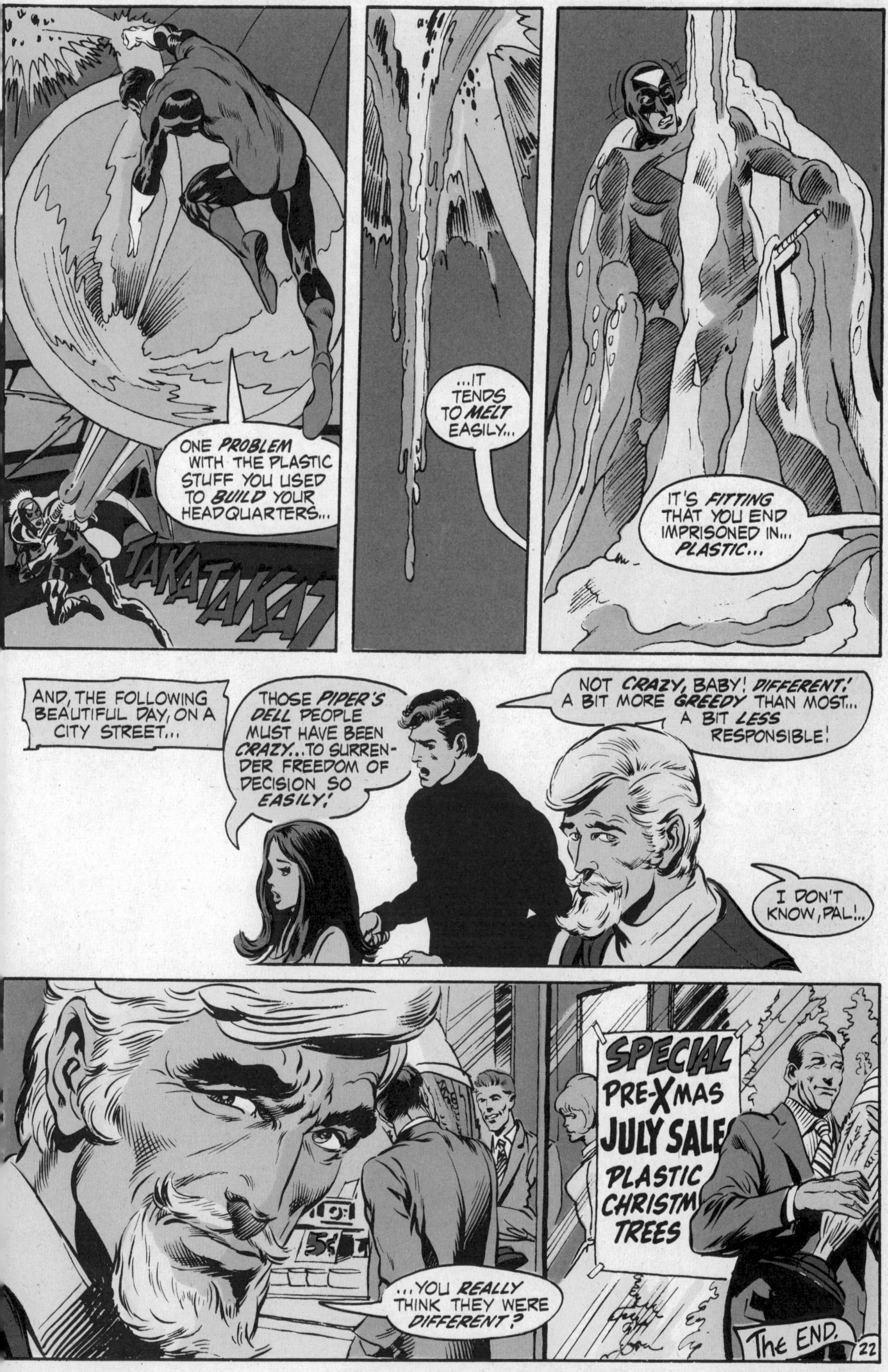
ONE PROBLEM WITH THE PLASTIC STUFF YOU USED TO BUILD YOUR HEADQUARTERS...
TAKATAKAT
...IT TENDS TO MELT EASILY...
IT'S FITTING THAT YOU END IMPRISONED IN... PLASTIC...
AND, THE FOLLOWING BEAUTIFUL DAY, ON A CITY STREET...
THOSE PIPER'S DELL PEOPLE MUST HAVE BEEN CRAZY...TO SURRENDER FREEDOM OF DECISION SO EASILY!
NOT CRAZY, BABY! DIFFERENT! A BIT MORE GREEDY THAN MOST... A BIT LESS RESPONSIBLE!
I DON'T KNOW, PAL!...
...YOU REALLY THINK THEY WERE DIFFERENT?
SPECIAL
PRE-XMAS
JULY SALE
PLASTIC
CHRISTM
TREES
THE END.
22

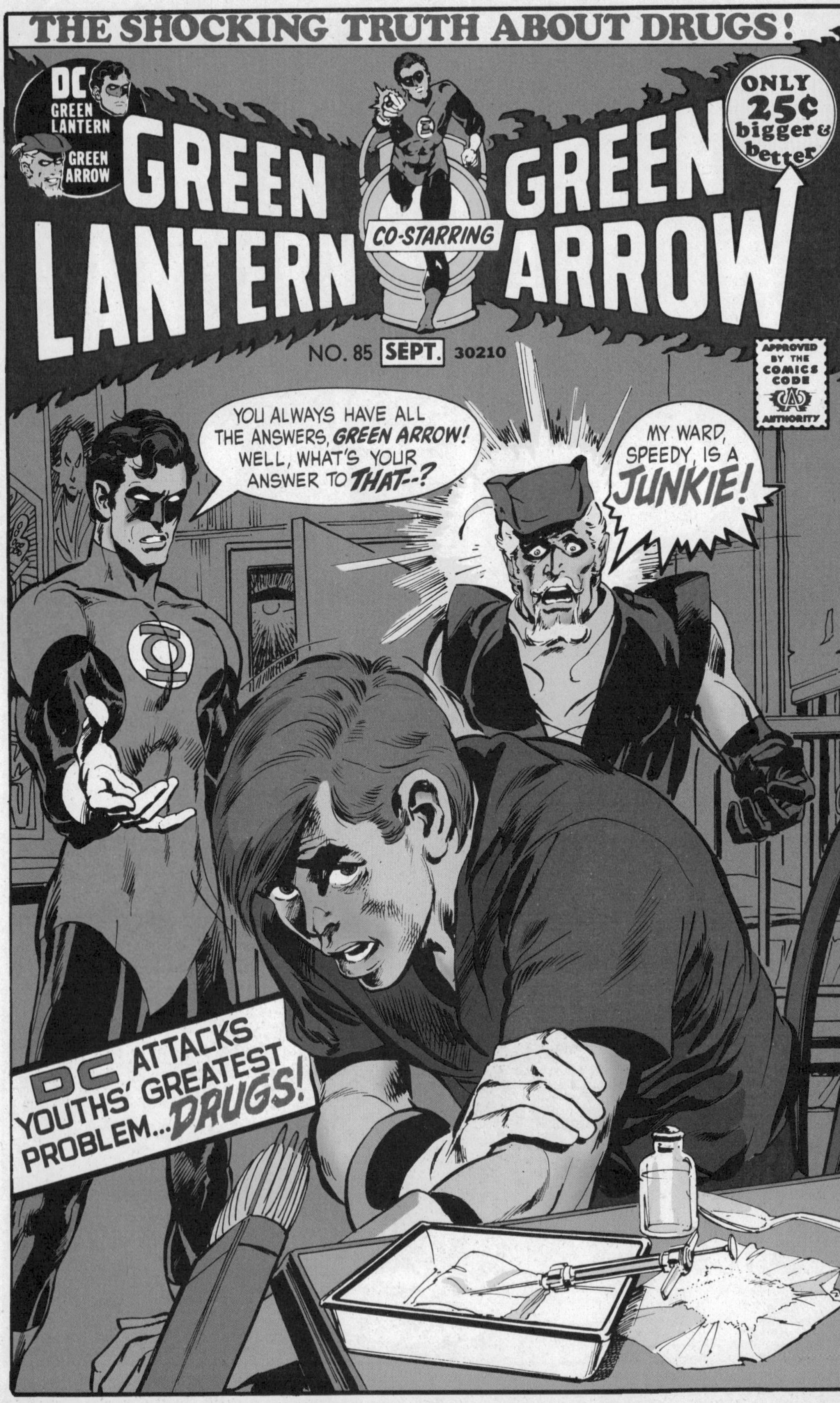
THE SHOCKING TRUTH ABOUT DRUGS!
DC GREEN LANTERN GREEN ARROW
ONLY 25¢ bigger & better
GREEN LANTERN
CO-STARRING
GREEN ARROW
NO. 85 SEPT. 30210
APPROVED BY THE COMICS CODE AUTHORITY
YOU ALWAYS HAVE ALL THE ANSWERS, GREEN ARROW! WELL, WHAT'S YOUR ANSWER TO THAT--?
MY WARD, SPEEDY, IS A JUNKIE!
DC ATTACKS YOUTHS' GREATEST PROBLEM...DRUGS!

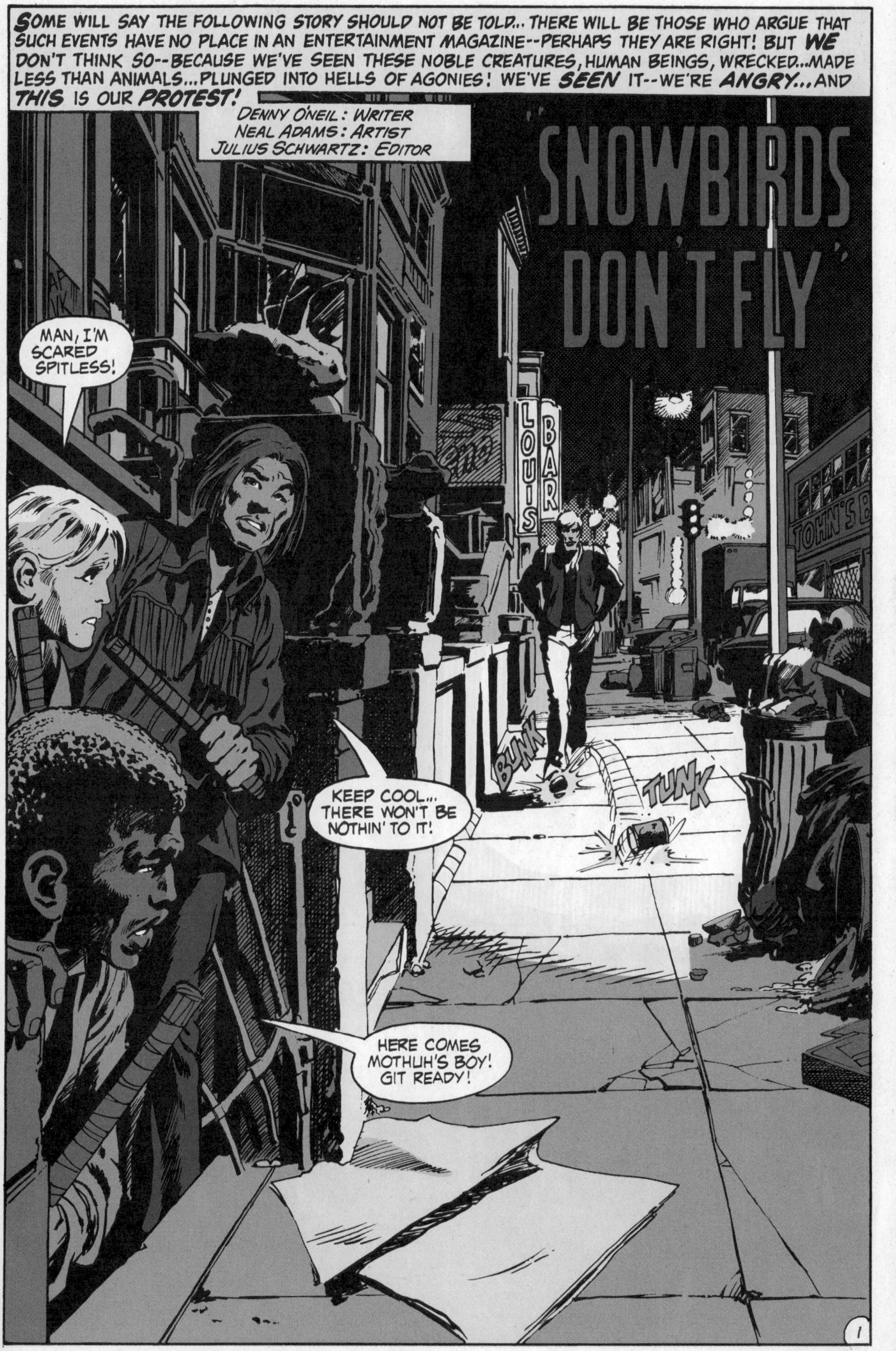
SOME WILL SAY THE FOLLOWING STORY SHOULD NOT BE TOLD.. THERE WILL BE THOSE WHO ARGUE THAT SUCH EVENTS HAVE NO PLACE IN AN ENTERTAINMENT MAGAZINE--PERHAPS THEY ARE RIGHT! BUT WE DON'T THINK SO--BECAUSE WE'VE SEEN THESE NOBLE CREATURES, HUMAN BEINGS, WRECKED...MADE LESS THAN ANIMALS...PLUNGED INTO HELLS OF AGONIES! WE'VE SEEN IT--WE'RE ANGRY...AND THIS IS OUR PROTEST!
DENNY O'NEIL: WRITER
NEAL ADAMS: ARTIST
JULIUS SCHWARTZ: EDITOR
SNOWBIRDS DON'T FLY
MAN, I'M SCARED SPITLESS!
LOUIS
BAR
JOHN'S
BUNK
TUNK
KEEP COOL... THERE WON'T BE NOTHIN' TO IT!
HERE COMES MOTHUH'S BOY! GIT READY!
1

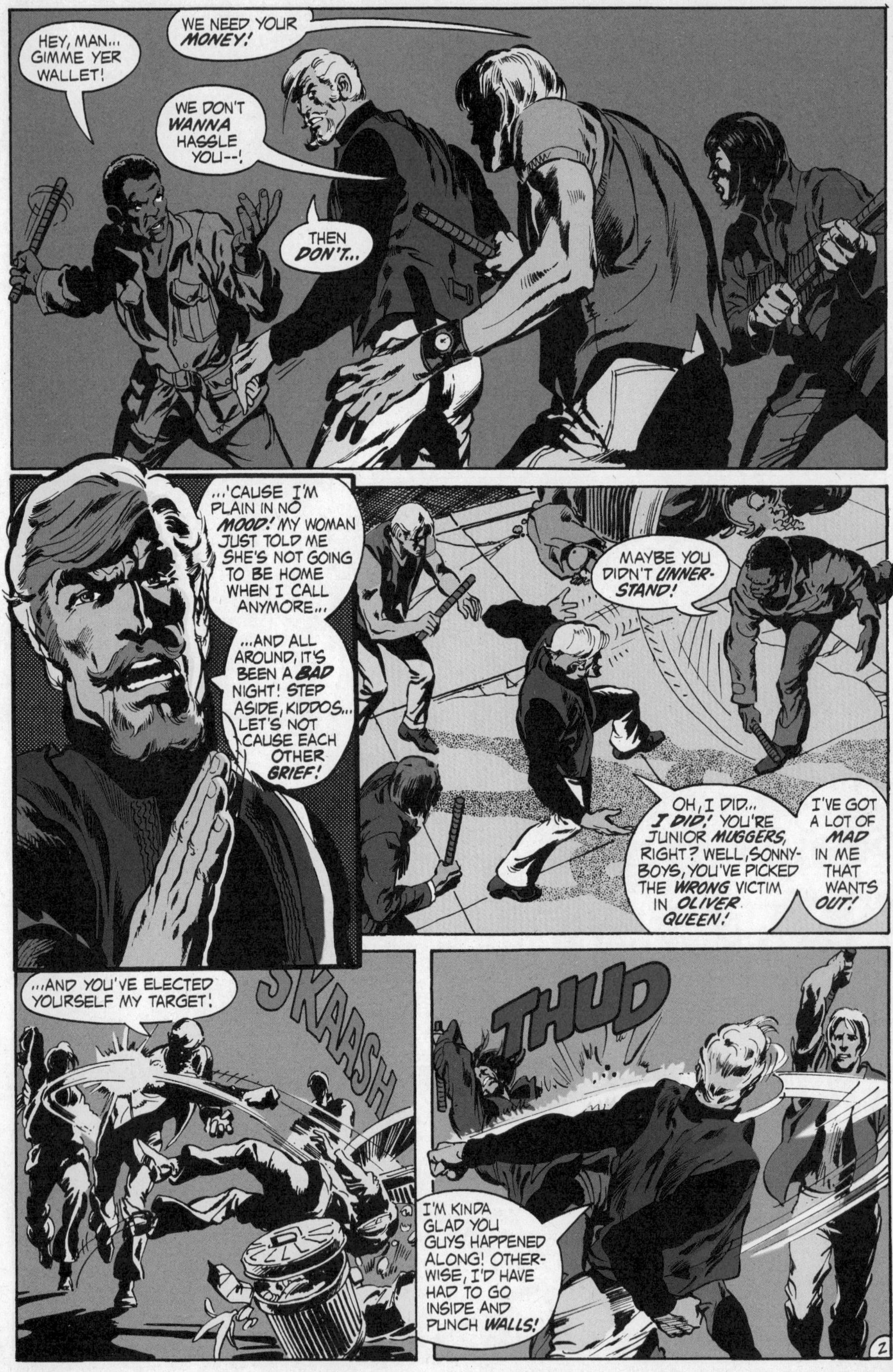
HEY, MAN... GIMME YER WALLET!
WE NEED YOUR MONEY!
WE DON'T WANNA HASSLE YOU--!
THEN DON'T...
...'CAUSE I'M PLAIN IN NO MOOD! MY WOMAN JUST TOLD ME SHE'S NOT GOING TO BE HOME WHEN I CALL ANYMORE...
...AND ALL AROUND, IT'S BEEN A BAD NIGHT! STEP ASIDE, KIDDOS... LET'S NOT CAUSE EACH OTHER GRIEF!
MAYBE YOU DIDN'T UNNER-STAND!
OH, I DID... I DID! YOU'RE JUNIOR MUGGERS, RIGHT? WELL, SONNY-BOYS, YOU'VE PICKED THE WRONG VICTIM IN OLIVER QUEEN!
I'VE GOT A LOT OF MAD IN ME THAT WANTS OUT!
...AND YOU'VE ELECTED YOURSELF MY TARGET!
SKAASH
THUD
I'M KINDA GLAD YOU GUYS HAPPENED ALONG! OTHER-WISE, I'D HAVE HAD TO GO INSIDE AND PUNCH WALLS!
2

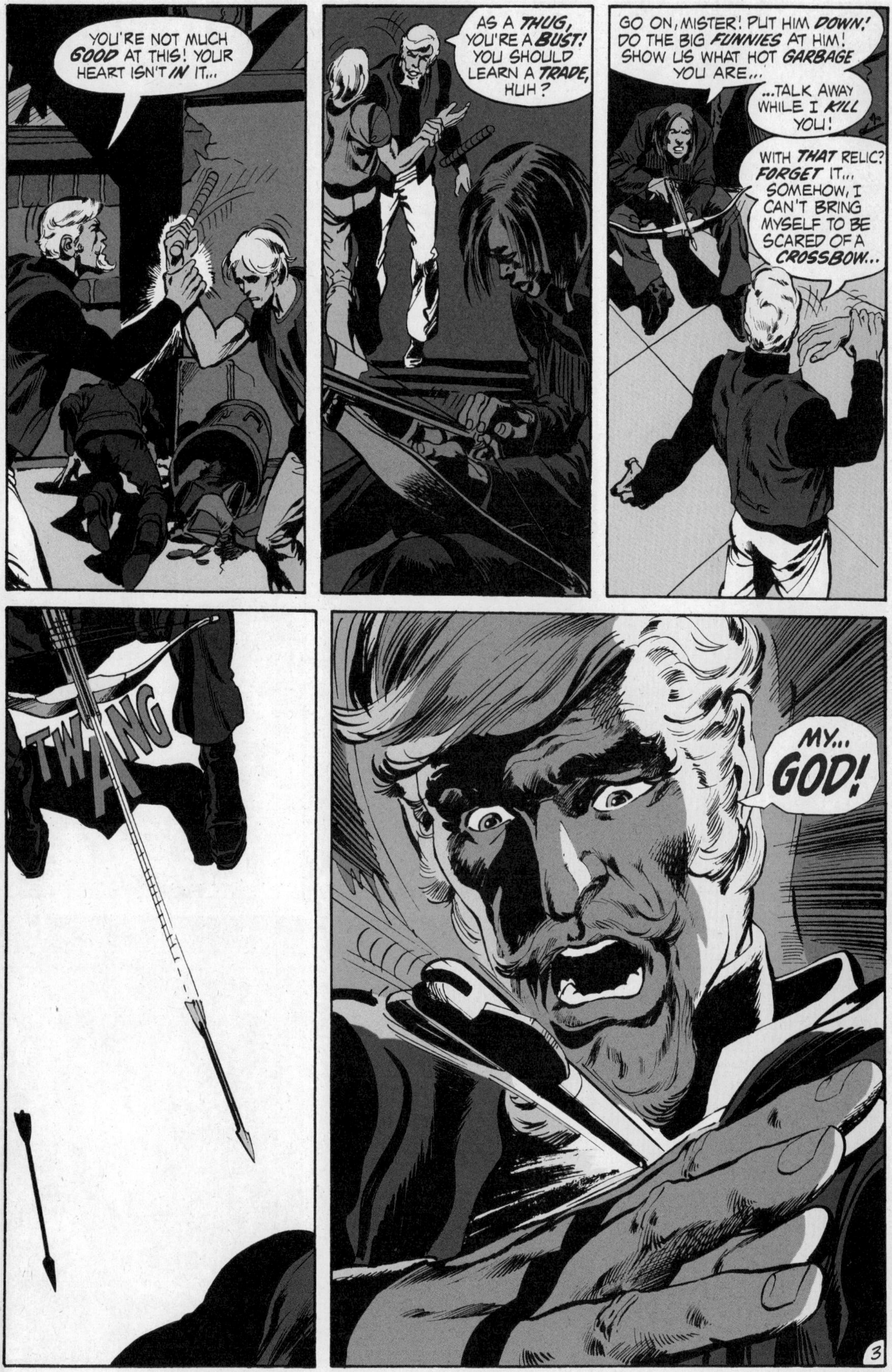
YOU'RE NOT MUCH GOOD AT THIS! YOUR HEART ISN'T IN IT...
AS A THUG, YOU'RE A BUST! YOU SHOULD LEARN A TRADE, HUH?
GO ON, MISTER! PUT HIM DOWN! DO THE BIG FUNNIES AT HIM! SHOW US WHAT HOT GARBAGE YOU ARE...
...TALK AWAY WHILE I KILL YOU!
WITH THAT RELIC? FORGET IT... SOMEHOW, I CAN'T BRING MYSELF TO BE SCARED OF A CROSSBOW...
TWANG
MY... GOD!
3

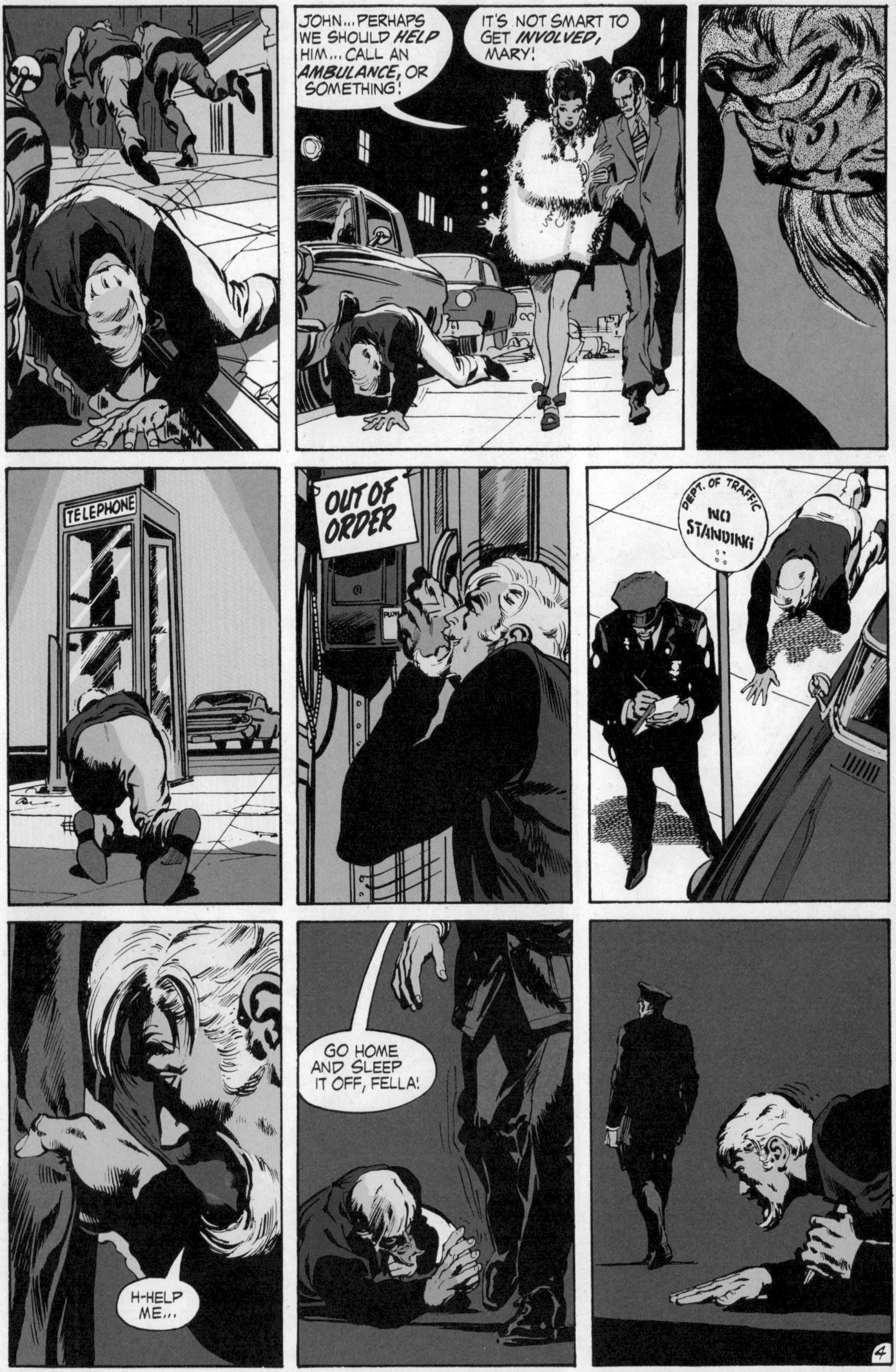
JOHN... PERHAPS WE SHOULD HELP HIM... CALL AN AMBULANCE, OR SOMETHING!
IT'S NOT SMART TO GET INVOLVED, MARY!
TELEPHONE
OUT OF ORDER
PUSH
DEPT. OF TRAFFIC
NO STANDINKI
H-HELP ME...
GO HOME AND SLEEP IT OFF, FELLA!
4

OFF TAXI DUTY

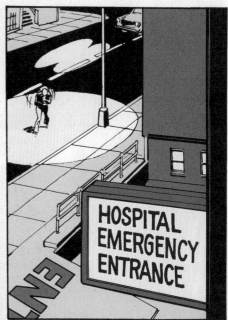

HOSPITAL EMERGENCY ENTRANCE

MISS... N-NEED A *DOCTOR!*

WE'RE VERY *BUSY* TONIGHT! COULD YOU COME BACK IN THE *MORNING?*

ISN'T MODERN CIVILIZATION... *WONDERFUL...?*

HOWEVER, NOT EVEN THE *BUSIEST* MEDICAL STAFF CAN IGNORE A MAN LYING ON THE FLOOR WITH AN ARROW JUTTING FROM HIS SHOULDER...ESPECIALLY WHEN HE'S BLOCKING THE CORRIDOR! THUS--

NASTY WOUND THERE...THE SHAFT CHIPPED THE BONE! BUT WE CAUGHT IT BEFORE INFECTION SET IN! DON'T USE THE ARM FOR A FEW WEEKS AND YOU SHOULD BE OKAY!

DOC.... CAN I SEE THE ARROW?

5

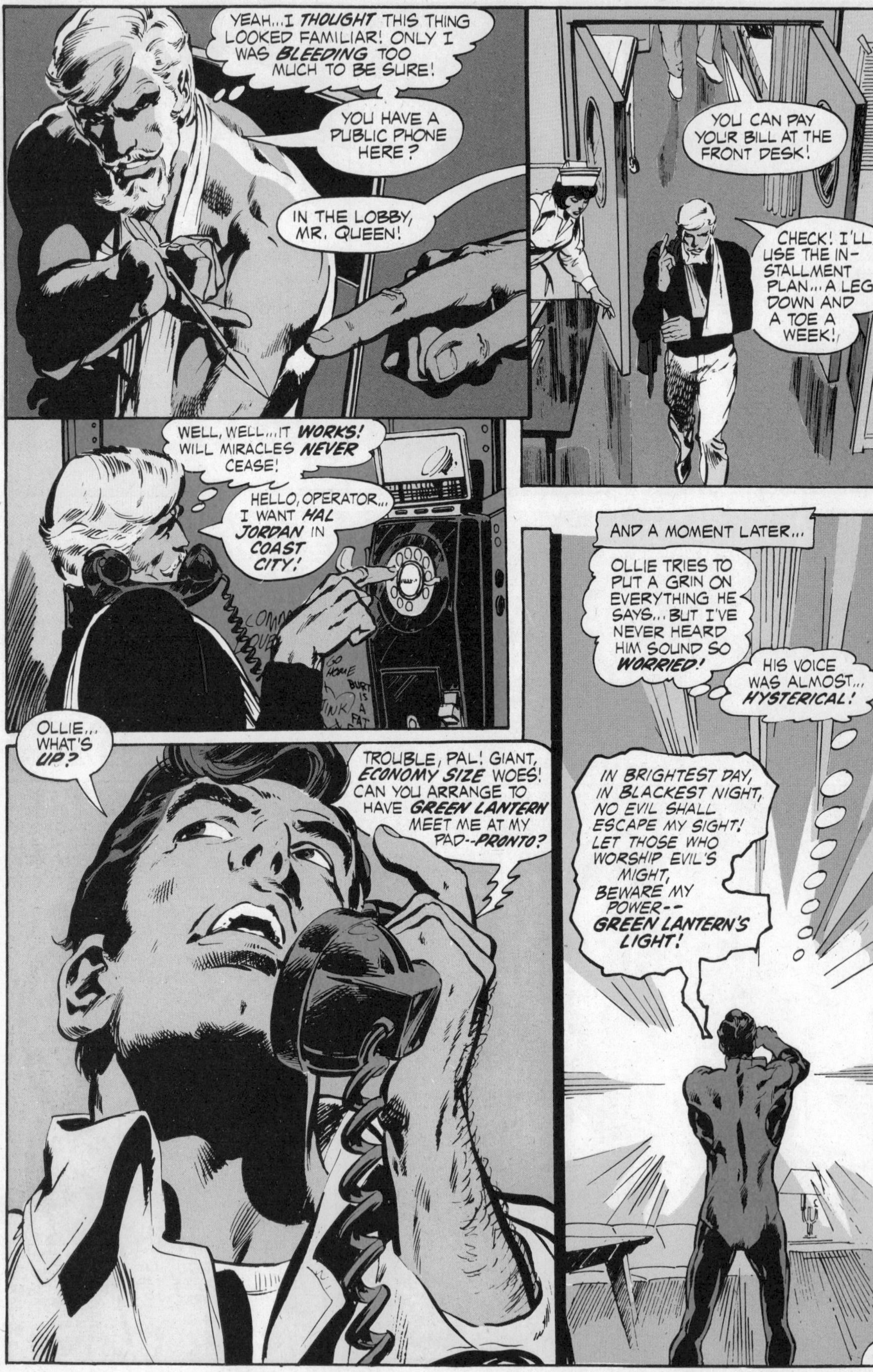

YEAH...I THOUGHT THIS THING LOOKED FAMILIAR! ONLY I WAS BLEEDING TOO MUCH TO BE SURE!
YOU HAVE A PUBLIC PHONE HERE?
IN THE LOBBY, MR. QUEEN!
YOU CAN PAY YOUR BILL AT THE FRONT DESK!
CHECK! I'LL USE THE IN-STALLMENT PLAN...A LEG DOWN AND A TOE A WEEK!
WELL, WELL...IT WORKS! WILL MIRACLES NEVER CEASE!
HELLO, OPERATOR... I WANT HAL JORDAN IN COAST CITY!
GO HOME
BURT IS A FAT
OLLIE... WHAT'S UP?
TROUBLE, PAL! GIANT, ECONOMY SIZE WOES! CAN YOU ARRANGE TO HAVE GREEN LANTERN MEET ME AT MY PAD--PRONTO?
AND A MOMENT LATER...
OLLIE TRIES TO PUT A GRIN ON EVERYTHING HE SAYS...BUT I'VE NEVER HEARD HIM SOUND SO WORRIED!
HIS VOICE WAS ALMOST... HYSTERICAL!
IN BRIGHTEST DAY, IN BLACKEST NIGHT, NO EVIL SHALL ESCAPE MY SIGHT! LET THOSE WHO WORSHIP EVIL'S MIGHT, BEWARE MY POWER-- GREEN LANTERN'S LIGHT!
6

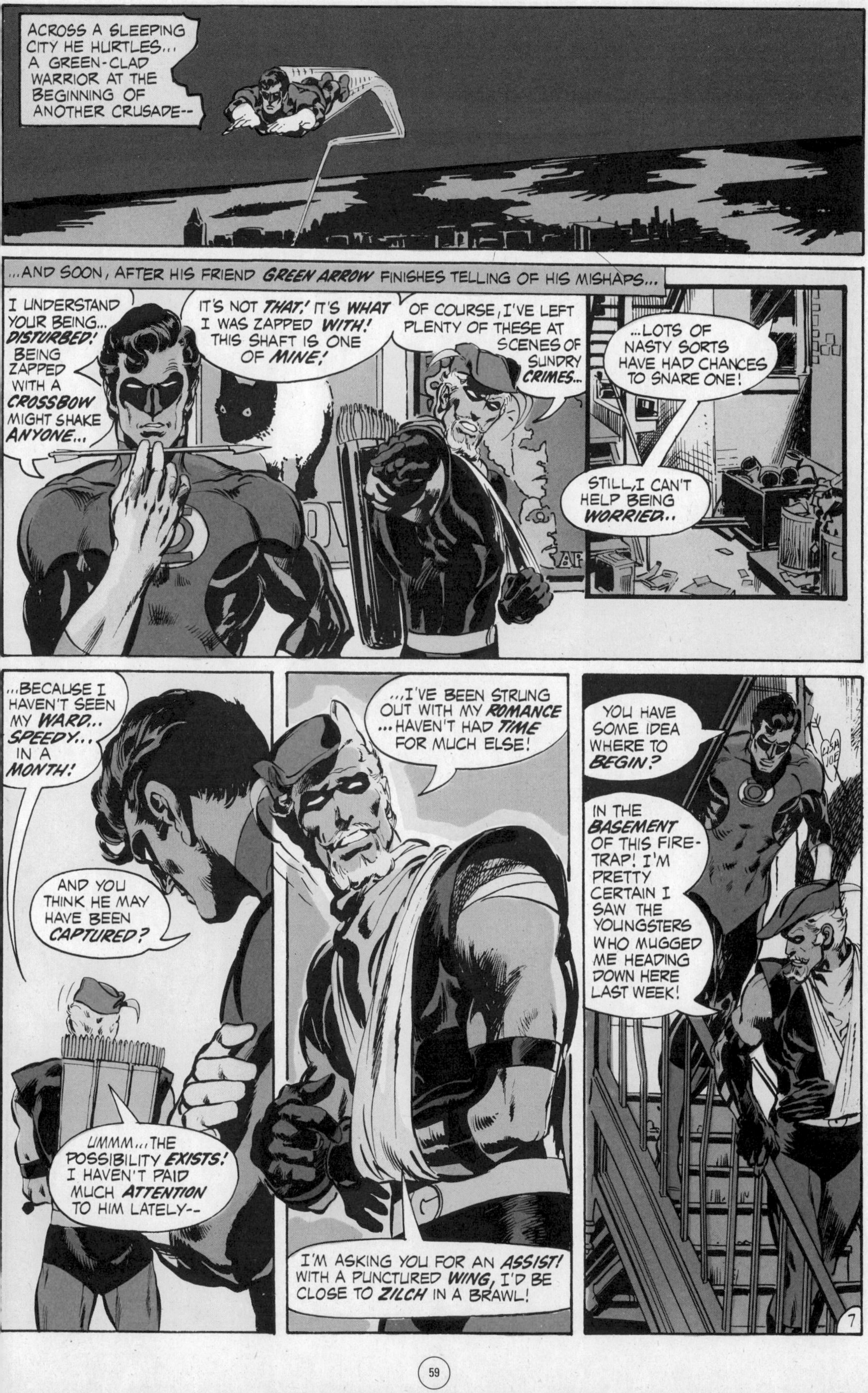
ACROSS A SLEEPING CITY HE HURTLES... A GREEN-CLAD WARRIOR AT THE BEGINNING OF ANOTHER CRUSADE--
...AND SOON, AFTER HIS FRIEND GREEN ARROW FINISHES TELLING OF HIS MISHAPS...
I UNDERSTAND YOUR BEING... DISTURBED! BEING ZAPPED WITH A CROSSBOW MIGHT SHAKE ANYONE...
IT'S NOT THAT! IT'S WHAT I WAS ZAPPED WITH! THIS SHAFT IS ONE OF MINE!
OF COURSE, I'VE LEFT PLENTY OF THESE AT SCENES OF SUNDRY CRIMES...
...LOTS OF NASTY SORTS HAVE HAD CHANCES TO SNARE ONE!
STILL, I CAN'T HELP BEING WORRIED...
...BECAUSE I HAVEN'T SEEN MY WARD... SPEEDY... IN A MONTH!
AND YOU THINK HE MAY HAVE BEEN CAPTURED?
UMMM... THE POSSIBILITY EXISTS! I HAVEN'T PAID MUCH ATTENTION TO HIM LATELY--
...I'VE BEEN STRUNG OUT WITH MY ROMANCE ...HAVEN'T HAD TIME FOR MUCH ELSE!
I'M ASKING YOU FOR AN ASSIST! WITH A PUNCTURED WING, I'D BE CLOSE TO ZILCH IN A BRAWL!
YOU HAVE SOME IDEA WHERE TO BEGIN?
IN THE BASEMENT OF THIS FIRE-TRAP! I'M PRETTY CERTAIN I SAW THE YOUNGSTERS WHO MUGGED ME HEADING DOWN HERE LAST WEEK!
7

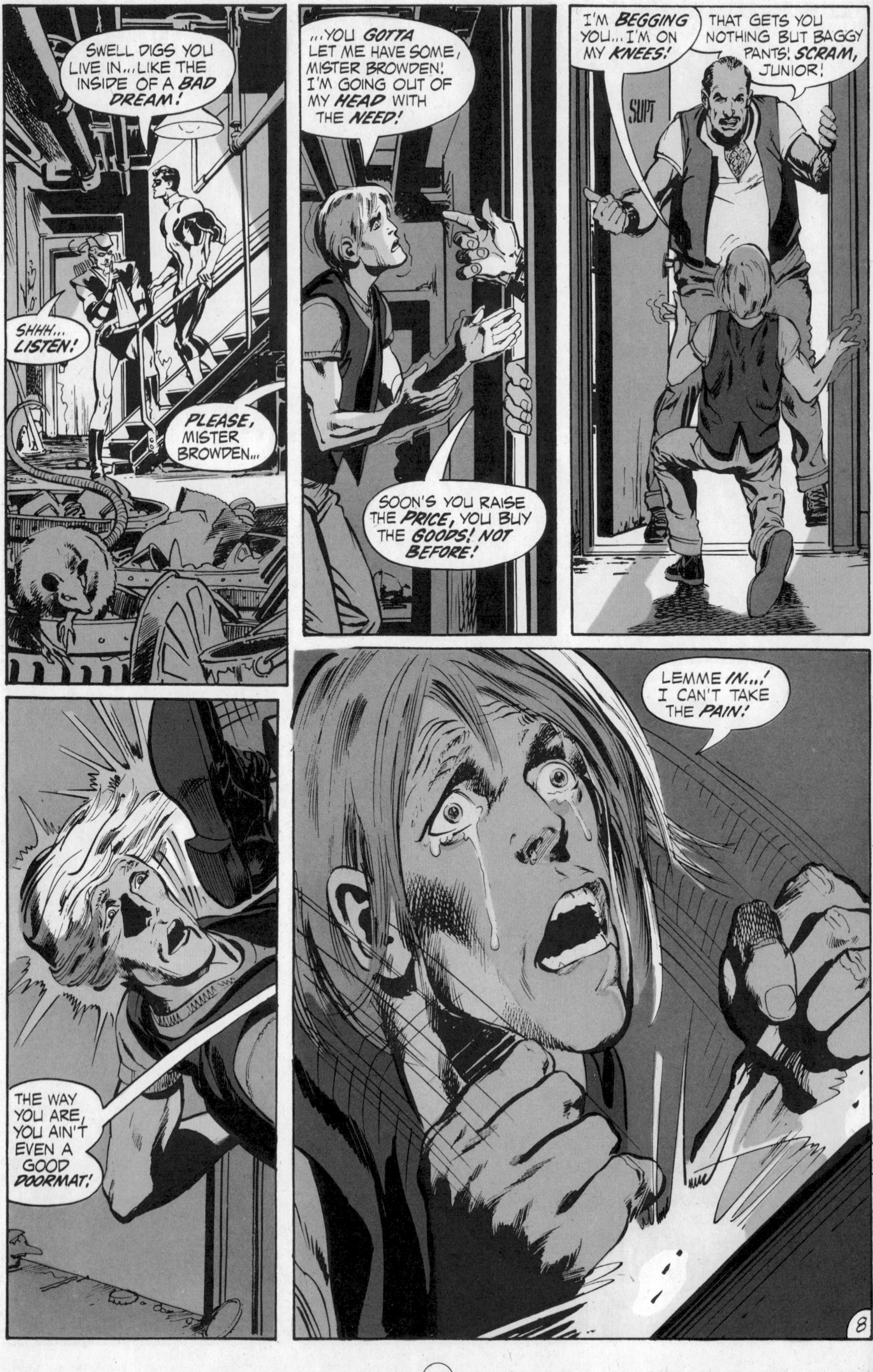
SWELL DIGS YOU LIVE IN...LIKE THE INSIDE OF A BAD DREAM!
SHHH... LISTEN!
PLEASE, MISTER BROWDEN...
...YOU GOTTA LET ME HAVE SOME, MISTER BROWDEN! I'M GOING OUT OF MY HEAD WITH THE NEED!
SOON'S YOU RAISE THE PRICE, YOU BUY THE GOODS! NOT BEFORE!
I'M BEGGING YOU...I'M ON MY KNEES!
THAT GETS YOU NOTHING BUT BAGGY PANTS! SCRAM, JUNIOR!
SUPT
THE WAY YOU ARE, YOU AIN'T EVEN A GOOD DOORMAT!
LEMME IN...! I CAN'T TAKE THE PAIN!
8

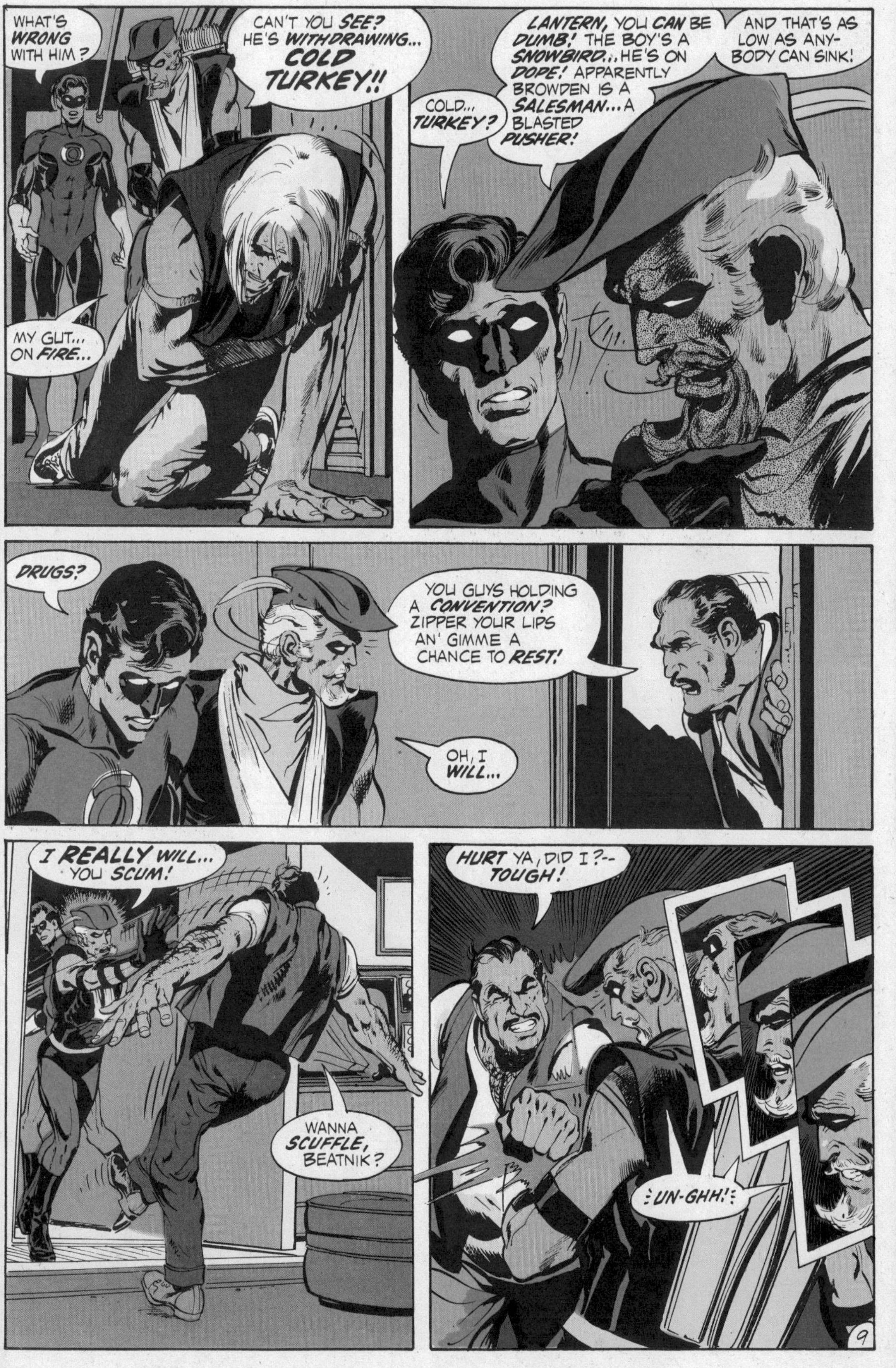
WHAT'S WRONG WITH HIM?
CAN'T YOU SEE? HE'S WITHDRAWING... COLD TURKEY!!
MY GUT... ON FIRE...
COLD... TURKEY?
LANTERN, YOU CAN BE DUMB! THE BOY'S A SNOWBIRD... HE'S ON DOPE! APPARENTLY BROWDEN IS A SALESMAN... A BLASTED PUSHER!
AND THAT'S AS LOW AS ANY-BODY CAN SINK!
DRUGS?
YOU GUYS HOLDING A CONVENTION? ZIPPER YOUR LIPS AN' GIMME A CHANCE TO REST!
OH, I WILL...
I REALLY WILL... YOU SCUM!
WANNA SCUFFLE, BEATNIK?
HURT YA, DID I?-- TOUGH!
UN-GHH!
9

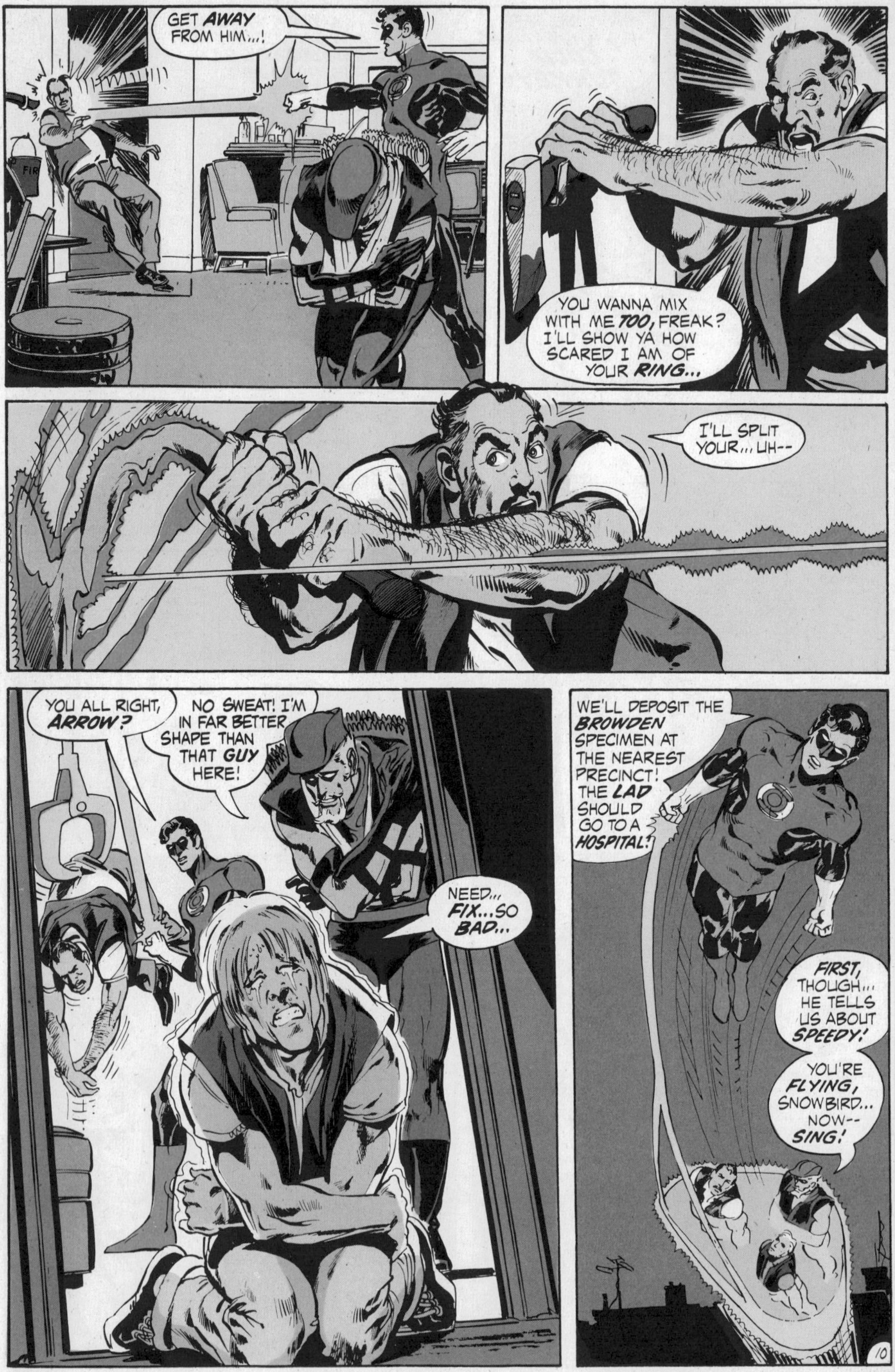
GET AWAY FROM HIM...!
YOU WANNA MIX WITH ME TOO, FREAK? I'LL SHOW YA HOW SCARED I AM OF YOUR RING...
I'LL SPLIT YOUR... UH--
YOU ALL RIGHT, ARROW?
NO SWEAT! I'M IN FAR BETTER SHAPE THAN THAT GUY HERE!
NEED... FIX... SO BAD...
WE'LL DEPOSIT THE BROWDEN SPECIMEN AT THE NEAREST PRECINCT! THE LAD SHOULD GO TO A HOSPITAL!
FIRST, THOUGH... HE TELLS US ABOUT SPEEDY!
YOU'RE FLYING, SNOWBIRD... NOW-- SING!
10

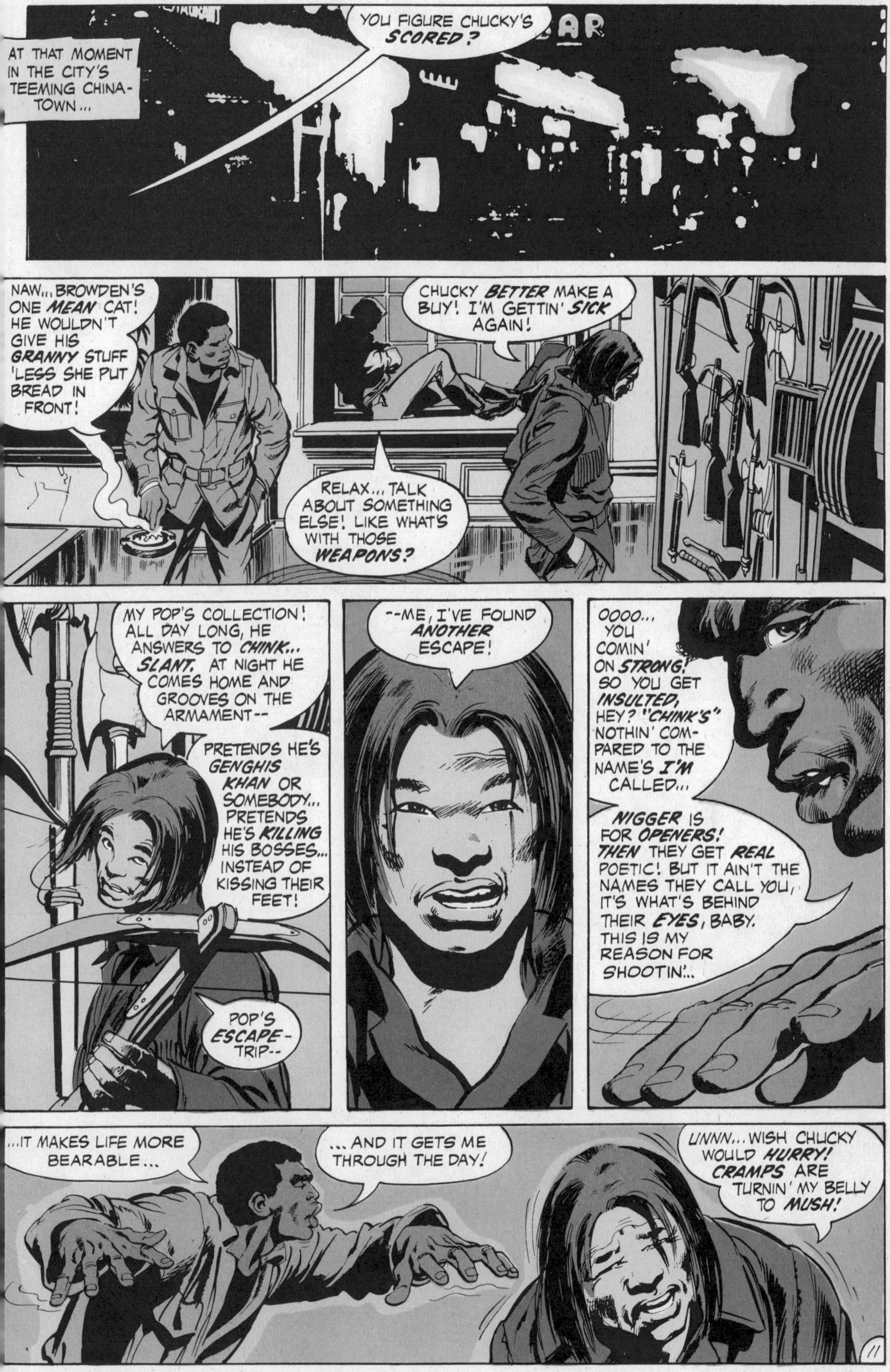

AT THAT MOMENT IN THE CITY'S TEEMING CHINA-TOWN...
YOU FIGURE CHUCKY'S SCORED?
NAW... BROWDEN'S ONE MEAN CAT! HE WOULDN'T GIVE HIS GRANNY STUFF 'LESS SHE PUT BREAD IN FRONT!
CHUCKY BETTER MAKE A BUY! I'M GETTIN' SICK AGAIN!
RELAX... TALK ABOUT SOMETHING ELSE! LIKE WHAT'S WITH THOSE WEAPONS?
MY POP'S COLLECTION! ALL DAY LONG, HE ANSWERS TO CHINK... SLANT. AT NIGHT HE COMES HOME AND GROOVES ON THE ARMAMENT--
PRETENDS HE'S GENGHIS KHAN OR SOMEBODY... PRETENDS HE'S KILLING HIS BOSSES... INSTEAD OF KISSING THEIR FEET!
POP'S ESCAPE-TRIP--
--ME, I'VE FOUND ANOTHER ESCAPE!
OOOO... YOU COMIN' ON STRONG! SO YOU GET INSULTED, HEY? "CHINK'S" NOTHIN' COM-PARED TO THE NAME'S I'M CALLED...
NIGGER IS FOR OPENERS! THEN THEY GET REAL POETIC! BUT IT AIN'T THE NAMES THEY CALL YOU, IT'S WHAT'S BEHIND THEIR EYES, BABY. THIS IS MY REASON FOR SHOOTIN'...
...IT MAKES LIFE MORE BEARABLE...
...AND IT GETS ME THROUGH THE DAY!
UNNN... WISH CHUCKY WOULD HURRY! CRAMPS ARE TURNIN' MY BELLY TO MUSH!
11

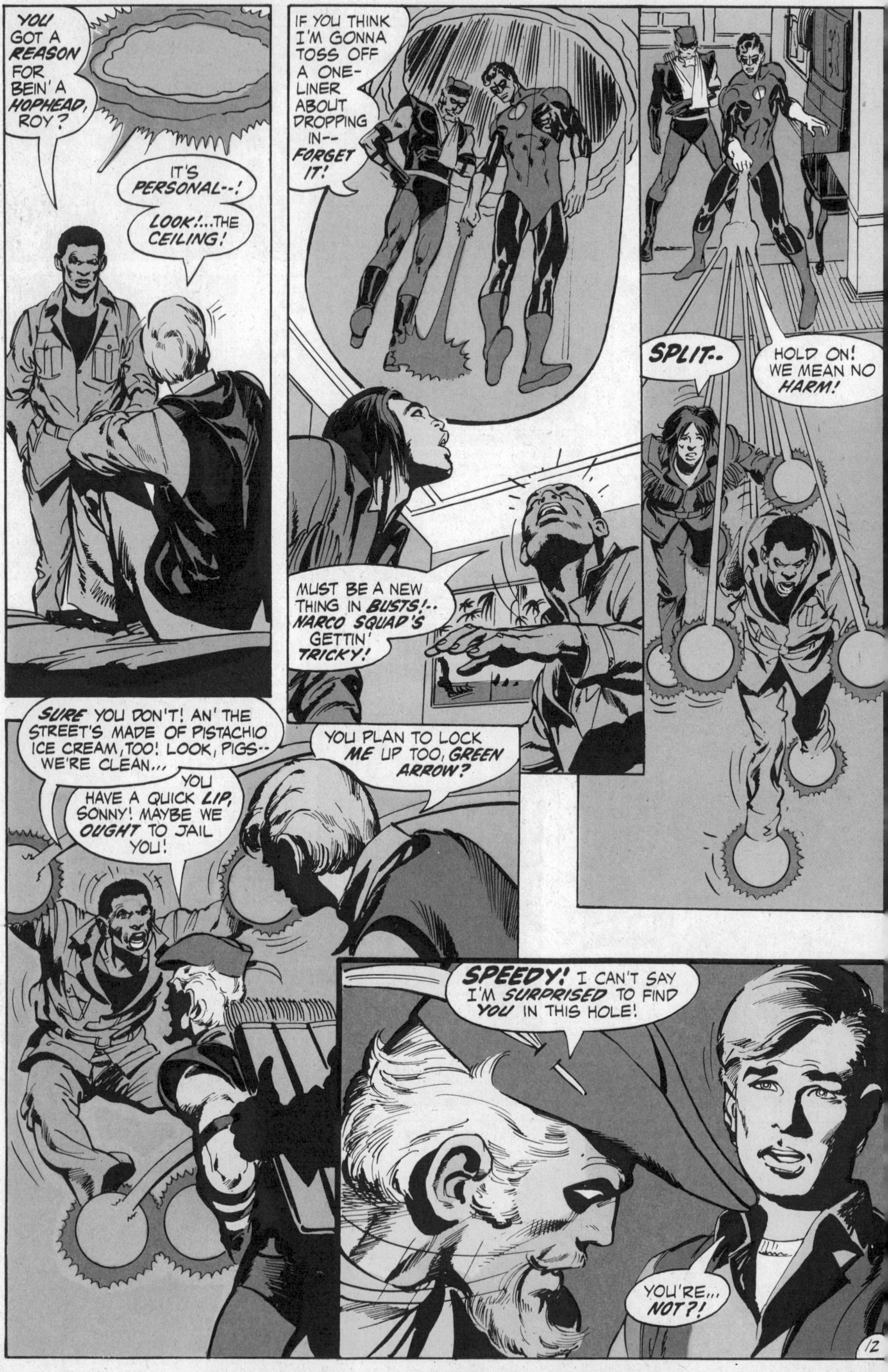
YOU GOT A REASON FOR BEIN' A HOPHEAD, ROY?
IT'S PERSONAL--!
LOOK!...THE CEILING!
IF YOU THINK I'M GONNA TOSS OFF A ONE-LINER ABOUT DROPPING IN-- FORGET IT!
MUST BE A NEW THING IN BUSTS!.. NARCO SQUAD'S GETTIN' TRICKY!
SPLIT--
HOLD ON! WE MEAN NO HARM!
SURE YOU DON'T! AN' THE STREET'S MADE OF PISTACHIO ICE CREAM, TOO! LOOK, PIGS-- WE'RE CLEAN...
YOU HAVE A QUICK LIP, SONNY! MAYBE WE OUGHT TO JAIL YOU!
YOU PLAN TO LOCK ME UP TOO, GREEN ARROW?
SPEEDY! I CAN'T SAY I'M SURPRISED TO FIND YOU IN THIS HOLE!
YOU'RE... NOT?!
12

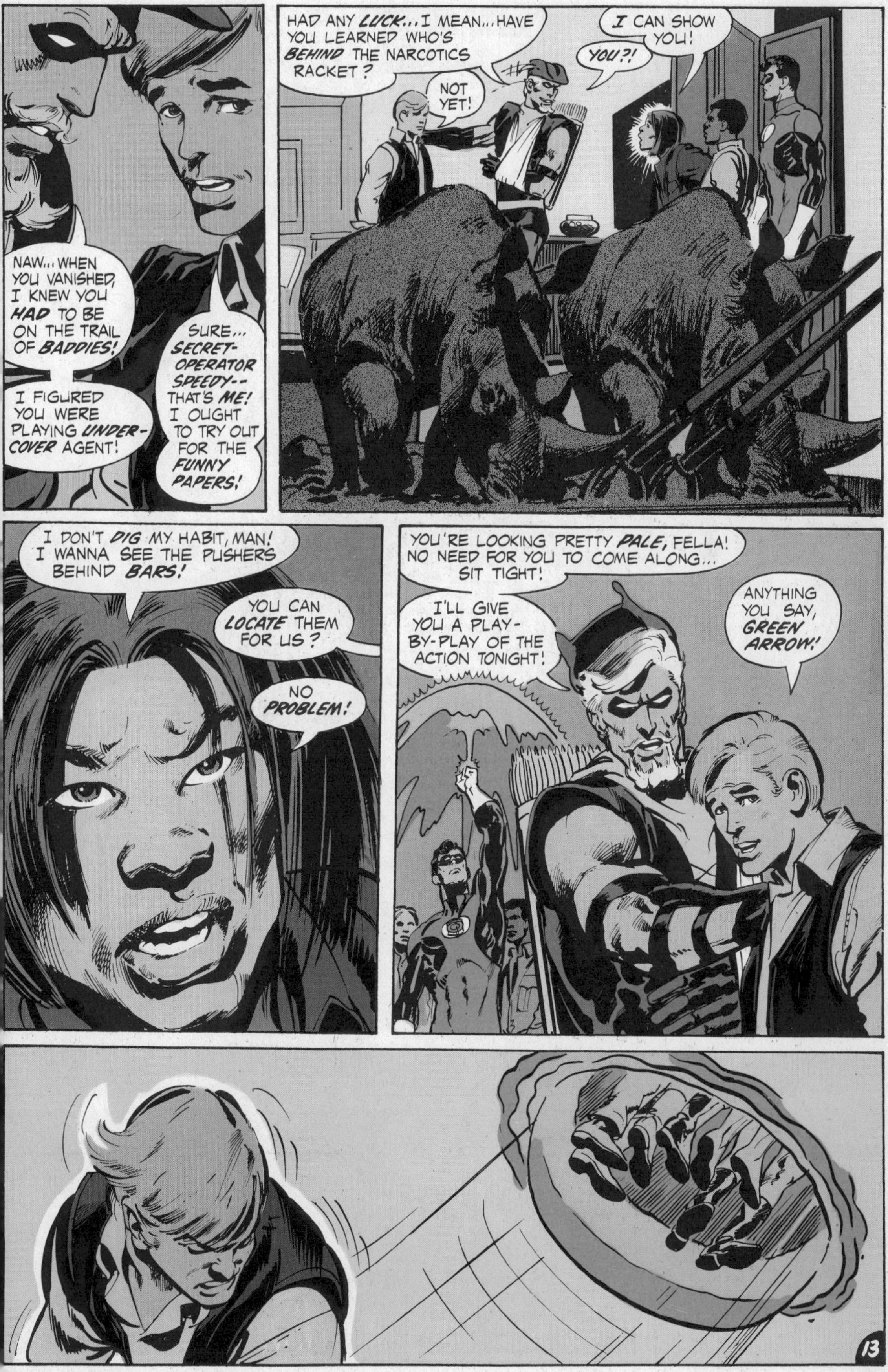
NAW... WHEN YOU VANISHED, I KNEW YOU HAD TO BE ON THE TRAIL OF BADDIES!
I FIGURED YOU WERE PLAYING UNDER-COVER AGENT!
SURE... SECRET-OPERATOR SPEEDY-- THAT'S ME! I OUGHT TO TRY OUT FOR THE FUNNY PAPERS!
HAD ANY LUCK... I MEAN... HAVE YOU LEARNED WHO'S BEHIND THE NARCOTICS RACKET?
NOT YET!
I CAN SHOW YOU!
YOU?!
I DON'T DIG MY HABIT, MAN! I WANNA SEE THE PUSHERS BEHIND BARS!
YOU CAN LOCATE THEM FOR US?
NO PROBLEM!
YOU'RE LOOKING PRETTY PALE, FELLA! NO NEED FOR YOU TO COME ALONG... SIT TIGHT!
I'LL GIVE YOU A PLAY-BY-PLAY OF THE ACTION TONIGHT!
ANYTHING YOU SAY, GREEN ARROW!
13

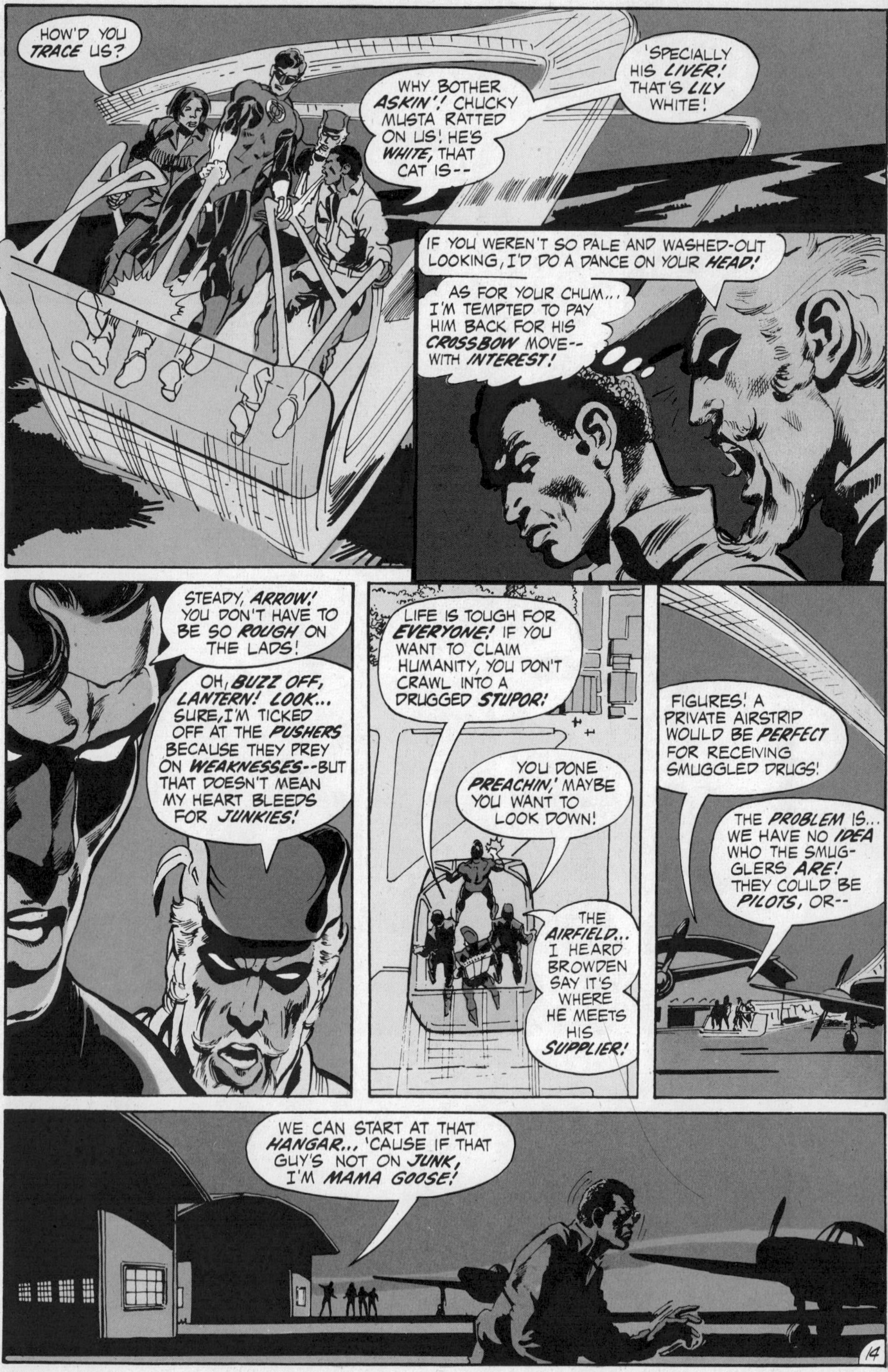

HOW'D YOU TRACE US?
WHY BOTHER ASKIN'! CHUCKY MUSTA RATTED ON US! HE'S WHITE, THAT CAT IS--
'SPECIALLY HIS LIVER! THAT'S LILY WHITE!
IF YOU WEREN'T SO PALE AND WASHED-OUT LOOKING, I'D DO A DANCE ON YOUR HEAD!
AS FOR YOUR CHUM... I'M TEMPTED TO PAY HIM BACK FOR HIS CROSSBOW MOVE--WITH INTEREST!
STEADY, ARROW! YOU DON'T HAVE TO BE SO ROUGH ON THE LADS!
OH, BUZZ OFF, LANTERN! LOOK... SURE, I'M TICKED OFF AT THE PUSHERS BECAUSE THEY PREY ON WEAKNESSES--BUT THAT DOESN'T MEAN MY HEART BLEEDS FOR JUNKIES!
LIFE IS TOUGH FOR EVERYONE! IF YOU WANT TO CLAIM HUMANITY, YOU DON'T CRAWL INTO A DRUGGED STUPOR!
YOU DONE PREACHIN,' MAYBE YOU WANT TO LOOK DOWN!
THE AIRFIELD... I HEARD BROWDEN SAY IT'S WHERE HE MEETS HIS SUPPLIER!
FIGURES! A PRIVATE AIRSTRIP WOULD BE PERFECT FOR RECEIVING SMUGGLED DRUGS!
THE PROBLEM IS... WE HAVE NO IDEA WHO THE SMUGGLERS ARE! THEY COULD BE PILOTS, OR--
WE CAN START AT THAT HANGAR... 'CAUSE IF THAT GUY'S NOT ON JUNK, I'M MAMA GOOSE!
14

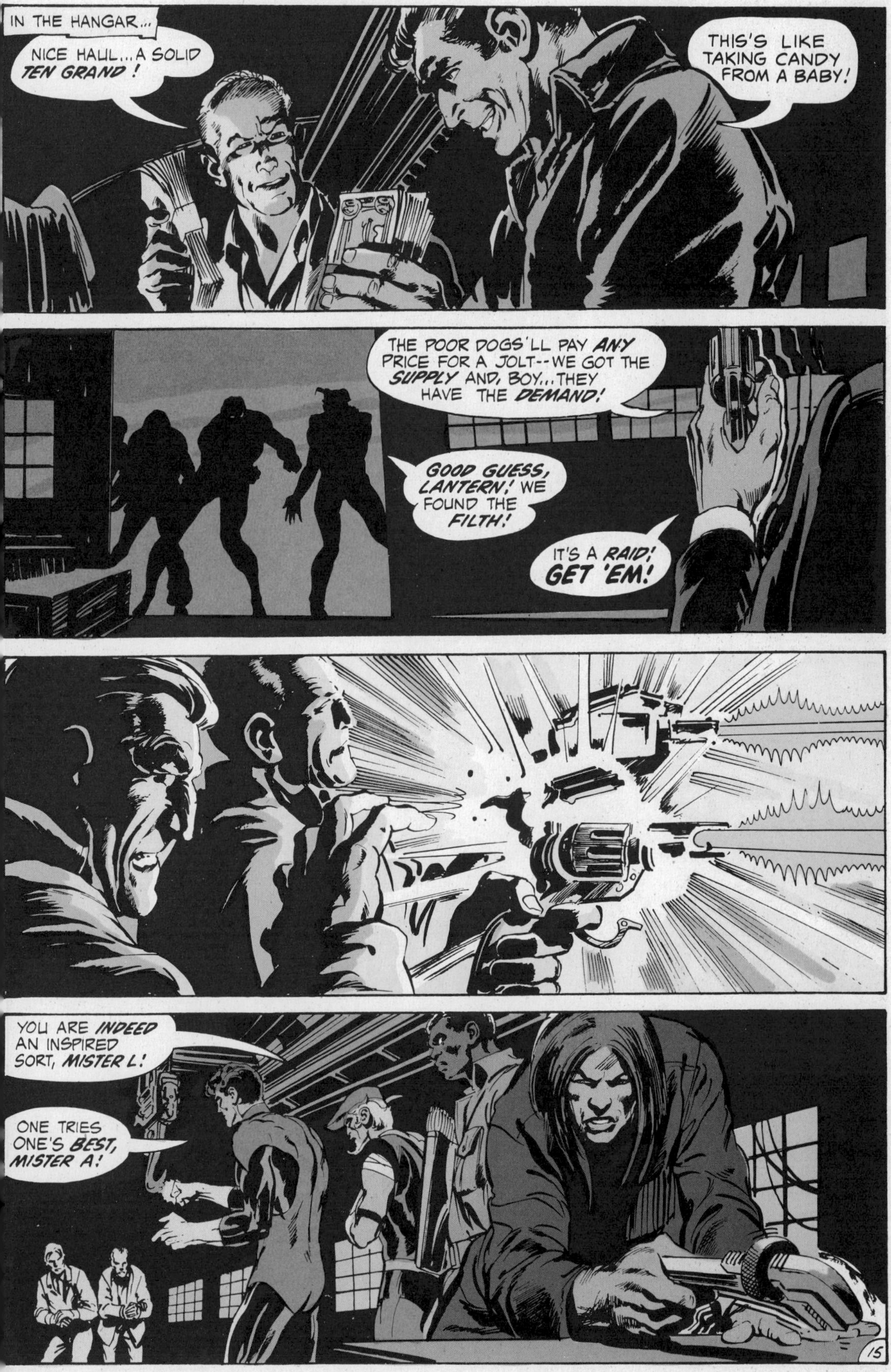
IN THE HANGAR...
NICE HAUL...A SOLID TEN GRAND!
THIS'S LIKE TAKING CANDY FROM A BABY!
THE POOR DOGS'LL PAY ANY PRICE FOR A JOLT--WE GOT THE SUPPLY AND, BOY...THEY HAVE THE DEMAND!
GOOD GUESS, LANTERN! WE FOUND THE FILTH!
IT'S A RAID! GET 'EM!
YOU ARE INDEED AN INSPIRED SORT, MISTER L!
ONE TRIES ONE'S BEST, MISTER A!
15

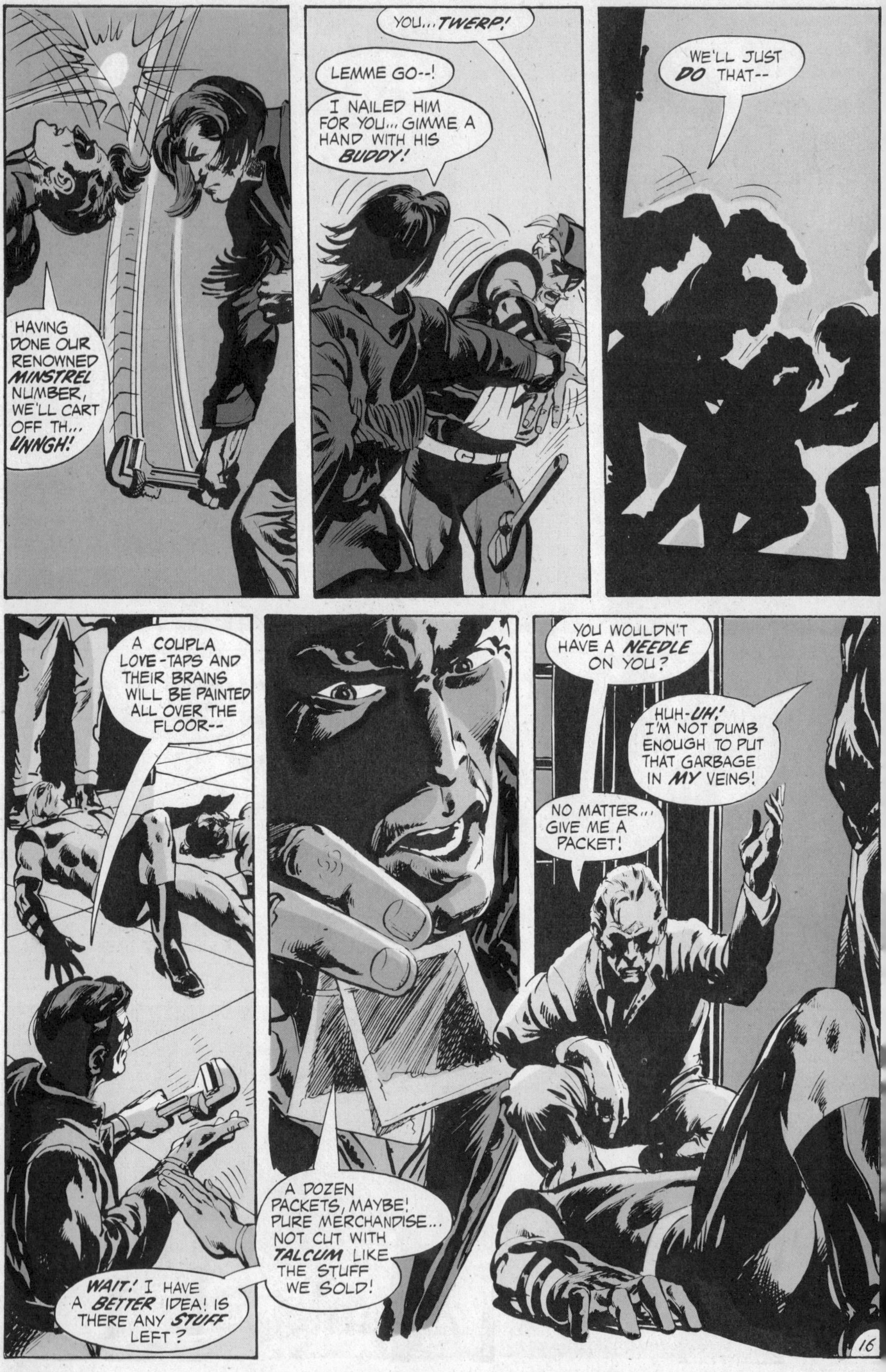
HAVING DONE OUR RENOWNED MINSTREL NUMBER, WE'LL CART OFF TH... UNNGH!
YOU... TWERP!
LEMME GO--!
I NAILED HIM FOR YOU... GIMME A HAND WITH HIS BUDDY!
WE'LL JUST DO THAT--
A COUPLA LOVE-TAPS AND THEIR BRAINS WILL BE PAINTED ALL OVER THE FLOOR--
WAIT! I HAVE A BETTER IDEA! IS THERE ANY STUFF LEFT?
A DOZEN PACKETS, MAYBE! PURE MERCHANDISE... NOT CUT WITH TALCUM LIKE THE STUFF WE SOLD!
YOU WOULDN'T HAVE A NEEDLE ON YOU?
HUH-UH! I'M NOT DUMB ENOUGH TO PUT THAT GARBAGE IN MY VEINS!
NO MATTER... GIVE ME A PACKET!
16

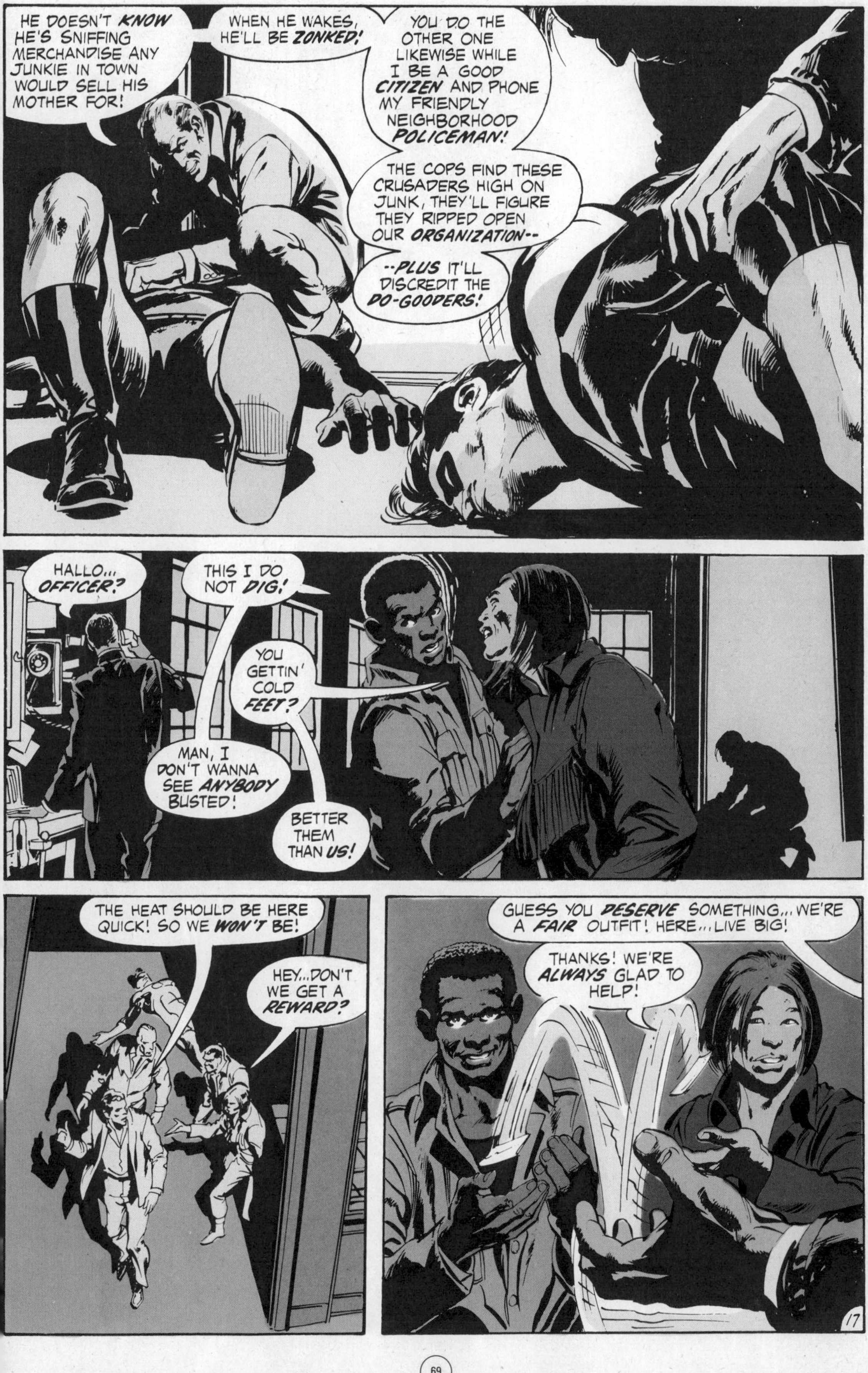
HE DOESN'T KNOW HE'S SNIFFING MERCHANDISE ANY JUNKIE IN TOWN WOULD SELL HIS MOTHER FOR!
WHEN HE WAKES, HE'LL BE ZONKED!
YOU DO THE OTHER ONE LIKEWISE WHILE I BE A GOOD CITIZEN AND PHONE MY FRIENDLY NEIGHBORHOOD POLICEMAN!
THE COPS FIND THESE CRUSADERS HIGH ON JUNK, THEY'LL FIGURE THEY RIPPED OPEN OUR ORGANIZATION--
--PLUS IT'LL DISCREDIT THE DO-GOODERS!
HALLO... OFFICER?
THIS I DO NOT DIG!
YOU GETTIN' COLD FEET?
MAN, I DON'T WANNA SEE ANYBODY BUSTED!
BETTER THEM THAN US!
THE HEAT SHOULD BE HERE QUICK! SO WE WON'T BE!
HEY...DON'T WE GET A REWARD?
GUESS YOU DESERVE SOMETHING... WE'RE A FAIR OUTFIT! HERE... LIVE BIG!
THANKS! WE'RE ALWAYS GLAD TO HELP!
17

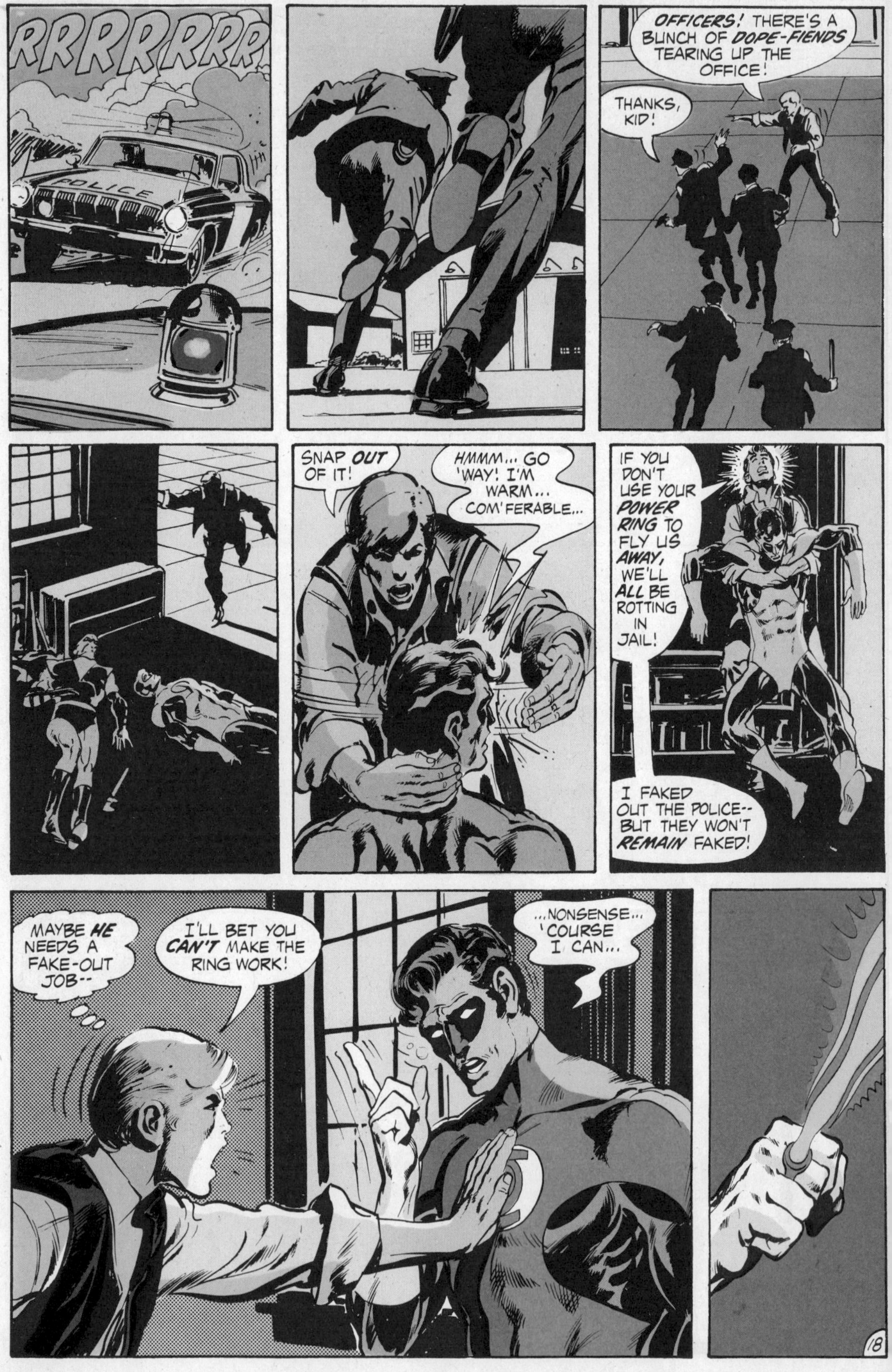
RRRRRRRR
POLICE
OFFICERS! THERE'S A BUNCH OF DOPE-FIENDS TEARING UP THE OFFICE!
THANKS, KID!
SNAP OUT OF IT!
HMMM... GO 'WAY! I'M WARM... COM'FERABLE...
IF YOU DON'T USE YOUR POWER RING TO FLY US AWAY, WE'LL ALL BE ROTTING IN JAIL!
I FAKED OUT THE POLICE-- BUT THEY WON'T REMAIN FAKED!
MAYBE HE NEEDS A FAKE-OUT JOB--
I'LL BET YOU CAN'T MAKE THE RING WORK!
...NONSENSE... 'COURSE I CAN...
18

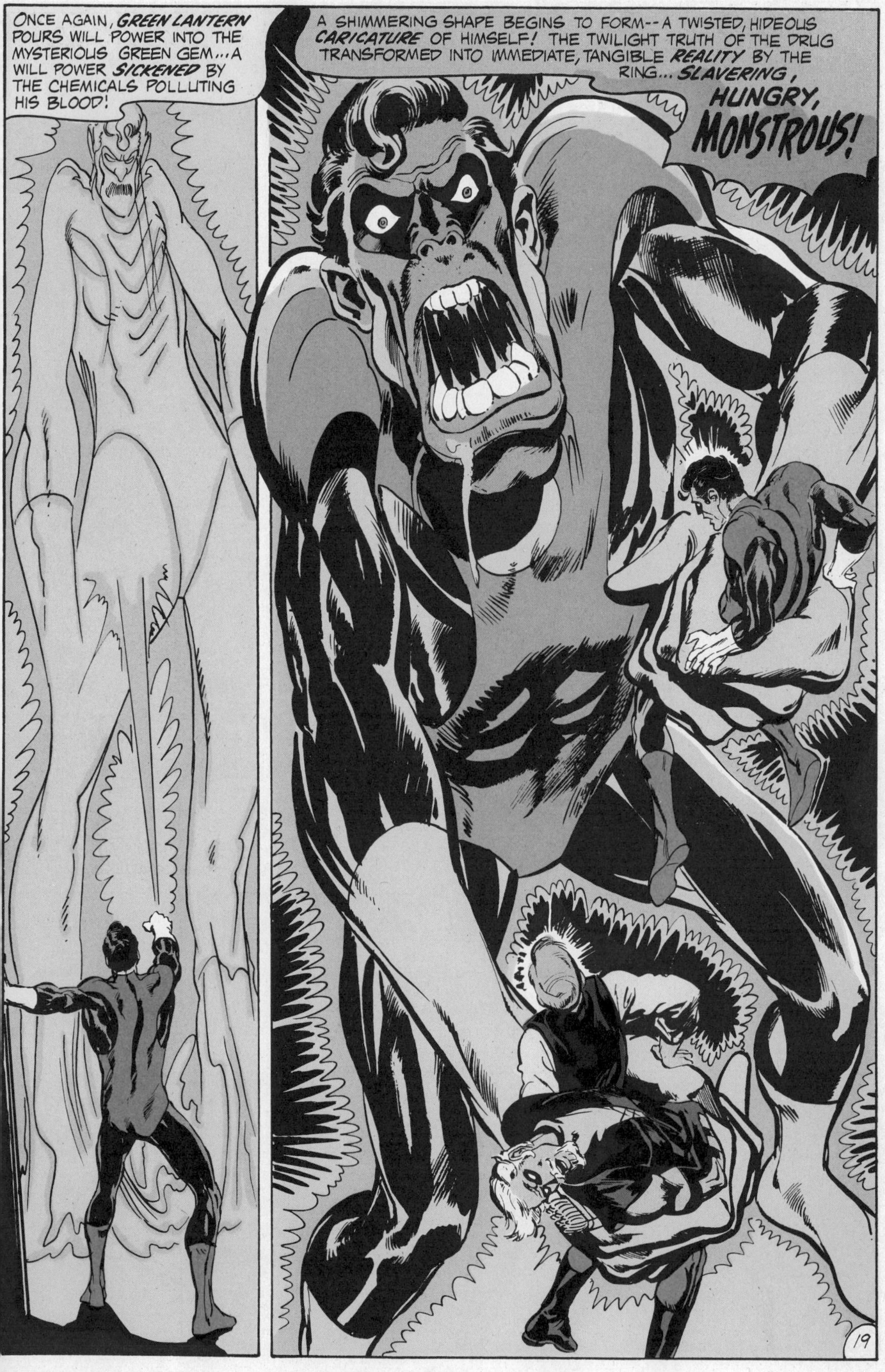
ONCE AGAIN, GREEN LANTERN POURS WILL POWER INTO THE MYSTERIOUS GREEN GEM... A WILL POWER SICKENED BY THE CHEMICALS POLLUTING HIS BLOOD!
A SHIMMERING SHAPE BEGINS TO FORM-- A TWISTED, HIDEOUS CARICATURE OF HIMSELF! THE TWILIGHT TRUTH OF THE DRUG TRANSFORMED INTO IMMEDIATE, TANGIBLE REALITY BY THE RING... SLAVERING,
HUNGRY, MONSTROUS!
19

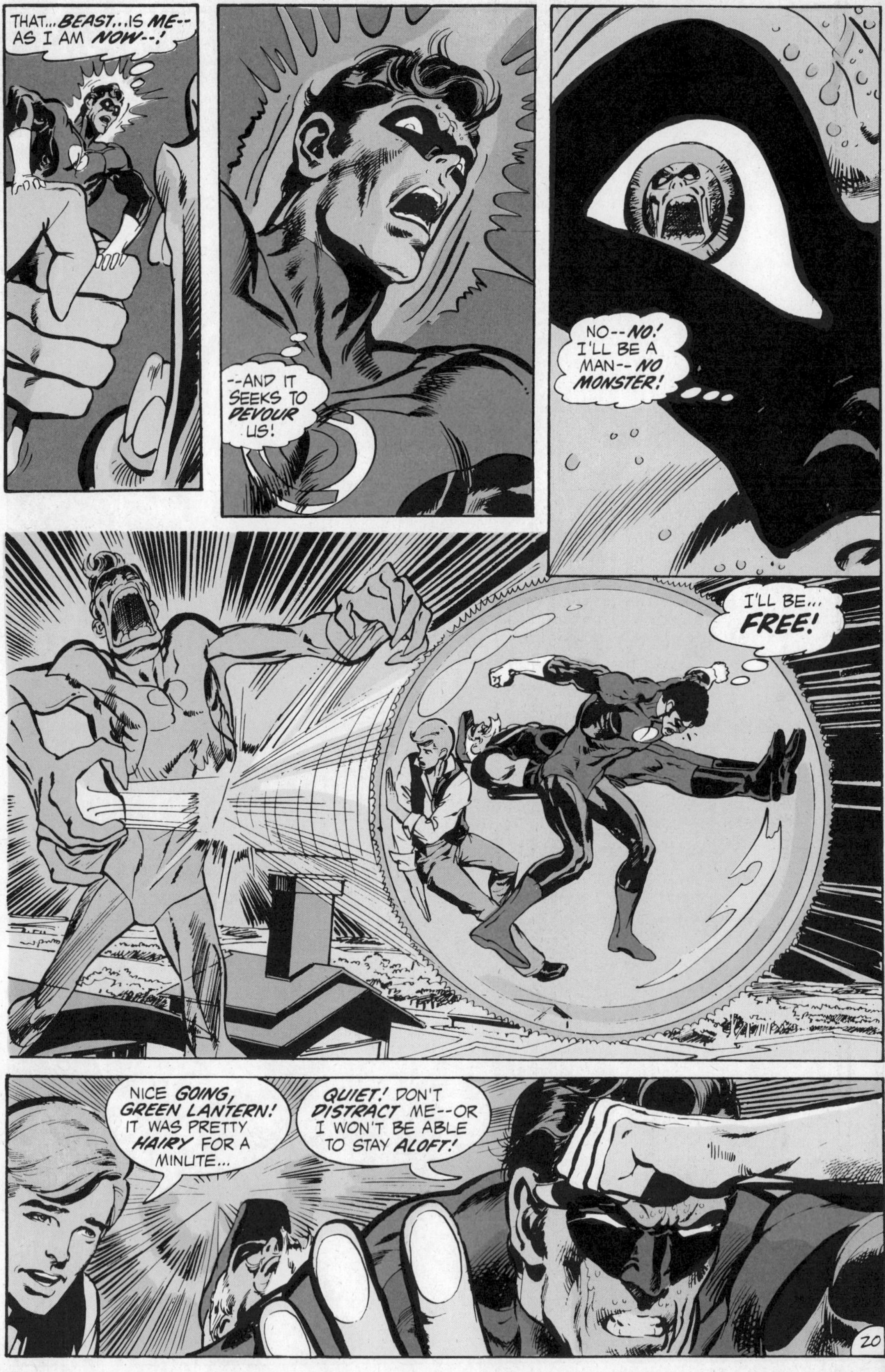

THAT... BEAST... IS ME-- AS I AM NOW--!
--AND IT SEEKS TO DEVOUR US!
NO--NO! I'LL BE A MAN--NO MONSTER!
I'LL BE... FREE!
NICE GOING, GREEN LANTERN! IT WAS PRETTY HAIRY FOR A MINUTE...
QUIET! DON'T DISTRACT ME--OR I WON'T BE ABLE TO STAY ALOFT!
20

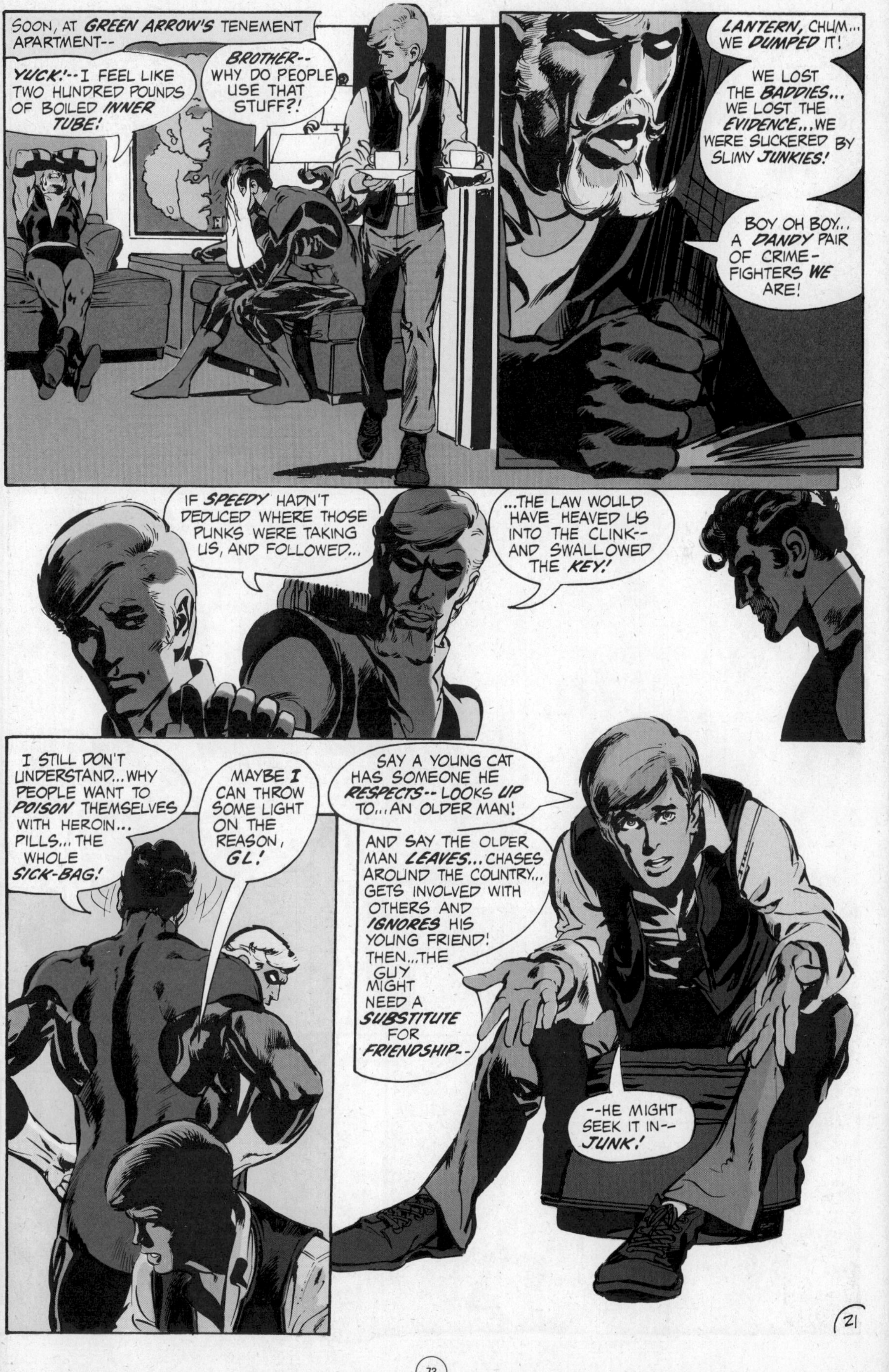

SOON, AT GREEN ARROW'S TENEMENT APARTMENT--
YUCK!--I FEEL LIKE TWO HUNDRED POUNDS OF BOILED INNER TUBE!
BROTHER-- WHY DO PEOPLE USE THAT STUFF?!
LANTERN, CHUM... WE DUMPED IT!
WE LOST THE BADDIES... WE LOST THE EVIDENCE...WE WERE SUCKERED BY SLIMY JUNKIES!
BOY OH BOY... A DANDY PAIR OF CRIME-FIGHTERS WE ARE!
IF SPEEDY HADN'T DEDUCED WHERE THOSE PUNKS WERE TAKING US, AND FOLLOWED...
...THE LAW WOULD HAVE HEAVED US INTO THE CLINK-- AND SWALLOWED THE KEY!
I STILL DON'T UNDERSTAND...WHY PEOPLE WANT TO POISON THEMSELVES WITH HEROIN... PILLS... THE WHOLE SICK-BAG!
MAYBE I CAN THROW SOME LIGHT ON THE REASON, GL!
SAY A YOUNG CAT HAS SOMEONE HE RESPECTS-- LOOKS UP TO...AN OLDER MAN!
AND SAY THE OLDER MAN LEAVES...CHASES AROUND THE COUNTRY... GETS INVOLVED WITH OTHERS AND IGNORES HIS YOUNG FRIEND! THEN...THE GUY MIGHT NEED A SUBSTITUTE FOR FRIENDSHIP--
--HE MIGHT SEEK IT IN-- JUNK!
21

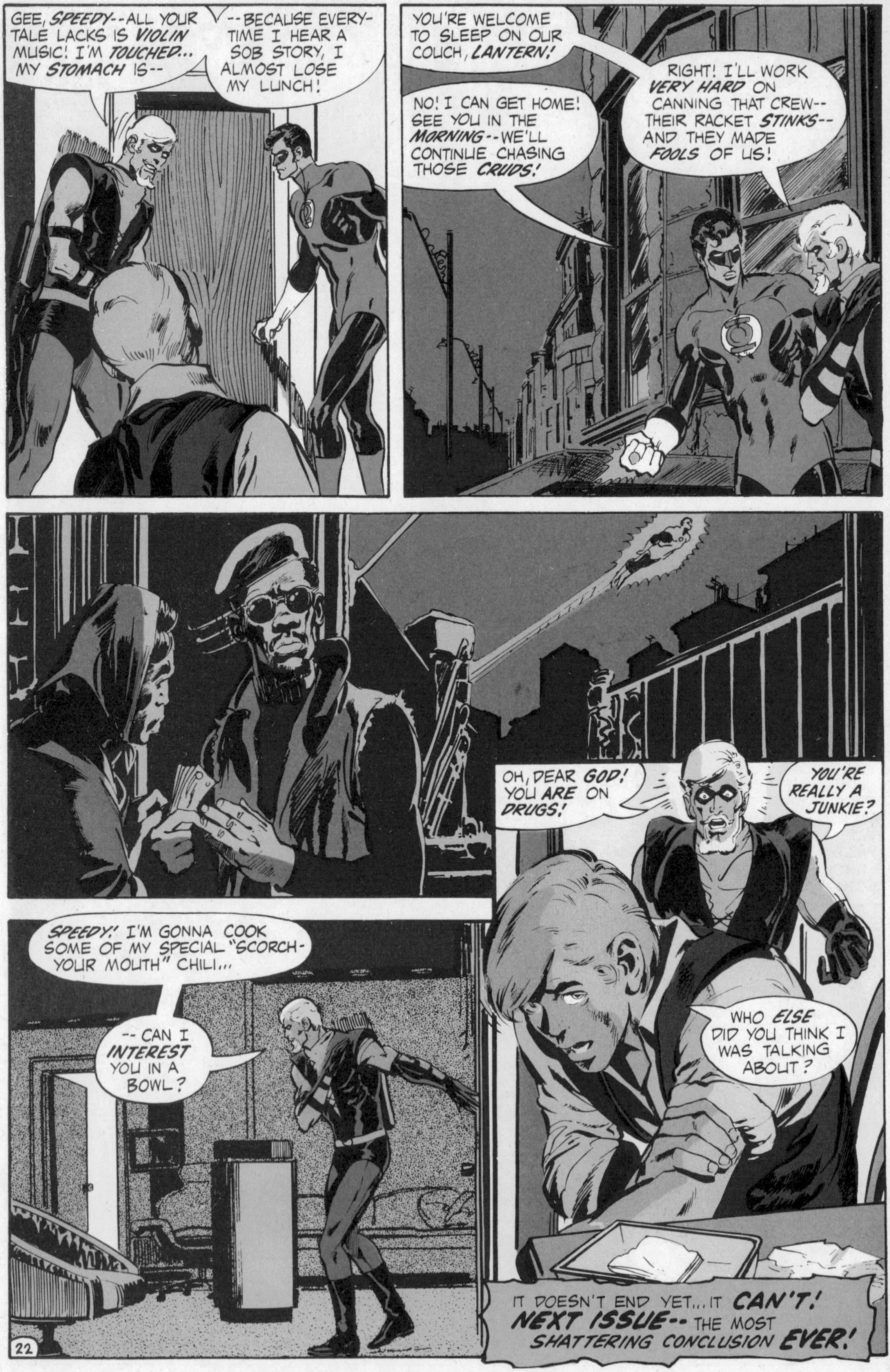
GEE, SPEEDY--ALL YOUR TALE LACKS IS VIOLIN MUSIC! I'M TOUCHED... MY STOMACH IS--
--BECAUSE EVERY-TIME I HEAR A SOB STORY, I ALMOST LOSE MY LUNCH!
YOU'RE WELCOME TO SLEEP ON OUR COUCH, LANTERN!
NO! I CAN GET HOME! SEE YOU IN THE MORNING--WE'LL CONTINUE CHASING THOSE CRUDS!
RIGHT! I'LL WORK VERY HARD ON CANNING THAT CREW--THEIR RACKET STINKS--AND THEY MADE FOOLS OF US!
SPEEDY! I'M GONNA COOK SOME OF MY SPECIAL "SCORCH-YOUR MOUTH" CHILI...
--CAN I INTEREST YOU IN A BOWL?
22
OH, DEAR GOD! YOU ARE ON DRUGS!
YOU'RE REALLY A JUNKIE?
WHO ELSE DID YOU THINK I WAS TALKING ABOUT?
IT DOESN'T END YET... IT CAN'T! NEXT ISSUE-- THE MOST SHATTERING CONCLUSION EVER!

AN IMPORTANT MESSAGE FROM THE HONORABLE JOHN V. LINDSAY
MAYOR OF NEW YORK CITY

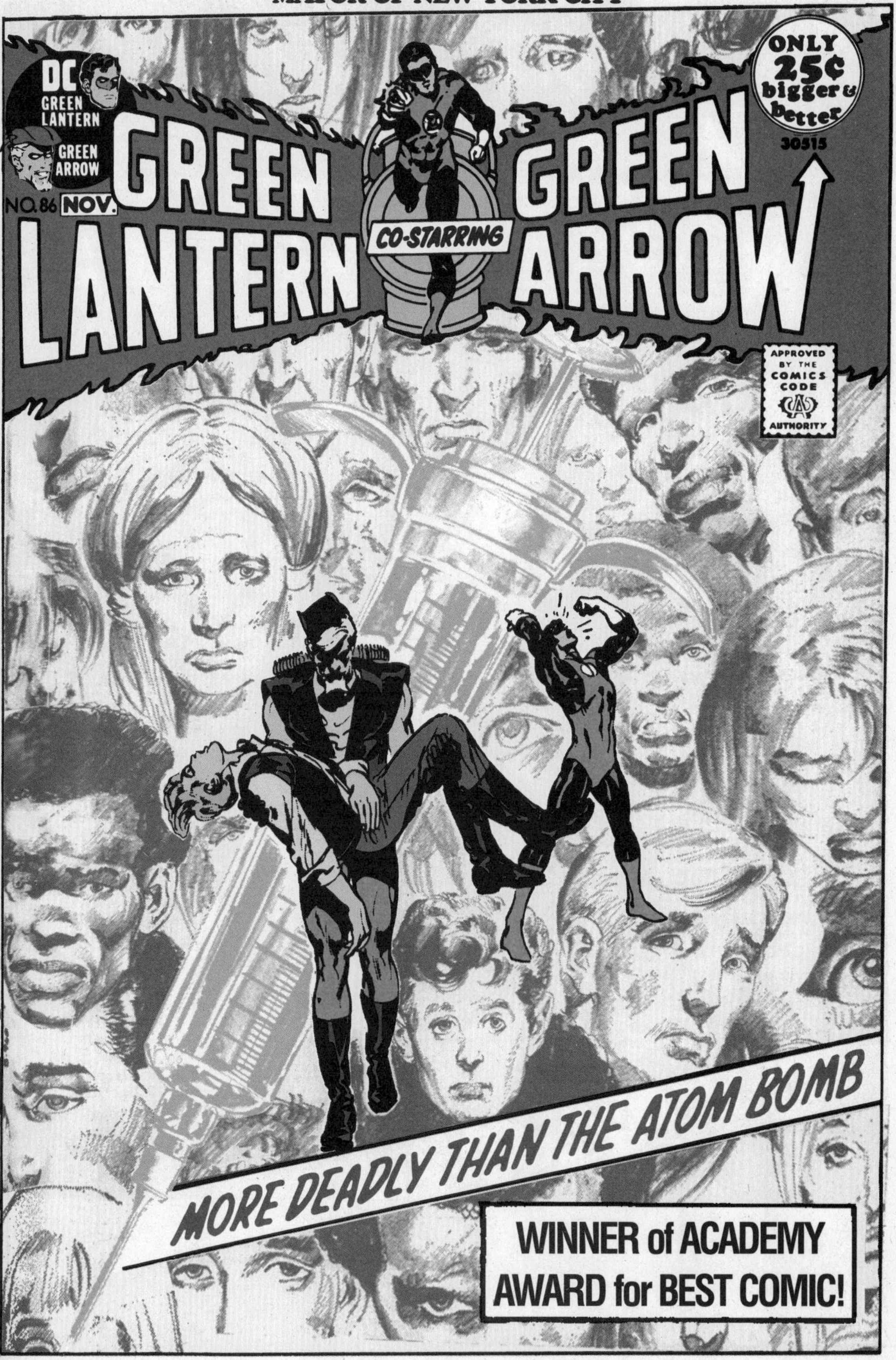
DC
GREEN LANTERN
GREEN ARROW
NO. 86 NOV.
GREEN LANTERN
CO-STARRING
GREEN ARROW
ONLY 25¢ bigger & better
30515
APPROVED BY THE COMICS CODE AUTHORITY
MORE DEADLY THAN THE ATOM BOMB
WINNER of ACADEMY AWARD for BEST COMIC!

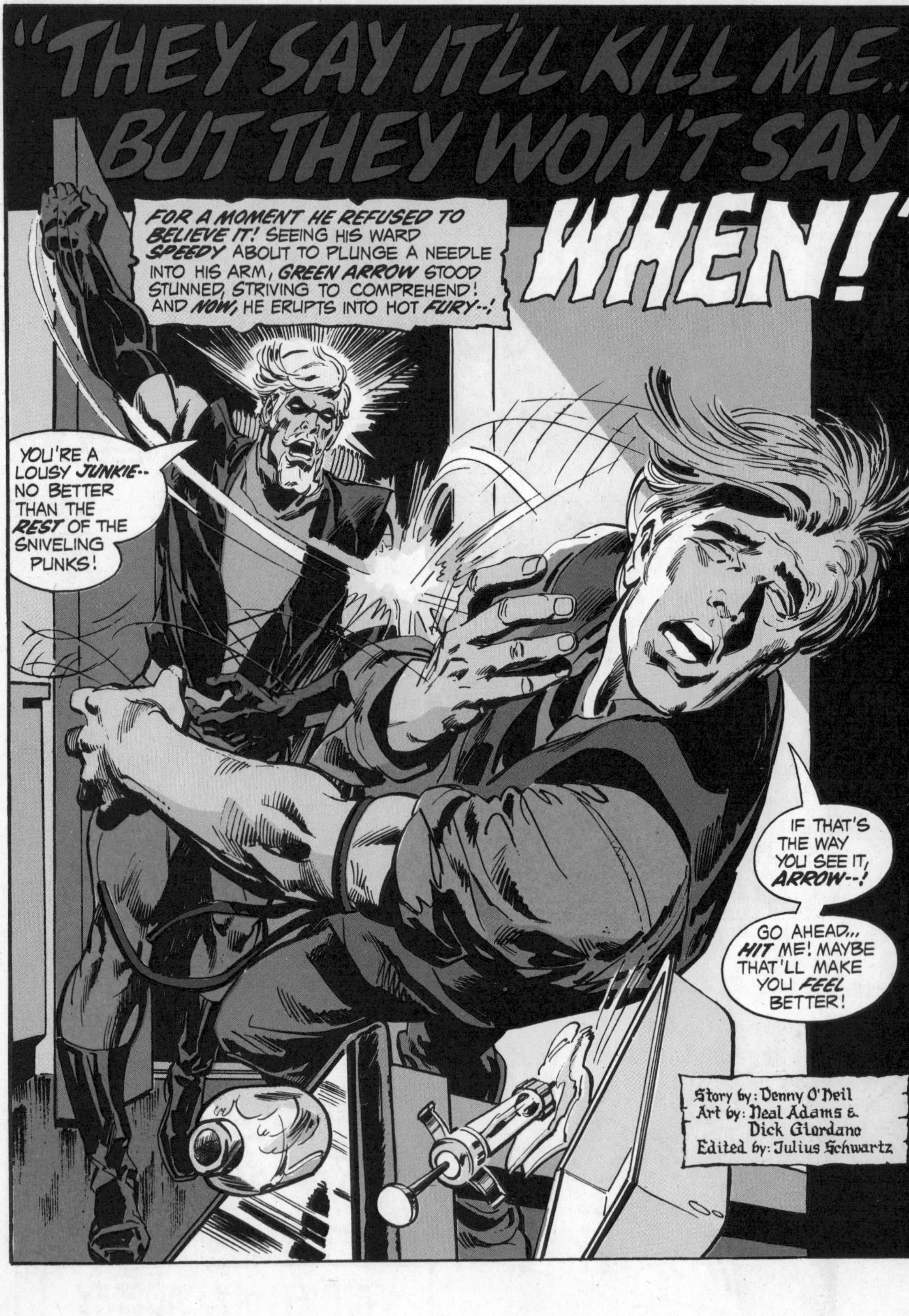
"THEY SAY IT'LL KILL ME... BUT THEY WON'T SAY WHEN!"
FOR A MOMENT HE REFUSED TO BELIEVE IT! SEEING HIS WARD SPEEDY ABOUT TO PLUNGE A NEEDLE INTO HIS ARM, GREEN ARROW STOOD STUNNED, STRIVING TO COMPREHEND! AND NOW, HE ERUPTS INTO HOT FURY--!
YOU'RE A LOUSY JUNKIE-- NO BETTER THAN THE REST OF THE SNIVELING PUNKS!
IF THAT'S THE WAY YOU SEE IT, ARROW--!
GO AHEAD... HIT ME! MAYBE THAT'LL MAKE YOU FEEL BETTER!
Story by: Denny O'Neil
Art by: Neal Adams & Dick Giordano
Edited by: Julius Schwartz

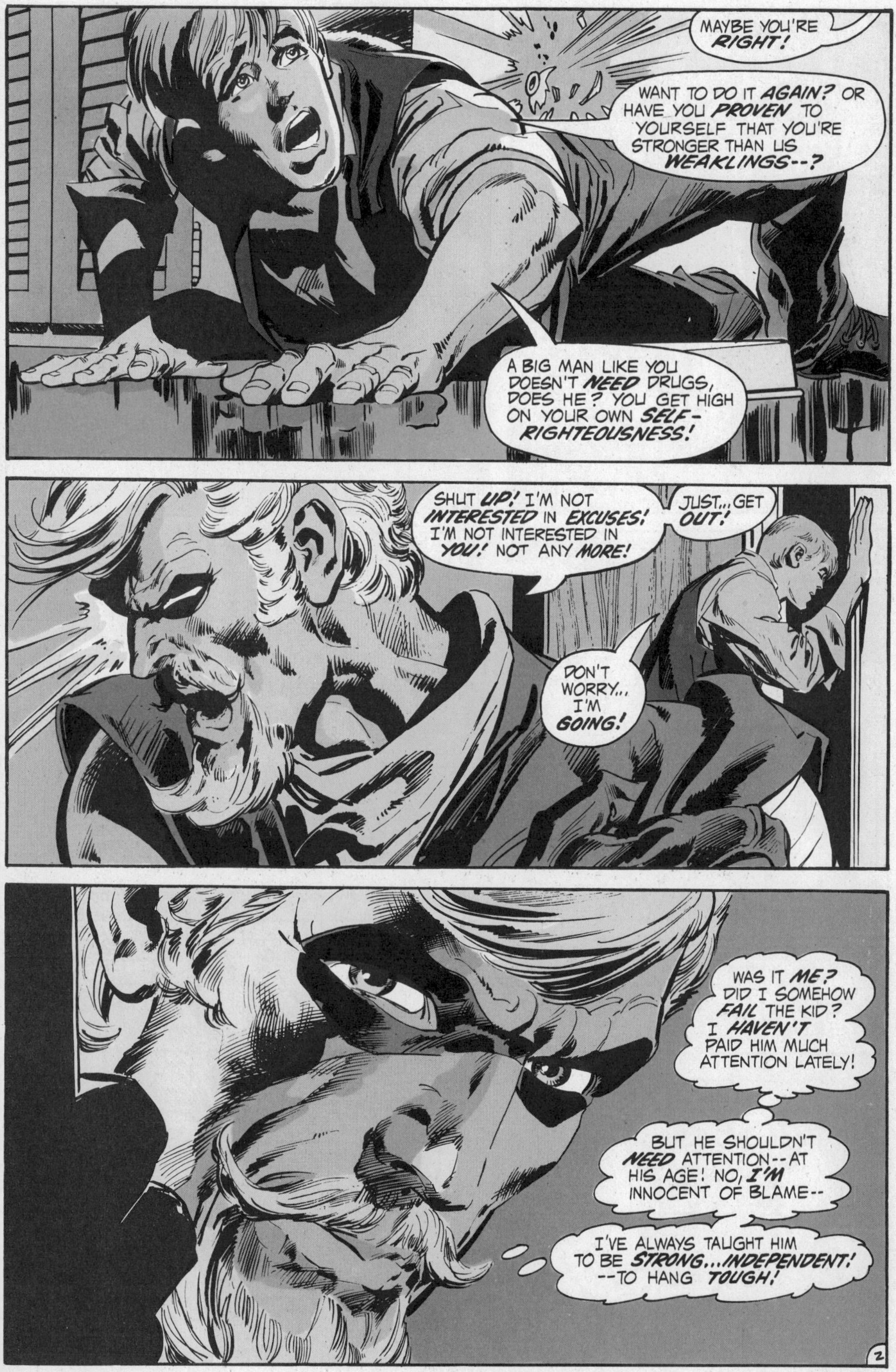
MAYBE YOU'RE RIGHT!
WANT TO DO IT AGAIN? OR HAVE YOU PROVEN TO YOURSELF THAT YOU'RE STRONGER THAN US WEAKLINGS--?
A BIG MAN LIKE YOU DOESN'T NEED DRUGS, DOES HE? YOU GET HIGH ON YOUR OWN SELF-RIGHTEOUSNESS!
SHUT UP! I'M NOT INTERESTED IN EXCUSES! I'M NOT INTERESTED IN YOU! NOT ANY MORE!
JUST... GET OUT!
DON'T WORRY... I'M GOING!
WAS IT ME? DID I SOMEHOW FAIL THE KID? I HAVEN'T PAID HIM MUCH ATTENTION LATELY!
BUT HE SHOULDN'T NEED ATTENTION--AT HIS AGE! NO, I'M INNOCENT OF BLAME--
I'VE ALWAYS TAUGHT HIM TO BE STRONG...INDEPENDENT! --TO HANG TOUGH!
2

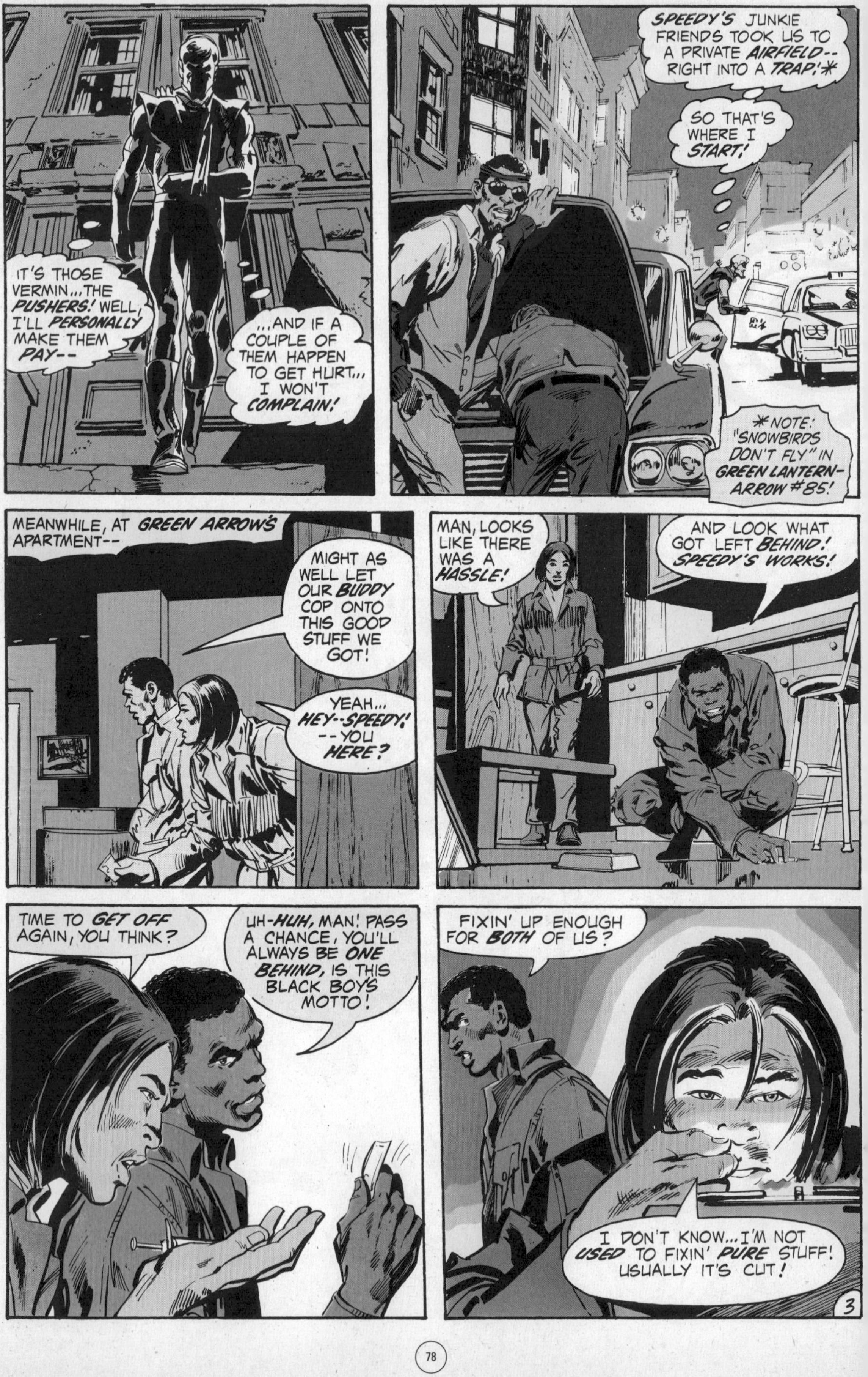

IT'S THOSE VERMIN... THE PUSHERS! WELL, I'LL PERSONALLY MAKE THEM PAY--
...AND IF A COUPLE OF THEM HAPPEN TO GET HURT... I WON'T COMPLAIN!
SPEEDY'S JUNKIE FRIENDS TOOK US TO A PRIVATE AIRFIELD-- RIGHT INTO A TRAP!*
SO THAT'S WHERE I START!
*NOTE: "SNOWBIRDS DON'T FLY" IN GREEN LANTERN-ARROW #85!
MEANWHILE, AT GREEN ARROW'S APARTMENT--
MIGHT AS WELL LET OUR BUDDY COP ONTO THIS GOOD STUFF WE GOT!
YEAH... HEY--SPEEDY! --YOU HERE?
MAN, LOOKS LIKE THERE WAS A HASSLE!
AND LOOK WHAT GOT LEFT BEHIND! SPEEDY'S WORKS!
TIME TO GET OFF AGAIN, YOU THINK?
UH-HUH, MAN! PASS A CHANCE, YOU'LL ALWAYS BE ONE BEHIND, IS THIS BLACK BOY'S MOTTO!
FIXIN' UP ENOUGH FOR BOTH OF US?
I DON'T KNOW... I'M NOT USED TO FIXIN' PURE STUFF! USUALLY IT'S CUT!
3

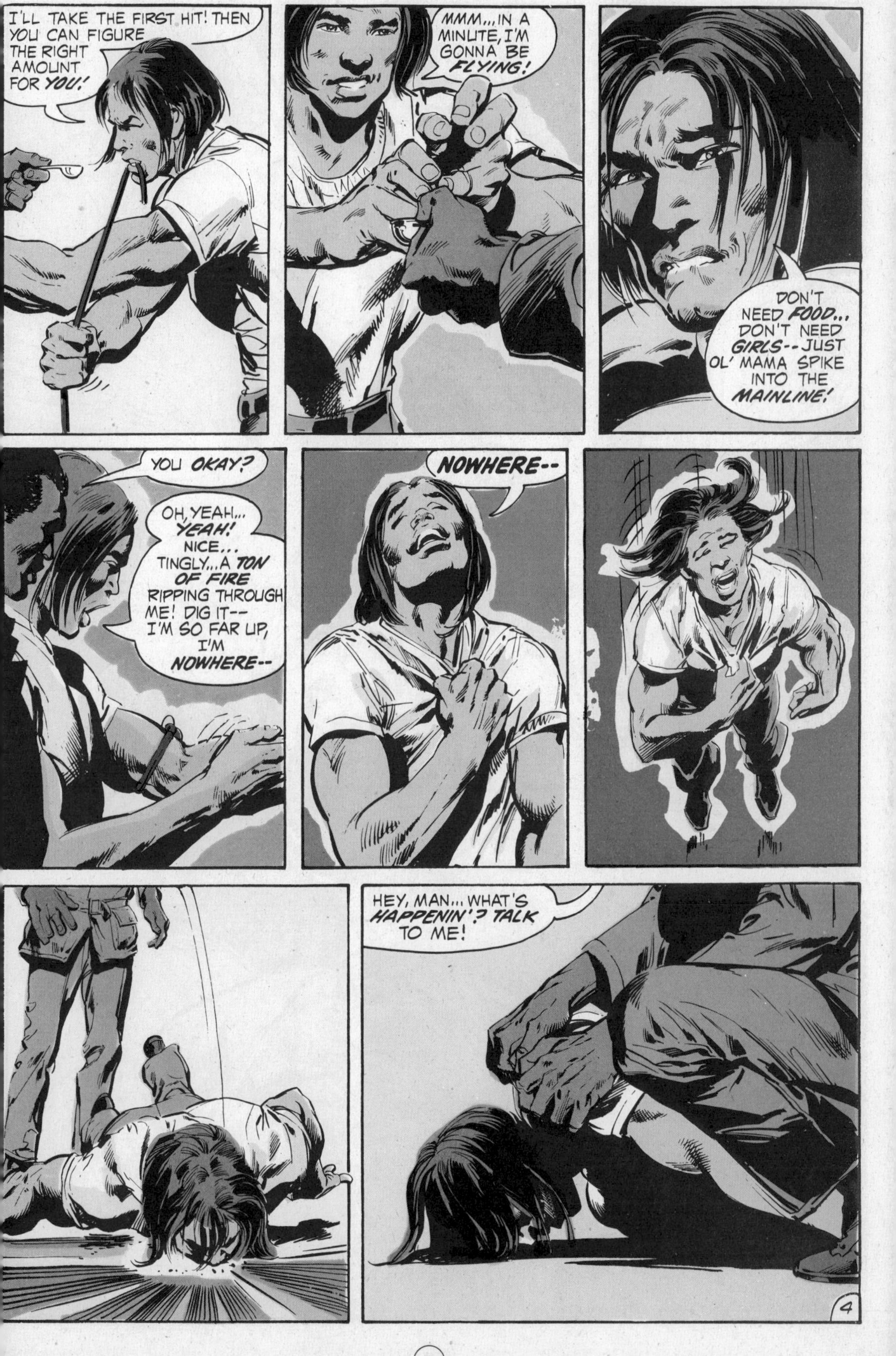
I'LL TAKE THE FIRST HIT! THEN YOU CAN FIGURE THE RIGHT AMOUNT FOR YOU!
MMM... IN A MINUTE, I'M GONNA BE FLYING!
DON'T NEED FOOD... DON'T NEED GIRLS-- JUST OL' MAMA SPIKE INTO THE MAINLINE!
YOU OKAY?
OH, YEAH... YEAH! NICE... TINGLY... A TON OF FIRE RIPPING THROUGH ME! DIG IT-- I'M SO FAR UP, I'M NOWHERE--
NOWHERE--
HEY, MAN... WHAT'S HAPPENIN'? TALK TO ME!
4

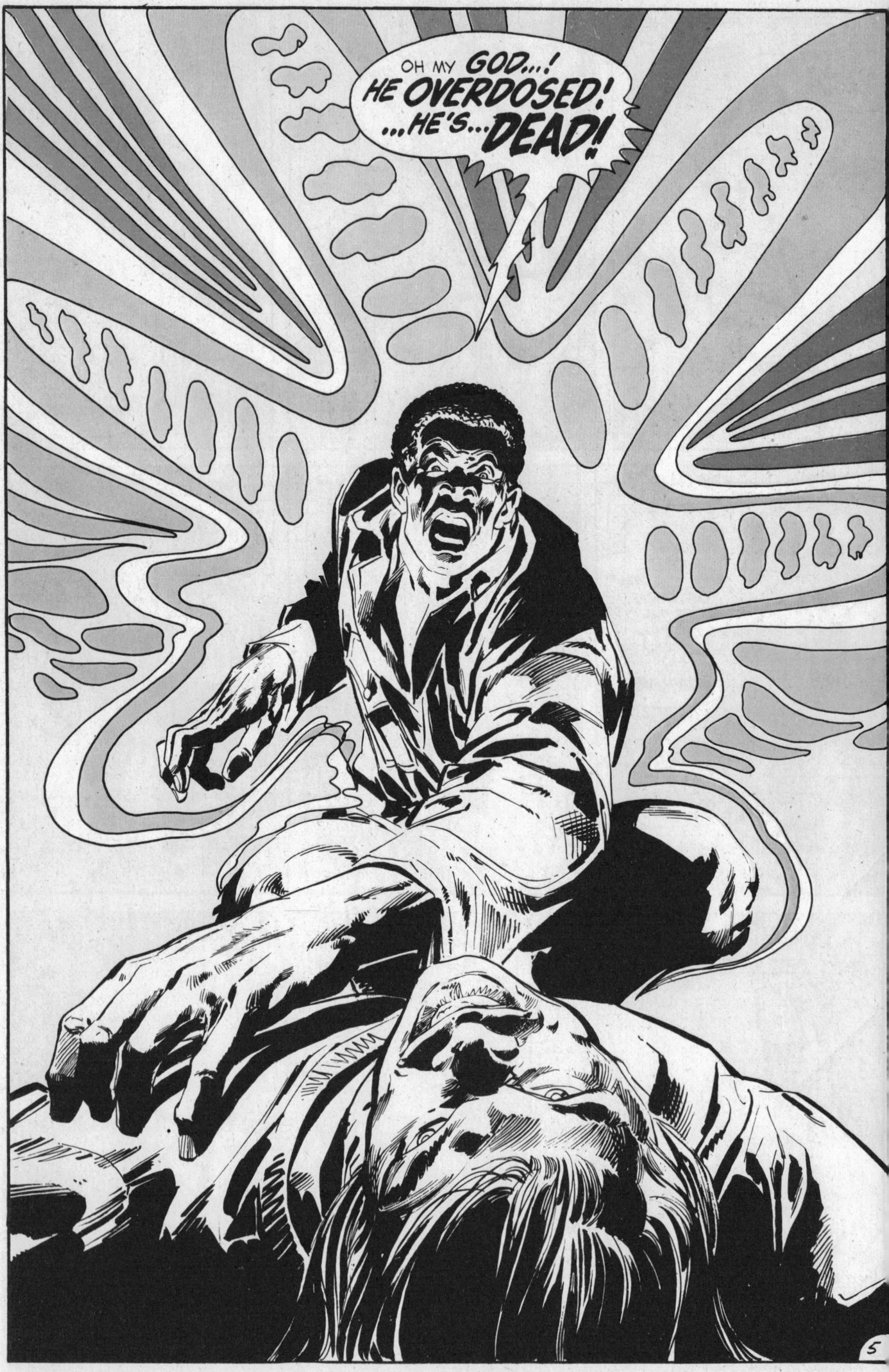
OH MY GOD...! HE OVERDOSED! ...HE'S...DEAD!
5

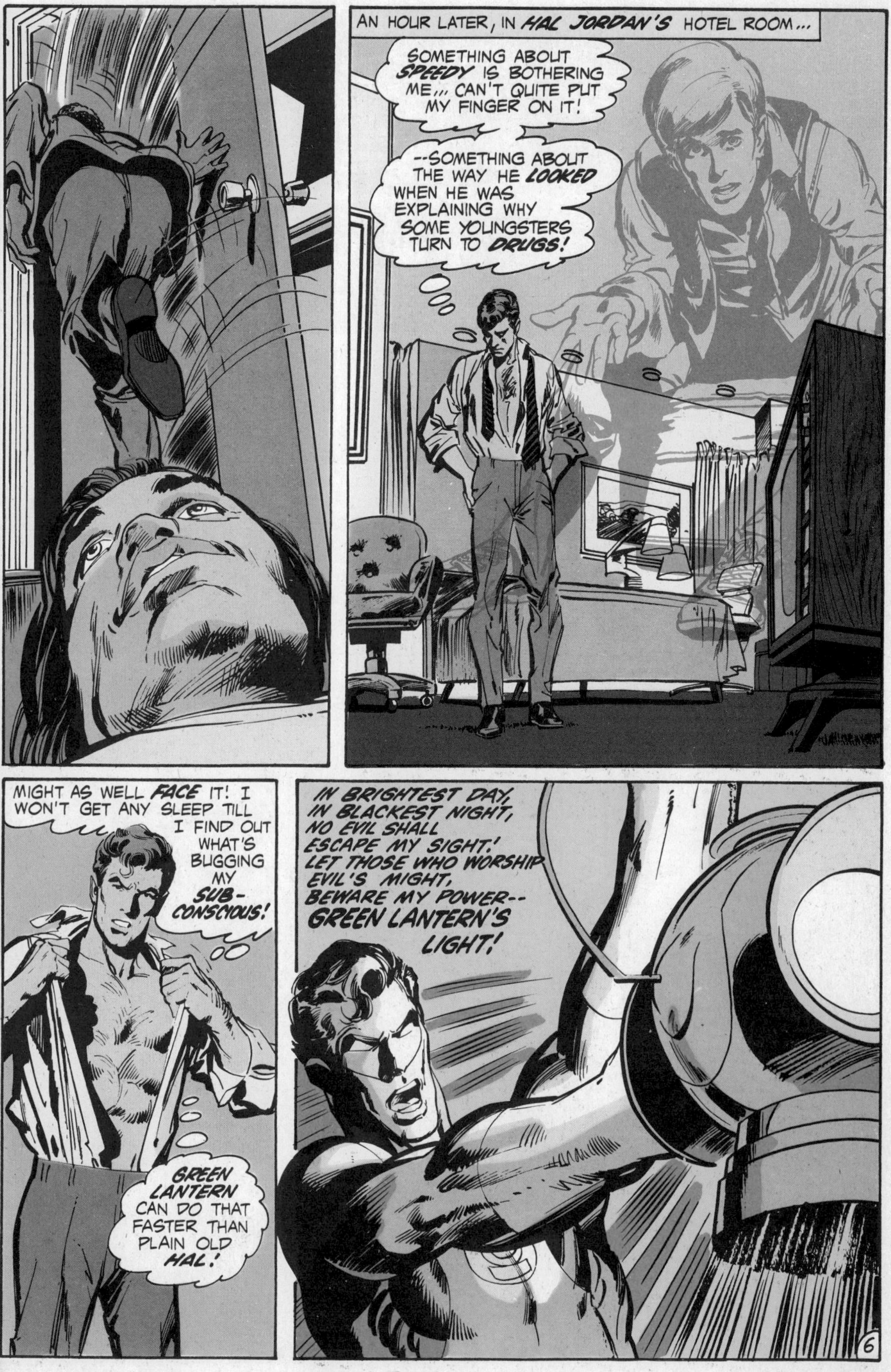
AN HOUR LATER, IN HAL JORDAN'S HOTEL ROOM...
SOMETHING ABOUT SPEEDY IS BOTHERING ME,,, CAN'T QUITE PUT MY FINGER ON IT!
--SOMETHING ABOUT THE WAY HE LOOKED WHEN HE WAS EXPLAINING WHY SOME YOUNGSTERS TURN TO DRUGS!
MIGHT AS WELL FACE IT! I WON'T GET ANY SLEEP TILL I FIND OUT WHAT'S BUGGING MY SUB-CONSCIOUS!
GREEN LANTERN CAN DO THAT FASTER THAN PLAIN OLD HAL!
IN BRIGHTEST DAY, IN BLACKEST NIGHT, NO EVIL SHALL ESCAPE MY SIGHT! LET THOSE WHO WORSHIP EVIL'S MIGHT, BEWARE MY POWER-- GREEN LANTERN'S LIGHT!
6

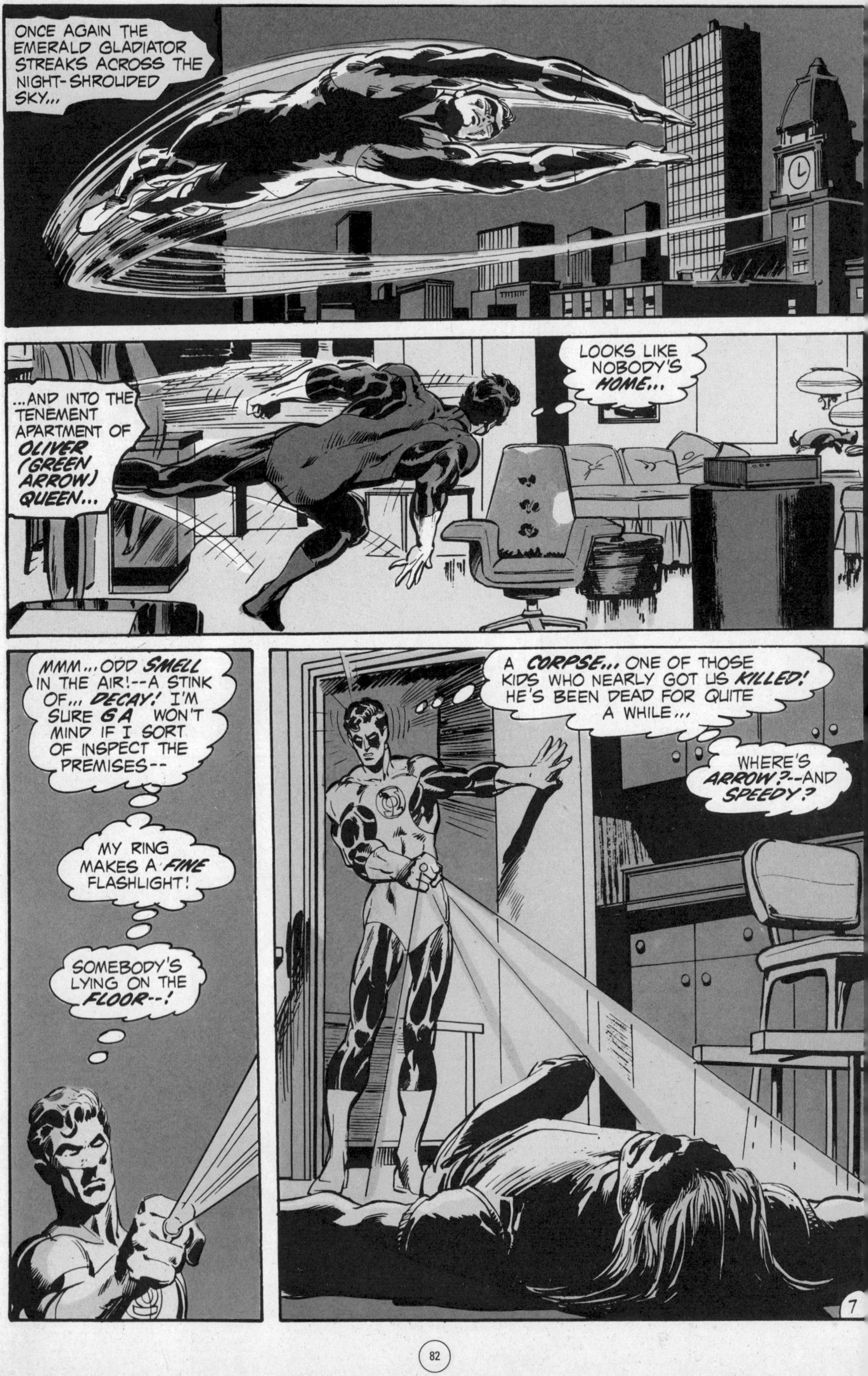
ONCE AGAIN THE EMERALD GLADIATOR STREAKS ACROSS THE NIGHT-SHROUDED SKY...
...AND INTO THE TENEMENT APARTMENT OF OLIVER (GREEN ARROW) QUEEN...
LOOKS LIKE NOBODY'S HOME...
MMM... ODD SMELL IN THE AIR!--A STINK OF... DECAY! I'M SURE GA WON'T MIND IF I SORT OF INSPECT THE PREMISES--
MY RING MAKES A FINE FLASHLIGHT!
SOMEBODY'S LYING ON THE FLOOR--!
A CORPSE... ONE OF THOSE KIDS WHO NEARLY GOT US KILLED! HE'S BEEN DEAD FOR QUITE A WHILE...
WHERE'S ARROW?--AND SPEEDY?
7

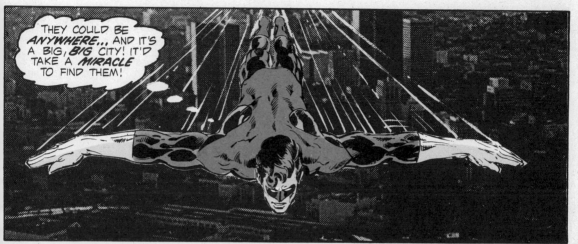

THEY COULD BE *ANYWHERE*... AND IT'S A BIG, *BIG* CITY! IT'D TAKE A *MIRACLE* TO FIND THEM!

EVEN AS *GREEN LANTERN* SWEEPS UPWARD, HIS FRIEND IS STEALTHILY ENTERING A PRIVATE AIR-FIELD...

THERE'S THE HANGAR WHERE THESE CREEPS *WAY-LAID* THE *LANTERN* AND ME! --SEEMS *DESERTED!*

JUST *MAYBE*... THEY LEFT A *CLUE* BEHIND!

PROBLEM IS, I'M NOT SURE WHAT I'M *LOOKING* FOR!

HEY....! FANCY-PANTS--

AIN'T NOBODY ALLOWED IN HERE WITHOUT THEY HAVE *PERMISSION!* YOU HOLDING SOME PERMISSION, TROT IT OUT!

EASY WITH THE GUN, MISTER! POINT IT IN ANOTHER DIRECTION AND I'LL *SHOW* YOU MY REASON FOR COMING IN--

8

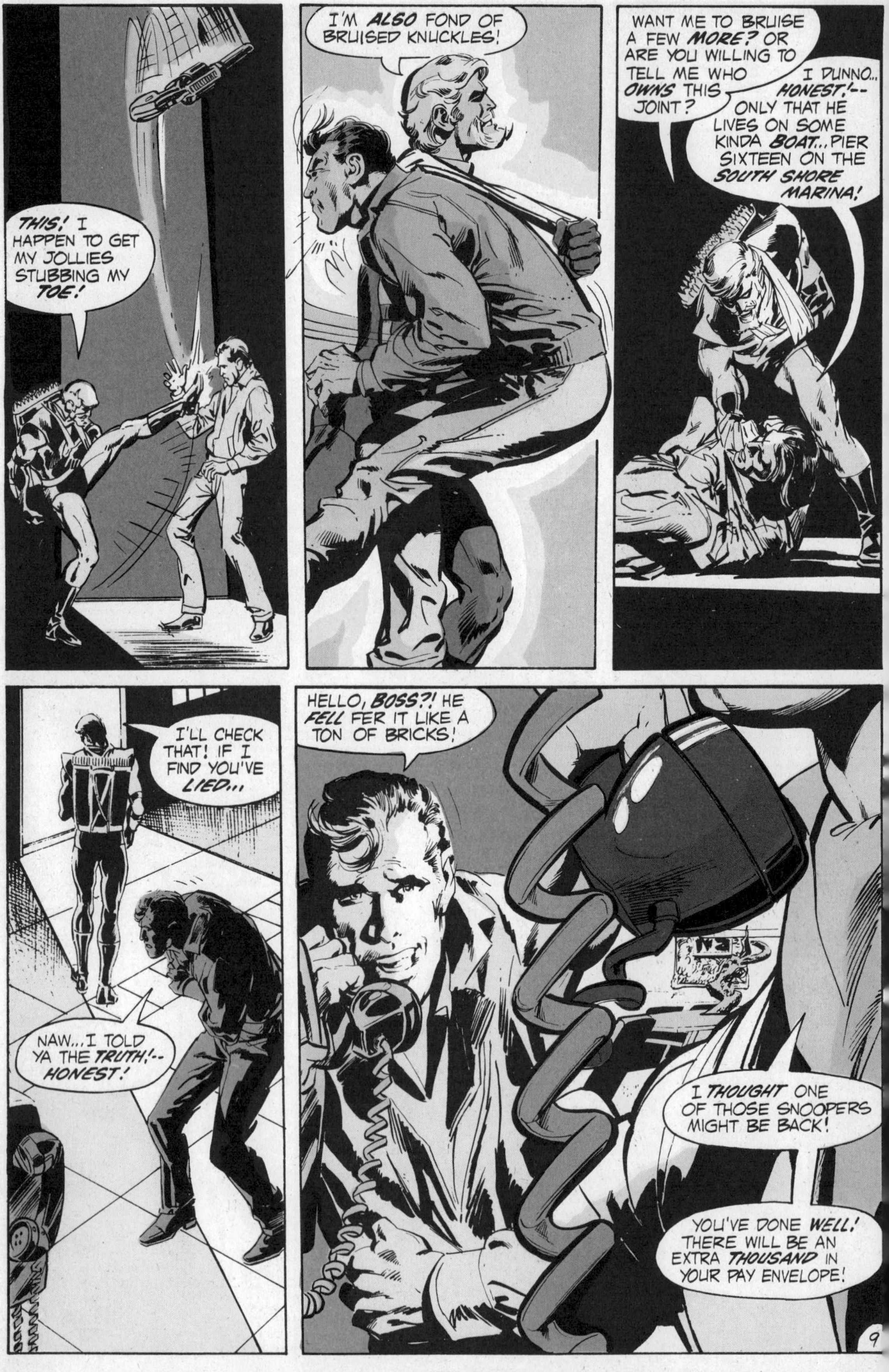
THIS! I HAPPEN TO GET MY JOLLIES STUBBING MY TOE!
I'M ALSO FOND OF BRUISED KNUCKLES!
WANT ME TO BRUISE A FEW MORE? OR ARE YOU WILLING TO TELL ME WHO OWNS THIS JOINT?
I DUNNO... HONEST!-- ONLY THAT HE LIVES ON SOME KINDA BOAT... PIER SIXTEEN ON THE SOUTH SHORE MARINA!
I'LL CHECK THAT! IF I FIND YOU'VE LIED...
NAW... I TOLD YA THE TRUTH!-- HONEST!
HELLO, BOSS?! HE FELL FER IT LIKE A TON OF BRICKS!
I THOUGHT ONE OF THOSE SNOOPERS MIGHT BE BACK!
YOU'VE DONE WELL! THERE WILL BE AN EXTRA THOUSAND IN YOUR PAY ENVELOPE!
9

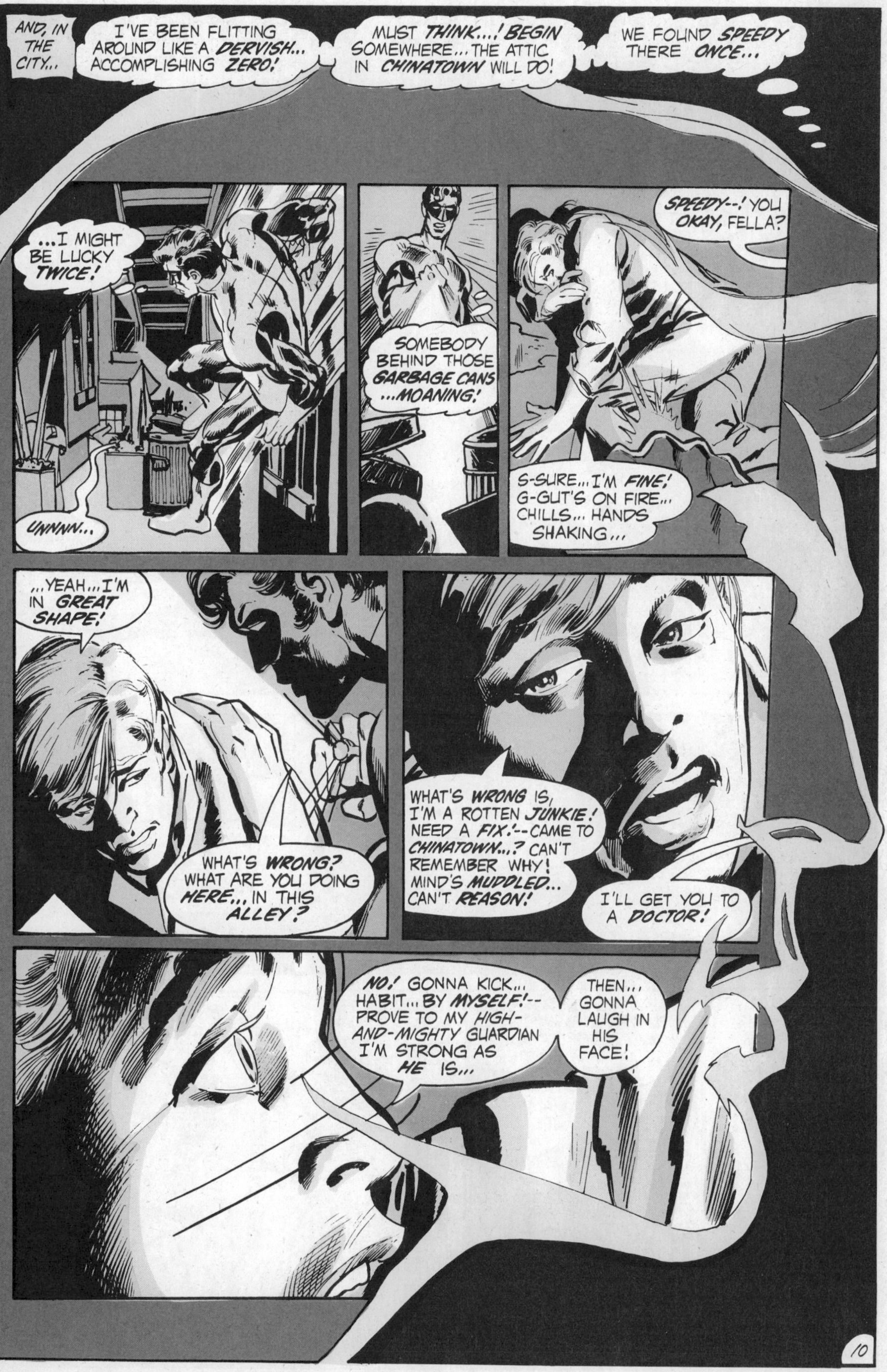
AND, IN THE CITY...
I'VE BEEN FLITTING AROUND LIKE A DERVISH... ACCOMPLISHING ZERO!
MUST THINK...! BEGIN SOMEWHERE... THE ATTIC IN CHINATOWN WILL DO!
WE FOUND SPEEDY THERE ONCE...
...I MIGHT BE LUCKY TWICE!
UNNNN...
SOMEBODY BEHIND THOSE GARBAGE CANS ...MOANING!
SPEEDY--! YOU OKAY, FELLA?
S-SURE... I'M FINE! G-GUT'S ON FIRE... CHILLS... HANDS SHAKING...
...YEAH... I'M IN GREAT SHAPE!
WHAT'S WRONG? WHAT ARE YOU DOING HERE... IN THIS ALLEY?
WHAT'S WRONG IS, I'M A ROTTEN JUNKIE! NEED A FIX!--CAME TO CHINATOWN...? CAN'T REMEMBER WHY! MIND'S MUDDLED... CAN'T REASON!
I'LL GET YOU TO A DOCTOR!
NO! GONNA KICK... HABIT... BY MYSELF!--PROVE TO MY HIGH-AND-MIGHTY GUARDIAN I'M STRONG AS HE IS...
THEN... GONNA LAUGH IN HIS FACE!
10

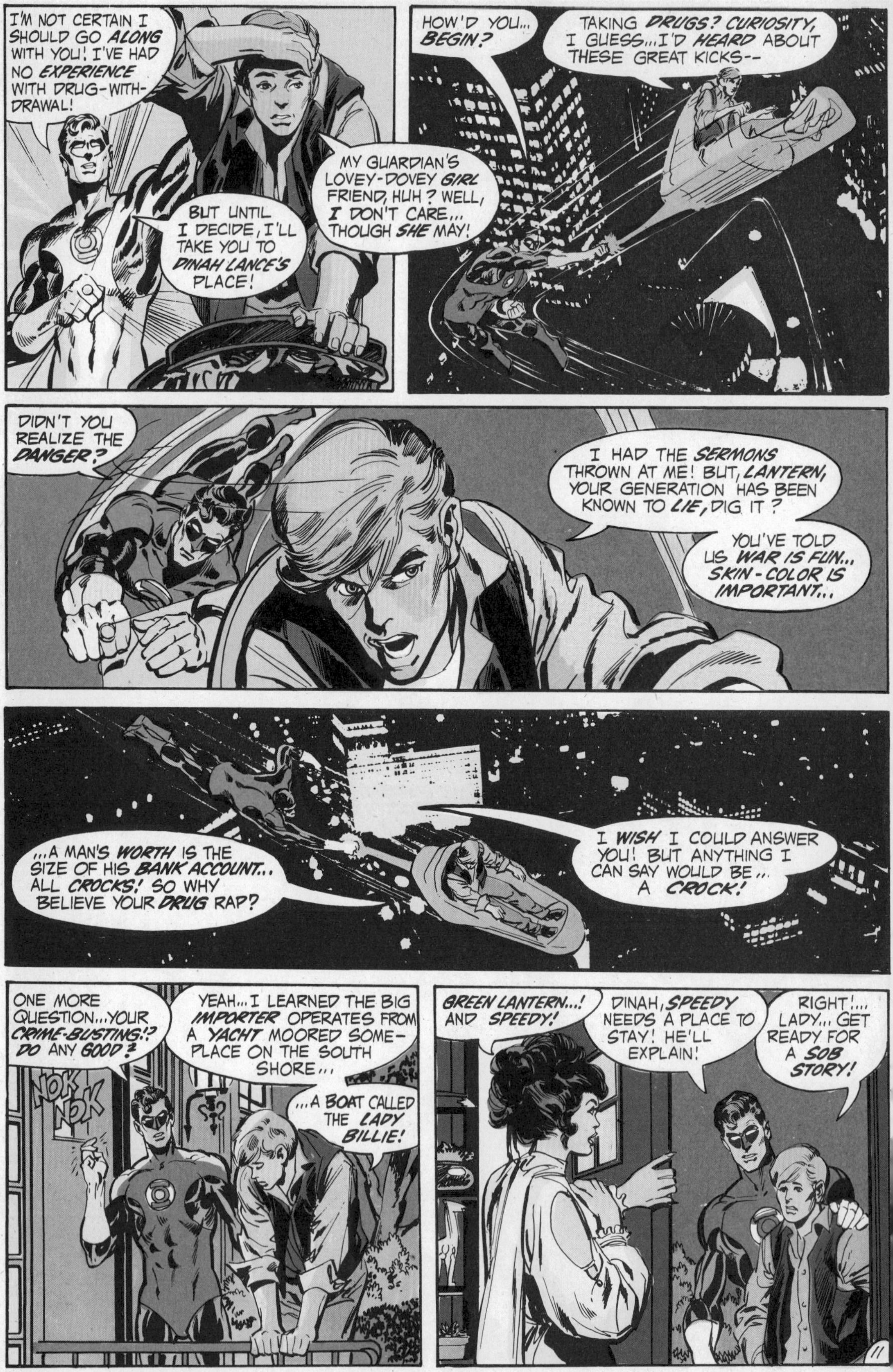
I'M NOT CERTAIN I SHOULD GO ALONG WITH YOU! I'VE HAD NO EXPERIENCE WITH DRUG-WITH-DRAWAL!
BUT UNTIL I DECIDE, I'LL TAKE YOU TO DINAH LANCE'S PLACE!
MY GUARDIAN'S LOVEY-DOVEY GIRL FRIEND, HUH? WELL, I DON'T CARE... THOUGH SHE MAY!
HOW'D YOU... BEGIN?
TAKING DRUGS? CURIOSITY, I GUESS...I'D HEARD ABOUT THESE GREAT KICKS--
DIDN'T YOU REALIZE THE DANGER?
I HAD THE SERMONS THROWN AT ME! BUT, LANTERN, YOUR GENERATION HAS BEEN KNOWN TO LIE, DIG IT?
YOU'VE TOLD US WAR IS FUN... SKIN-COLOR IS IMPORTANT...
...A MAN'S WORTH IS THE SIZE OF HIS BANK ACCOUNT... ALL CROCKS! SO WHY BELIEVE YOUR DRUG RAP?
I WISH I COULD ANSWER YOU! BUT ANYTHING I CAN SAY WOULD BE... A CROCK!
ONE MORE QUESTION...YOUR CRIME-BUSTING!? DO ANY GOOD?
YEAH...I LEARNED THE BIG IMPORTER OPERATES FROM A YACHT MOORED SOME-PLACE ON THE SOUTH SHORE...
NOK NOK
...A BOAT CALLED THE LADY BILLIE!
GREEN LANTERN...! AND SPEEDY!
DINAH, SPEEDY NEEDS A PLACE TO STAY! HE'LL EXPLAIN!
RIGHT!... LADY... GET READY FOR A SOB STORY!
11

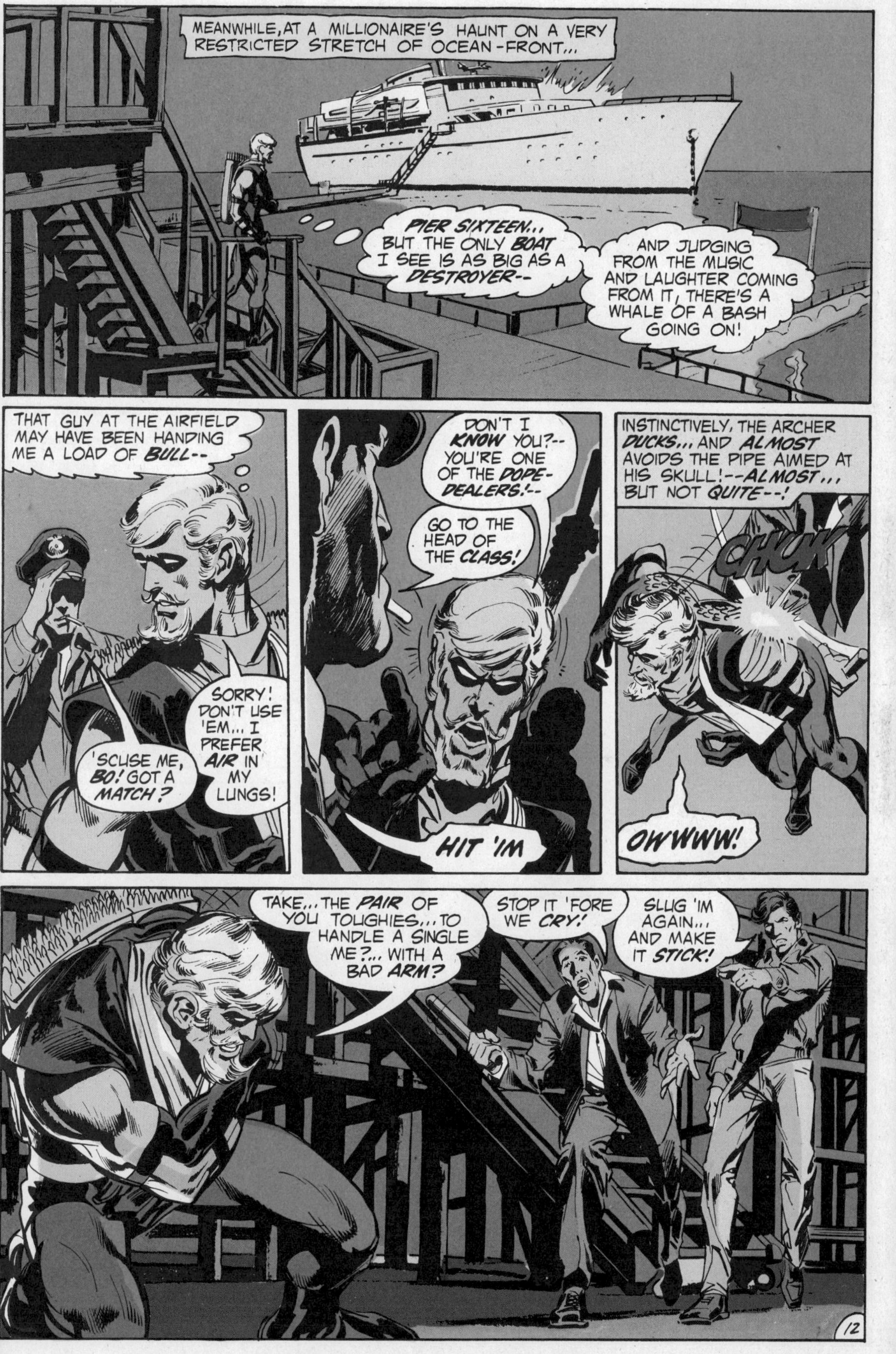
MEANWHILE, AT A MILLIONAIRE'S HAUNT ON A VERY RESTRICTED STRETCH OF OCEAN-FRONT...
PIER SIXTEEN... BUT THE ONLY BOAT I SEE IS AS BIG AS A DESTROYER--
AND JUDGING FROM THE MUSIC AND LAUGHTER COMING FROM IT, THERE'S A WHALE OF A BASH GOING ON!
THAT GUY AT THE AIRFIELD MAY HAVE BEEN HANDING ME A LOAD OF BULL--
'SCUSE ME, BO! GOT A MATCH?
SORRY! DON'T USE 'EM... I PREFER AIR IN MY LUNGS!
DON'T I KNOW YOU?-- YOU'RE ONE OF THE DOPE-DEALERS!--
GO TO THE HEAD OF THE CLASS!
HIT 'IM
INSTINCTIVELY, THE ARCHER DUCKS... AND ALMOST AVOIDS THE PIPE AIMED AT HIS SKULL!--ALMOST... BUT NOT QUITE--!
CHUK
OWWWW!
TAKE... THE PAIR OF YOU TOUGHIES... TO HANDLE A SINGLE ME?... WITH A BAD ARM?
STOP IT 'FORE WE CRY!
SLUG 'IM AGAIN... AND MAKE IT STICK!
12

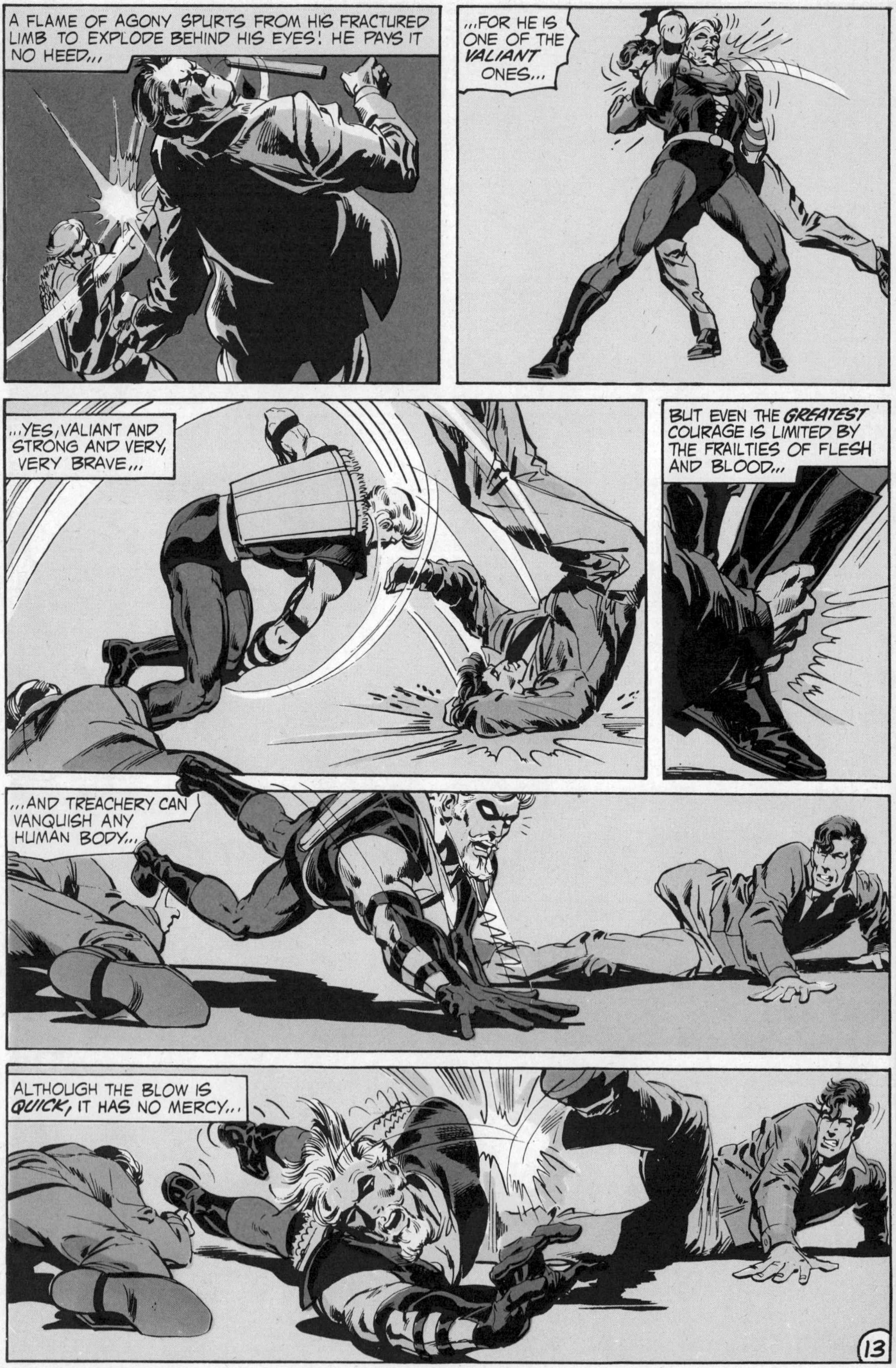
A FLAME OF AGONY SPURTS FROM HIS FRACTURED LIMB TO EXPLODE BEHIND HIS EYES! HE PAYS IT NO HEED...
...FOR HE IS ONE OF THE VALIANT ONES...
...YES, VALIANT AND STRONG AND VERY, VERY BRAVE...
BUT EVEN THE GREATEST COURAGE IS LIMITED BY THE FRAILTIES OF FLESH AND BLOOD...
...AND TREACHERY CAN VANQUISH ANY HUMAN BODY...
ALTHOUGH THE BLOW IS QUICK, IT HAS NO MERCY...
13

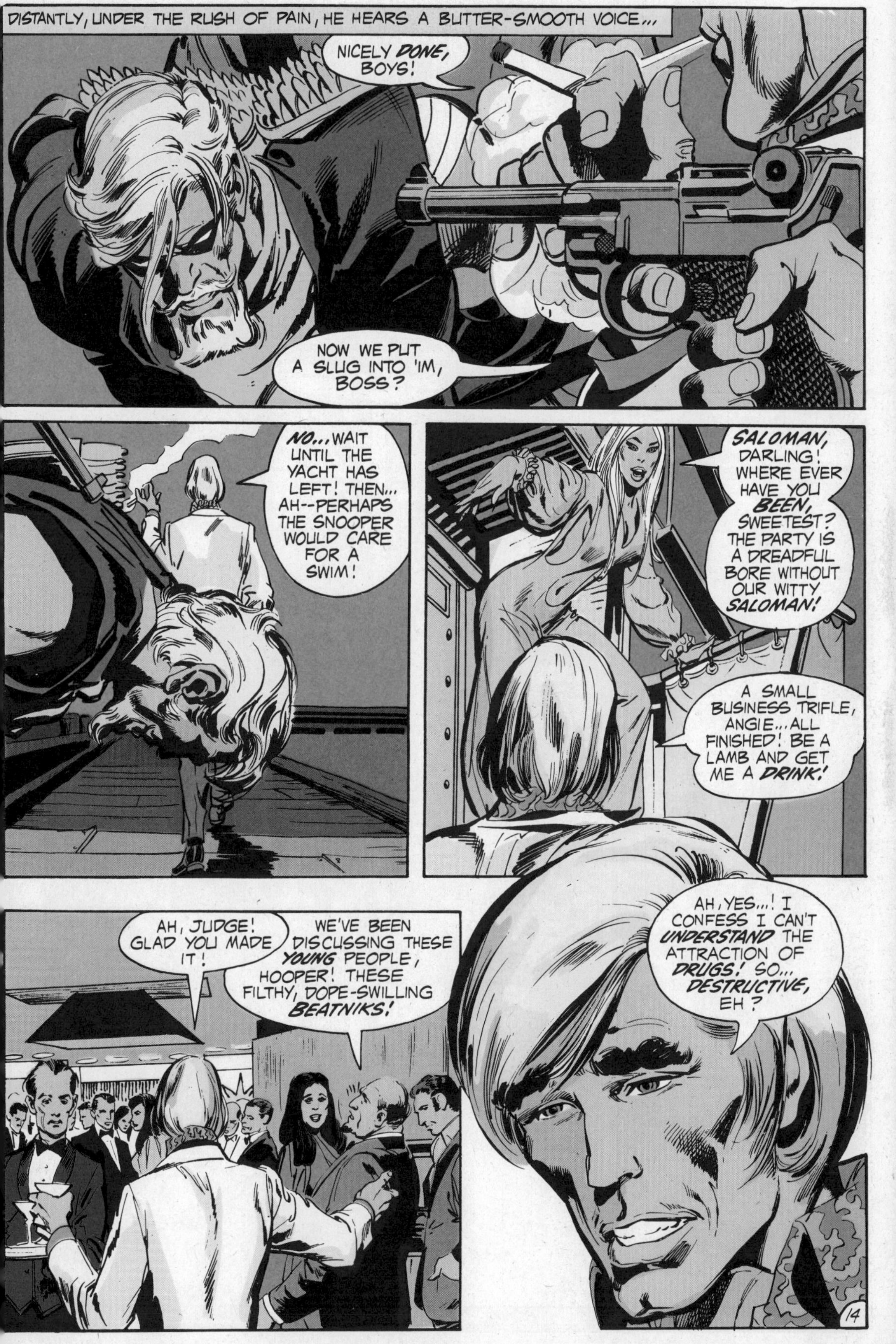
DISTANTLY, UNDER THE RUSH OF PAIN, HE HEARS A BUTTER-SMOOTH VOICE...
NICELY DONE, BOYS!
NOW WE PUT A SLUG INTO 'IM, BOSS?
NO... WAIT UNTIL THE YACHT HAS LEFT! THEN... AH--PERHAPS THE SNOOPER WOULD CARE FOR A SWIM!
SALOMAN, DARLING! WHERE EVER HAVE YOU BEEN, SWEETEST? THE PARTY IS A DREADFUL BORE WITHOUT OUR WITTY SALOMAN!
A SMALL BUSINESS TRIFLE, ANGIE... ALL FINISHED! BE A LAMB AND GET ME A DRINK!
AH, JUDGE! GLAD YOU MADE IT!
WE'VE BEEN DISCUSSING THESE YOUNG PEOPLE, HOOPER! THESE FILTHY, DOPE-SWILLING BEATNIKS!
AH, YES...! I CONFESS I CAN'T UNDERSTAND THE ATTRACTION OF DRUGS! SO... DESTRUCTIVE, EH?
14

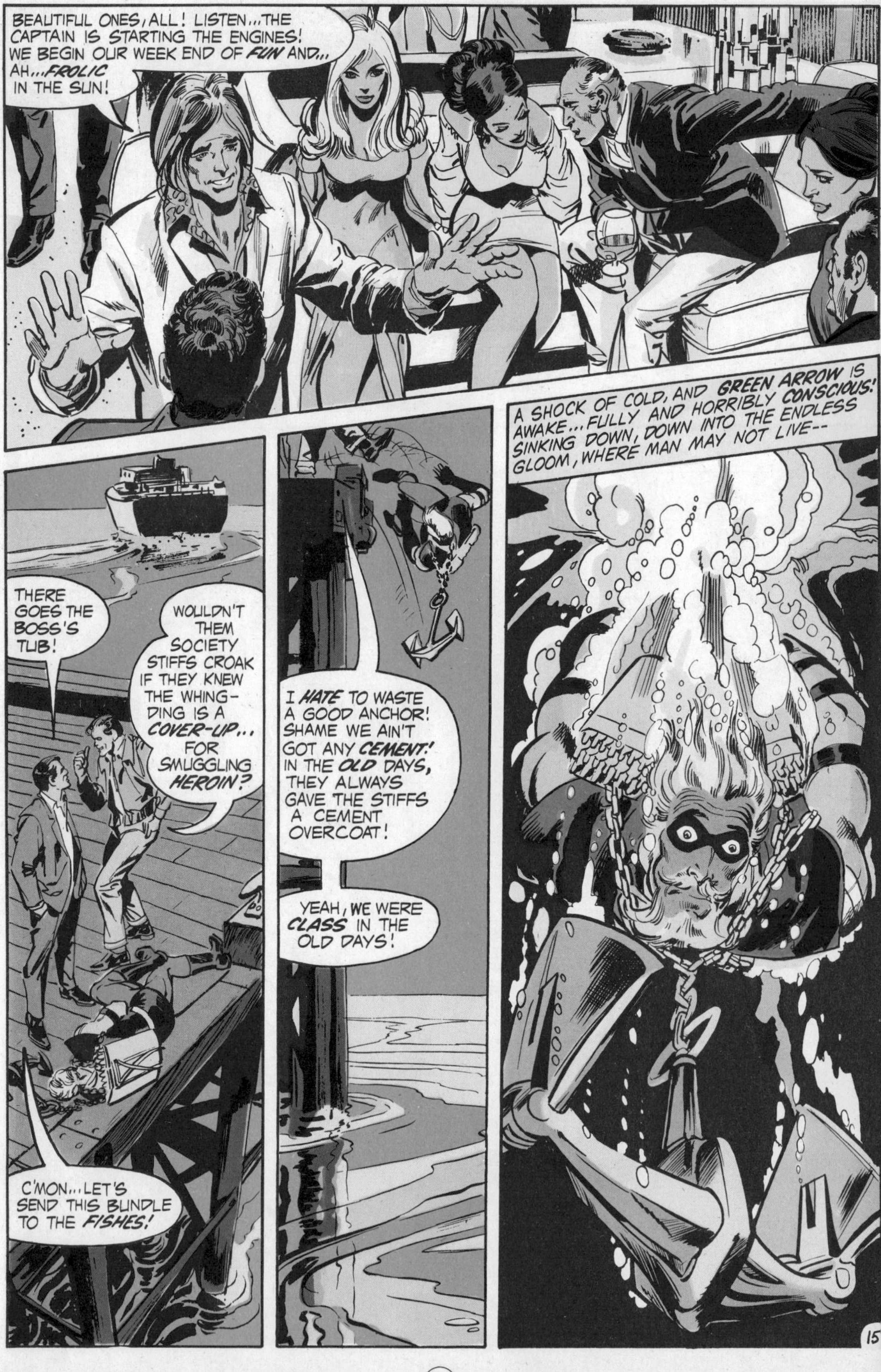

BEAUTIFUL ONES, ALL! LISTEN... THE CAPTAIN IS STARTING THE ENGINES! WE BEGIN OUR WEEK END OF FUN AND... AH... FROLIC IN THE SUN!
THERE GOES THE BOSS'S TUB!
WOULDN'T THEM SOCIETY STIFFS CROAK IF THEY KNEW THE WHING-DING IS A COVER-UP... FOR SMUGGLING HEROIN?
C'MON... LET'S SEND THIS BUNDLE TO THE FISHES!
I HATE TO WASTE A GOOD ANCHOR! SHAME WE AIN'T GOT ANY CEMENT! IN THE OLD DAYS, THEY ALWAYS GAVE THE STIFFS A CEMENT OVERCOAT!
YEAH, WE WERE CLASS IN THE OLD DAYS!
A SHOCK OF COLD, AND GREEN ARROW IS AWAKE... FULLY AND HORRIBLY CONSCIOUS! SINKING DOWN, DOWN INTO THE ENDLESS GLOOM, WHERE MAN MAY NOT LIVE--
15

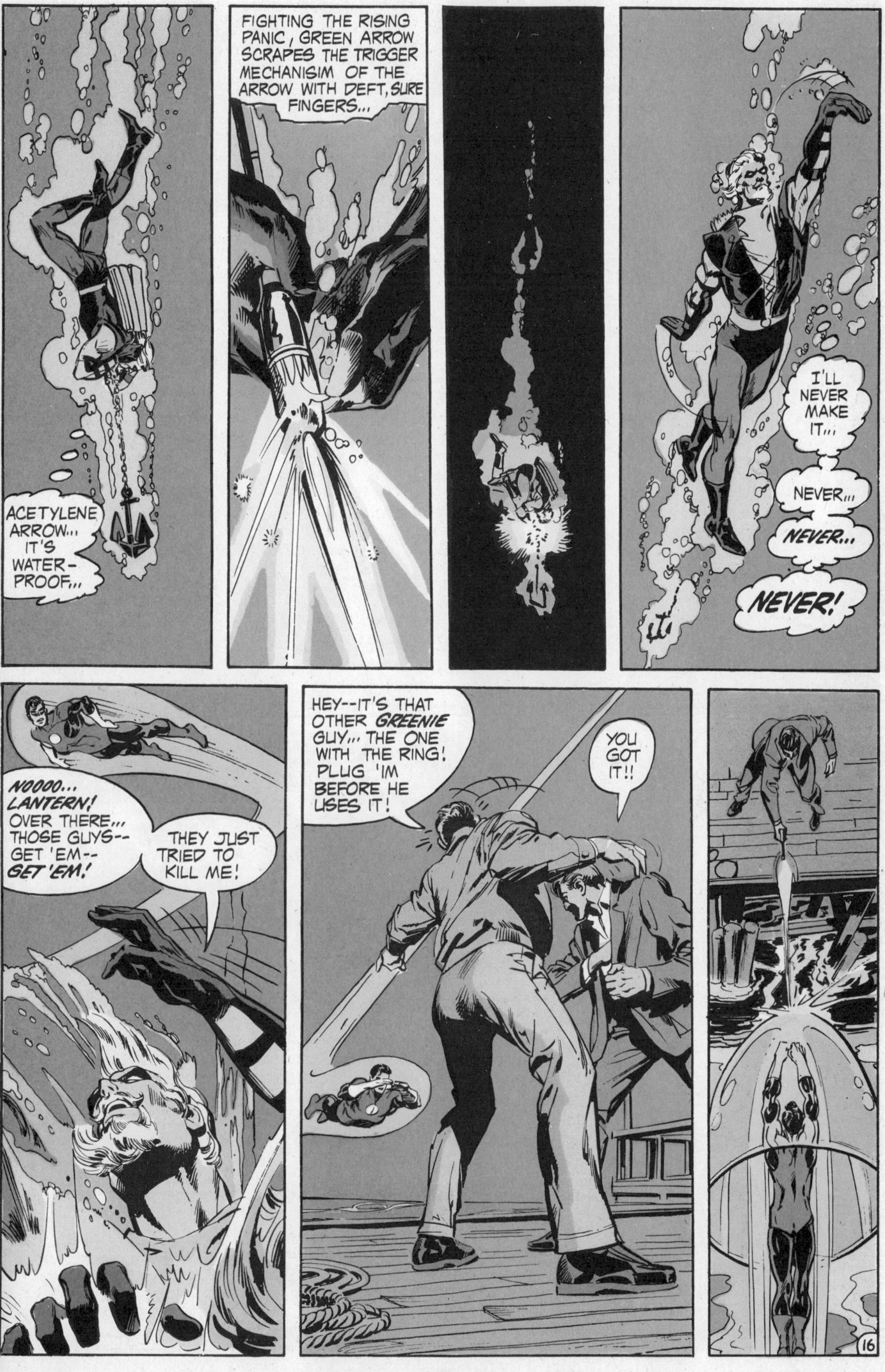
ACETYLENE ARROW... IT'S WATER-PROOF...
FIGHTING THE RISING PANIC, GREEN ARROW SCRAPES THE TRIGGER MECHANISIM OF THE ARROW WITH DEFT, SURE FINGERS...
I'LL NEVER MAKE IT...
NEVER...
NEVER...
NEVER!
NOOOO... LANTERN! OVER THERE... THOSE GUYS-- GET 'EM-- GET 'EM!
THEY JUST TRIED TO KILL ME!
HEY--IT'S THAT OTHER GREENIE GUY... THE ONE WITH THE RING! PLUG 'IM BEFORE HE USES IT!
YOU GOT IT!!
16

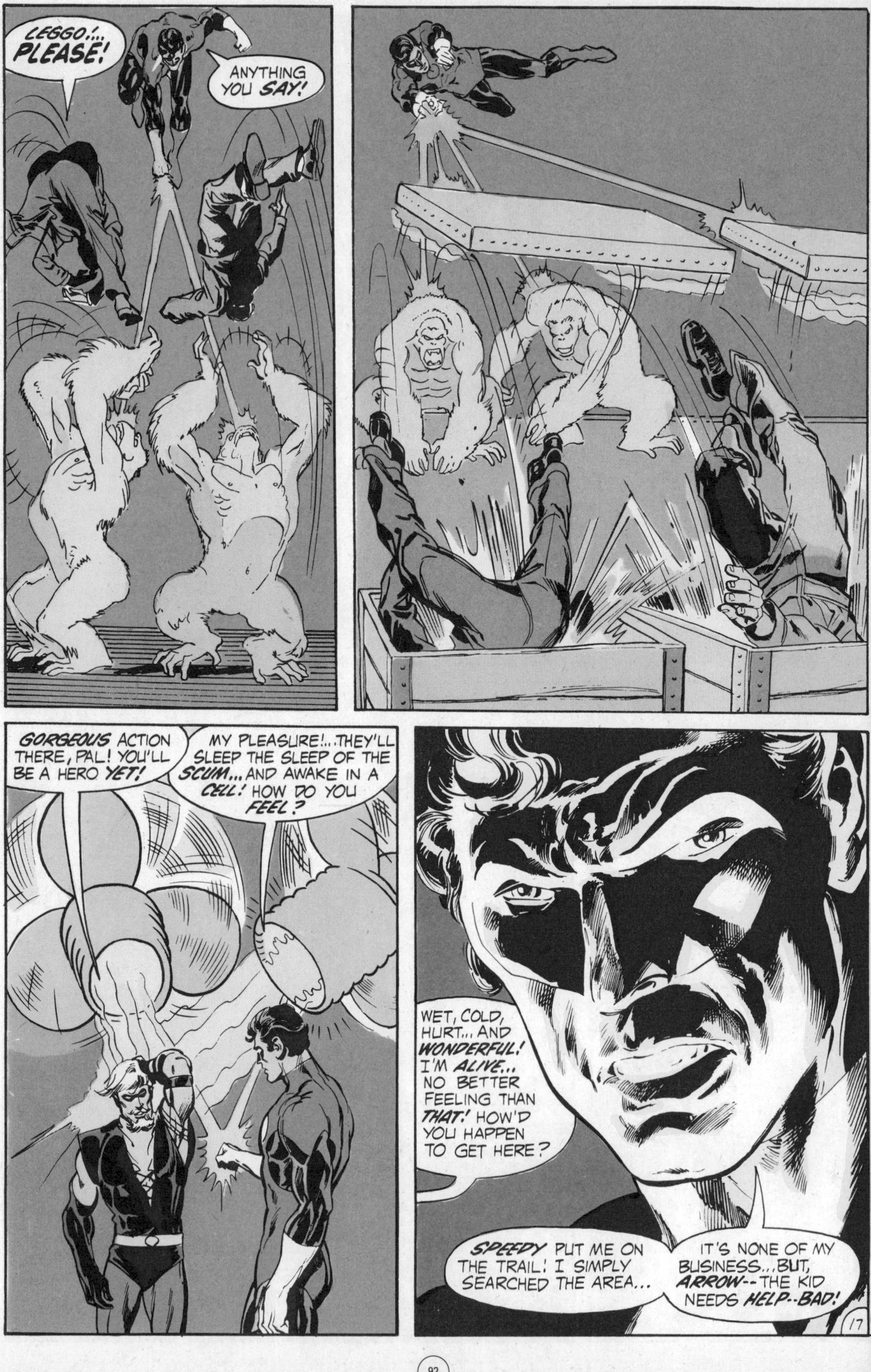
LEGGO!... PLEASE!
ANYTHING YOU SAY!
GORGEOUS ACTION THERE, PAL! YOU'LL BE A HERO YET!
MY PLEASURE!...THEY'LL SLEEP THE SLEEP OF THE SCUM...AND AWAKE IN A CELL! HOW DO YOU FEEL?
WET, COLD, HURT... AND WONDERFUL! I'M ALIVE... NO BETTER FEELING THAN THAT! HOW'D YOU HAPPEN TO GET HERE?
SPEEDY PUT ME ON THE TRAIL! I SIMPLY SEARCHED THE AREA...
IT'S NONE OF MY BUSINESS...BUT, ARROW--THE KID NEEDS HELP--BAD!
17

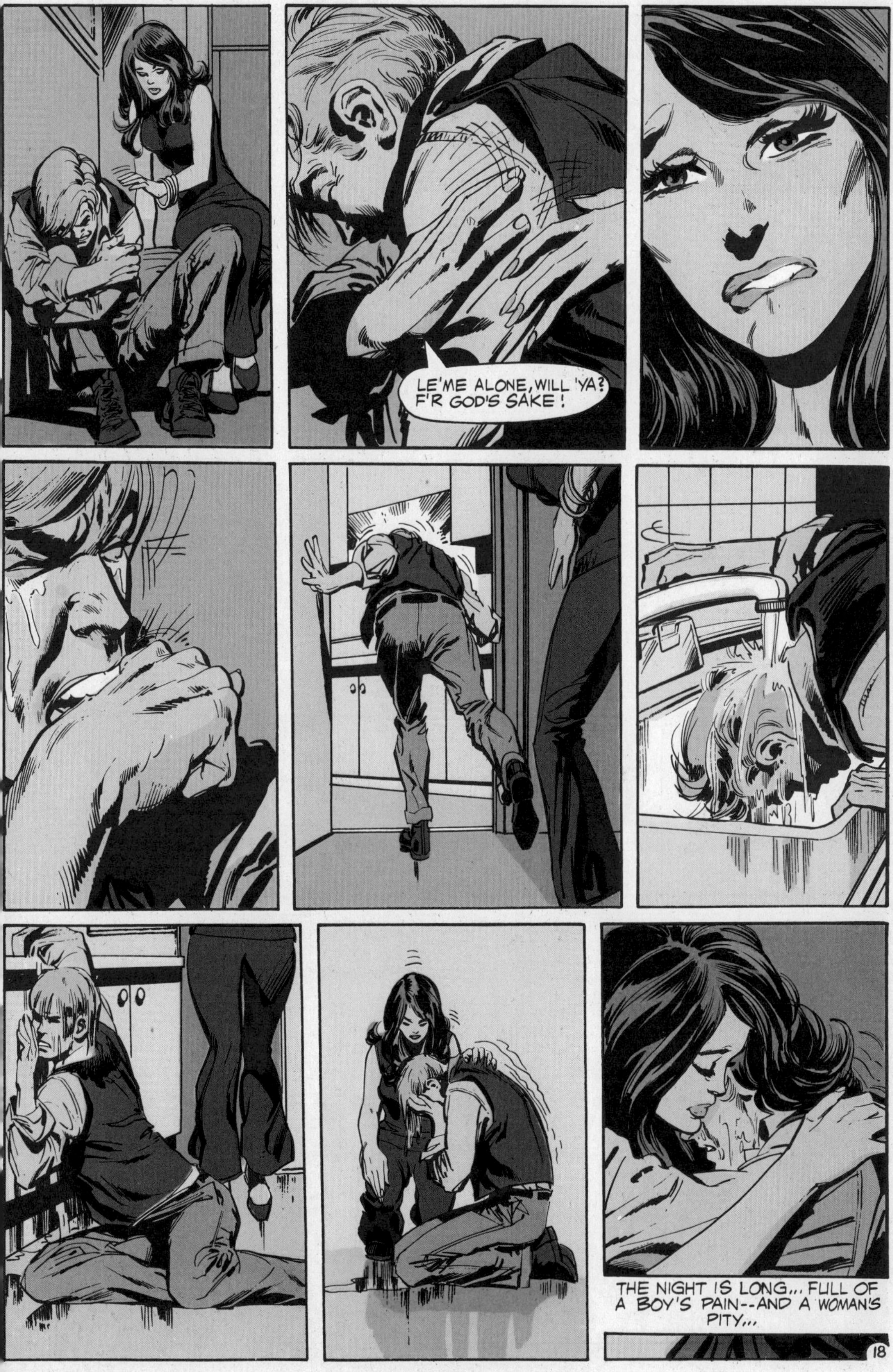

LE'ME ALONE, WILL 'YA? F'R GOD'S SAKE!
THE NIGHT IS LONG... FULL OF A BOY'S PAIN--AND A WOMAN'S PITY...
18

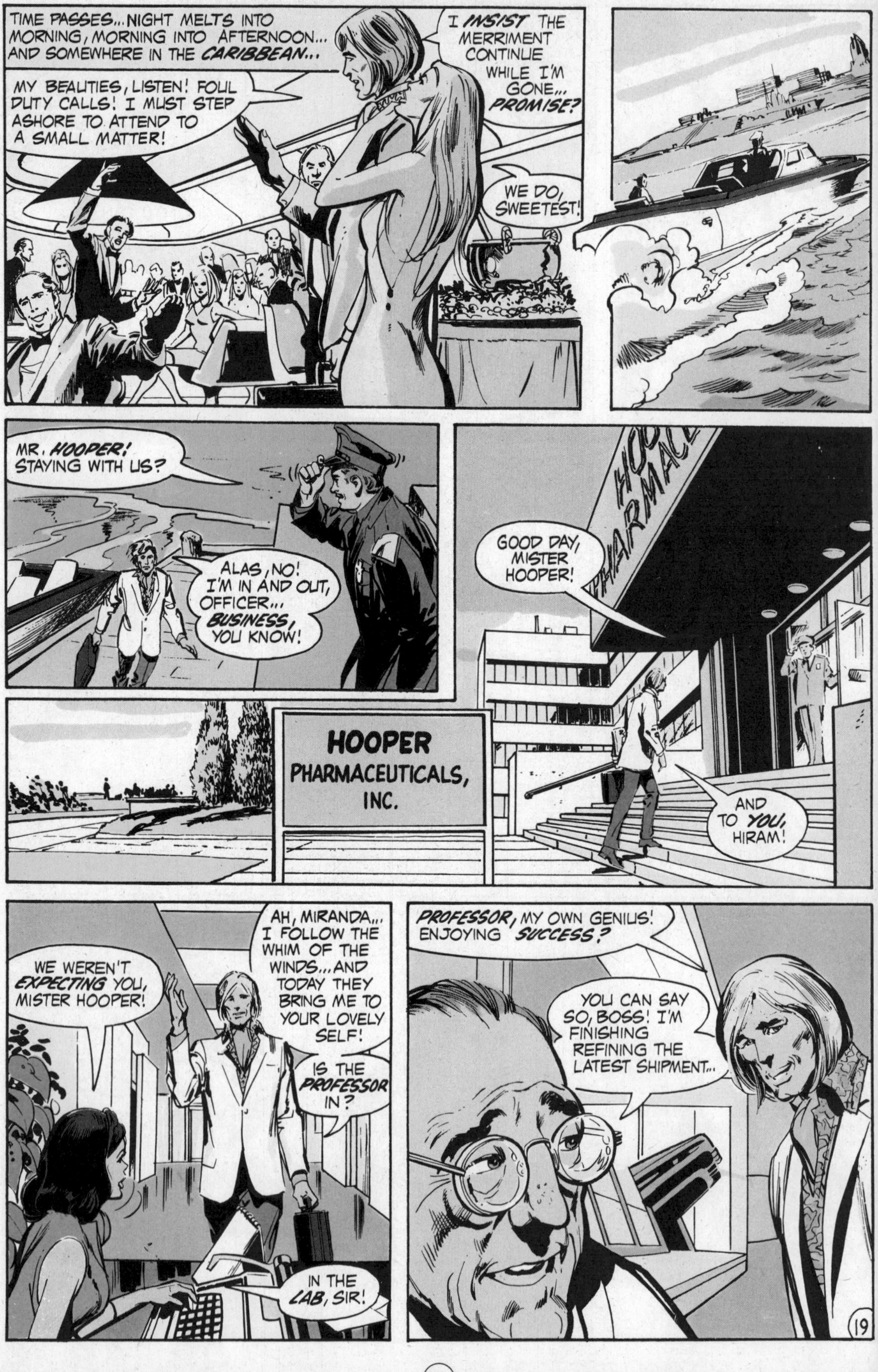
TIME PASSES... NIGHT MELTS INTO MORNING, MORNING INTO AFTERNOON... AND SOMEWHERE IN THE CARIBBEAN...
MY BEAUTIES, LISTEN! FOUL DUTY CALLS! I MUST STEP ASHORE TO ATTEND TO A SMALL MATTER!
I INSIST THE MERRIMENT CONTINUE WHILE I'M GONE... PROMISE?
WE DO, SWEETEST!
MR. HOOPER! STAYING WITH US?
ALAS, NO! I'M IN AND OUT, OFFICER... BUSINESS, YOU KNOW!
HOO PHARMAC
GOOD DAY, MISTER HOOPER!
HOOPER PHARMACEUTICALS, INC.
AND TO YOU, HIRAM!
WE WEREN'T EXPECTING YOU, MISTER HOOPER!
AH, MIRANDA... I FOLLOW THE WHIM OF THE WINDS... AND TODAY THEY BRING ME TO YOUR LOVELY SELF!
IS THE PROFESSOR IN?
IN THE LAB, SIR!
PROFESSOR, MY OWN GENIUS! ENJOYING SUCCESS?
YOU CAN SAY SO, BOSS! I'M FINISHING REFINING THE LATEST SHIPMENT...
19

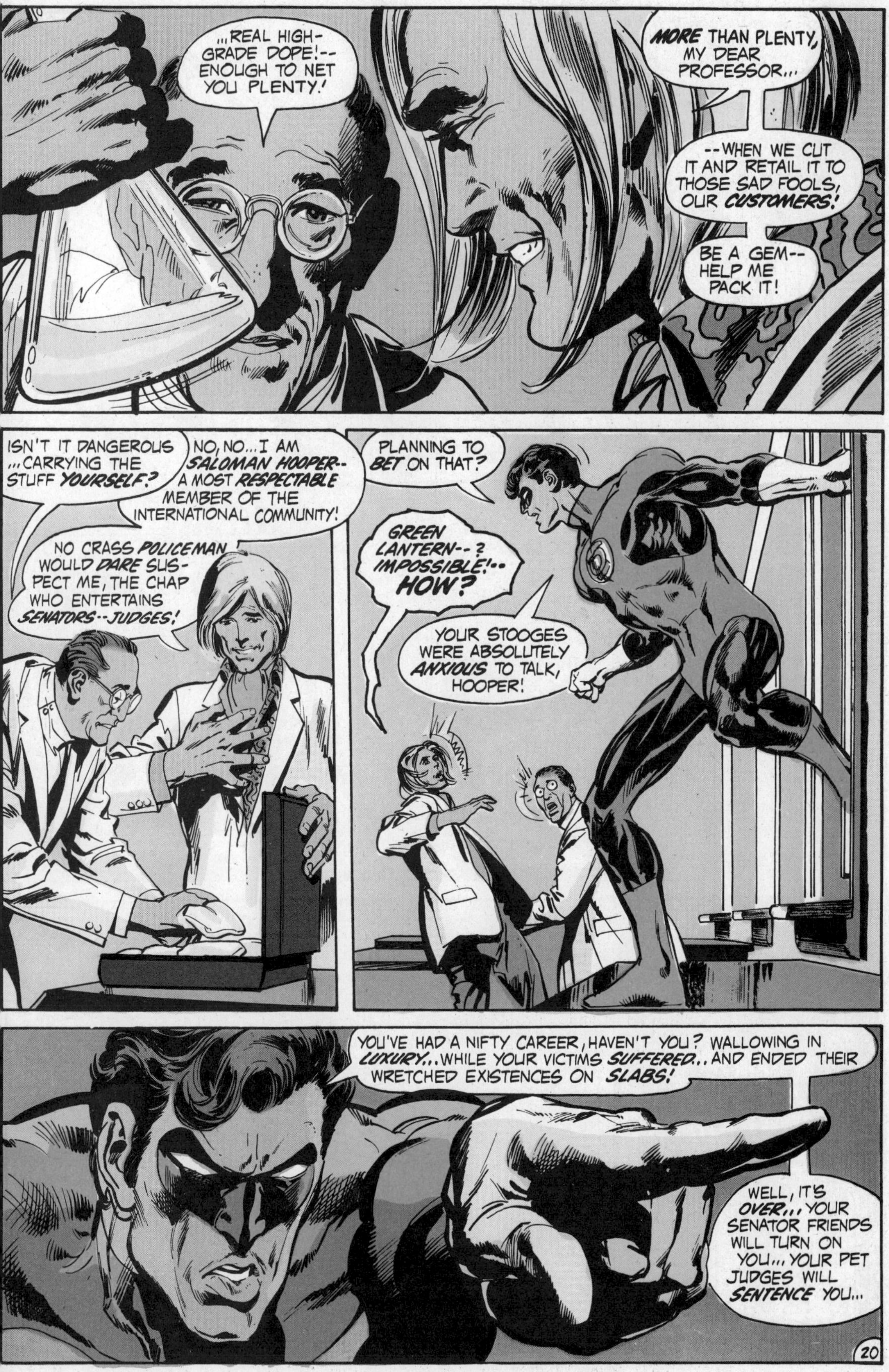
...REAL HIGH-GRADE DOPE!--ENOUGH TO NET YOU PLENTY!
MORE THAN PLENTY, MY DEAR PROFESSOR...
--WHEN WE CUT IT AND RETAIL IT TO THOSE SAD FOOLS, OUR CUSTOMERS!
BE A GEM--HELP ME PACK IT!
ISN'T IT DANGEROUS ...CARRYING THE STUFF YOURSELF?
NO, NO...I AM SALOMAN HOOPER--A MOST RESPECTABLE MEMBER OF THE INTERNATIONAL COMMUNITY!
NO CRASS POLICEMAN WOULD DARE SUSPECT ME, THE CHAP WHO ENTERTAINS SENATORS--JUDGES!
PLANNING TO BET ON THAT?
GREEN LANTERN--? IMPOSSIBLE!--HOW?
YOUR STOOGES WERE ABSOLUTELY ANXIOUS TO TALK, HOOPER!
YOU'VE HAD A NIFTY CAREER, HAVEN'T YOU? WALLOWING IN LUXURY...WHILE YOUR VICTIMS SUFFERED...AND ENDED THEIR WRETCHED EXISTENCES ON SLABS!
WELL, IT'S OVER... YOUR SENATOR FRIENDS WILL TURN ON YOU... YOUR PET JUDGES WILL SENTENCE YOU...
20

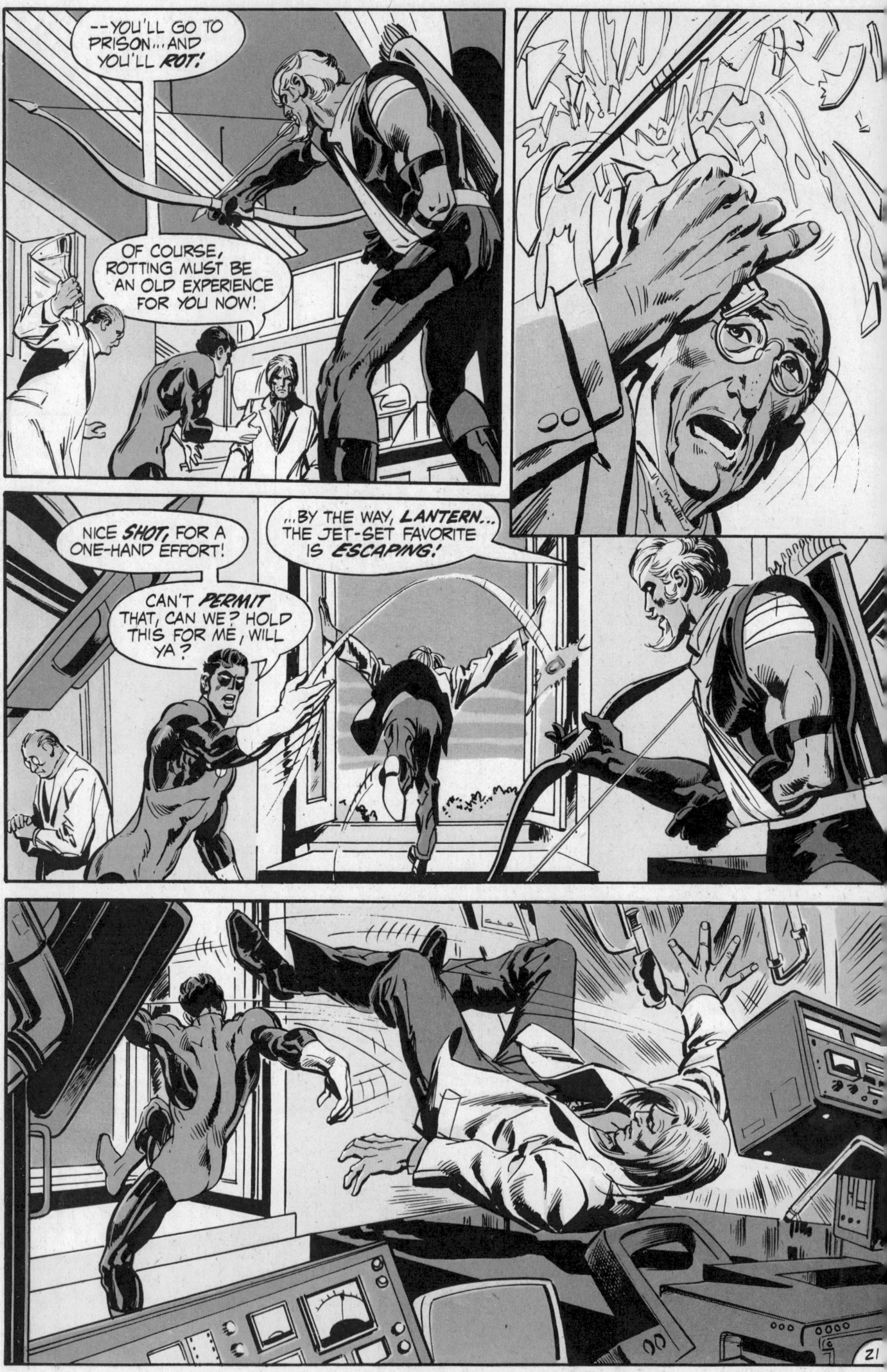
--YOU'LL GO TO PRISON...AND YOU'LL ROT!
OF COURSE, ROTTING MUST BE AN OLD EXPERIENCE FOR YOU NOW!
NICE SHOT, FOR A ONE-HAND EFFORT!
CAN'T PERMIT THAT, CAN WE? HOLD THIS FOR ME, WILL YA?
...BY THE WAY, LANTERN... THE JET-SET FAVORITE IS ESCAPING!
21

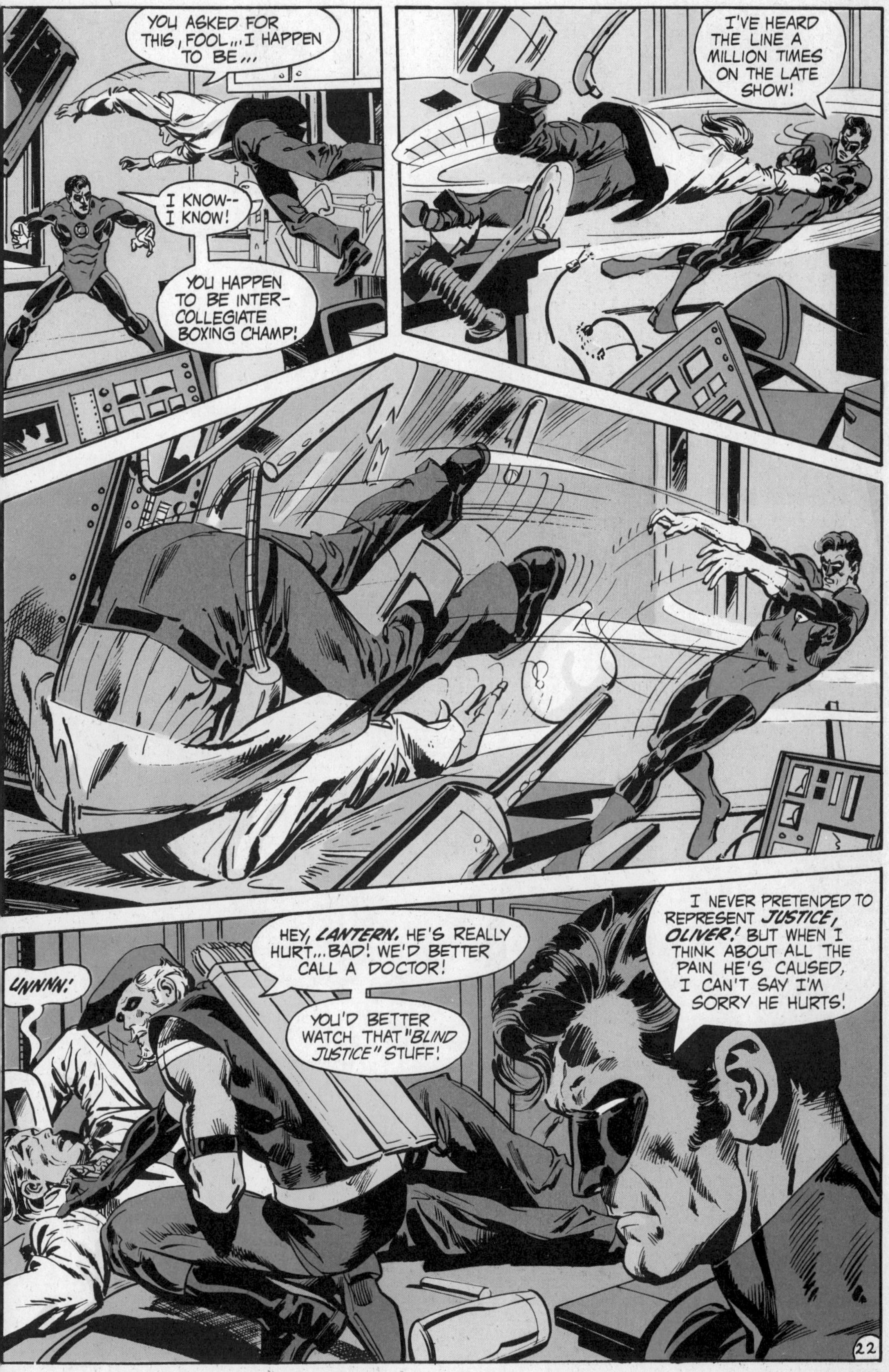
YOU ASKED FOR THIS, FOOL... I HAPPEN TO BE...
I KNOW-- I KNOW!
YOU HAPPEN TO BE INTER-COLLEGIATE BOXING CHAMP!
I'VE HEARD THE LINE A MILLION TIMES ON THE LATE SHOW!
UNNNN!
HEY, LANTERN. HE'S REALLY HURT... BAD! WE'D BETTER CALL A DOCTOR!
YOU'D BETTER WATCH THAT "BLIND JUSTICE" STUFF!
I NEVER PRETENDED TO REPRESENT JUSTICE, OLIVER! BUT WHEN I THINK ABOUT ALL THE PAIN HE'S CAUSED, I CAN'T SAY I'M SORRY HE HURTS!
22

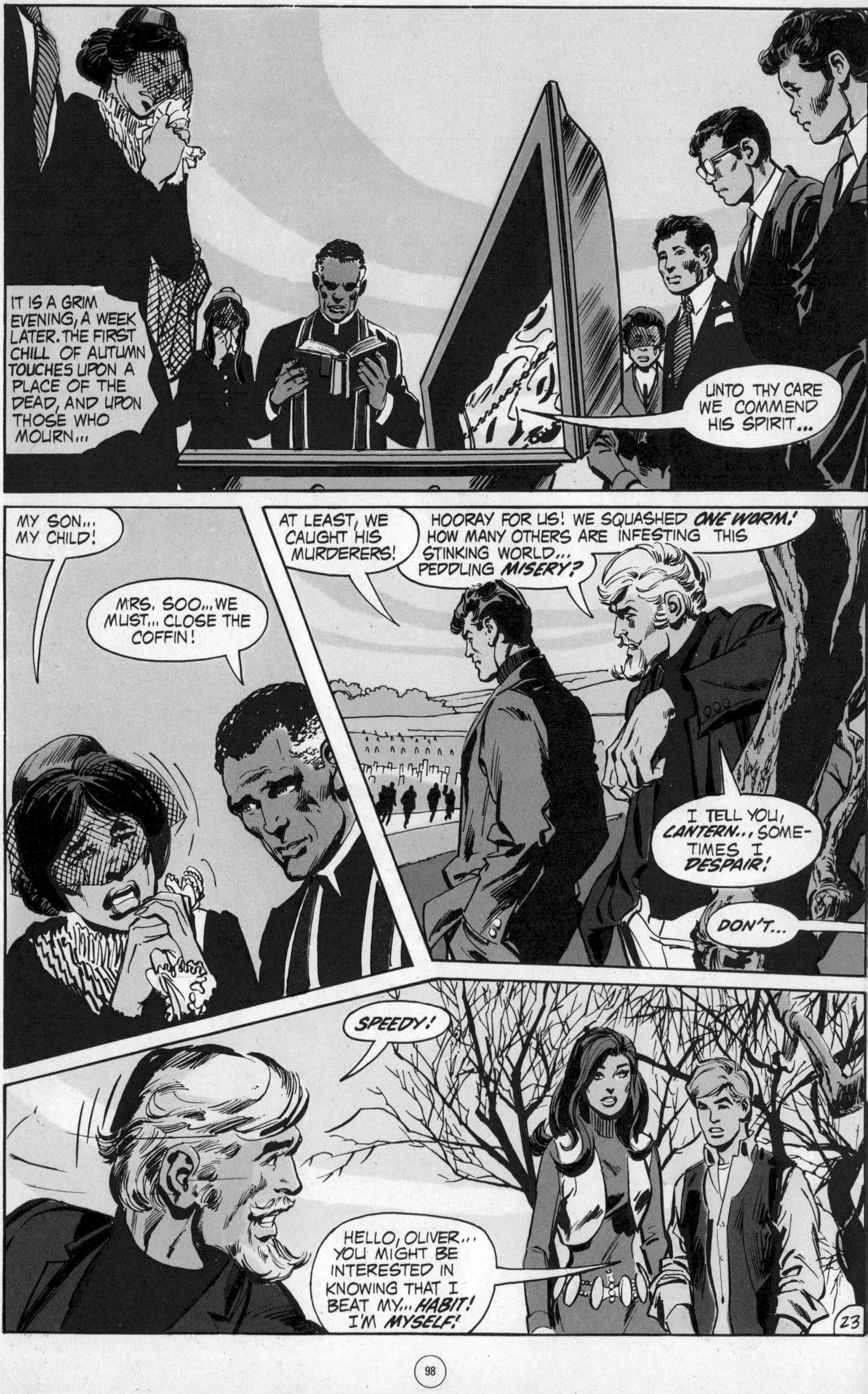
IT IS A GRIM EVENING, A WEEK LATER. THE FIRST CHILL OF AUTUMN TOUCHES UPON A PLACE OF THE DEAD, AND UPON THOSE WHO MOURN...
UNTO THY CARE WE COMMEND HIS SPIRIT...
MY SON... MY CHILD!
MRS. SOO... WE MUST... CLOSE THE COFFIN!
AT LEAST, WE CAUGHT HIS MURDERERS!
HOORAY FOR US! WE SQUASHED ONE WORM! HOW MANY OTHERS ARE INFESTING THIS STINKING WORLD... PEDDLING MISERY?
I TELL YOU, LANTERN..., SOMETIMES I DESPAIR!
DON'T...
SPEEDY!
HELLO, OLIVER... YOU MIGHT BE INTERESTED IN KNOWING THAT I BEAT MY... HABIT! I'M MYSELF!
23

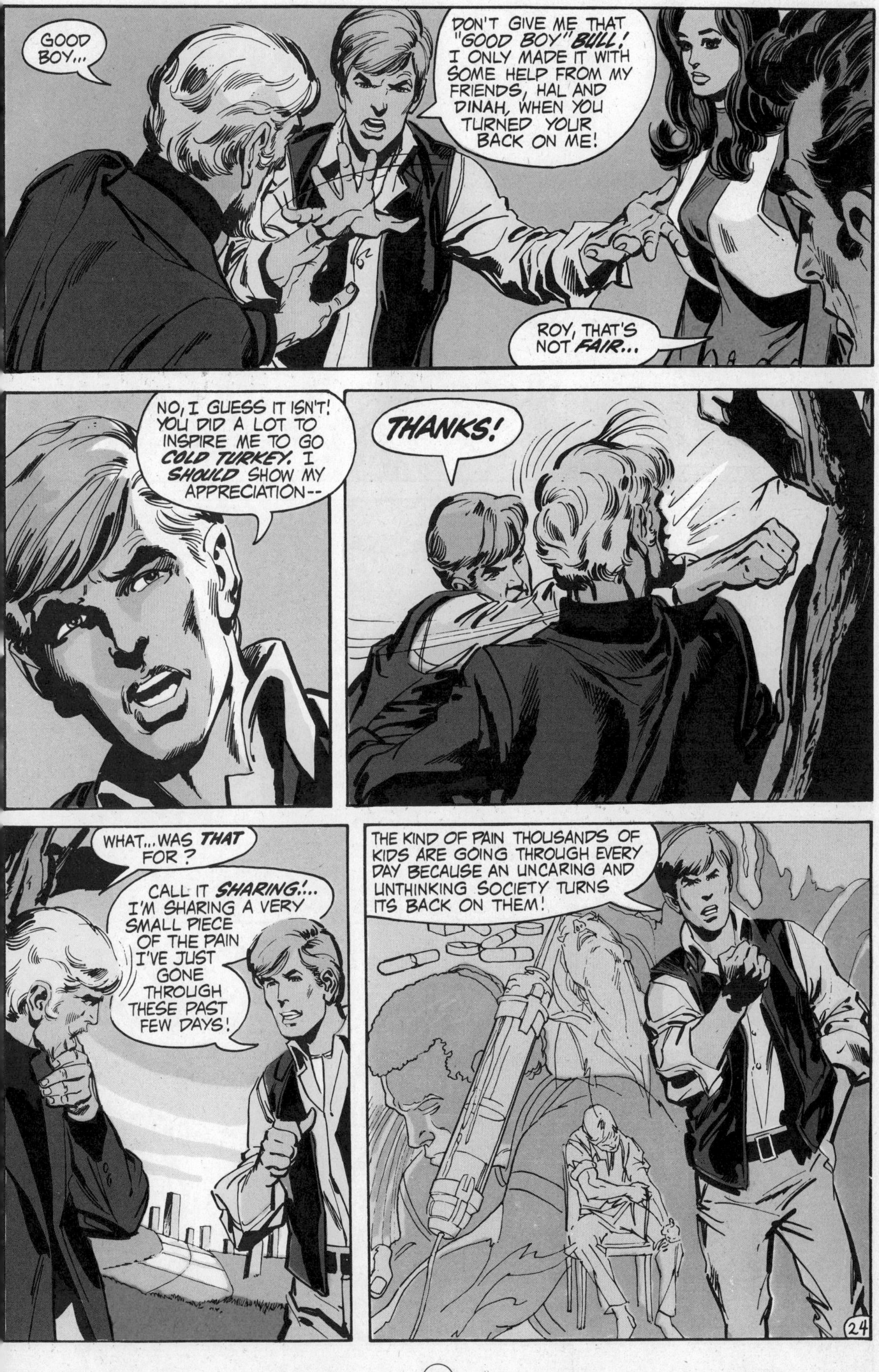
GOOD BOY...
DON'T GIVE ME THAT "GOOD BOY" BULL! I ONLY MADE IT WITH SOME HELP FROM MY FRIENDS, HAL AND DINAH, WHEN YOU TURNED YOUR BACK ON ME!
ROY, THAT'S NOT FAIR...
NO, I GUESS IT ISN'T! YOU DID A LOT TO INSPIRE ME TO GO COLD TURKEY. I SHOULD SHOW MY APPRECIATION--
THANKS!
WHAT...WAS THAT FOR?
CALL IT SHARING!... I'M SHARING A VERY SMALL PIECE OF THE PAIN I'VE JUST GONE THROUGH THESE PAST FEW DAYS!
THE KIND OF PAIN THOUSANDS OF KIDS ARE GOING THROUGH EVERY DAY BECAUSE AN UNCARING AND UNTHINKING SOCIETY TURNS ITS BACK ON THEM!
24

DRUGS ARE A SYMPTOM...AND *YOU*... LIKE THE REST OF SOCIETY... ATTACK THE SYMPTOM...NOT THE DISEASE! BUT THIS *SYMPTOM* IS WORSE THAN MOST--

IT MAIMS...IT PAINS...IT DIMS *YOU*! IT DRIVES YOU TO THE EDGE OF INSANITY AND *OVER*... AND ONE DAY ENDS YOUR TRIP ON A SLAB IN THE MORGUE...WITH A TAG AROUND YOUR TOE!

GOTTA GO NOW...

ROY...

THANKS FOR THE HAND, SISTER-- BUT *HE* NEEDS YOUR HELP *NOW* MORE THAN I DO-- ONLY HE DOESN'T KNOW IT...

HE'S KINDA DUMB... IN A LOTTA WAYS...

I'M LIKE HIM A *LOT!* I'M COCKY ENOUGH TO THINK I CAN HELP SOME OF MY FRIENDS AVOID THAT SLAB! SEE YOU "STRAIGHTS" AROUND!

IT'S A *VERY LARGE* LUMP OF *PRIDE* WHICH FORMS IN THE THROAT OF OLIVER QUEEN-- AS HIS *BOY* BECOMES A *MAN!*

25

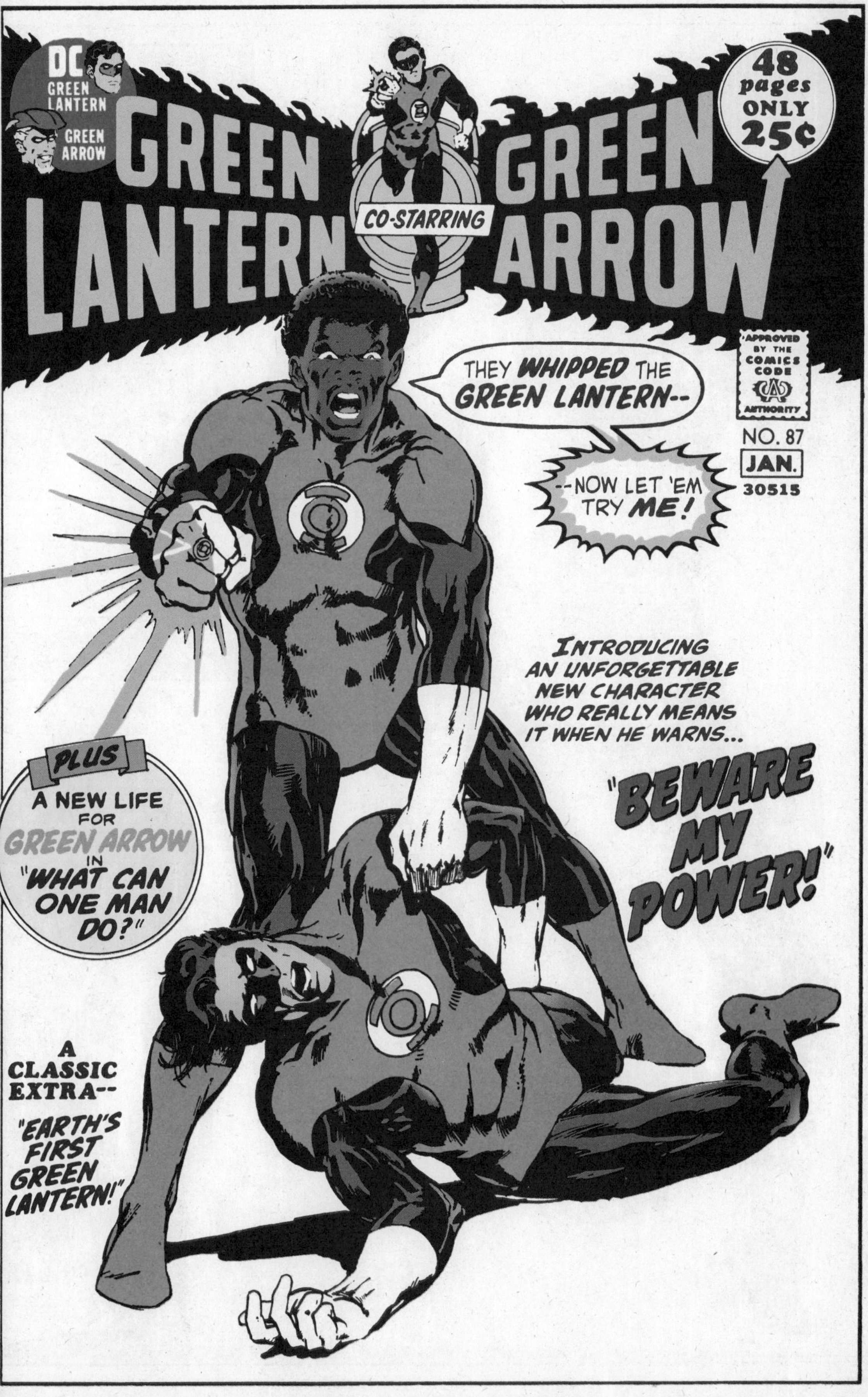

DC
GREEN LANTERN
GREEN ARROW
GREEN LANTERN
CO-STARRING
GREEN ARROW
48 pages ONLY 25¢
APPROVED BY THE COMICS CODE AUTHORITY
NO. 87
JAN.
30515
THEY WHIPPED THE GREEN LANTERN--
--NOW LET 'EM TRY ME!
INTRODUCING AN UNFORGETTABLE NEW CHARACTER WHO REALLY MEANS IT WHEN HE WARNS...
"BEWARE MY POWER!"
PLUS
A NEW LIFE FOR GREEN ARROW IN "WHAT CAN ONE MAN DO?"
A CLASSIC EXTRA--
"EARTH'S FIRST GREEN LANTERN!"

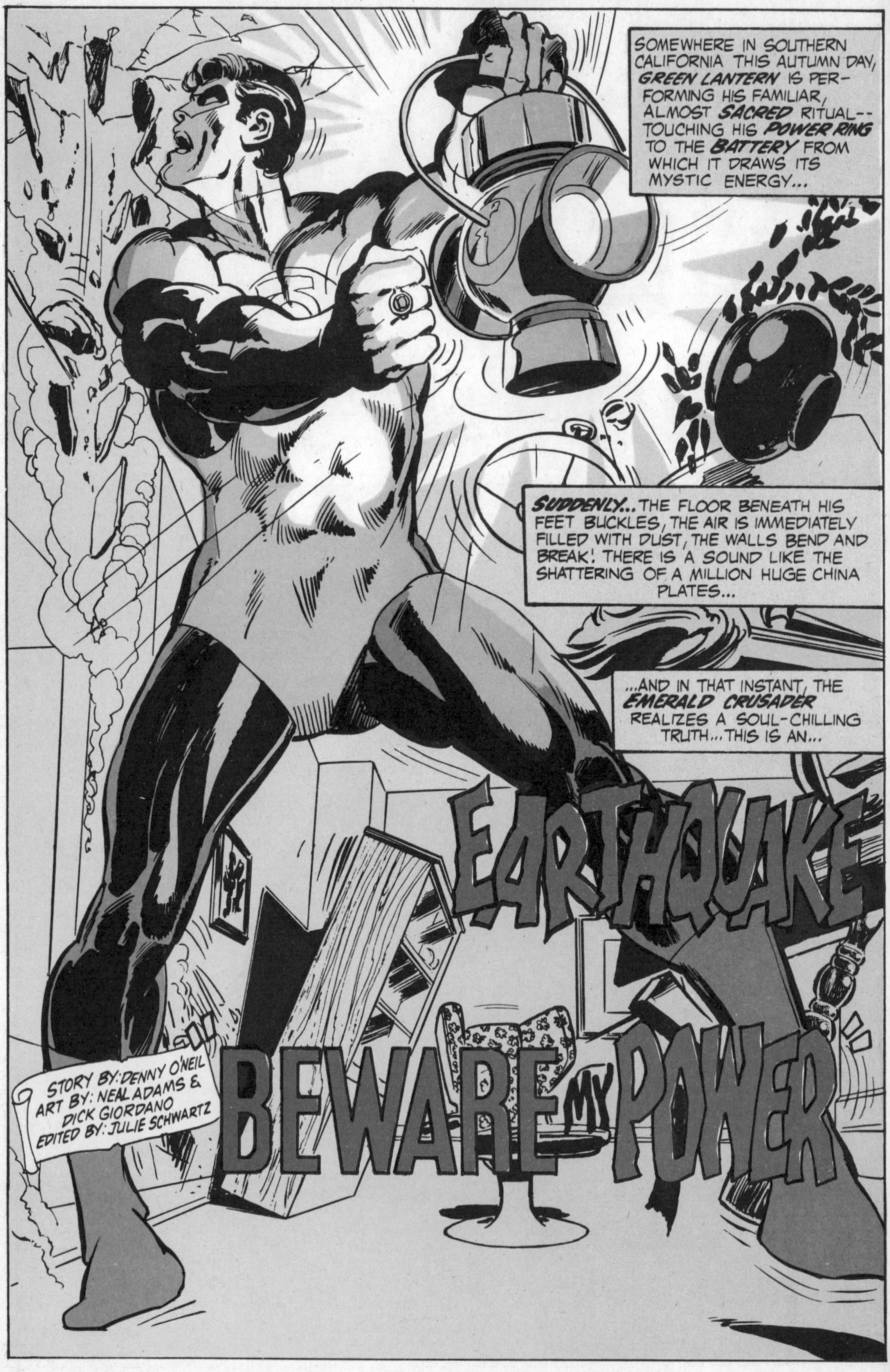

SOMEWHERE IN SOUTHERN CALIFORNIA THIS AUTUMN DAY, GREEN LANTERN IS PERFORMING HIS FAMILIAR, ALMOST SACRED RITUAL-- TOUCHING HIS POWER RING TO THE BATTERY FROM WHICH IT DRAWS ITS MYSTIC ENERGY...
SUDDENLY... THE FLOOR BENEATH HIS FEET BUCKLES, THE AIR IS IMMEDIATELY FILLED WITH DUST, THE WALLS BEND AND BREAK! THERE IS A SOUND LIKE THE SHATTERING OF A MILLION HUGE CHINA PLATES...
...AND IN THAT INSTANT, THE EMERALD CRUSADER REALIZES A SOUL-CHILLING TRUTH... THIS IS AN...
EARTHQUAKE
"BEWARE MY POWER"
STORY BY: DENNY O'NEIL
ART BY: NEAL ADAMS & DICK GIORDANO
EDITED BY: JULIE SCHWARTZ

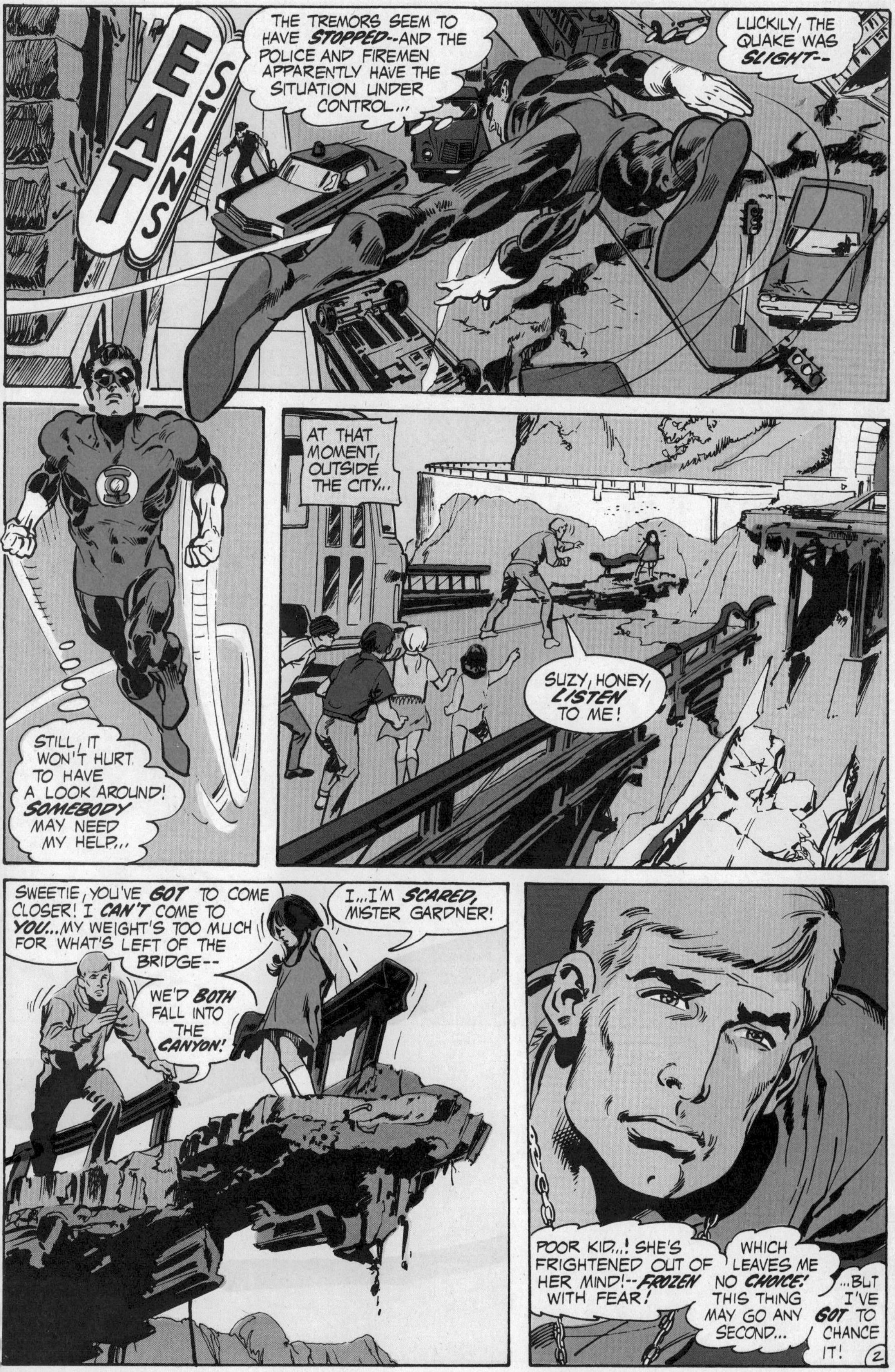
EAT
STANS
THE TREMORS SEEM TO HAVE STOPPED--AND THE POLICE AND FIREMEN APPARENTLY HAVE THE SITUATION UNDER CONTROL...
LUCKILY, THE QUAKE WAS SLIGHT--
STILL, IT WON'T HURT TO HAVE A LOOK AROUND! SOMEBODY MAY NEED MY HELP...
AT THAT MOMENT, OUTSIDE THE CITY...
SUZY, HONEY, LISTEN TO ME!
SWEETIE, YOU'VE GOT TO COME CLOSER! I CAN'T COME TO YOU...MY WEIGHT'S TOO MUCH FOR WHAT'S LEFT OF THE BRIDGE--
I...I'M SCARED, MISTER GARDNER!
WE'D BOTH FALL INTO THE CANYON!
POOR KID...! SHE'S FRIGHTENED OUT OF HER MIND!--FROZEN WITH FEAR!
WHICH LEAVES ME NO CHOICE! THIS THING MAY GO ANY SECOND...
...BUT I'VE GOT TO CHANCE IT!
2

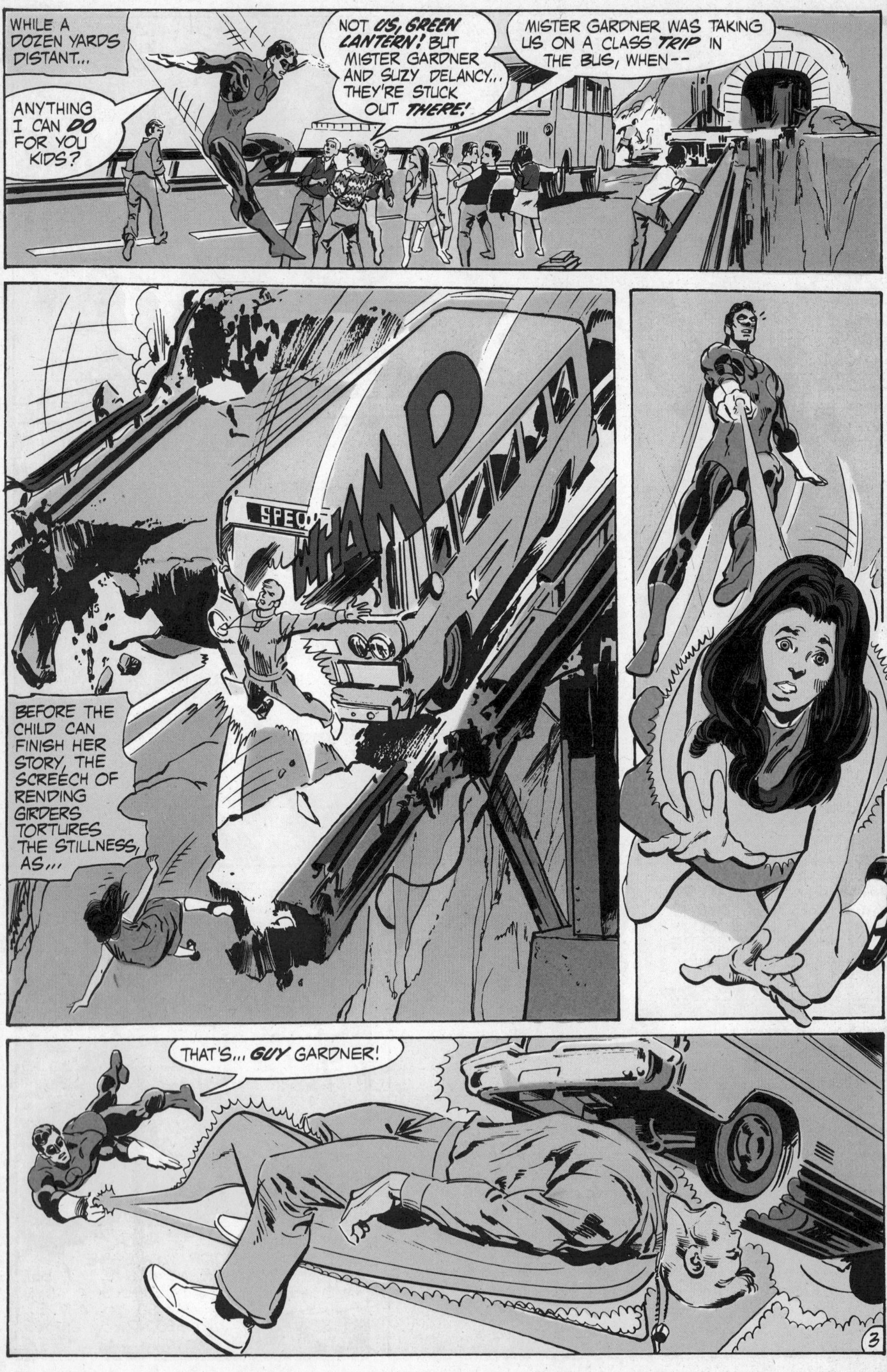

WHILE A DOZEN YARDS DISTANT...
ANYTHING I CAN DO FOR YOU KIDS?
NOT US, GREEN LANTERN! BUT MISTER GARDNER AND SUZY DELANCY... THEY'RE STUCK OUT THERE!
MISTER GARDNER WAS TAKING US ON A CLASS TRIP IN THE BUS, WHEN--
SPEC
WHAMP
BEFORE THE CHILD CAN FINISH HER STORY, THE SCREECH OF RENDING GIRDERS TORTURES THE STILLNESS, AS...
THAT'S... GUY GARDNER!
3

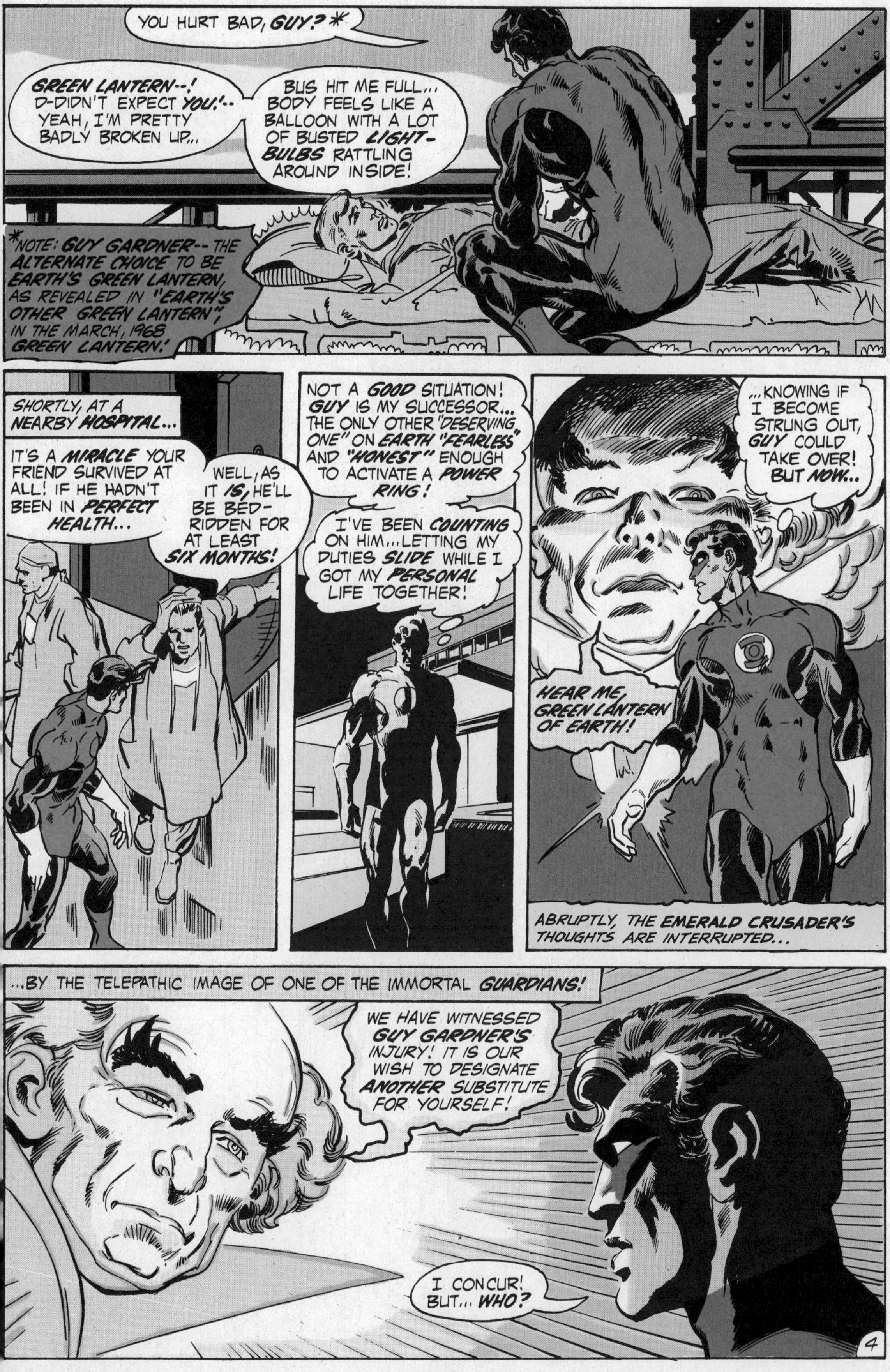
YOU HURT BAD, GUY?*
GREEN LANTERN--! D-DIDN'T EXPECT YOU!-- YEAH, I'M PRETTY BADLY BROKEN UP...
BUS HIT ME FULL... BODY FEELS LIKE A BALLOON WITH A LOT OF BUSTED LIGHT-BULBS RATTLING AROUND INSIDE!
*NOTE: GUY GARDNER--THE ALTERNATE CHOICE TO BE EARTH'S GREEN LANTERN, AS REVEALED IN "EARTH'S OTHER GREEN LANTERN", IN THE MARCH, 1968 GREEN LANTERN!
SHORTLY, AT A NEARBY HOSPITAL...
IT'S A MIRACLE YOUR FRIEND SURVIVED AT ALL! IF HE HADN'T BEEN IN PERFECT HEALTH...
WELL, AS IT IS, HE'LL BE BED-RIDDEN FOR AT LEAST SIX MONTHS!
NOT A GOOD SITUATION! GUY IS MY SUCCESSOR... THE ONLY OTHER "DESERVING ONE" ON EARTH "FEARLESS" AND "HONEST" ENOUGH TO ACTIVATE A POWER RING!
I'VE BEEN COUNTING ON HIM... LETTING MY DUTIES SLIDE WHILE I GOT MY PERSONAL LIFE TOGETHER!
...KNOWING IF I BECOME STRUNG OUT, GUY COULD TAKE OVER! BUT NOW...
HEAR ME, GREEN LANTERN OF EARTH!
ABRUPTLY, THE EMERALD CRUSADER'S THOUGHTS ARE INTERRUPTED...
...BY THE TELEPATHIC IMAGE OF ONE OF THE IMMORTAL GUARDIANS!
WE HAVE WITNESSED GUY GARDNER'S INJURY! IT IS OUR WISH TO DESIGNATE ANOTHER SUBSTITUTE FOR YOURSELF!
I CONCUR! BUT... WHO?
4

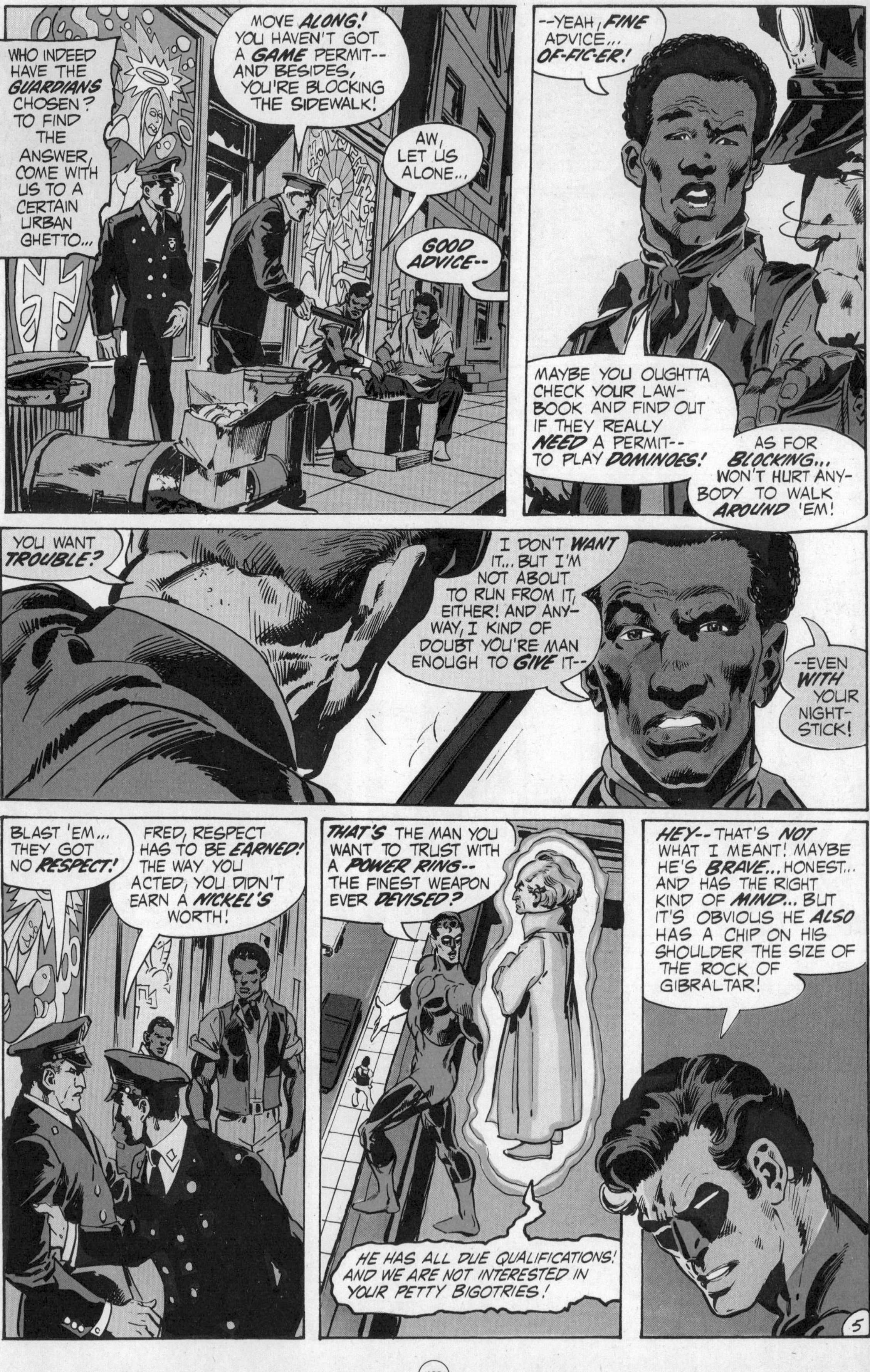

WHO INDEED HAVE THE GUARDIANS CHOSEN? TO FIND THE ANSWER, COME WITH US TO A CERTAIN URBAN GHETTO...
MOVE ALONG! YOU HAVEN'T GOT A GAME PERMIT-- AND BESIDES, YOU'RE BLOCKING THE SIDEWALK!
AW, LET US ALONE...
GOOD ADVICE--
--YEAH, FINE ADVICE... OF-FIC-ER!
MAYBE YOU OUGHTTA CHECK YOUR LAW-BOOK AND FIND OUT IF THEY REALLY NEED A PERMIT-- TO PLAY DOMINOES!
AS FOR BLOCKING... WON'T HURT ANY-BODY TO WALK AROUND 'EM!
YOU WANT TROUBLE?
I DON'T WANT IT... BUT I'M NOT ABOUT TO RUN FROM IT, EITHER! AND ANY-WAY, I KIND OF DOUBT YOU'RE MAN ENOUGH TO GIVE IT--
--EVEN WITH YOUR NIGHT-STICK!
BLAST 'EM... THEY GOT NO RESPECT!
FRED, RESPECT HAS TO BE EARNED! THE WAY YOU ACTED, YOU DIDN'T EARN A NICKEL'S WORTH!
THAT'S THE MAN YOU WANT TO TRUST WITH A POWER RING-- THE FINEST WEAPON EVER DEVISED?
HE HAS ALL DUE QUALIFICATIONS! AND WE ARE NOT INTERESTED IN YOUR PETTY BIGOTRIES!
HEY-- THAT'S NOT WHAT I MEANT! MAYBE HE'S BRAVE... HONEST... AND HAS THE RIGHT KIND OF MIND... BUT IT'S OBVIOUS HE ALSO HAS A CHIP ON HIS SHOULDER THE SIZE OF THE ROCK OF GIBRALTAR!
5

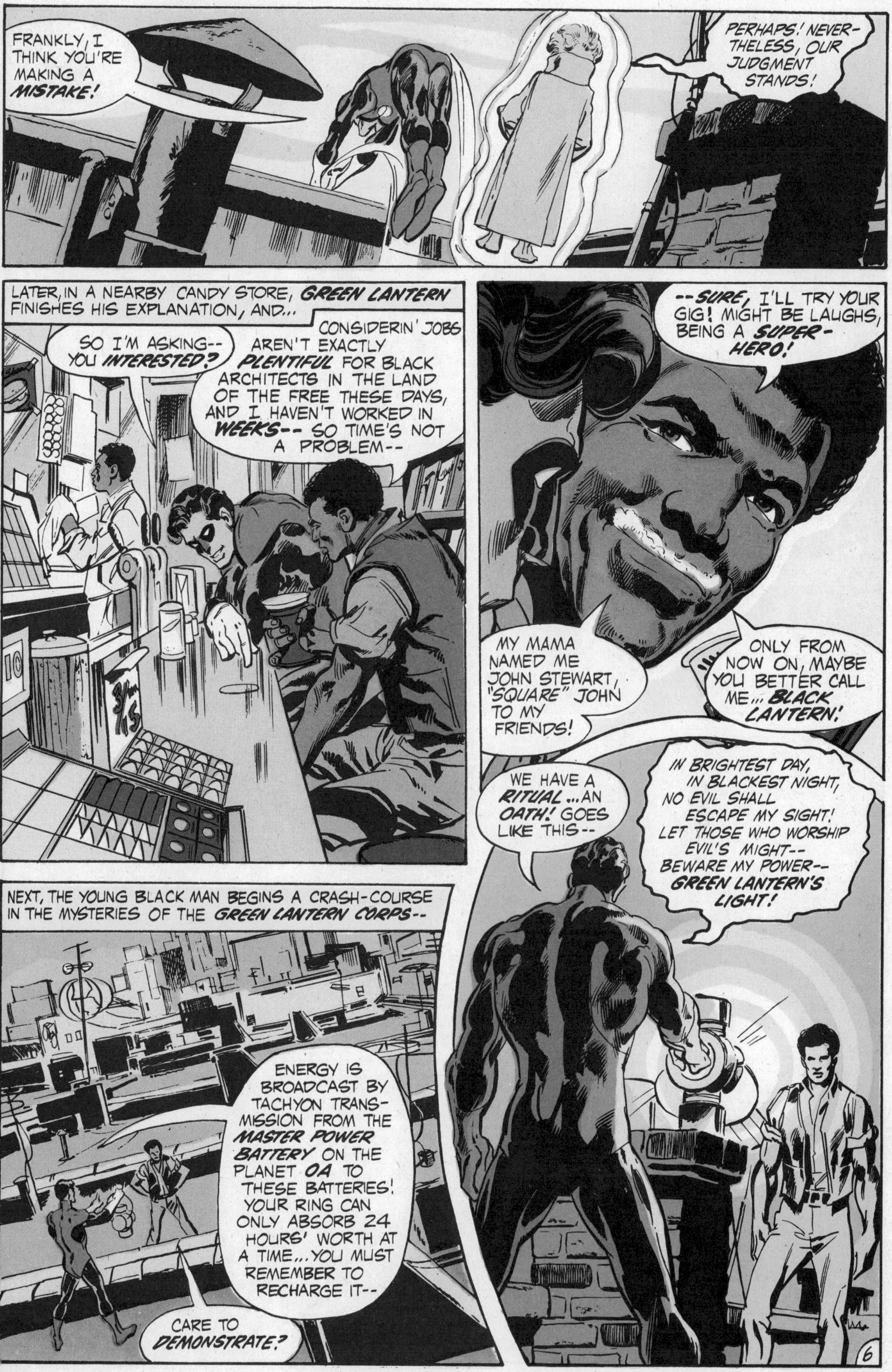

FRANKLY, I THINK YOU'RE MAKING A MISTAKE!
PERHAPS! NEVERTHELESS, OUR JUDGMENT STANDS!
LATER, IN A NEARBY CANDY STORE, GREEN LANTERN FINISHES HIS EXPLANATION, AND...
SO I'M ASKING-- YOU INTERESTED?
CONSIDERIN' JOBS AREN'T EXACTLY PLENTIFUL FOR BLACK ARCHITECTS IN THE LAND OF THE FREE THESE DAYS, AND I HAVEN'T WORKED IN WEEKS-- SO TIME'S NOT A PROBLEM--
--SURE, I'LL TRY YOUR GIG! MIGHT BE LAUGHS, BEING A SUPER-HERO!
MY MAMA NAMED ME JOHN STEWART, "SQUARE" JOHN TO MY FRIENDS!
ONLY FROM NOW ON, MAYBE YOU BETTER CALL ME... BLACK LANTERN!
NEXT, THE YOUNG BLACK MAN BEGINS A CRASH-COURSE IN THE MYSTERIES OF THE GREEN LANTERN CORPS--
ENERGY IS BROADCAST BY TACHYON TRANSMISSION FROM THE MASTER POWER BATTERY ON THE PLANET OA TO THESE BATTERIES! YOUR RING CAN ONLY ABSORB 24 HOURS' WORTH AT A TIME... YOU MUST REMEMBER TO RECHARGE IT--
CARE TO DEMONSTRATE?
WE HAVE A RITUAL... AN OATH! GOES LIKE THIS--
IN BRIGHTEST DAY, IN BLACKEST NIGHT, NO EVIL SHALL ESCAPE MY SIGHT! LET THOSE WHO WORSHIP EVIL'S MIGHT-- BEWARE MY POWER-- GREEN LANTERN'S LIGHT!
6

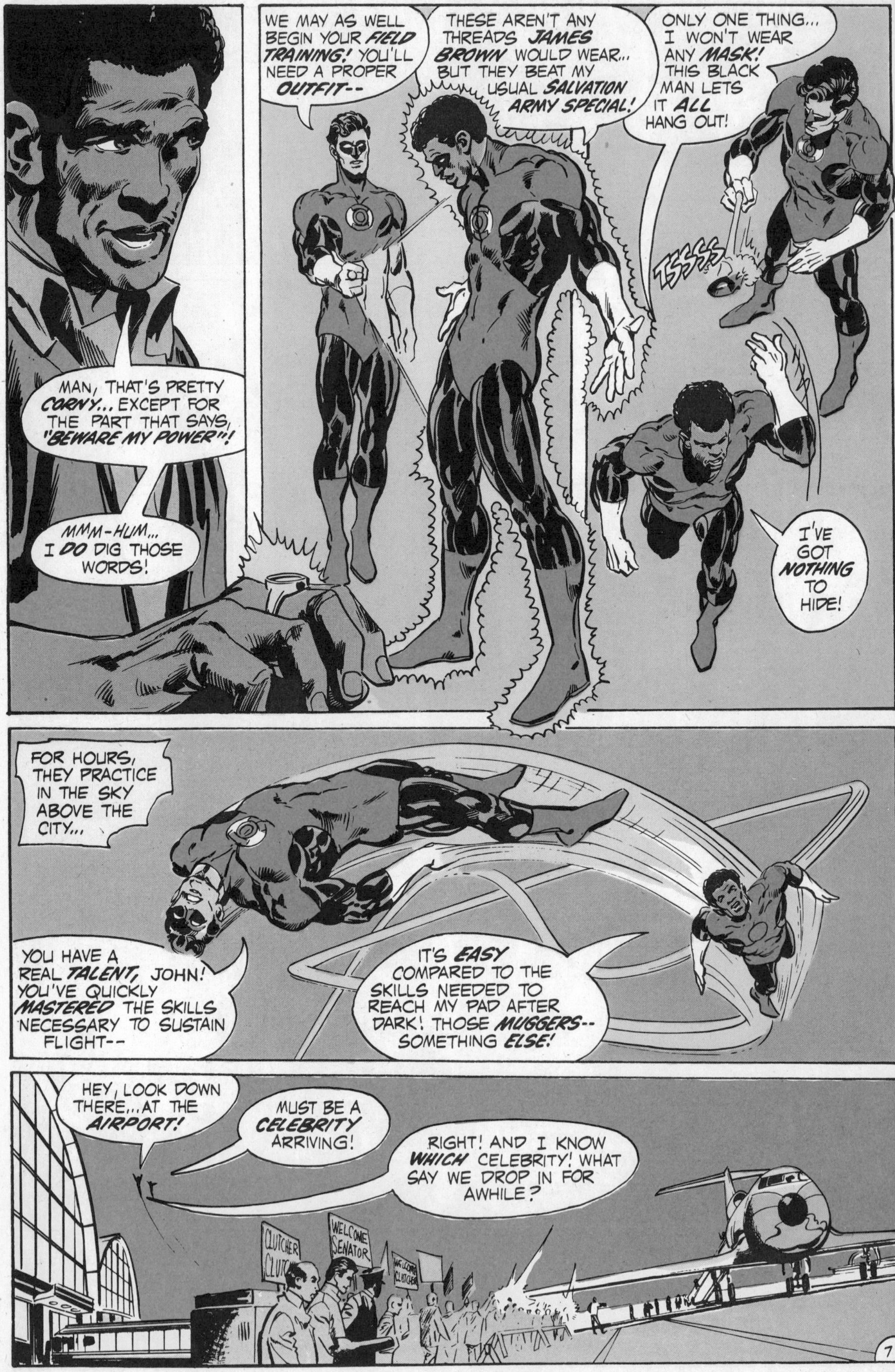
MAN, THAT'S PRETTY CORNY... EXCEPT FOR THE PART THAT SAYS, "BEWARE MY POWER"!
MMM-HUM... I DO DIG THOSE WORDS!
WE MAY AS WELL BEGIN YOUR FIELD TRAINING! YOU'LL NEED A PROPER OUTFIT--
THESE AREN'T ANY THREADS JAMES BROWN WOULD WEAR... BUT THEY BEAT MY USUAL SALVATION ARMY SPECIAL!
ONLY ONE THING... I WON'T WEAR ANY MASK! THIS BLACK MAN LETS IT ALL HANG OUT!
TSSSS
I'VE GOT NOTHING TO HIDE!
FOR HOURS, THEY PRACTICE IN THE SKY ABOVE THE CITY...
YOU HAVE A REAL TALENT, JOHN! YOU'VE QUICKLY MASTERED THE SKILLS NECESSARY TO SUSTAIN FLIGHT--
IT'S EASY COMPARED TO THE SKILLS NEEDED TO REACH MY PAD AFTER DARK! THOSE MUGGERS-- SOMETHING ELSE!
HEY, LOOK DOWN THERE... AT THE AIRPORT!
MUST BE A CELEBRITY ARRIVING!
RIGHT! AND I KNOW WHICH CELEBRITY! WHAT SAY WE DROP IN FOR AWHILE?
CLUTCHER
WELCOME SENATOR
7

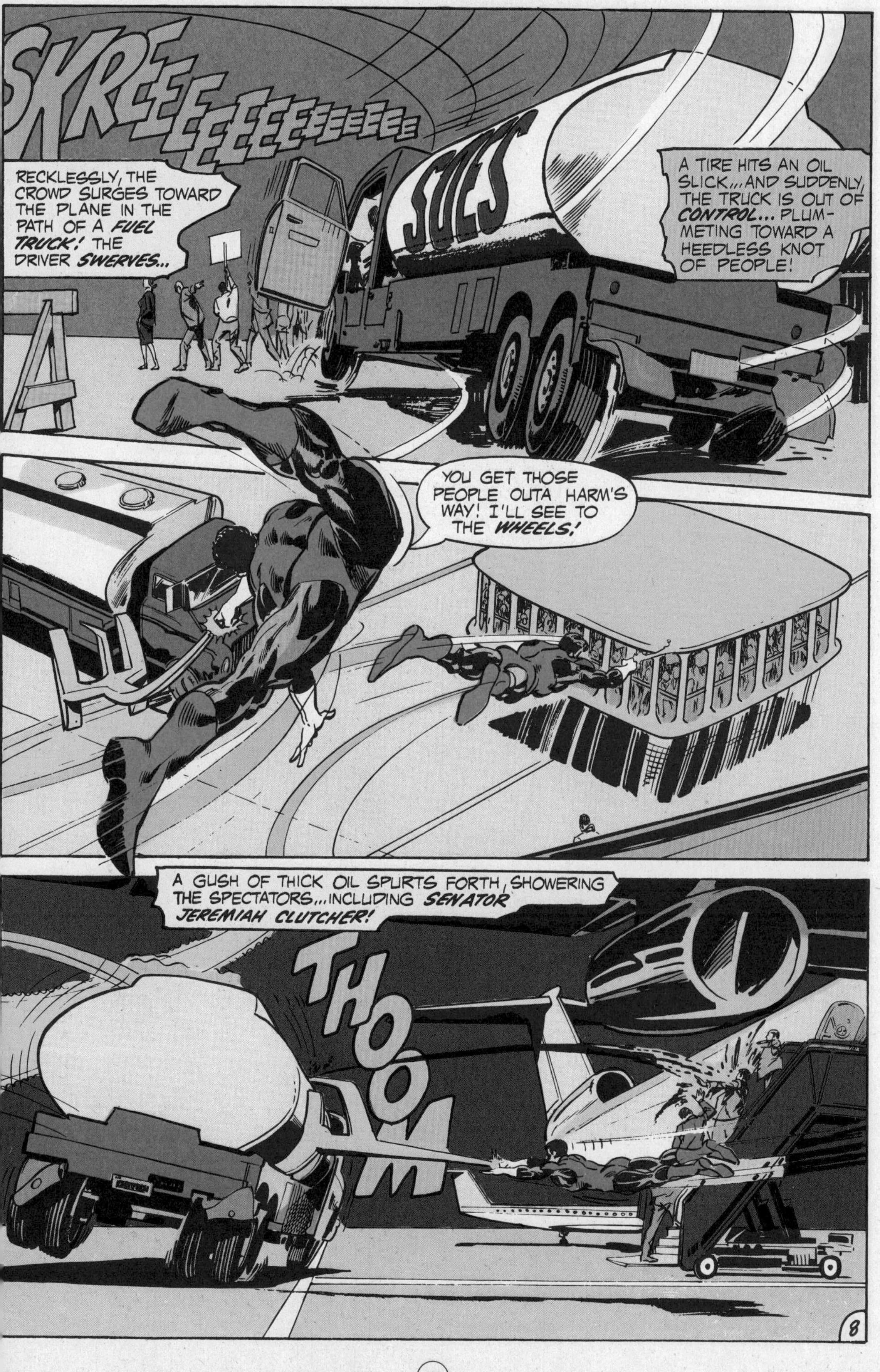
SKREEEEEEEEEEEEEE
RECKLESSLY, THE CROWD SURGES TOWARD THE PLANE IN THE PATH OF A FUEL TRUCK! THE DRIVER SWERVES...
A TIRE HITS AN OIL SLICK,,,AND SUDDENLY, THE TRUCK IS OUT OF CONTROL... PLUMMETING TOWARD A HEEDLESS KNOT OF PEOPLE!
YOU GET THOSE PEOPLE OUTA HARM'S WAY! I'LL SEE TO THE WHEELS!
A GUSH OF THICK OIL SPURTS FORTH, SHOWERING THE SPECTATORS,,,INCLUDING SENATOR JEREMIAH CLUTCHER!
THOOM
8

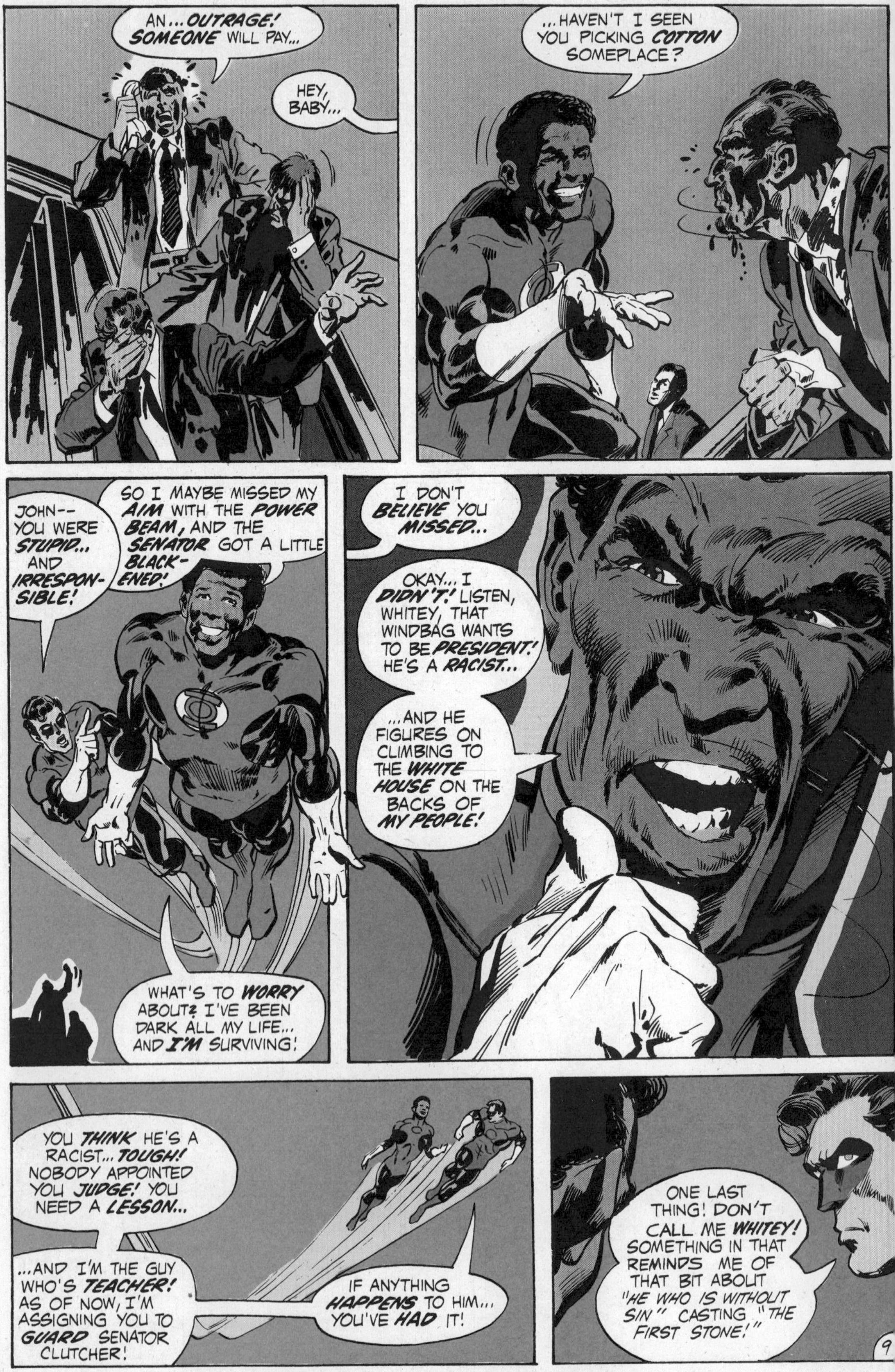
AN... OUTRAGE! SOMEONE WILL PAY...
HEY, BABY...
...HAVEN'T I SEEN YOU PICKING COTTON SOMEPLACE?
JOHN-- YOU WERE STUPID... AND IRRESPONSIBLE!
SO I MAYBE MISSED MY AIM WITH THE POWER BEAM, AND THE SENATOR GOT A LITTLE BLACKENED!
WHAT'S TO WORRY ABOUT? I'VE BEEN DARK ALL MY LIFE... AND I'M SURVIVING!
I DON'T BELIEVE YOU MISSED...
OKAY... I DIDN'T! LISTEN, WHITEY, THAT WINDBAG WANTS TO BE PRESIDENT! HE'S A RACIST...
...AND HE FIGURES ON CLIMBING TO THE WHITE HOUSE ON THE BACKS OF MY PEOPLE!
YOU THINK HE'S A RACIST... TOUGH! NOBODY APPOINTED YOU JUDGE! YOU NEED A LESSON...
...AND I'M THE GUY WHO'S TEACHER! AS OF NOW, I'M ASSIGNING YOU TO GUARD SENATOR CLUTCHER!
IF ANYTHING HAPPENS TO HIM... YOU'VE HAD IT!
ONE LAST THING! DON'T CALL ME WHITEY! SOMETHING IN THAT REMINDS ME OF THAT BIT ABOUT "HE WHO IS WITHOUT SIN" CASTING "THE FIRST STONE!"
9

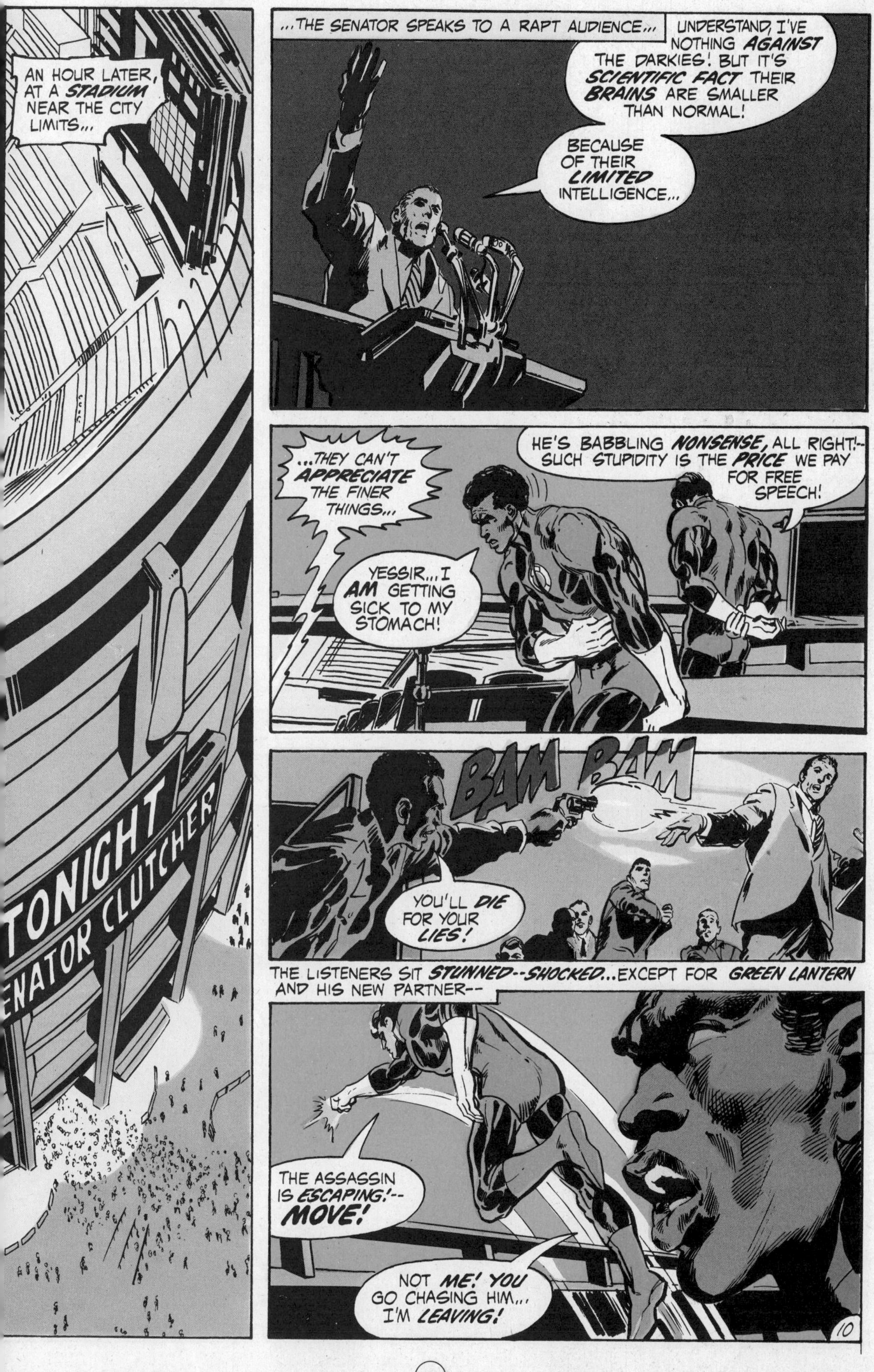
AN HOUR LATER, AT A STADIUM NEAR THE CITY LIMITS...
TONIGHT
SENATOR CLUTCHER
...THE SENATOR SPEAKS TO A RAPT AUDIENCE...
UNDERSTAND, I'VE NOTHING AGAINST THE DARKIES! BUT IT'S SCIENTIFIC FACT THEIR BRAINS ARE SMALLER THAN NORMAL!
BECAUSE OF THEIR LIMITED INTELLIGENCE...
...THEY CAN'T APPRECIATE THE FINER THINGS...
HE'S BABBLING NONSENSE, ALL RIGHT!-- SUCH STUPIDITY IS THE PRICE WE PAY FOR FREE SPEECH!
YESSIR... I AM GETTING SICK TO MY STOMACH!
BAM BAM
YOU'LL DIE FOR YOUR LIES!
THE LISTENERS SIT STUNNED--SHOCKED...EXCEPT FOR GREEN LANTERN AND HIS NEW PARTNER--
THE ASSASSIN IS ESCAPING!-- MOVE!
NOT ME! YOU GO CHASING HIM... I'M LEAVING!
10

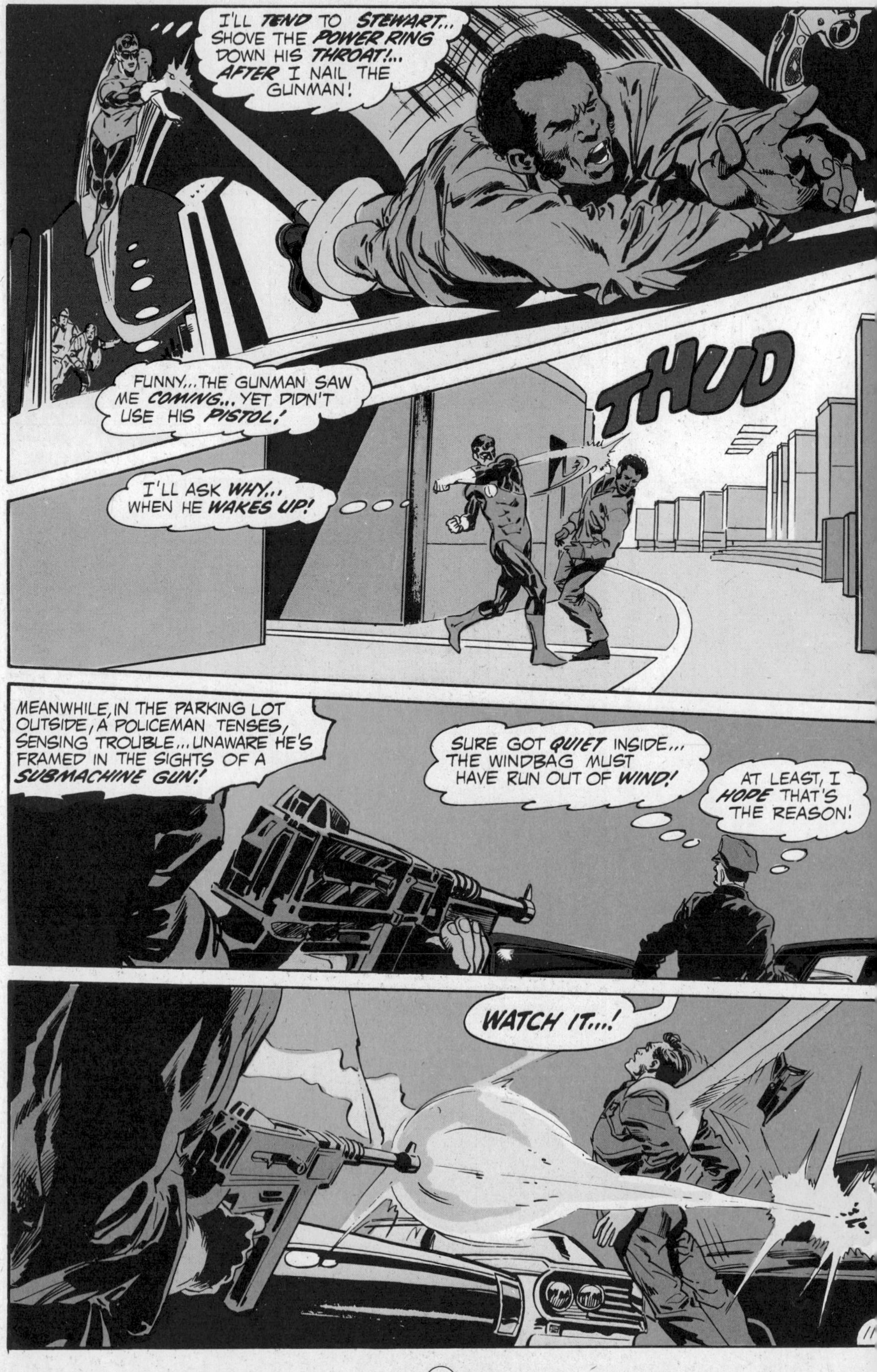
I'LL TEND TO STEWART... SHOVE THE POWER RING DOWN HIS THROAT!... AFTER I NAIL THE GUNMAN!
FUNNY... THE GUNMAN SAW ME COMING... YET DIDN'T USE HIS PISTOL!
THUD
I'LL ASK WHY... WHEN HE WAKES UP!
MEANWHILE, IN THE PARKING LOT OUTSIDE, A POLICEMAN TENSES, SENSING TROUBLE... UNAWARE HE'S FRAMED IN THE SIGHTS OF A SUBMACHINE GUN!
SURE GOT QUIET INSIDE... THE WINDBAG MUST HAVE RUN OUT OF WIND!
AT LEAST, I HOPE THAT'S THE REASON!
WATCH IT...!
11

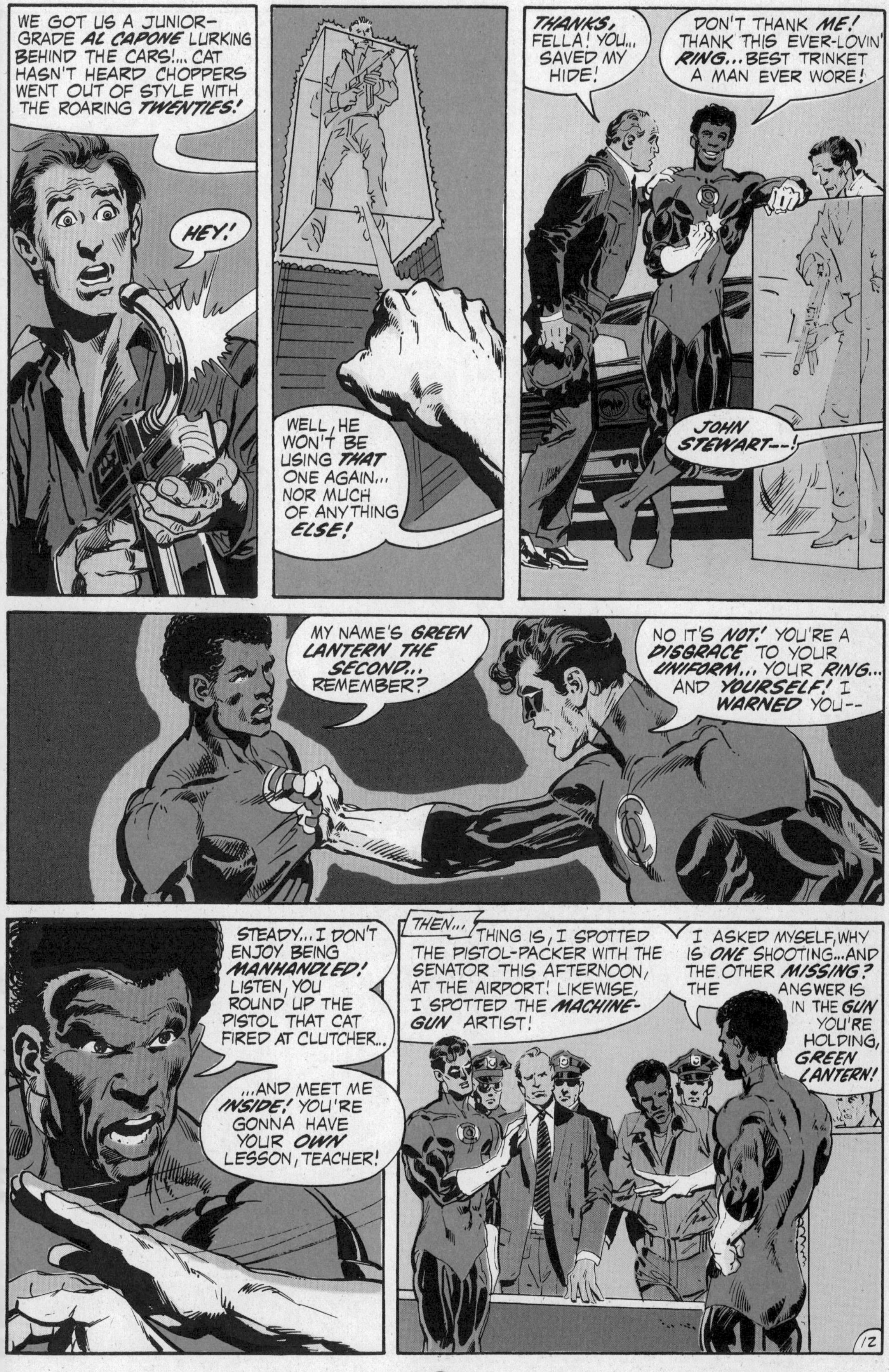
WE GOT US A JUNIOR-GRADE AL CAPONE LURKING BEHIND THE CARS!... CAT HASN'T HEARD CHOPPERS WENT OUT OF STYLE WITH THE ROARING TWENTIES!
HEY!
WELL, HE WON'T BE USING THAT ONE AGAIN... NOR MUCH OF ANYTHING ELSE!
THANKS, FELLA! YOU... SAVED MY HIDE!
DON'T THANK ME! THANK THIS EVER-LOVIN' RING... BEST TRINKET A MAN EVER WORE!
JOHN STEWART--!
MY NAME'S GREEN LANTERN THE SECOND... REMEMBER?
NO IT'S NOT! YOU'RE A DISGRACE TO YOUR UNIFORM... YOUR RING... AND YOURSELF! I WARNED YOU--
STEADY... I DON'T ENJOY BEING MANHANDLED! LISTEN, YOU ROUND UP THE PISTOL THAT CAT FIRED AT CLUTCHER...
...AND MEET ME INSIDE! YOU'RE GONNA HAVE YOUR OWN LESSON, TEACHER!
THEN...
THING IS, I SPOTTED THE PISTOL-PACKER WITH THE SENATOR THIS AFTERNOON, AT THE AIRPORT! LIKEWISE, I SPOTTED THE MACHINE-GUN ARTIST!
I ASKED MYSELF, WHY IS ONE SHOOTING... AND THE OTHER MISSING? THE ANSWER IS IN THE GUN YOU'RE HOLDING, GREEN LANTERN!
12

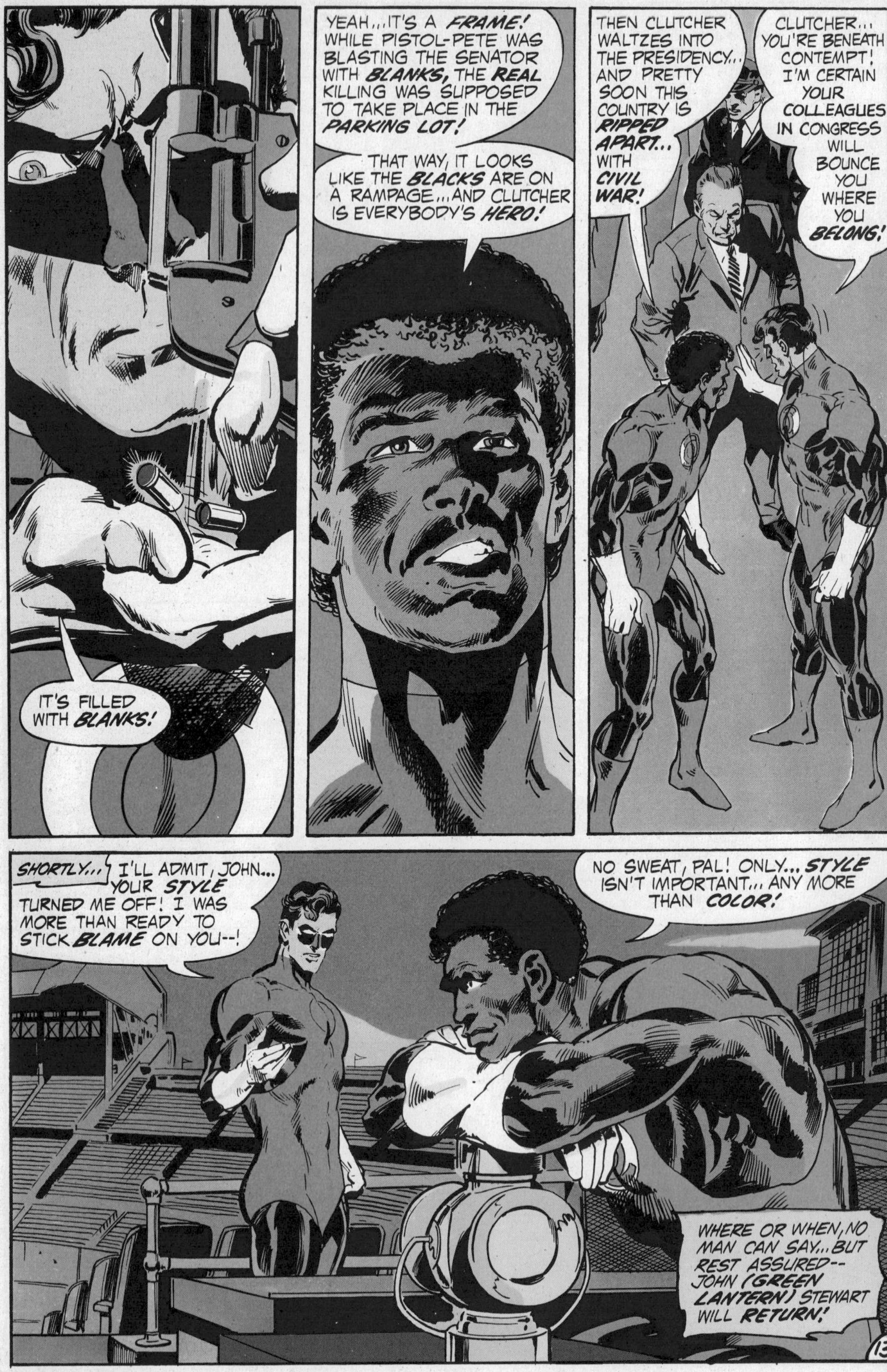

IT'S FILLED WITH BLANKS!
YEAH...IT'S A FRAME! WHILE PISTOL-PETE WAS BLASTING THE SENATOR WITH BLANKS, THE REAL KILLING WAS SUPPOSED TO TAKE PLACE IN THE PARKING LOT!
THAT WAY, IT LOOKS LIKE THE BLACKS ARE ON A RAMPAGE...AND CLUTCHER IS EVERYBODY'S HERO!
THEN CLUTCHER WALTZES INTO THE PRESIDENCY... AND PRETTY SOON THIS COUNTRY IS RIPPED APART... WITH CIVIL WAR!
CLUTCHER... YOU'RE BENEATH CONTEMPT! I'M CERTAIN YOUR COLLEAGUES IN CONGRESS WILL BOUNCE YOU WHERE YOU BELONG!
SHORTLY...
I'LL ADMIT, JOHN... YOUR STYLE TURNED ME OFF! I WAS MORE THAN READY TO STICK BLAME ON YOU--!
NO SWEAT, PAL! ONLY... STYLE ISN'T IMPORTANT... ANY MORE THAN COLOR!
WHERE OR WHEN, NO MAN CAN SAY...BUT REST ASSURED-- JOHN (GREEN LANTERN) STEWART WILL RETURN!
13

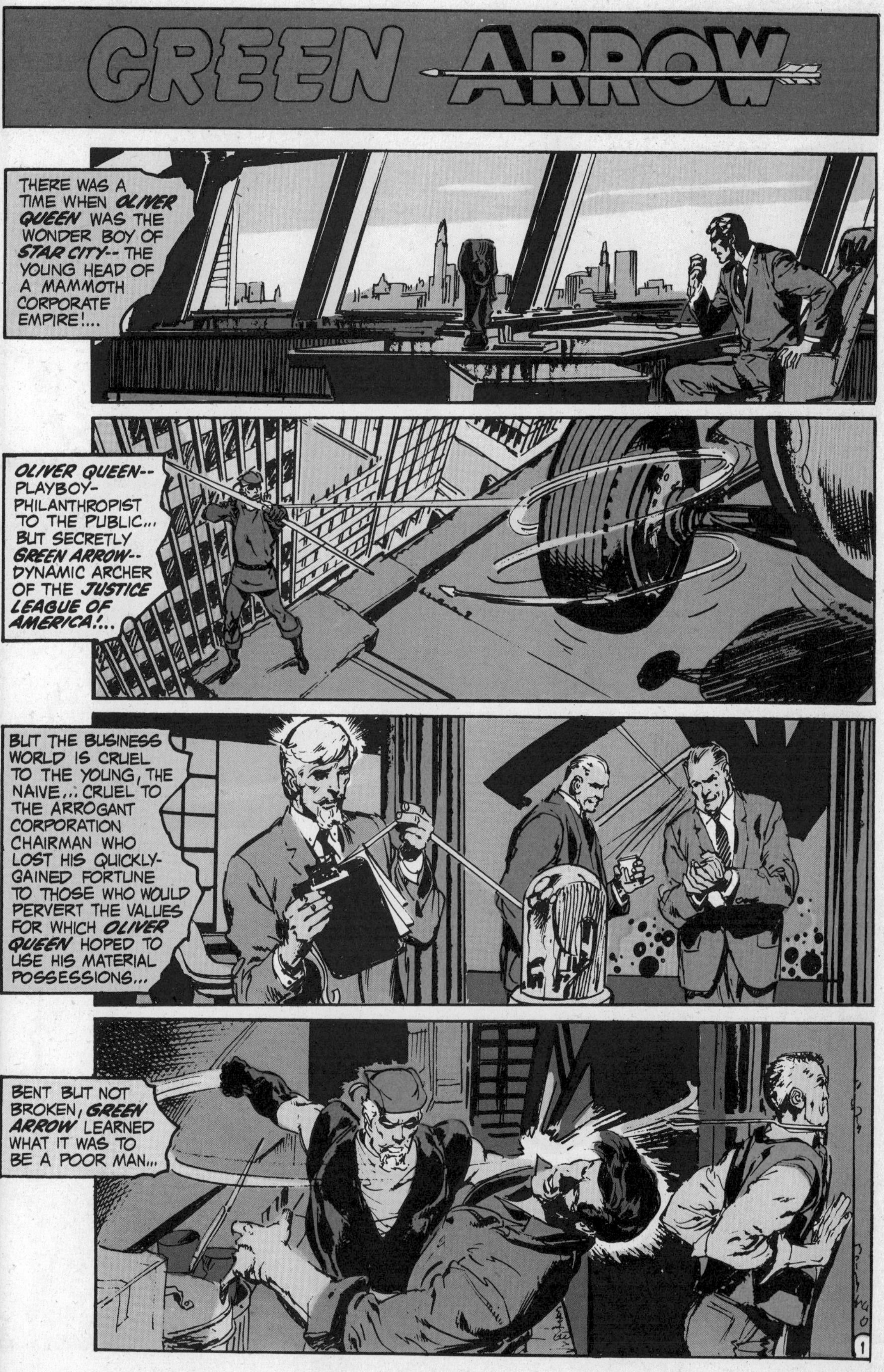
GREEN ARROW
THERE WAS A TIME WHEN OLIVER QUEEN WAS THE WONDER BOY OF STAR CITY-- THE YOUNG HEAD OF A MAMMOTH CORPORATE EMPIRE!...
OLIVER QUEEN-- PLAYBOY-PHILANTHROPIST TO THE PUBLIC... BUT SECRETLY GREEN ARROW-- DYNAMIC ARCHER OF THE JUSTICE LEAGUE OF AMERICA!...
BUT THE BUSINESS WORLD IS CRUEL TO THE YOUNG, THE NAIVE... CRUEL TO THE ARROGANT CORPORATION CHAIRMAN WHO LOST HIS QUICKLY-GAINED FORTUNE TO THOSE WHO WOULD PERVERT THE VALUES FOR WHICH OLIVER QUEEN HOPED TO USE HIS MATERIAL POSSESSIONS...
BENT BUT NOT BROKEN, GREEN ARROW LEARNED WHAT IT WAS TO BE A POOR MAN...
1

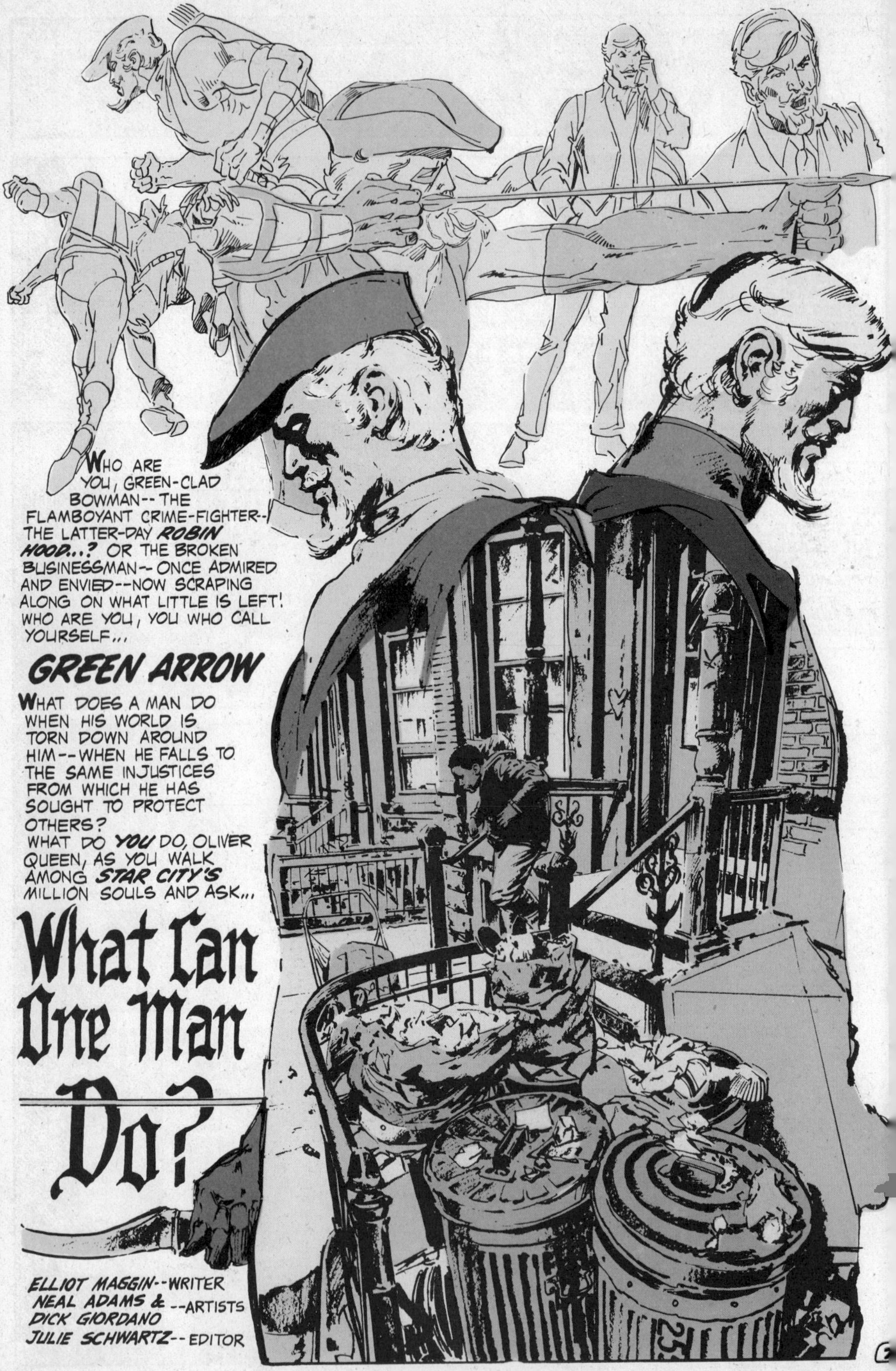

WHO ARE YOU, GREEN-CLAD BOWMAN-- THE FLAMBOYANT CRIME-FIGHTER-- THE LATTER-DAY ROBIN HOOD...? OR THE BROKEN BUSINESSMAN-- ONCE ADMIRED AND ENVIED--NOW SCRAPING ALONG ON WHAT LITTLE IS LEFT! WHO ARE YOU, YOU WHO CALL YOURSELF...
GREEN ARROW
WHAT DOES A MAN DO WHEN HIS WORLD IS TORN DOWN AROUND HIM--WHEN HE FALLS TO THE SAME INJUSTICES FROM WHICH HE HAS SOUGHT TO PROTECT OTHERS? WHAT DO YOU DO, OLIVER QUEEN, AS YOU WALK AMONG STAR CITY'S MILLION SOULS AND ASK...
What Can One Man Do?
ELLIOT MAGGIN--WRITER
NEAL ADAMS & DICK GIORDANO --ARTISTS
JULIE SCHWARTZ--EDITOR

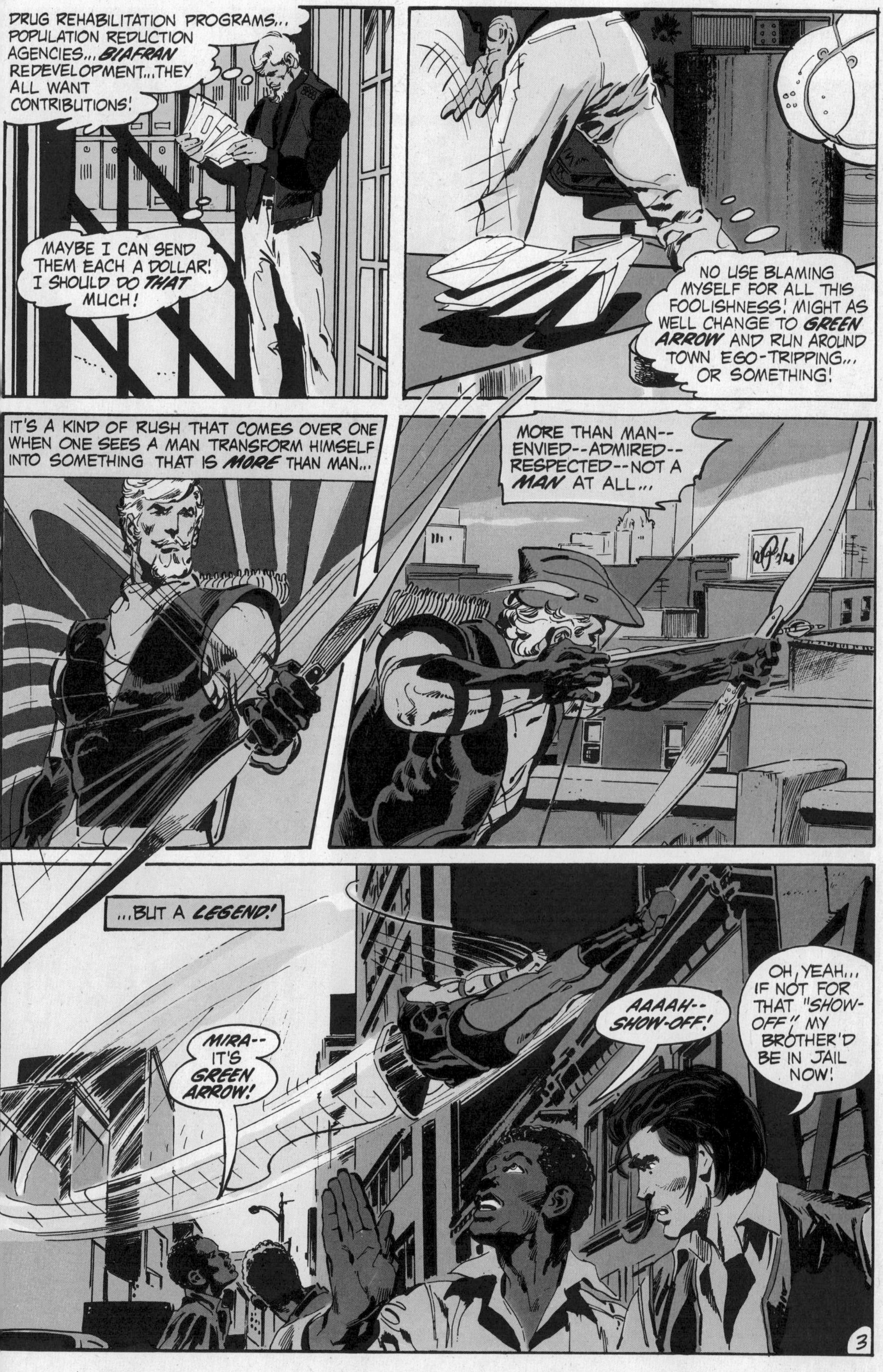
DRUG REHABILITATION PROGRAMS... POPULATION REDUCTION AGENCIES... BIAFRAN REDEVELOPMENT... THEY ALL WANT CONTRIBUTIONS!
MAYBE I CAN SEND THEM EACH A DOLLAR! I SHOULD DO THAT MUCH!
NO USE BLAMING MYSELF FOR ALL THIS FOOLISHNESS! MIGHT AS WELL CHANGE TO GREEN ARROW AND RUN AROUND TOWN EGO-TRIPPING... OR SOMETHING!
IT'S A KIND OF RUSH THAT COMES OVER ONE WHEN ONE SEES A MAN TRANSFORM HIMSELF INTO SOMETHING THAT IS MORE THAN MAN...
MORE THAN MAN-- ENVIED--ADMIRED-- RESPECTED--NOT A MAN AT ALL...
...BUT A LEGEND!
MIRA-- IT'S GREEN ARROW!
AAAAH-- SHOW-OFF!
OH, YEAH... IF NOT FOR THAT "SHOW-OFF," MY BROTHER'D BE IN JAIL NOW!
3

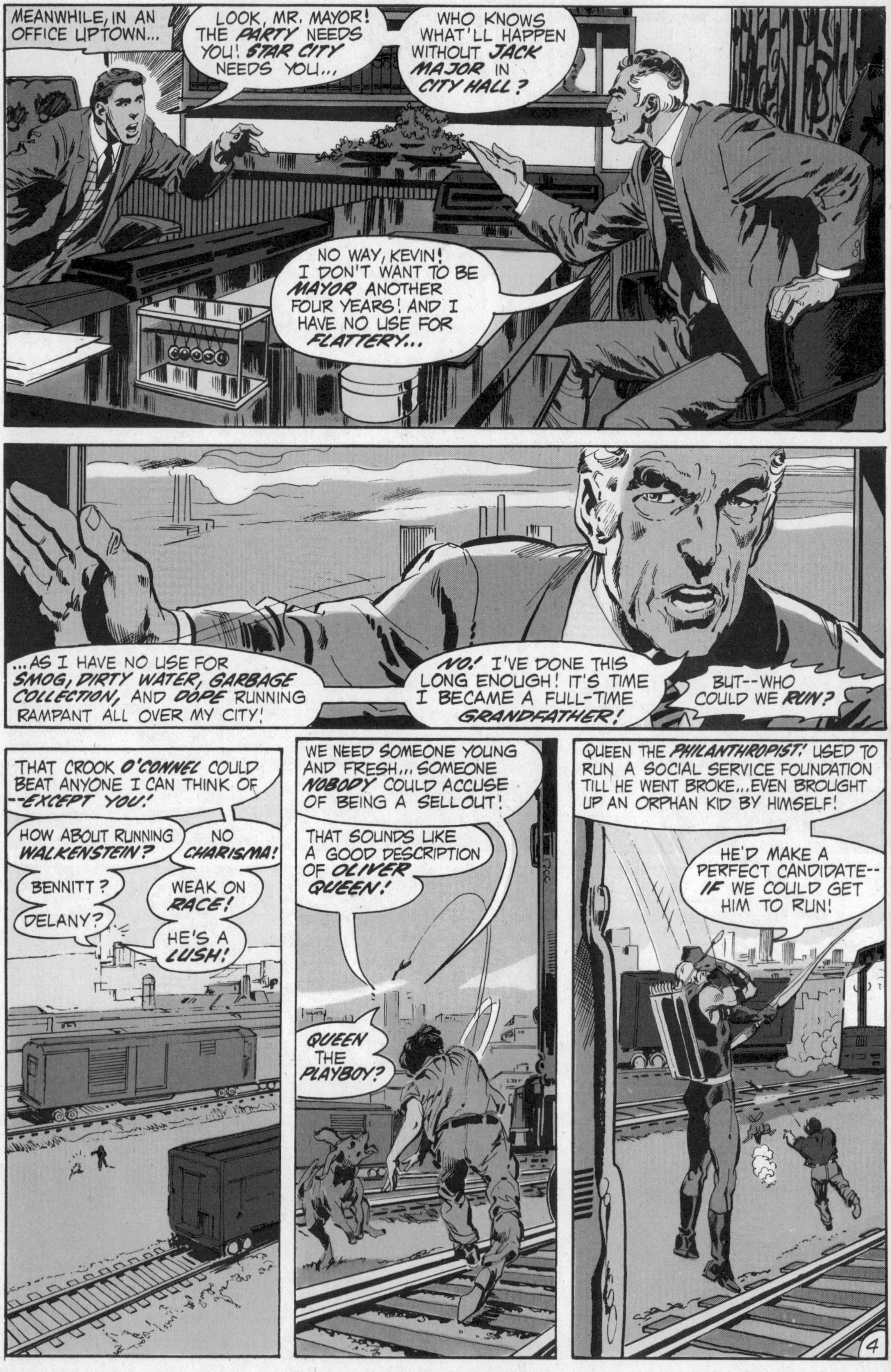
MEANWHILE, IN AN OFFICE UPTOWN...
LOOK, MR. MAYOR! THE PARTY NEEDS YOU! STAR CITY NEEDS YOU...
WHO KNOWS WHAT'LL HAPPEN WITHOUT JACK MAJOR IN CITY HALL?
NO WAY, KEVIN! I DON'T WANT TO BE MAYOR ANOTHER FOUR YEARS! AND I HAVE NO USE FOR FLATTERY...
...AS I HAVE NO USE FOR SMOG, DIRTY WATER, GARBAGE COLLECTION, AND DOPE RUNNING RAMPANT ALL OVER MY CITY!
NO! I'VE DONE THIS LONG ENOUGH! IT'S TIME I BECAME A FULL-TIME GRANDFATHER!
BUT--WHO COULD WE RUN?
THAT CROOK O'CONNEL COULD BEAT ANYONE I CAN THINK OF --EXCEPT YOU!
HOW ABOUT RUNNING WALKENSTEIN?
NO CHARISMA!
BENNITT?
WEAK ON RACE!
DELANY?
HE'S A LUSH!
WE NEED SOMEONE YOUNG AND FRESH... SOMEONE NOBODY COULD ACCUSE OF BEING A SELLOUT!
THAT SOUNDS LIKE A GOOD DESCRIPTION OF OLIVER QUEEN!
QUEEN THE PLAYBOY?
QUEEN THE PHILANTHROPIST! USED TO RUN A SOCIAL SERVICE FOUNDATION TILL HE WENT BROKE... EVEN BROUGHT UP AN ORPHAN KID BY HIMSELF!
HE'D MAKE A PERFECT CANDIDATE-- IF WE COULD GET HIM TO RUN!
4

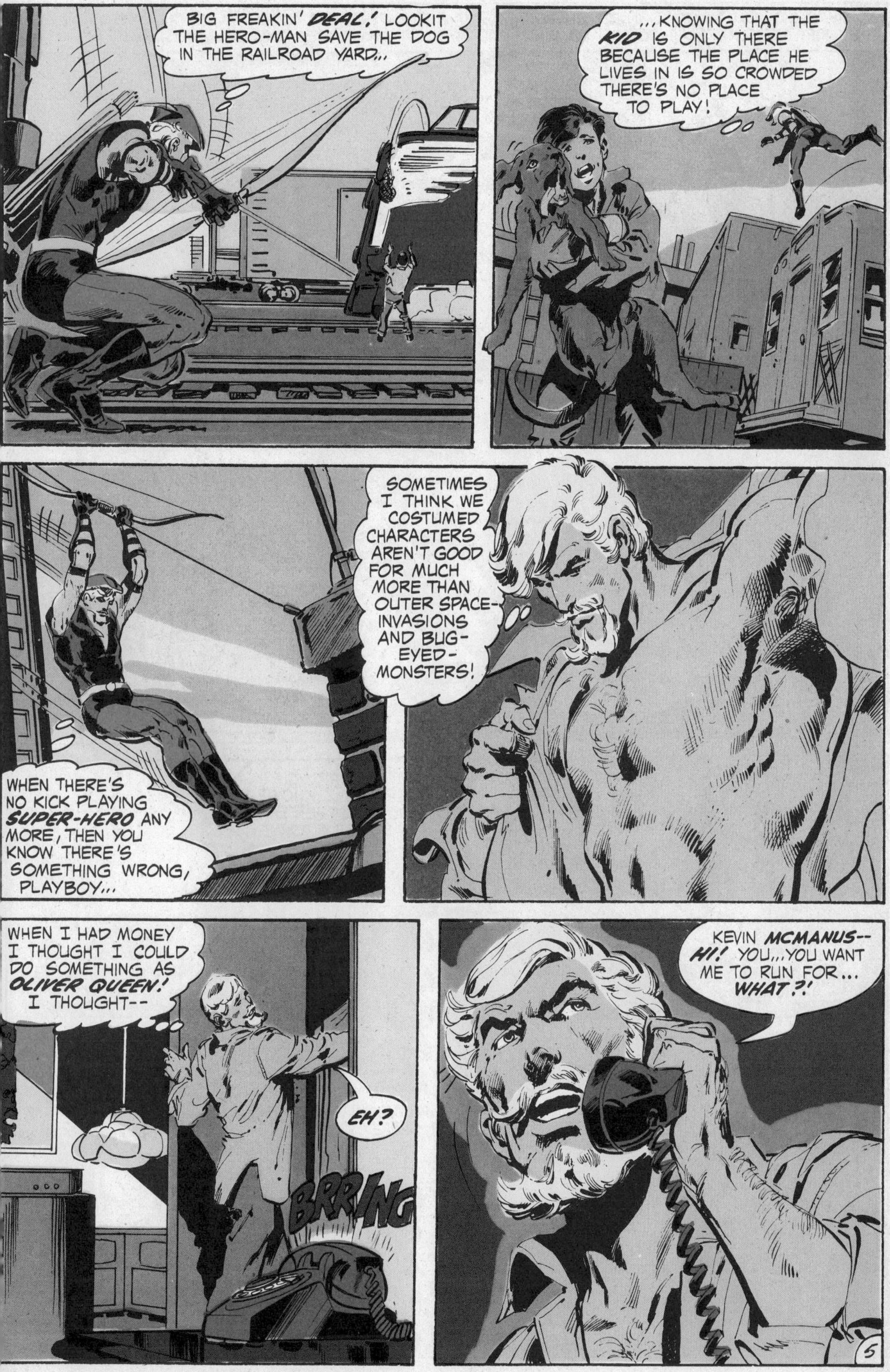
BIG FREAKIN' DEAL! LOOKIT THE HERO-MAN SAVE THE DOG IN THE RAILROAD YARD...
...KNOWING THAT THE KID IS ONLY THERE BECAUSE THE PLACE HE LIVES IN IS SO CROWDED THERE'S NO PLACE TO PLAY!
WHEN THERE'S NO KICK PLAYING SUPER-HERO ANY MORE, THEN YOU KNOW THERE'S SOMETHING WRONG, PLAYBOY...
SOMETIMES I THINK WE COSTUMED CHARACTERS AREN'T GOOD FOR MUCH MORE THAN OUTER SPACE-INVASIONS AND BUG-EYED-MONSTERS!
WHEN I HAD MONEY I THOUGHT I COULD DO SOMETHING AS OLIVER QUEEN! I THOUGHT--
EH?
BRRING
KEVIN MCMANUS-- HI! YOU... YOU WANT ME TO RUN FOR... WHAT?!
5

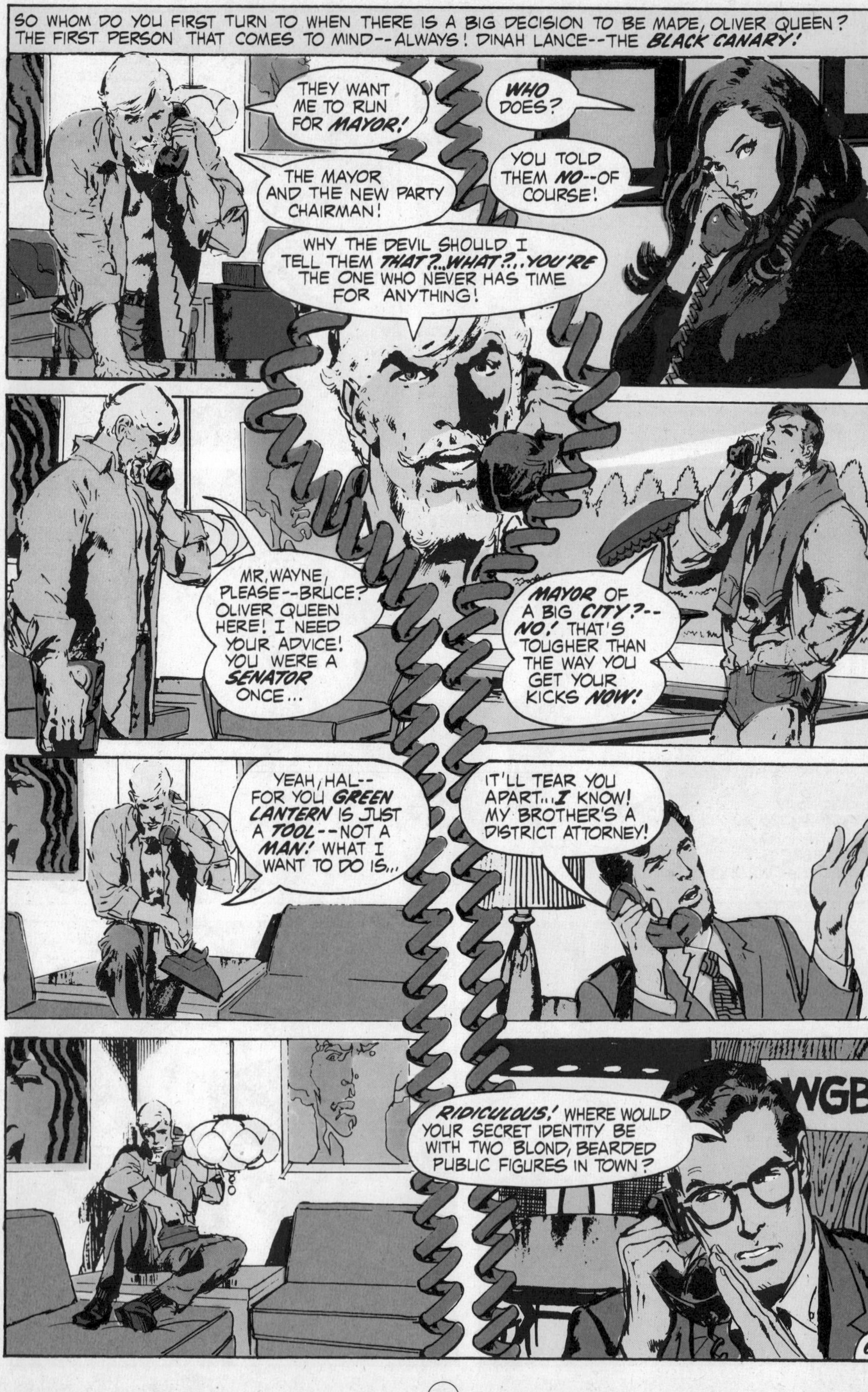
SO WHOM DO YOU FIRST TURN TO WHEN THERE IS A BIG DECISION TO BE MADE, OLIVER QUEEN? THE FIRST PERSON THAT COMES TO MIND--ALWAYS! DINAH LANCE--THE BLACK CANARY!
THEY WANT ME TO RUN FOR MAYOR!
WHO DOES?
THE MAYOR AND THE NEW PARTY CHAIRMAN!
YOU TOLD THEM NO--OF COURSE!
WHY THE DEVIL SHOULD I TELL THEM THAT?...WHAT?...YOU'RE THE ONE WHO NEVER HAS TIME FOR ANYTHING!
MR. WAYNE, PLEASE--BRUCE? OLIVER QUEEN HERE! I NEED YOUR ADVICE! YOU WERE A SENATOR ONCE...
MAYOR OF A BIG CITY?--NO! THAT'S TOUGHER THAN THE WAY YOU GET YOUR KICKS NOW!
YEAH, HAL--FOR YOU GREEN LANTERN IS JUST A TOOL--NOT A MAN! WHAT I WANT TO DO IS...
IT'LL TEAR YOU APART...I KNOW! MY BROTHER'S A DISTRICT ATTORNEY!
WGBS
RIDICULOUS! WHERE WOULD YOUR SECRET IDENTITY BE WITH TWO BLOND, BEARDED PUBLIC FIGURES IN TOWN?
6

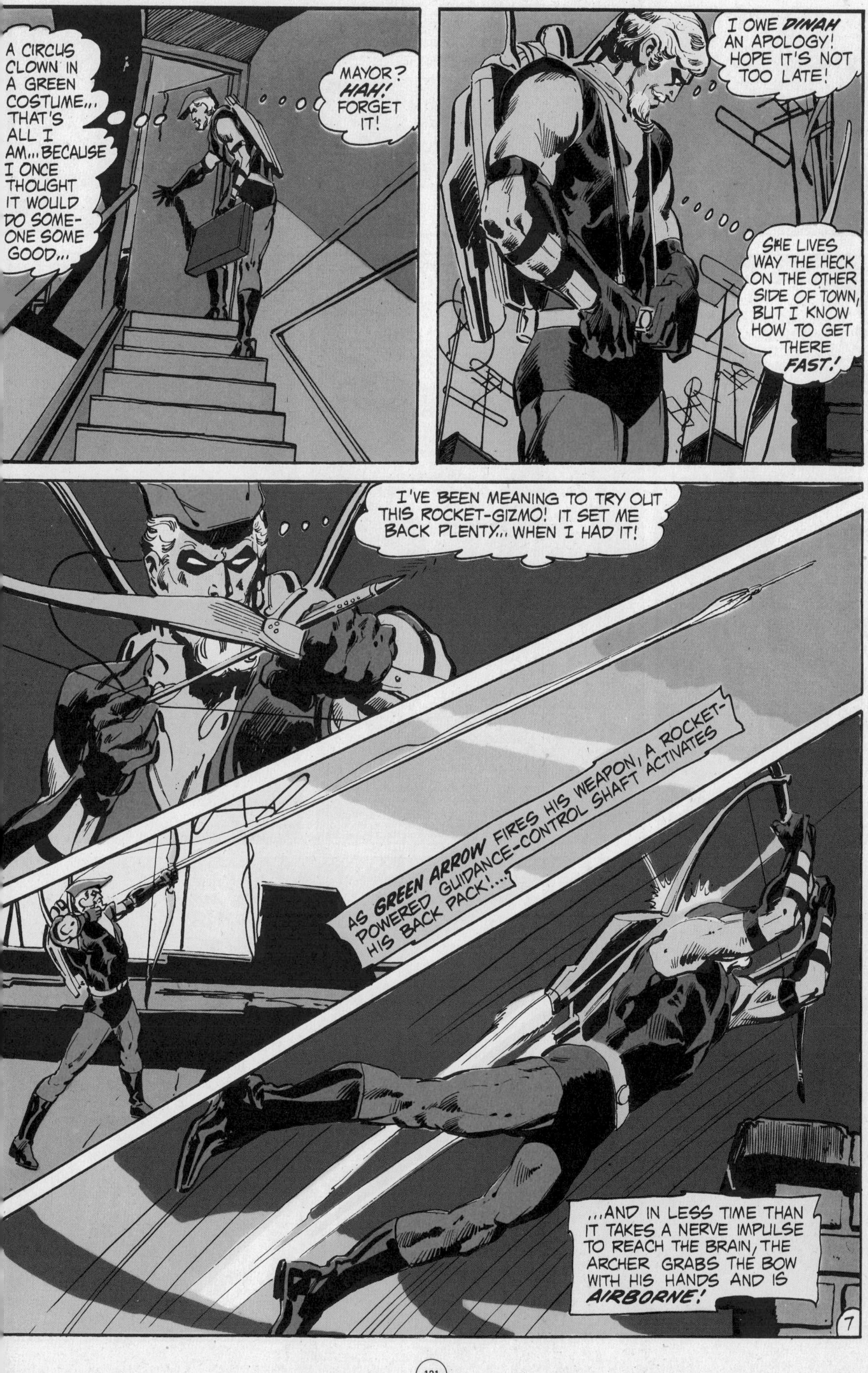
A CIRCUS CLOWN IN A GREEN COSTUME... THAT'S ALL I AM... BECAUSE I ONCE THOUGHT IT WOULD DO SOME-ONE SOME GOOD...
MAYOR? HAH! FORGET IT!
I OWE DINAH AN APOLOGY! HOPE IT'S NOT TOO LATE!
SHE LIVES WAY THE HECK ON THE OTHER SIDE OF TOWN, BUT I KNOW HOW TO GET THERE FAST!
I'VE BEEN MEANING TO TRY OUT THIS ROCKET-GIZMO! IT SET ME BACK PLENTY... WHEN I HAD IT!
AS GREEN ARROW FIRES HIS WEAPON, A ROCKET-POWERED GUIDANCE-CONTROL SHAFT ACTIVATES HIS BACK PACK!...
...AND IN LESS TIME THAN IT TAKES A NERVE IMPULSE TO REACH THE BRAIN, THE ARCHER GRABS THE BOW WITH HIS HANDS AND IS AIRBORNE!
7

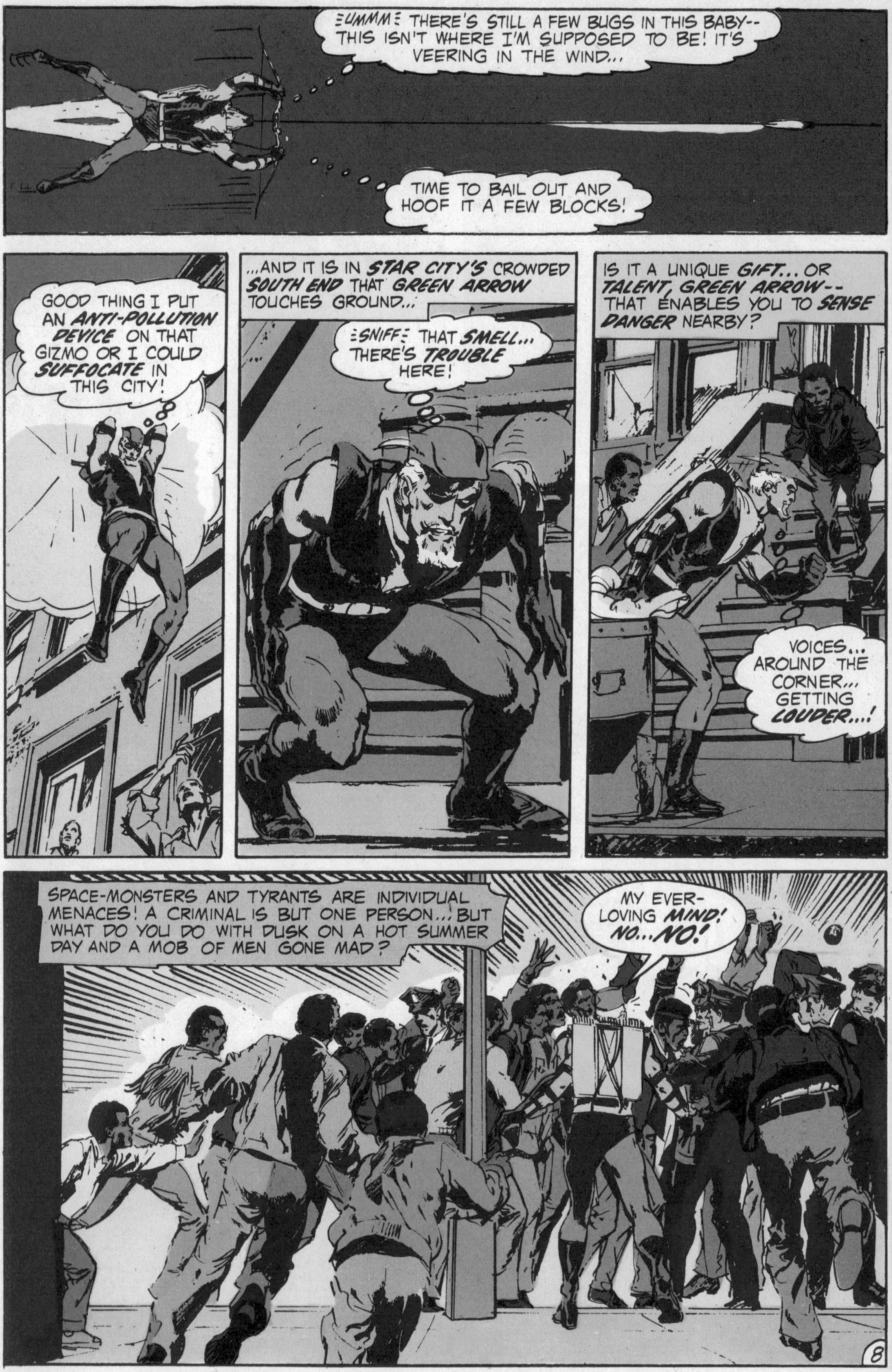
≡UMMM≡ THERE'S STILL A FEW BUGS IN THIS BABY-- THIS ISN'T WHERE I'M SUPPOSED TO BE! IT'S VEERING IN THE WIND...
TIME TO BAIL OUT AND HOOF IT A FEW BLOCKS!
GOOD THING I PUT AN ANTI-POLLUTION DEVICE ON THAT GIZMO OR I COULD SUFFOCATE IN THIS CITY!
...AND IT IS IN STAR CITY'S CROWDED SOUTH END THAT GREEN ARROW TOUCHES GROUND...
≡SNIFF≡ THAT SMELL... THERE'S TROUBLE HERE!
IS IT A UNIQUE GIFT... OR TALENT, GREEN ARROW-- THAT ENABLES YOU TO SENSE DANGER NEARBY?
VOICES... AROUND THE CORNER... GETTING LOUDER...!
SPACE-MONSTERS AND TYRANTS ARE INDIVIDUAL MENACES! A CRIMINAL IS BUT ONE PERSON... BUT WHAT DO YOU DO WITH DUSK ON A HOT SUMMER DAY AND A MOB OF MEN GONE MAD?
MY EVER-LOVING MIND! NO...NO!
8

WHOSE FAULT IS THIS, *OLIVER (GREEN ARROW) QUEEN?* AND AT WHOM DO YOU DIRECT YOUR *JUSTICE*... YOUR *ANGER?*

WHO'S FAULT? THE *BLACK*, THE *RED*, THE *YELLOW*...

...THE POOR, THE MEEK, THE PEACEFUL, HERDED INTO A SMALL SPECK OF EARTH...

...WHERE MOVEMENT AT ALL CANNOT BE OUTWARD...

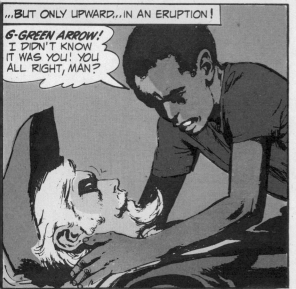

...BUT ONLY UPWARD...IN AN ERUPTION!

G-GREEN ARROW! I DIDN'T KNOW IT WAS YOU! YOU ALL RIGHT, MAN?

YEAH! I'M OKAY! HEY! WHAT ARE YOU DOING RUNNING AROUND WITH THAT *STICK?*

I'M SORRY! I HADDA DO *SOMETHIN'*! BUT, HONEST... I DIDN'T KNOW IT WAS *YOU!*

9

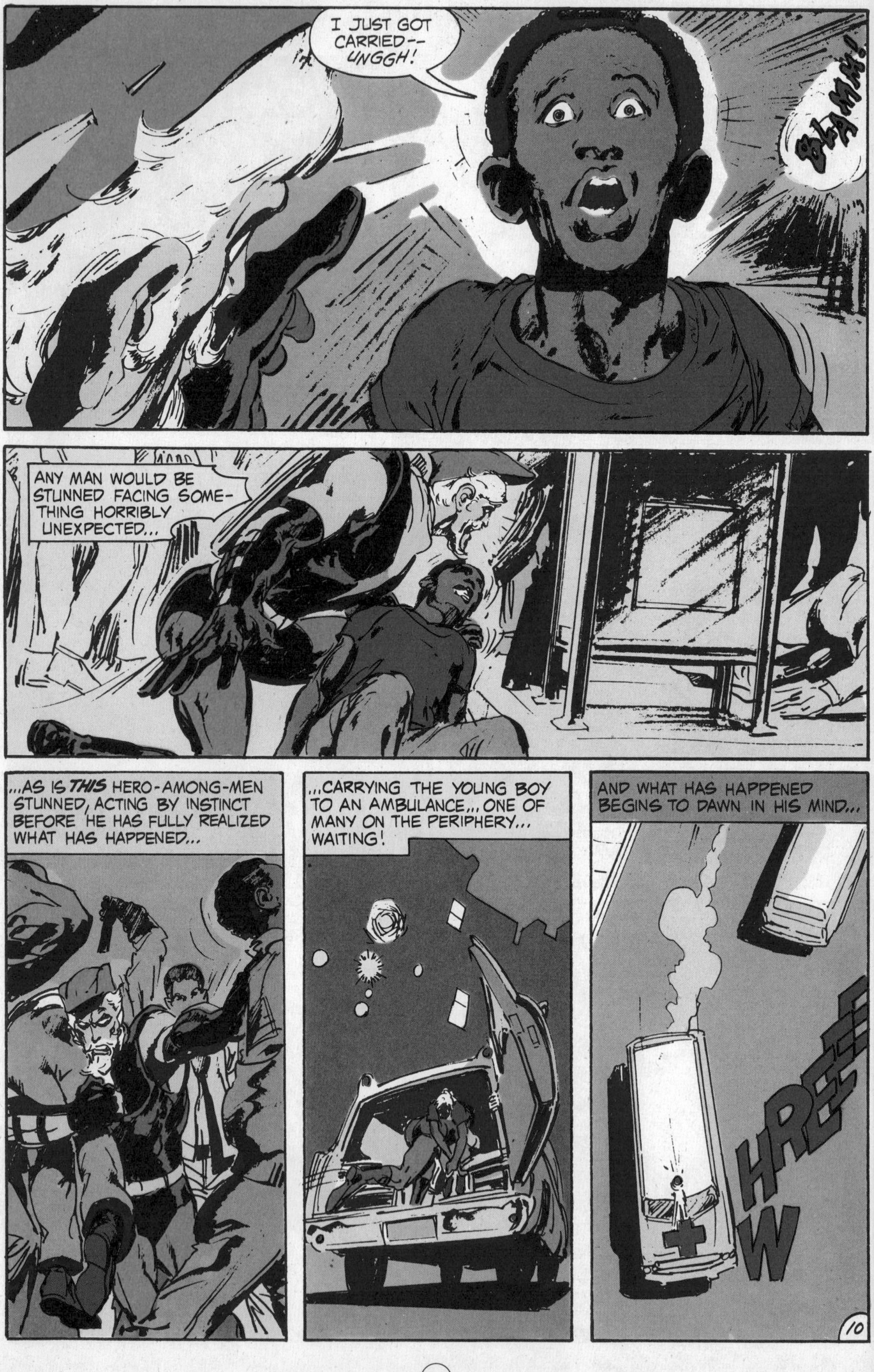

I JUST GOT CARRIED-- UNGGH!
BLAMM!
ANY MAN WOULD BE STUNNED FACING SOMETHING HORRIBLY UNEXPECTED...
...AS IS THIS HERO-AMONG-MEN STUNNED, ACTING BY INSTINCT BEFORE HE HAS FULLY REALIZED WHAT HAS HAPPENED...
...CARRYING THE YOUNG BOY TO AN AMBULANCE... ONE OF MANY ON THE PERIPHERY... WAITING!
AND WHAT HAS HAPPENED BEGINS TO DAWN IN HIS MIND...
HREEEEW
10

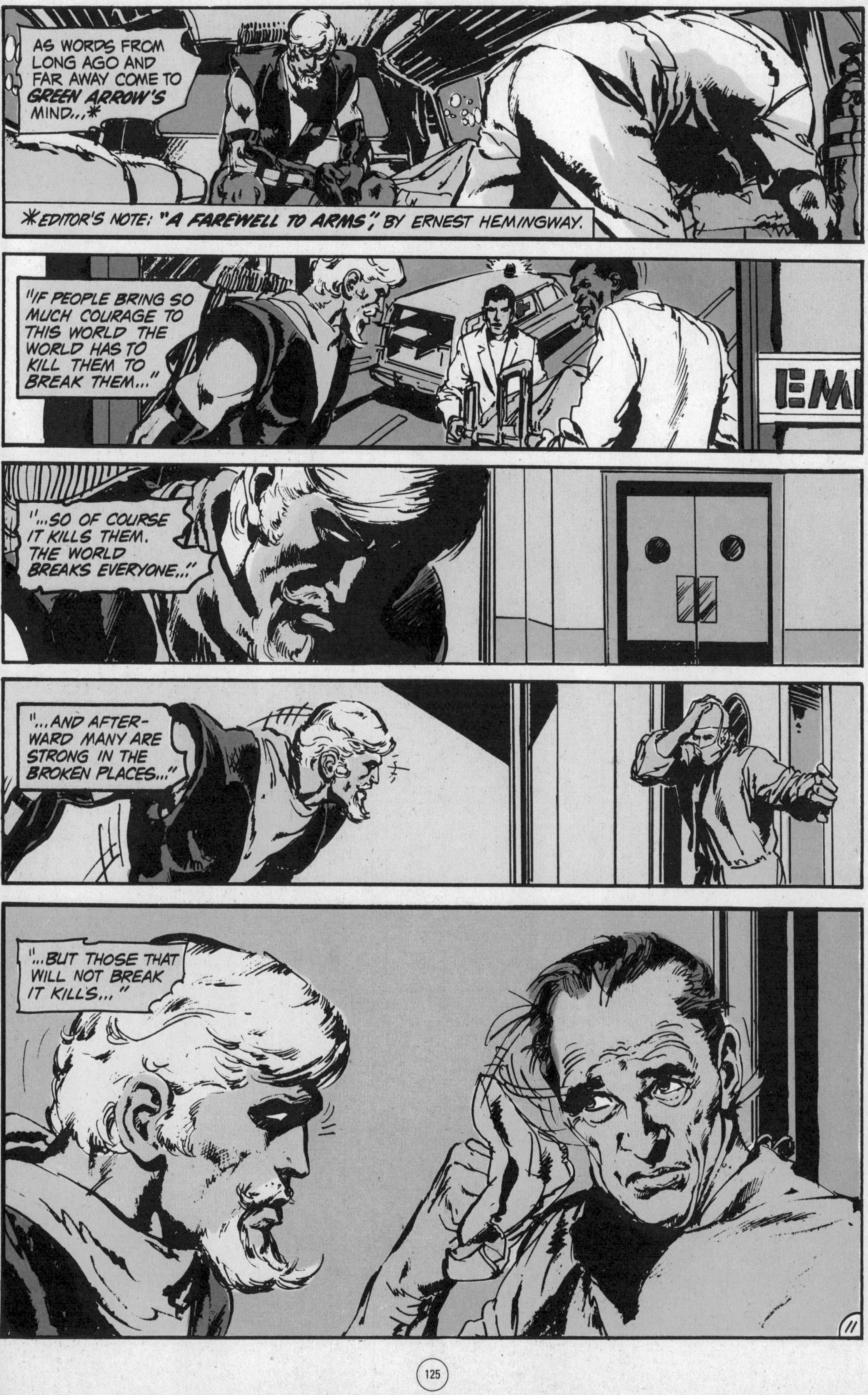
AS WORDS FROM LONG AGO AND FAR AWAY COME TO GREEN ARROW'S MIND...*
*EDITOR'S NOTE: "A FAREWELL TO ARMS", BY ERNEST HEMINGWAY.
"IF PEOPLE BRING SO MUCH COURAGE TO THIS WORLD THE WORLD HAS TO KILL THEM TO BREAK THEM..."
EM
"...SO OF COURSE IT KILLS THEM. THE WORLD BREAKS EVERYONE..."
"...AND AFTER-WARD MANY ARE STRONG IN THE BROKEN PLACES..."
"...BUT THOSE THAT WILL NOT BREAK IT KILLS..."
11

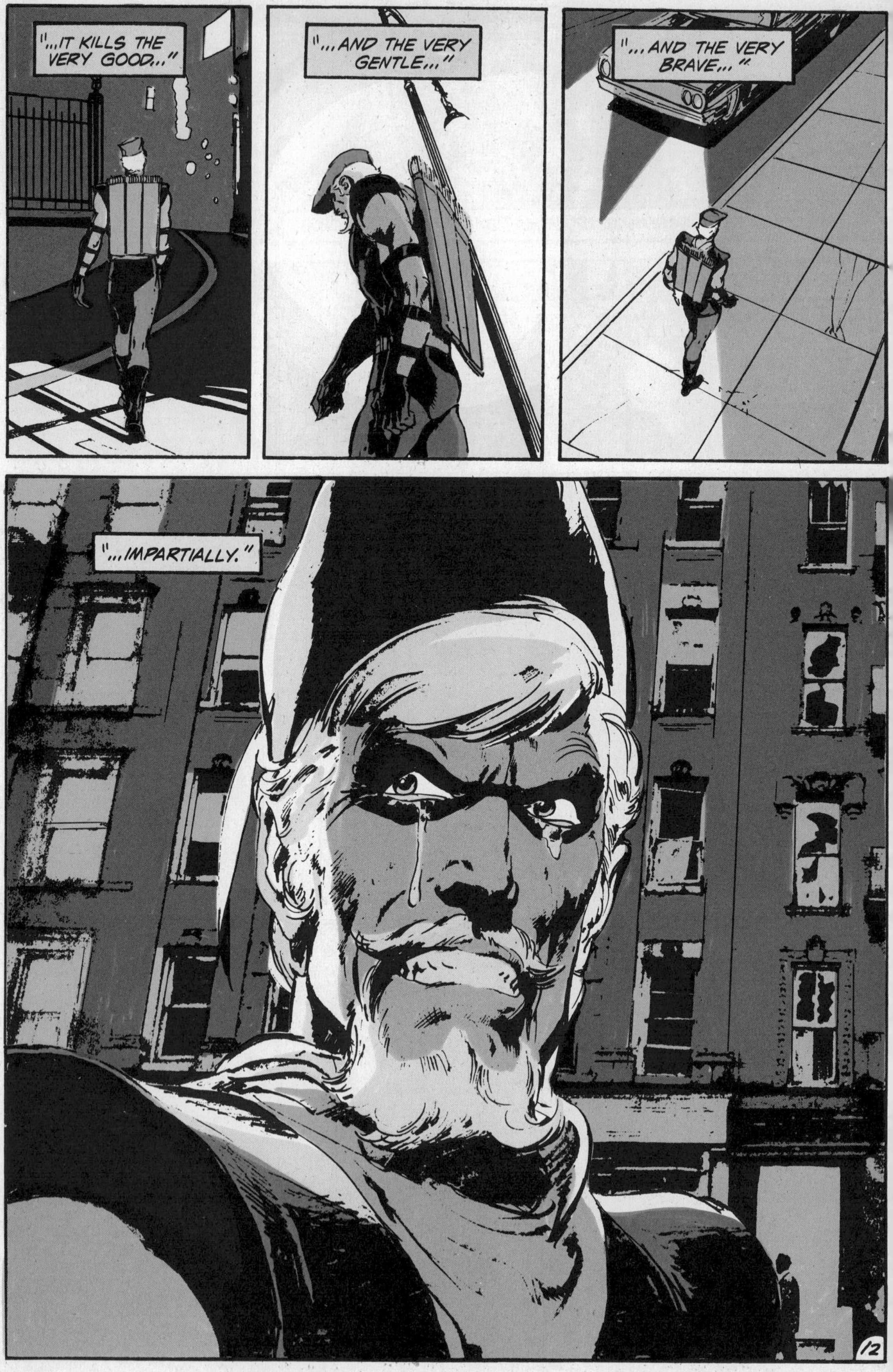
"...IT KILLS THE VERY GOOD..."
"...AND THE VERY GENTLE..."
"...AND THE VERY BRAVE..."
"...IMPARTIALLY."
12

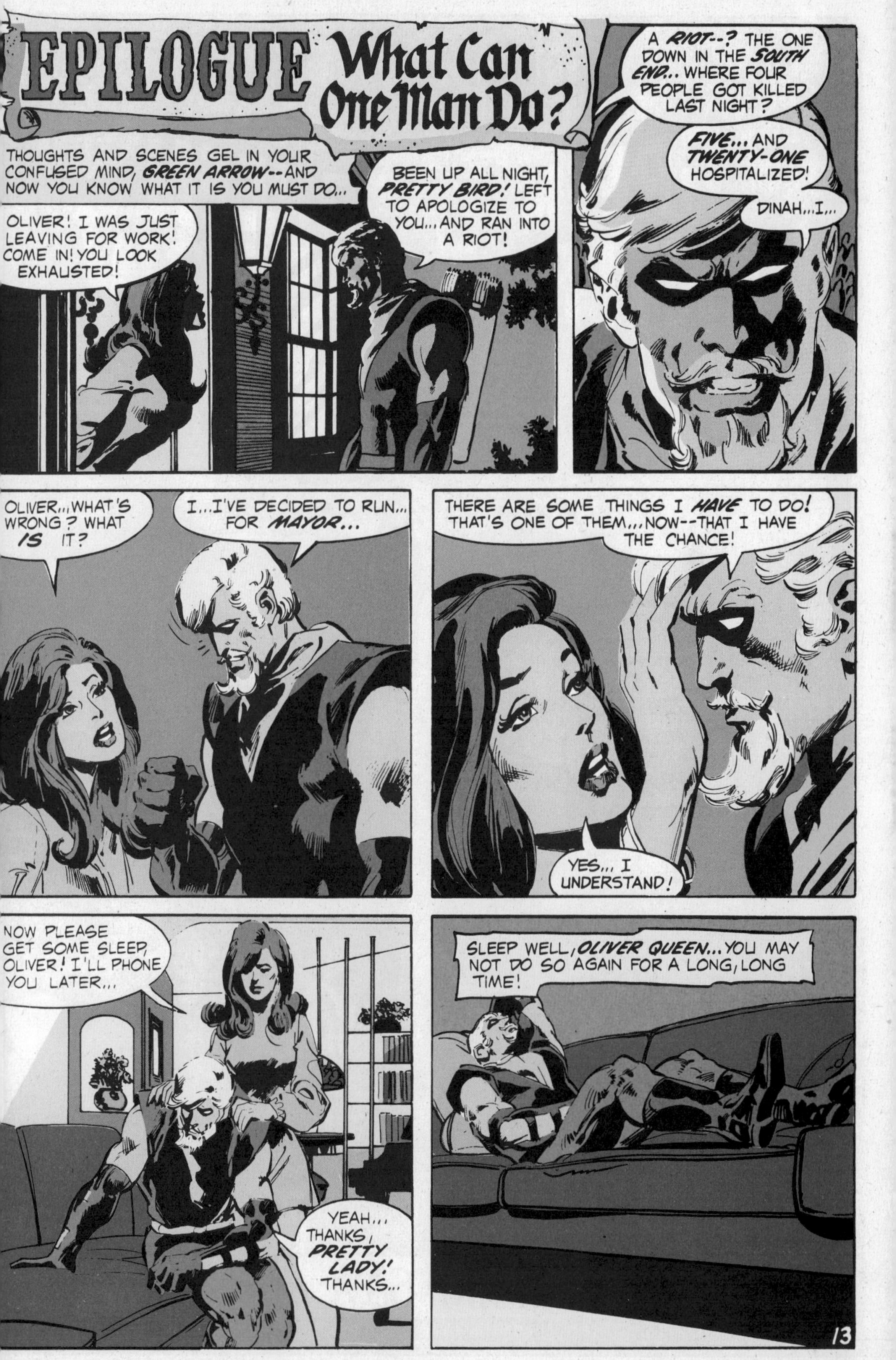
EPILOGUE
What Can One Man Do?
THOUGHTS AND SCENES GEL IN YOUR CONFUSED MIND, GREEN ARROW--AND NOW YOU KNOW WHAT IT IS YOU MUST DO...
OLIVER! I WAS JUST LEAVING FOR WORK! COME IN! YOU LOOK EXHAUSTED!
BEEN UP ALL NIGHT, PRETTY BIRD! LEFT TO APOLOGIZE TO YOU... AND RAN INTO A RIOT!
A RIOT--? THE ONE DOWN IN THE SOUTH END... WHERE FOUR PEOPLE GOT KILLED LAST NIGHT?
FIVE... AND TWENTY-ONE HOSPITALIZED!
DINAH... I...
OLIVER... WHAT'S WRONG? WHAT IS IT?
I... I'VE DECIDED TO RUN... FOR MAYOR...
THERE ARE SOME THINGS I HAVE TO DO! THAT'S ONE OF THEM... NOW--THAT I HAVE THE CHANCE!
YES... I UNDERSTAND!
NOW PLEASE GET SOME SLEEP, OLIVER! I'LL PHONE YOU LATER...
YEAH... THANKS, PRETTY LADY! THANKS...
SLEEP WELL, OLIVER QUEEN... YOU MAY NOT DO SO AGAIN FOR A LONG, LONG TIME!
13

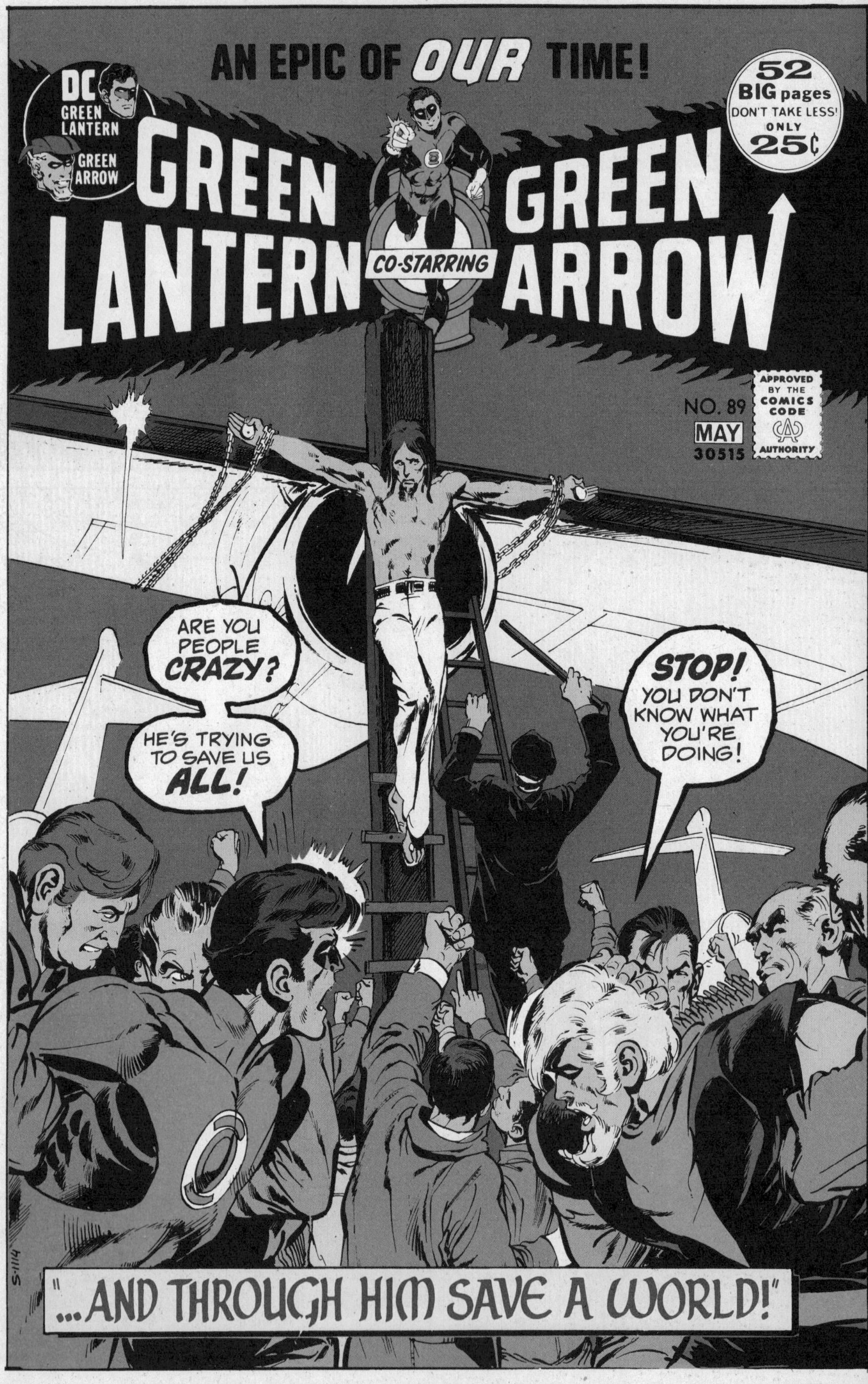
AN EPIC OF OUR TIME!
DC GREEN LANTERN GREEN ARROW
52 BIG pages DON'T TAKE LESS! ONLY 25¢
GREEN LANTERN
CO-STARRING
GREEN ARROW
NO. 89
MAY
30515
APPROVED BY THE COMICS CODE AUTHORITY
ARE YOU PEOPLE CRAZY?
HE'S TRYING TO SAVE US ALL!
STOP! YOU DON'T KNOW WHAT YOU'RE DOING!
S-1114
"...AND THROUGH HIM SAVE A WORLD!"

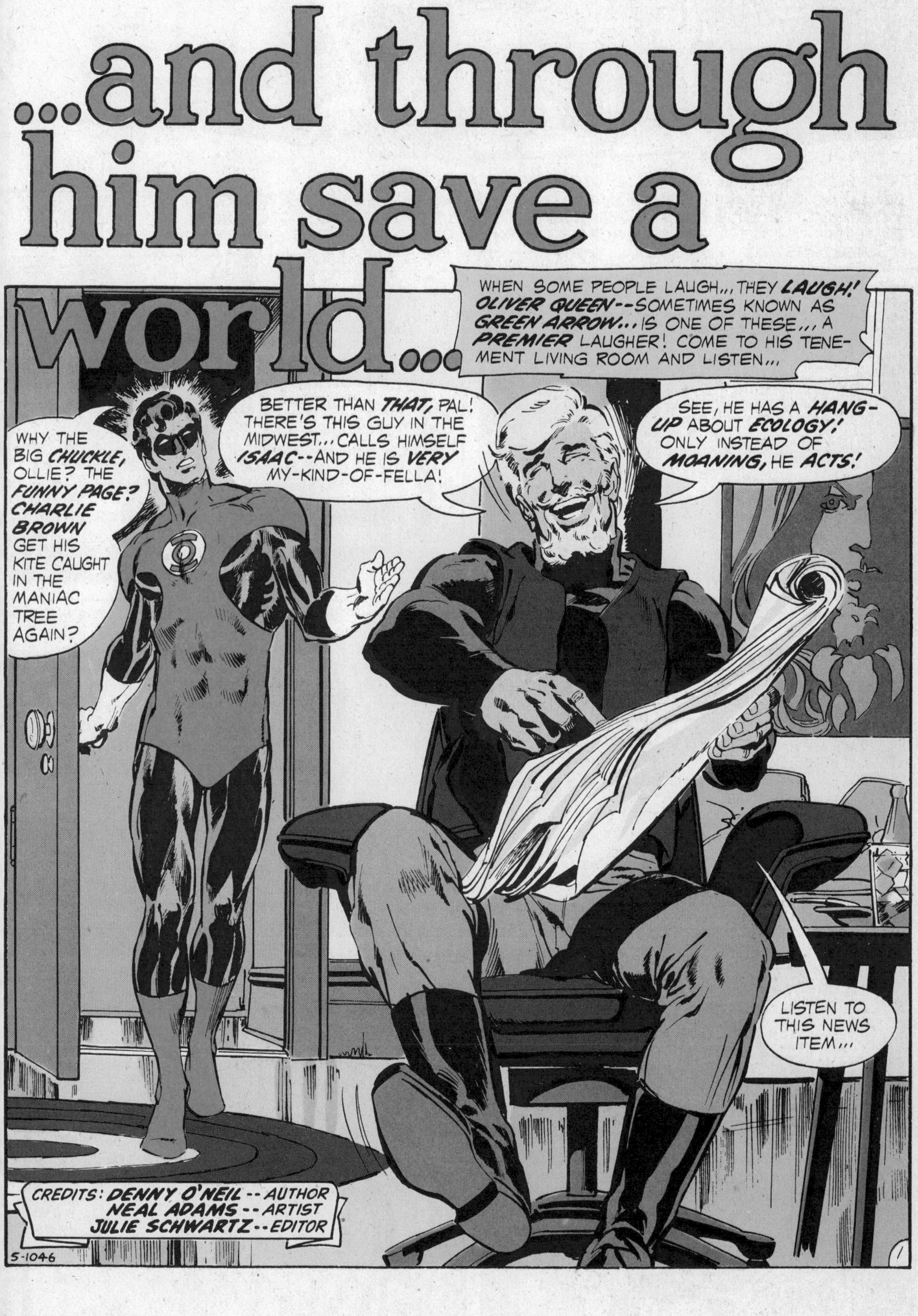
...and through him save a world...
WHEN SOME PEOPLE LAUGH... THEY LAUGH! OLIVER QUEEN--SOMETIMES KNOWN AS GREEN ARROW... IS ONE OF THESE... A PREMIER LAUGHER! COME TO HIS TENEMENT LIVING ROOM AND LISTEN...
WHY THE BIG CHUCKLE, OLLIE? THE FUNNY PAGE? CHARLIE BROWN GET HIS KITE CAUGHT IN THE MANIAC TREE AGAIN?
BETTER THAN THAT, PAL! THERE'S THIS GUY IN THE MIDWEST... CALLS HIMSELF ISAAC--AND HE IS VERY MY-KIND-OF-FELLA!
SEE, HE HAS A HANG-UP ABOUT ECOLOGY! ONLY INSTEAD OF MOANING, HE ACTS!
LISTEN TO THIS NEWS ITEM...
CREDITS: DENNY O'NEIL -- AUTHOR
NEAL ADAMS -- ARTIST
JULIE SCHWARTZ -- EDITOR
S-1046
1

IT'S DATE-LINED *ABRAHAM*...WHICH I GATHER IS A SMALLISH CITY... AND BEGINS...

"THE MYSTERIOUS VANDAL WHO CALLS HIMSELF *ISAAC* STRUCK AGAIN EARLY YESTERDAY MORNING. ACCORDING TO POLICE REPORTS, HE ENTERED THE LOCAL OFFICE OF THE FERRIS AIRCRAFT COMPANY AT APPROXIMATELY 9:15 A.M."

"POLICE SAY HE APPROACHED A RECEPTIONIST, MISS BARBI DOLE, AND REPRESENTED HIMSELF AS A HOUSE-PAINTER HIRED TO REDECORATE THE PREMISES."

"FOR THE NEXT HOUR, HE SPREAD LIQUID FROM TWO BUCKETS HE CARRIED OVER THE WALLS AND RUG OF THE RECEPTION AREA."

"MISS DOLE TOLD REPORTERS THAT HE THANKED HER POLITELY, AND LEFT THE BUILDING AT ABOUT 10:30 P.M."

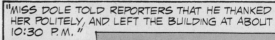

"I BEGAN TO NOTICE A SORT OF FUNNY SMELL, LIKE ROTTEN EGGS," MISS DOLE CONTINUED. MISS DOLE THEN SUMMONED HER SUPERIOR, MR. BARNABY CATTS, THE INSTALLATION'S OFFICE MANAGER."

"MISTER CATTS EXAMINED THE LIQUID THE ALLEGED PAINTER HAD SMEARED ON THE WALLS,"

2

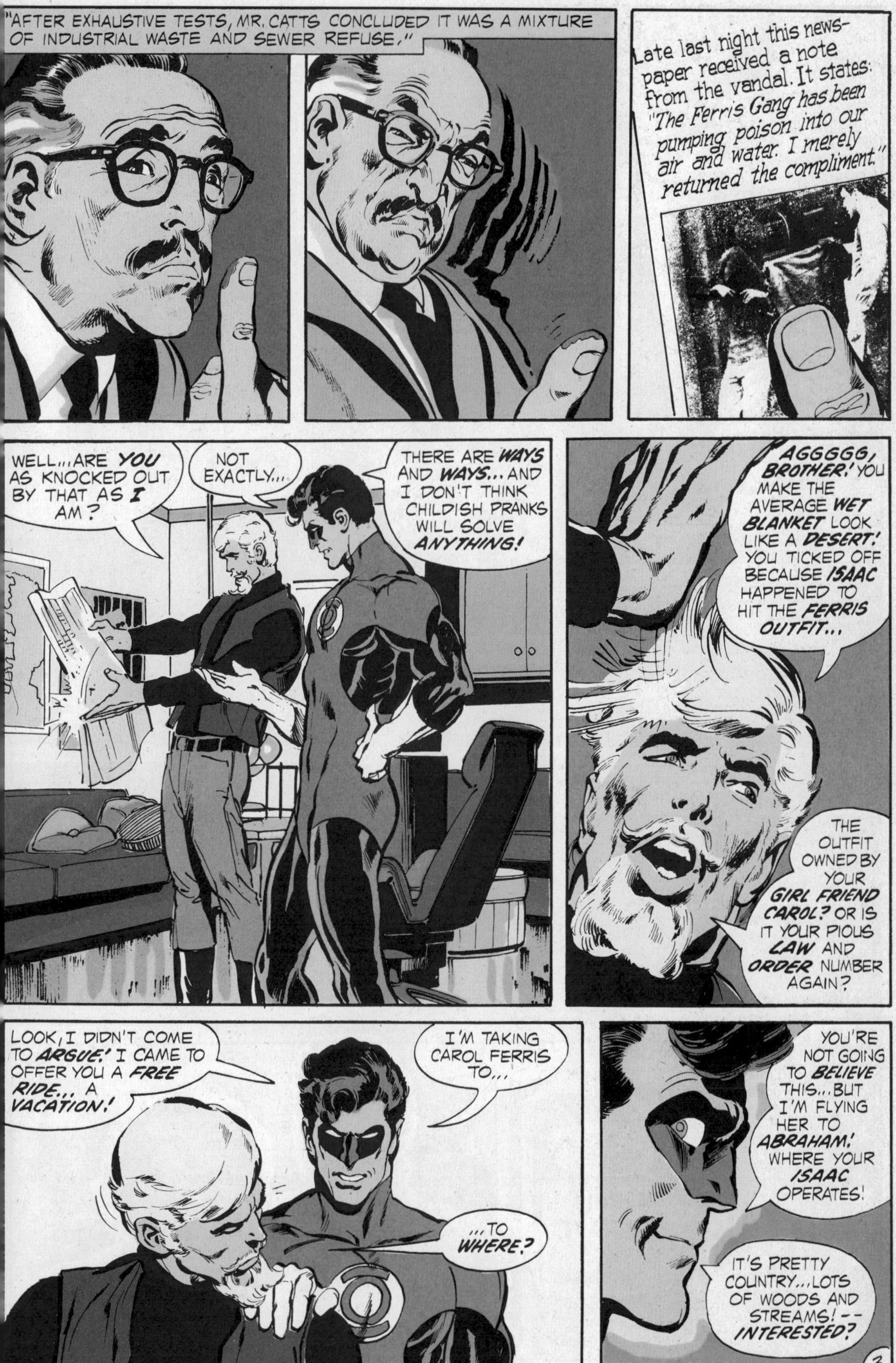
"AFTER EXHAUSTIVE TESTS, MR. CATTS CONCLUDED IT WAS A MIXTURE OF INDUSTRIAL WASTE AND SEWER REFUSE."
Late last night this newspaper received a note from the vandal. It states: "The Ferris Gang has been pumping poison into our air and water. I merely returned the compliment."
WELL... ARE YOU AS KNOCKED OUT BY THAT AS I AM?
NOT EXACTLY...
THERE ARE WAYS AND WAYS... AND I DON'T THINK CHILDISH PRANKS WILL SOLVE ANYTHING!
AGGGGG, BROTHER! YOU MAKE THE AVERAGE WET BLANKET LOOK LIKE A DESERT! YOU TICKED OFF BECAUSE ISAAC HAPPENED TO HIT THE FERRIS OUTFIT...
THE OUTFIT OWNED BY YOUR GIRL FRIEND CAROL? OR IS IT YOUR PIOUS LAW AND ORDER NUMBER AGAIN?
LOOK, I DIDN'T COME TO ARGUE! I CAME TO OFFER YOU A FREE RIDE... A VACATION!
I'M TAKING CAROL FERRIS TO...
...TO WHERE?
YOU'RE NOT GOING TO BELIEVE THIS... BUT I'M FLYING HER TO ABRAHAM! WHERE YOUR ISAAC OPERATES!
IT'S PRETTY COUNTRY... LOTS OF WOODS AND STREAMS! -- INTERESTED?
3

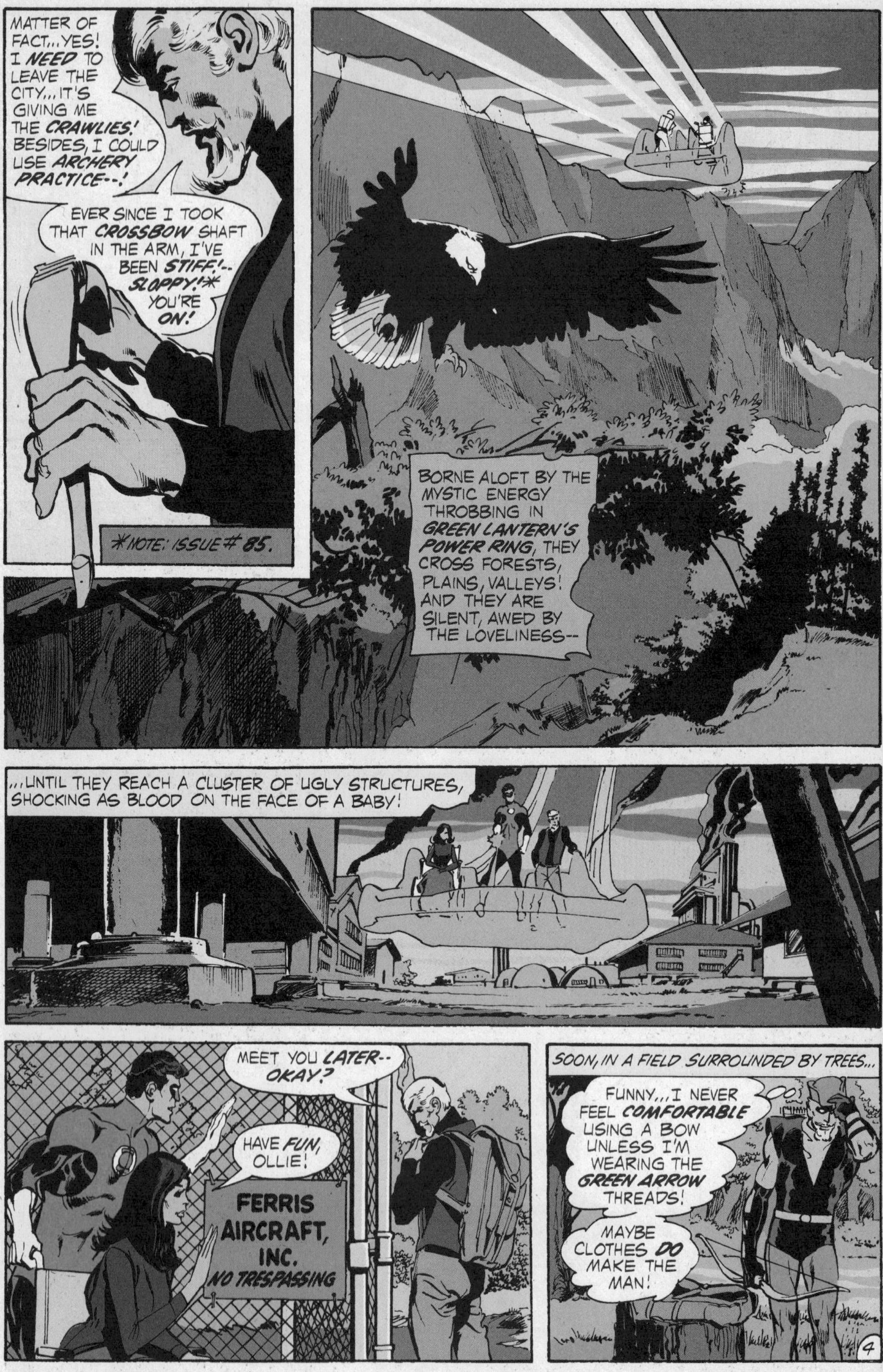
MATTER OF FACT... YES! I NEED TO LEAVE THE CITY... IT'S GIVING ME THE CRAWLIES! BESIDES, I COULD USE ARCHERY PRACTICE--!
EVER SINCE I TOOK THAT CROSSBOW SHAFT IN THE ARM, I'VE BEEN STIFF!.. SLOPPY!* YOU'RE ON!
*NOTE: ISSUE # 85.
BORNE ALOFT BY THE MYSTIC ENERGY THROBBING IN GREEN LANTERN'S POWER RING, THEY CROSS FORESTS, PLAINS, VALLEYS! AND THEY ARE SILENT, AWED BY THE LOVELINESS--
...UNTIL THEY REACH A CLUSTER OF UGLY STRUCTURES, SHOCKING AS BLOOD ON THE FACE OF A BABY!
MEET YOU LATER-- OKAY?
HAVE FUN, OLLIE!
FERRIS AIRCRAFT, INC. NO TRESPASSING
SOON, IN A FIELD SURROUNDED BY TREES...
FUNNY... I NEVER FEEL COMFORTABLE USING A BOW UNLESS I'M WEARING THE GREEN ARROW THREADS!
MAYBE CLOTHES DO MAKE THE MAN!
4

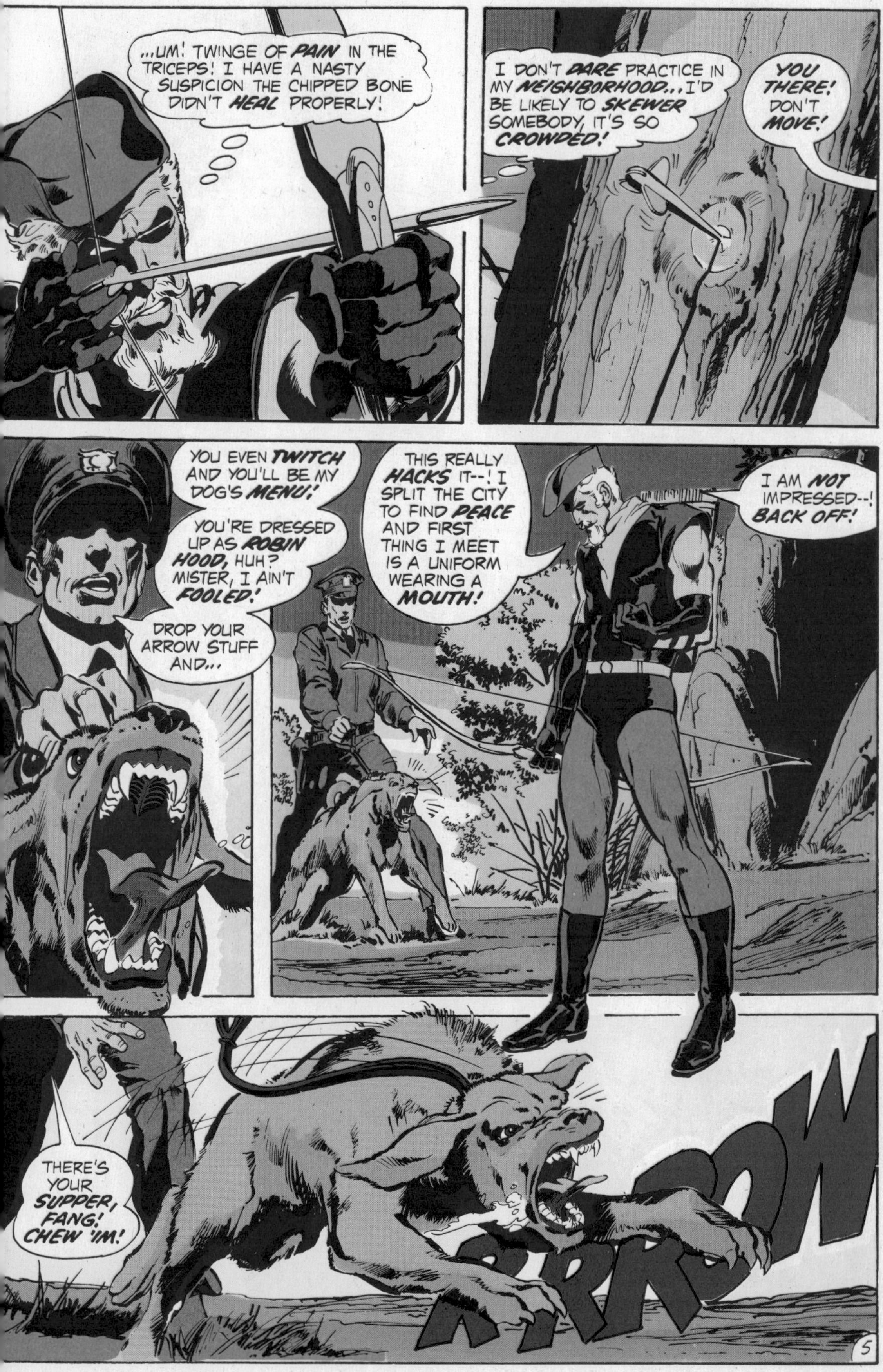
...UM! TWINGE OF PAIN IN THE TRICEPS! I HAVE A NASTY SUSPICION THE CHIPPED BONE DIDN'T HEAL PROPERLY!
I DON'T DARE PRACTICE IN MY NEIGHBORHOOD... I'D BE LIKELY TO SKEWER SOMEBODY, IT'S SO CROWDED!
YOU THERE! DON'T MOVE!
YOU EVEN TWITCH AND YOU'LL BE MY DOG'S MENU!
YOU'RE DRESSED UP AS ROBIN HOOD, HUH? MISTER, I AIN'T FOOLED!
DROP YOUR ARROW STUFF AND...
THIS REALLY HACKS IT--! I SPLIT THE CITY TO FIND PEACE AND FIRST THING I MEET IS A UNIFORM WEARING A MOUTH!
I AM NOT IMPRESSED--! BACK OFF!
THERE'S YOUR SUPPER, FANG! CHEW 'IM!
ARRROOW
5

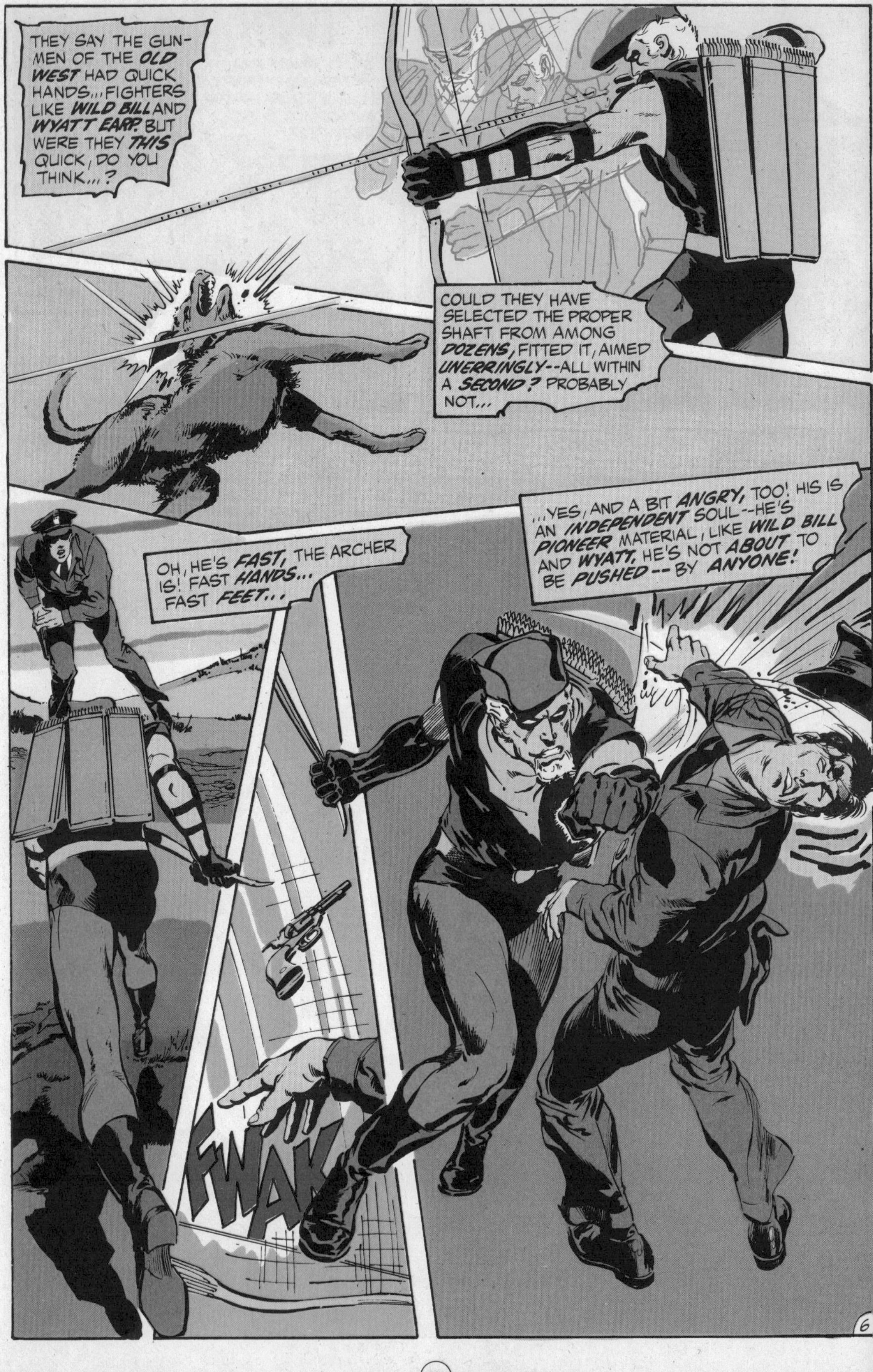

THEY SAY THE GUNMEN OF THE OLD WEST HAD QUICK HANDS... FIGHTERS LIKE WILD BILL AND WYATT EARP. BUT WERE THEY THIS QUICK, DO YOU THINK...?
COULD THEY HAVE SELECTED THE PROPER SHAFT FROM AMONG DOZENS, FITTED IT, AIMED UNERRINGLY--ALL WITHIN A SECOND? PROBABLY NOT...
OH, HE'S FAST, THE ARCHER IS! FAST HANDS... FAST FEET...
...YES, AND A BIT ANGRY, TOO! HIS IS AN INDEPENDENT SOUL--HE'S PIONEER MATERIAL, LIKE WILD BILL AND WYATT. HE'S NOT ABOUT TO BE PUSHED--BY ANYONE!
FWAK
6

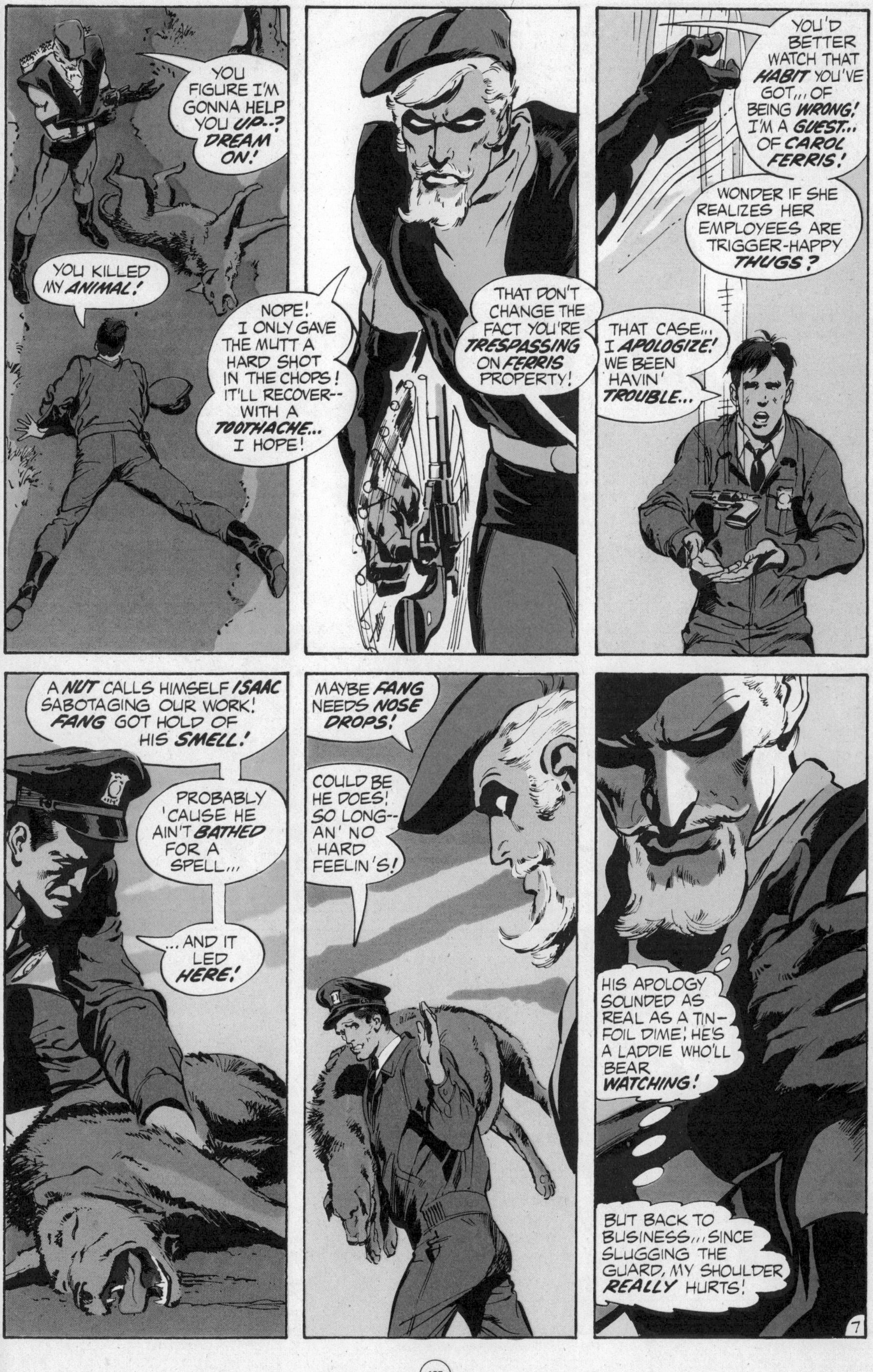
YOU FIGURE I'M GONNA HELP YOU UP..? DREAM ON!
YOU KILLED MY ANIMAL!
NOPE! I ONLY GAVE THE MUTT A HARD SHOT IN THE CHOPS! IT'LL RECOVER-- WITH A TOOTHACHE... I HOPE!
THAT DON'T CHANGE THE FACT YOU'RE TRESPASSING ON FERRIS PROPERTY!
YOU'D BETTER WATCH THAT HABIT YOU'VE GOT... OF BEING WRONG! I'M A GUEST... OF CAROL FERRIS!
WONDER IF SHE REALIZES HER EMPLOYEES ARE TRIGGER-HAPPY THUGS?
THAT CASE... I APOLOGIZE! WE BEEN HAVIN' TROUBLE...
A NUT CALLS HIMSELF ISAAC SABOTAGING OUR WORK! FANG GOT HOLD OF HIS SMELL!
PROBABLY 'CAUSE HE AIN'T BATHED FOR A SPELL...
... AND IT LED HERE!
MAYBE FANG NEEDS NOSE DROPS!
COULD BE HE DOES! SO LONG-- AN' NO HARD FEELIN'S!
HIS APOLOGY SOUNDED AS REAL AS A TIN-FOIL DIME; HE'S A LADDIE WHO'LL BEAR WATCHING!
BUT BACK TO BUSINESS... SINCE SLUGGING THE GUARD, MY SHOULDER REALLY HURTS!
7

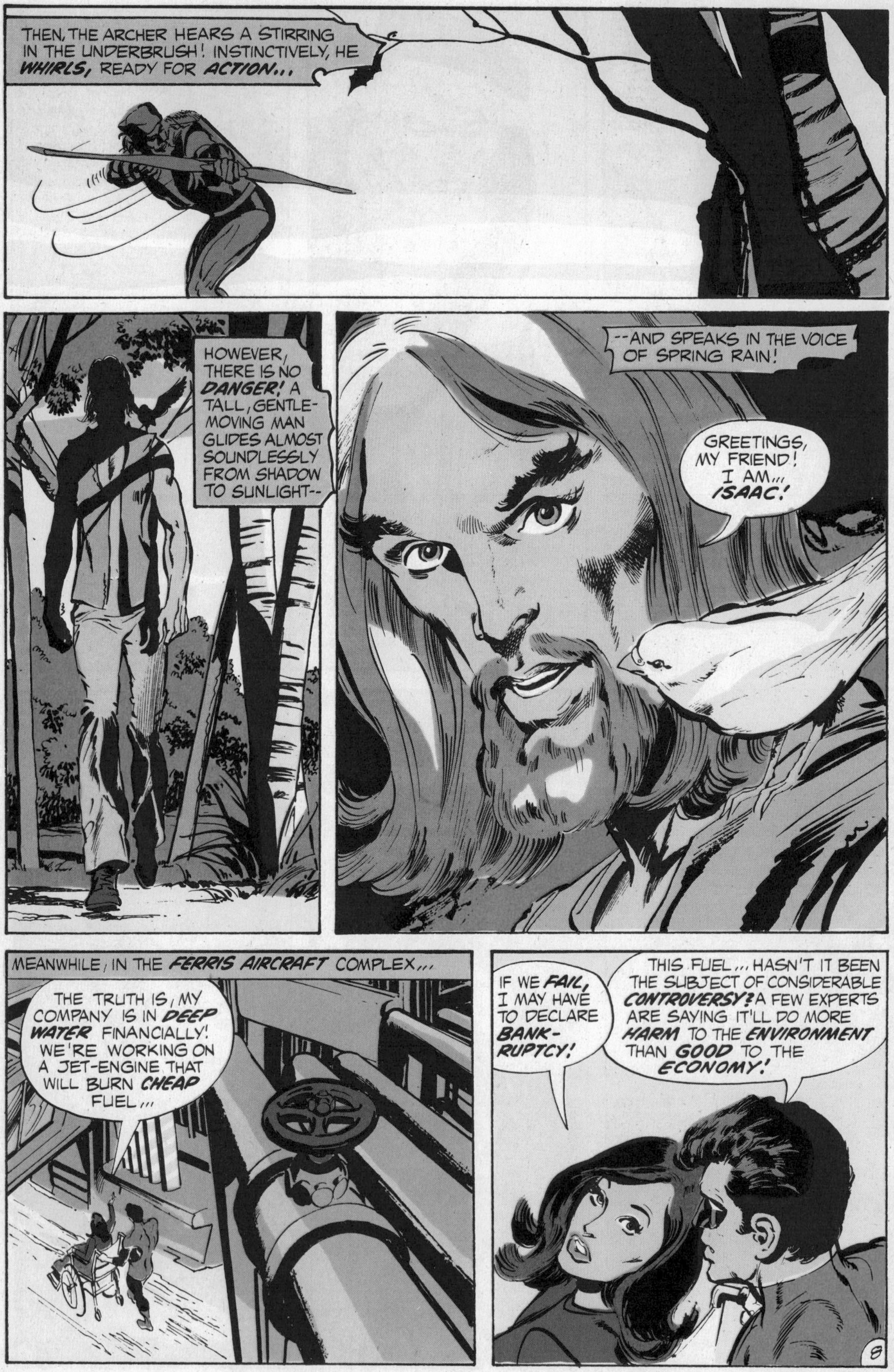

THEN, THE ARCHER HEARS A STIRRING IN THE UNDERBRUSH! INSTINCTIVELY, HE WHIRLS, READY FOR ACTION...
HOWEVER, THERE IS NO DANGER! A TALL, GENTLE-MOVING MAN GLIDES ALMOST SOUNDLESSLY FROM SHADOW TO SUNLIGHT--
--AND SPEAKS IN THE VOICE OF SPRING RAIN!
GREETINGS, MY FRIEND! I AM... ISAAC!
MEANWHILE, IN THE FERRIS AIRCRAFT COMPLEX...
THE TRUTH IS, MY COMPANY IS IN DEEP WATER FINANCIALLY! WE'RE WORKING ON A JET-ENGINE THAT WILL BURN CHEAP FUEL...
IF WE FAIL, I MAY HAVE TO DECLARE BANK-RUPTCY!
THIS FUEL... HASN'T IT BEEN THE SUBJECT OF CONSIDERABLE CONTROVERSY? A FEW EXPERTS ARE SAYING IT'LL DO MORE HARM TO THE ENVIRONMENT THAN GOOD TO THE ECONOMY!
8

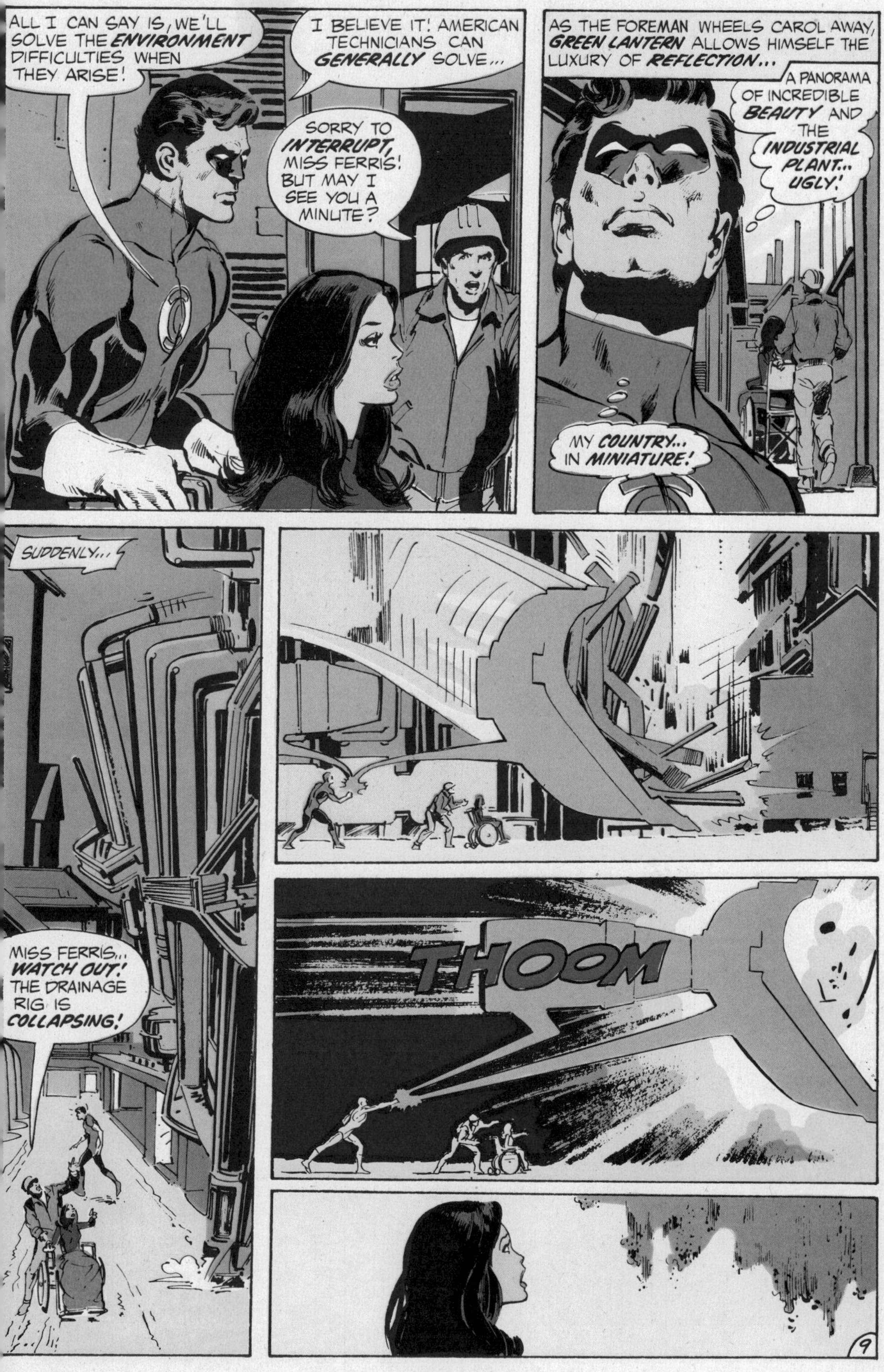
ALL I CAN SAY IS, WE'LL SOLVE THE ENVIRONMENT DIFFICULTIES WHEN THEY ARISE!
I BELIEVE IT! AMERICAN TECHNICIANS CAN GENERALLY SOLVE...
SORRY TO INTERRUPT, MISS FERRIS! BUT MAY I SEE YOU A MINUTE?
AS THE FOREMAN WHEELS CAROL AWAY, GREEN LANTERN ALLOWS HIMSELF THE LUXURY OF REFLECTION...
A PANORAMA OF INCREDIBLE BEAUTY AND THE INDUSTRIAL PLANT... UGLY!
MY COUNTRY... IN MINIATURE!
SUDDENLY...
MISS FERRIS... WATCH OUT! THE DRAINAGE RIG IS COLLAPSING!
THOOM
9

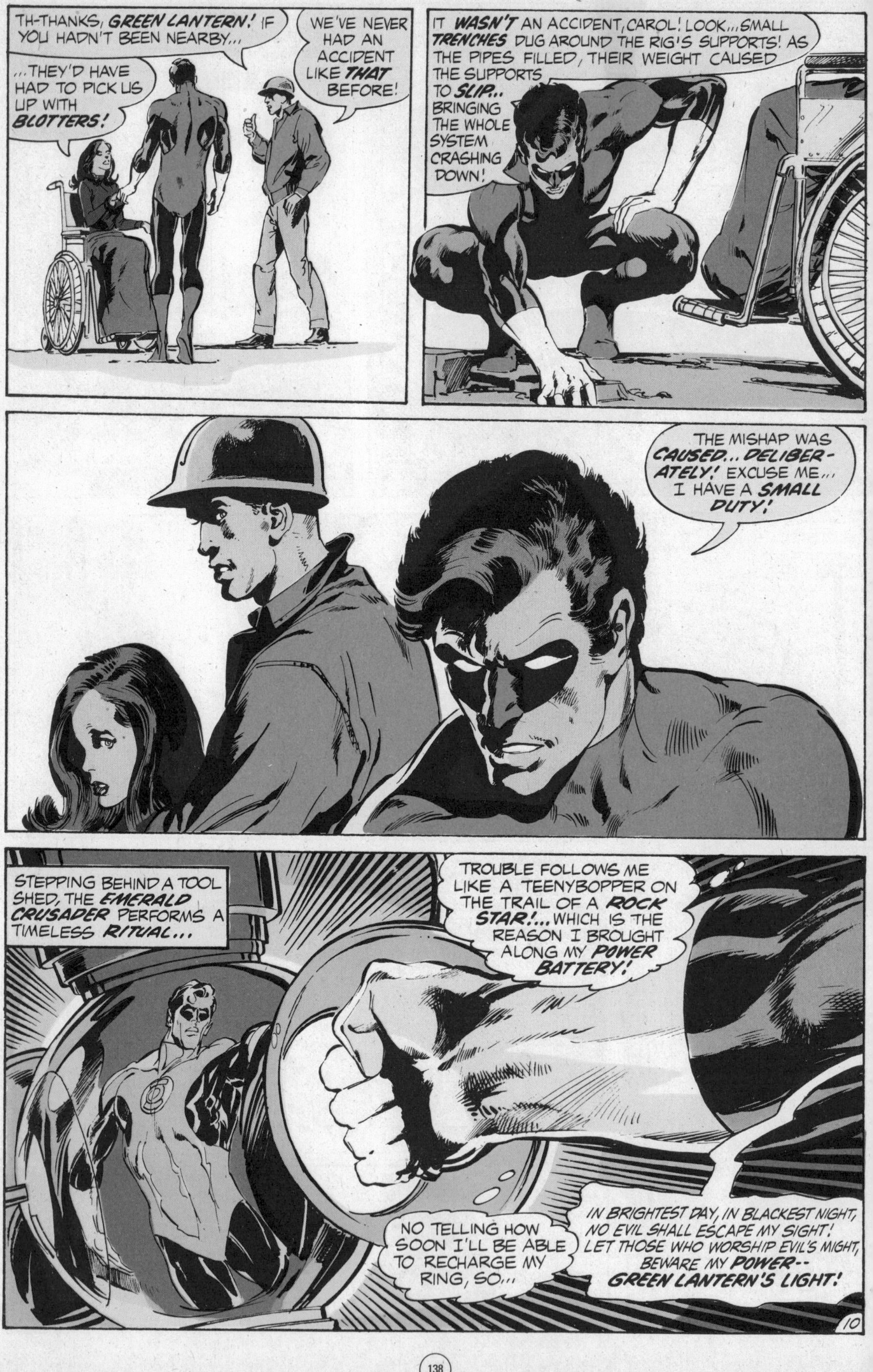
TH-THANKS, GREEN LANTERN! IF YOU HADN'T BEEN NEARBY...
...THEY'D HAVE HAD TO PICK US UP WITH BLOTTERS!
WE'VE NEVER HAD AN ACCIDENT LIKE THAT BEFORE!
IT WASN'T AN ACCIDENT, CAROL! LOOK... SMALL TRENCHES DUG AROUND THE RIG'S SUPPORTS! AS THE PIPES FILLED, THEIR WEIGHT CAUSED THE SUPPORTS TO SLIP.. BRINGING THE WHOLE SYSTEM CRASHING DOWN!
THE MISHAP WAS CAUSED... DELIBERATELY! EXCUSE ME... I HAVE A SMALL DUTY!
STEPPING BEHIND A TOOL SHED, THE EMERALD CRUSADER PERFORMS A TIMELESS RITUAL...
TROUBLE FOLLOWS ME LIKE A TEENYBOPPER ON THE TRAIL OF A ROCK STAR!... WHICH IS THE REASON I BROUGHT ALONG MY POWER BATTERY!
NO TELLING HOW SOON I'LL BE ABLE TO RECHARGE MY RING, SO...
IN BRIGHTEST DAY, IN BLACKEST NIGHT, NO EVIL SHALL ESCAPE MY SIGHT! LET THOSE WHO WORSHIP EVIL'S MIGHT, BEWARE MY POWER-- GREEN LANTERN'S LIGHT!
10

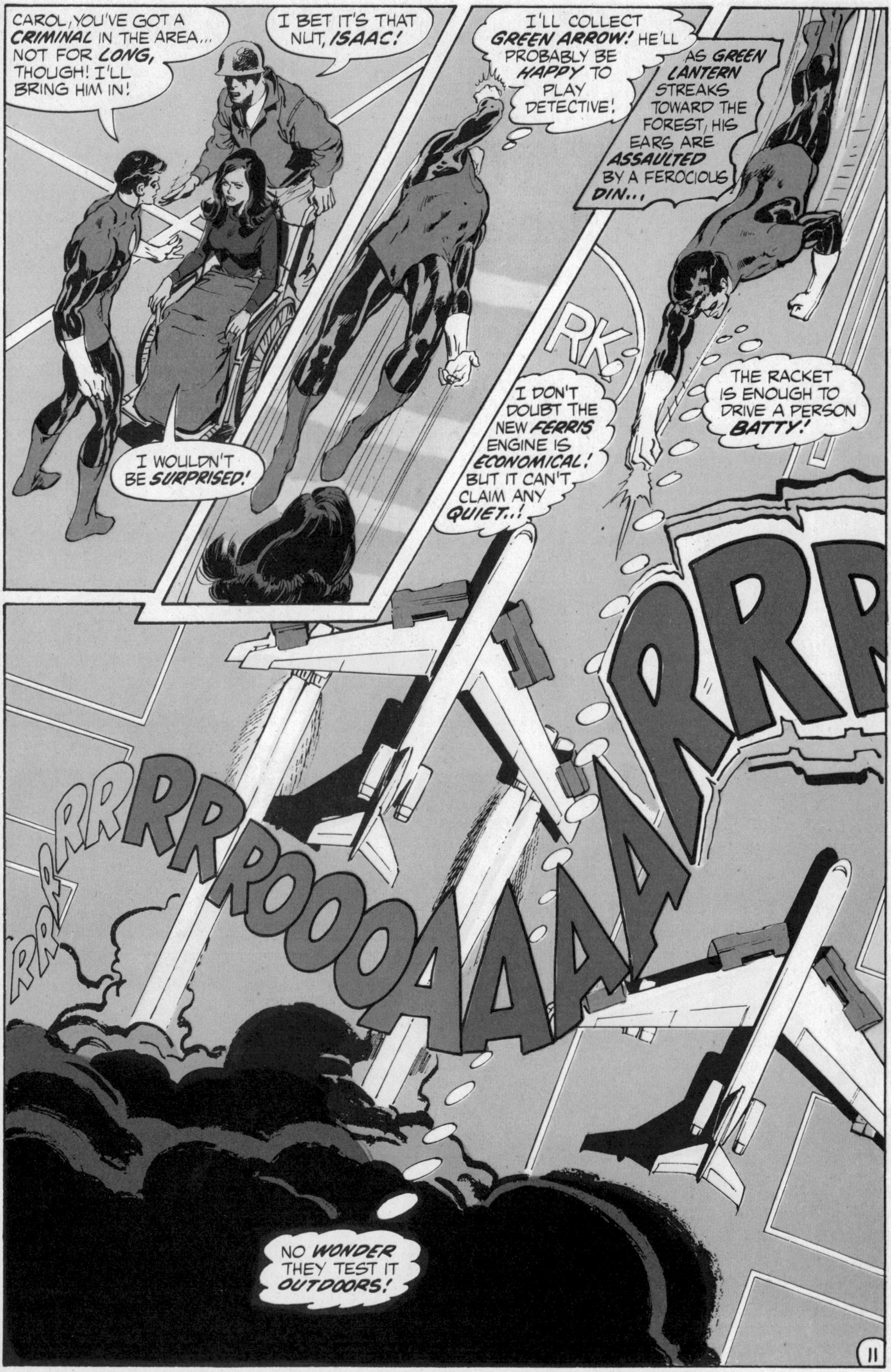
CAROL, YOU'VE GOT A CRIMINAL IN THE AREA... NOT FOR LONG, THOUGH! I'LL BRING HIM IN!
I BET IT'S THAT NUT, ISAAC!
I WOULDN'T BE SURPRISED!
I'LL COLLECT GREEN ARROW! HE'LL PROBABLY BE HAPPY TO PLAY DETECTIVE!
AS GREEN LANTERN STREAKS TOWARD THE FOREST, HIS EARS ARE ASSAULTED BY A FEROCIOUS DIN...
RK
I DON'T DOUBT THE NEW FERRIS ENGINE IS ECONOMICAL! BUT IT CAN'T CLAIM ANY QUIET..!
THE RACKET IS ENOUGH TO DRIVE A PERSON BATTY!
RRRRRRROOOOAAAAARRR
NO WONDER THEY TEST IT OUTDOORS!
11

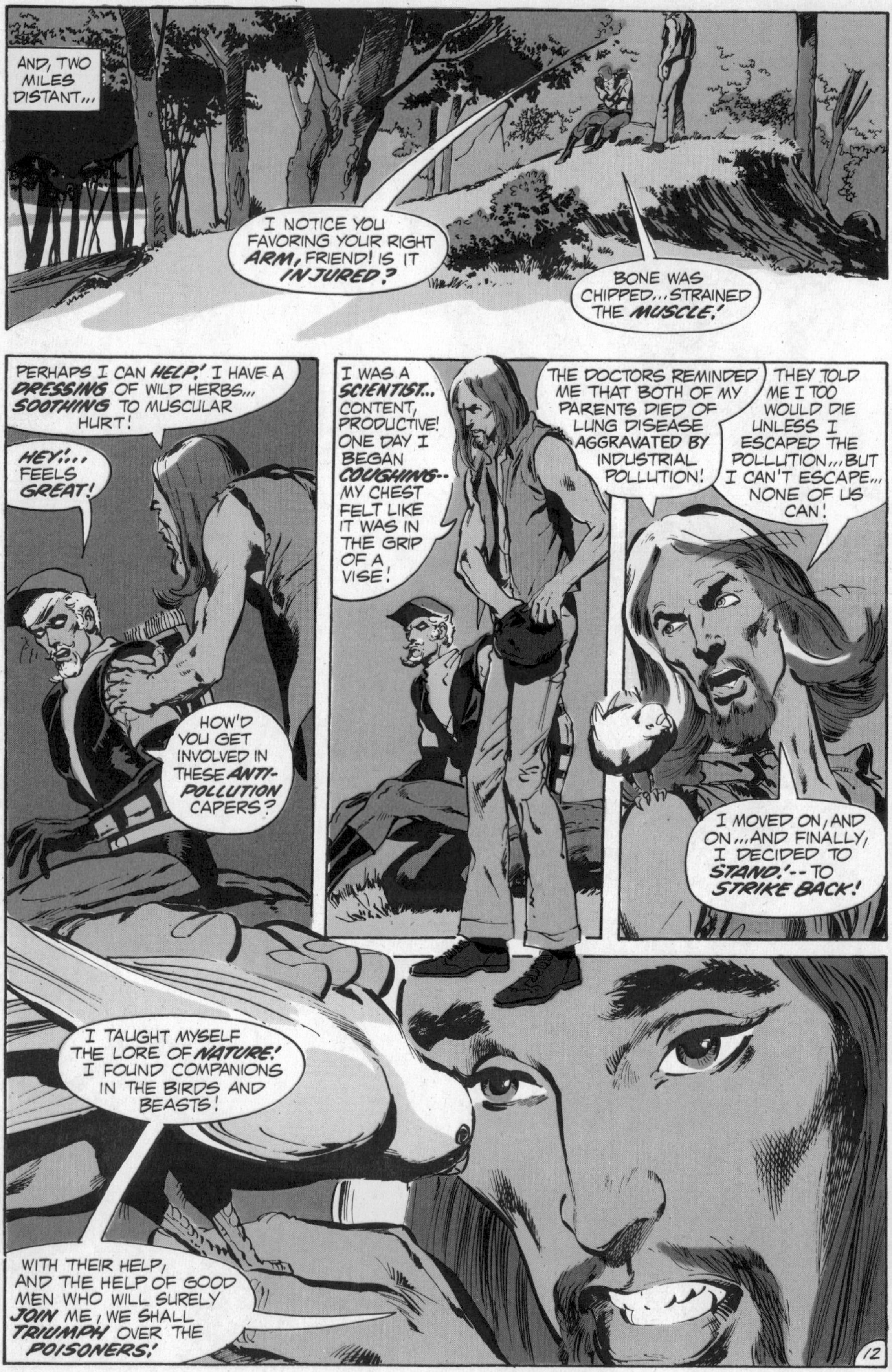

AND, TWO MILES DISTANT...
I NOTICE YOU FAVORING YOUR RIGHT ARM, FRIEND! IS IT INJURED?
BONE WAS CHIPPED... STRAINED THE MUSCLE!
PERHAPS I CAN HELP! I HAVE A DRESSING OF WILD HERBS... SOOTHING TO MUSCULAR HURT!
HEY!... FEELS GREAT!
HOW'D YOU GET INVOLVED IN THESE ANTI-POLLUTION CAPERS?
I WAS A SCIENTIST... CONTENT, PRODUCTIVE! ONE DAY I BEGAN COUGHING-- MY CHEST FELT LIKE IT WAS IN THE GRIP OF A VISE!
THE DOCTORS REMINDED ME THAT BOTH OF MY PARENTS DIED OF LUNG DISEASE AGGRAVATED BY INDUSTRIAL POLLUTION!
THEY TOLD ME I TOO WOULD DIE UNLESS I ESCAPED THE POLLUTION... BUT I CAN'T ESCAPE... NONE OF US CAN!
I MOVED ON, AND ON... AND FINALLY, I DECIDED TO STAND!-- TO STRIKE BACK!
I TAUGHT MYSELF THE LORE OF NATURE! I FOUND COMPANIONS IN THE BIRDS AND BEASTS!
WITH THEIR HELP, AND THE HELP OF GOOD MEN WHO WILL SURELY JOIN ME, WE SHALL TRIUMPH OVER THE POISONERS!
12

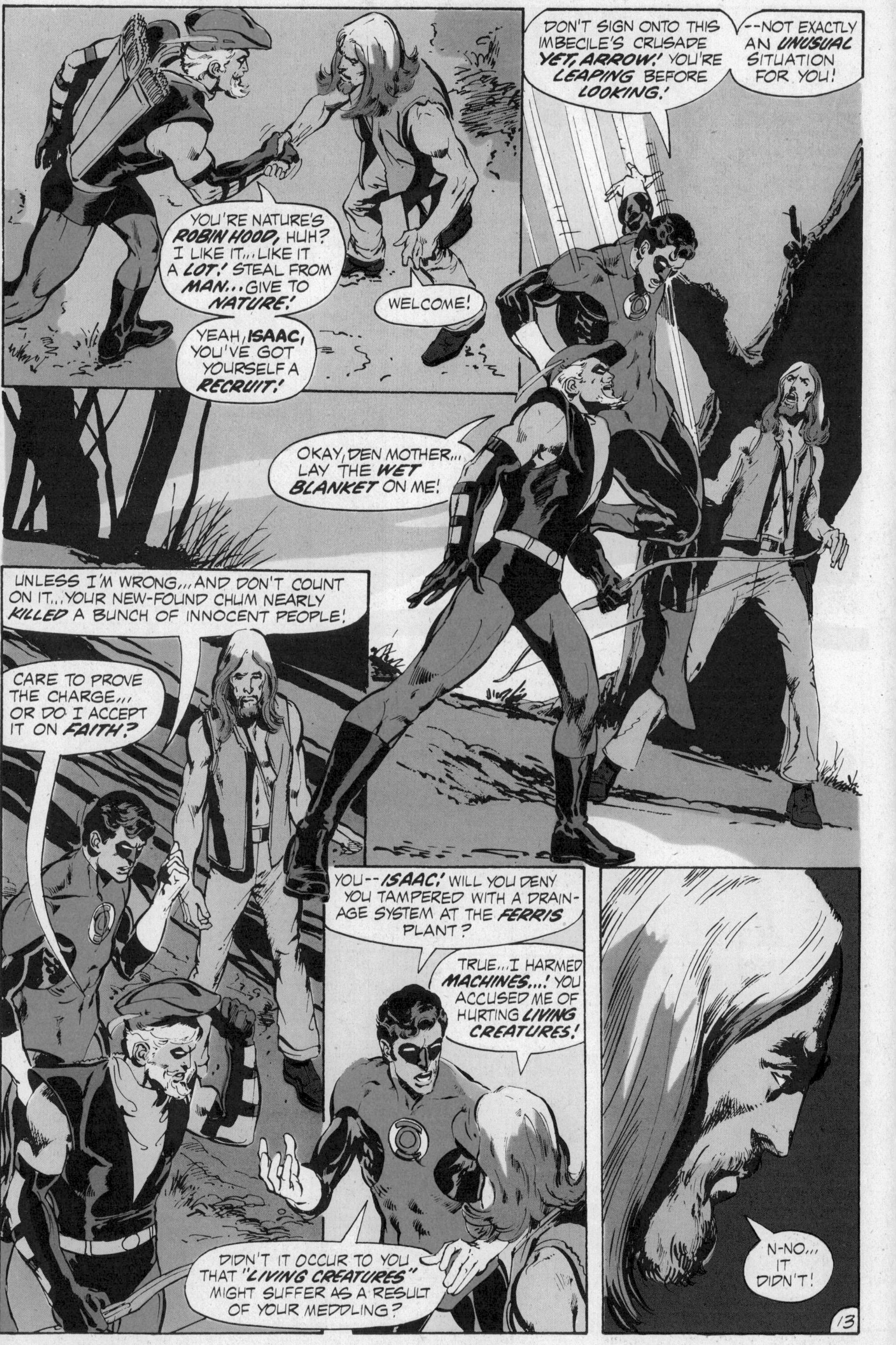
DON'T SIGN ONTO THIS IMBECILE'S CRUSADE YET, ARROW! YOU'RE LEAPING BEFORE LOOKING!
--NOT EXACTLY AN UNUSUAL SITUATION FOR YOU!
YOU'RE NATURE'S ROBIN HOOD, HUH? I LIKE IT... LIKE IT A LOT! STEAL FROM MAN... GIVE TO NATURE!
WELCOME!
YEAH, ISAAC, YOU'VE GOT YOURSELF A RECRUIT!
OKAY, DEN MOTHER... LAY THE WET BLANKET ON ME!
UNLESS I'M WRONG... AND DON'T COUNT ON IT... YOUR NEW-FOUND CHUM NEARLY KILLED A BUNCH OF INNOCENT PEOPLE!
CARE TO PROVE THE CHARGE... OR DO I ACCEPT IT ON FAITH?
YOU--ISAAC! WILL YOU DENY YOU TAMPERED WITH A DRAIN-AGE SYSTEM AT THE FERRIS PLANT?
TRUE... I HARMED MACHINES...! YOU ACCUSED ME OF HURTING LIVING CREATURES!
DIDN'T IT OCCUR TO YOU THAT "LIVING CREATURES" MIGHT SUFFER AS A RESULT OF YOUR MEDDLING?
N-NO... IT DIDN'T!
13

LANTERN... YOU'RE *DENSE!* CAN'T YOU UNDERSTAND *ISAAC'S* OBEYING A *HIGHER LAW* THAN ANY OF *MAN'S?*

A FEW OF *FERRIS'S* LACKEYS ARE *INCONVENIENCED!* IS THAT WORSE THAN THE *RUIN* OF A PLANET... *OUR WORLD?*

REASONING WITH *GREEN ARROW* IS AS HOPELESS AS REASONING WITH A *BROKEN RECORD!*

ISAAC...YOU BROKE A *LAW...* AND YOU'LL BE *TRIED...* IN COURT!

NO *CHANCE,* RING-SLINGER...

ISAAC...HOLD YOUR *BREATH!*

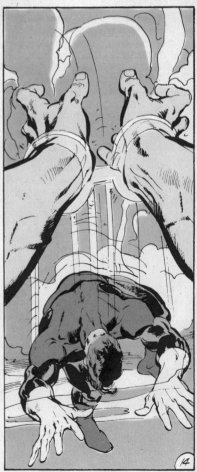

A THICK VAPOR BILLOWS FROM THE SPEEDING SHAFT--THICK AND CHOKING...

14

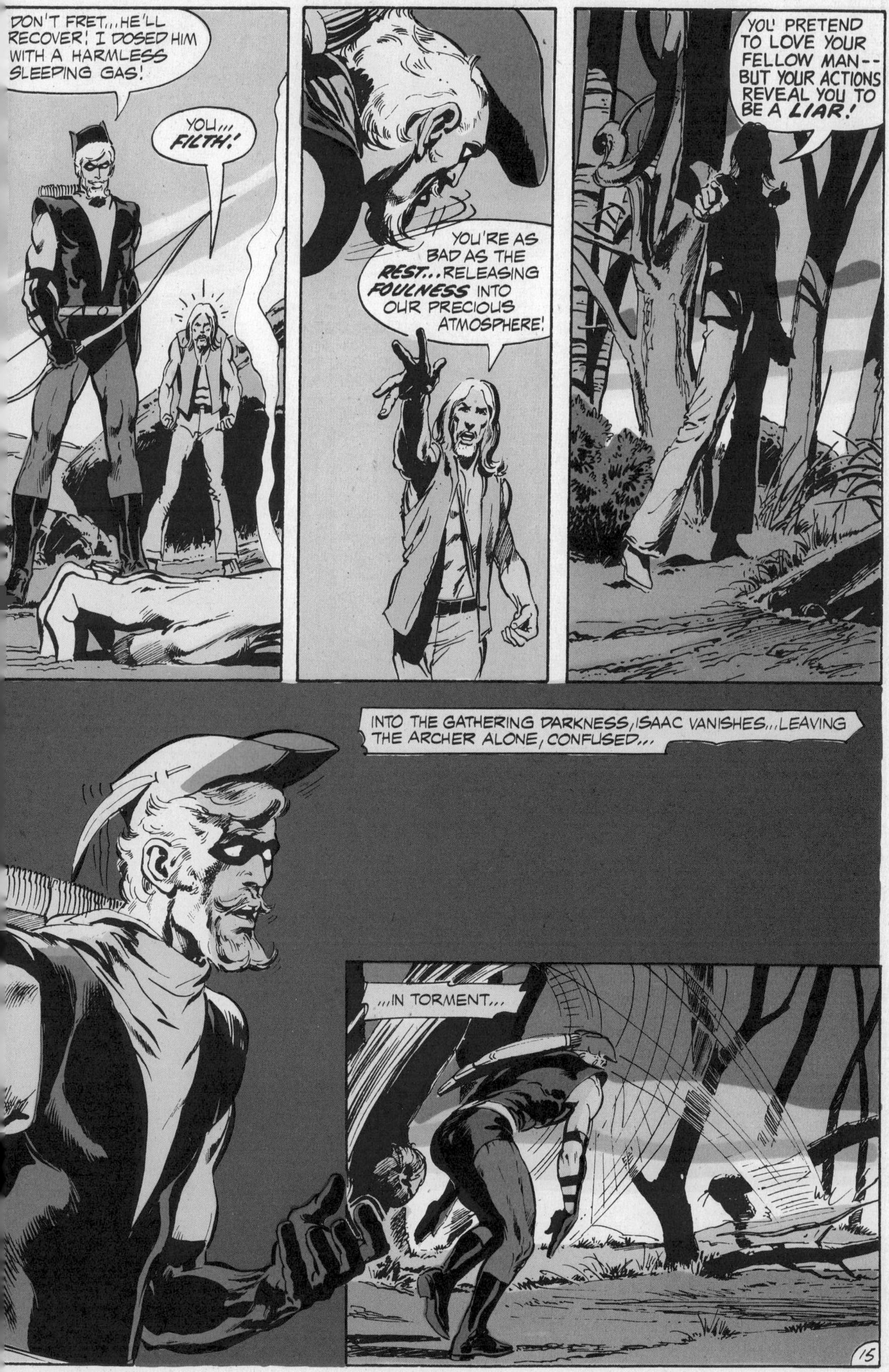
DON'T FRET... HE'LL RECOVER! I DOSED HIM WITH A HARMLESS SLEEPING GAS!
YOU... FILTH!
YOU'RE AS BAD AS THE REST... RELEASING FOULNESS INTO OUR PRECIOUS ATMOSPHERE!
YOU! PRETEND TO LOVE YOUR FELLOW MAN-- BUT YOUR ACTIONS REVEAL YOU TO BE A LIAR!
INTO THE GATHERING DARKNESS, ISAAC VANISHES... LEAVING THE ARCHER ALONE, CONFUSED...
...IN TORMENT...
15

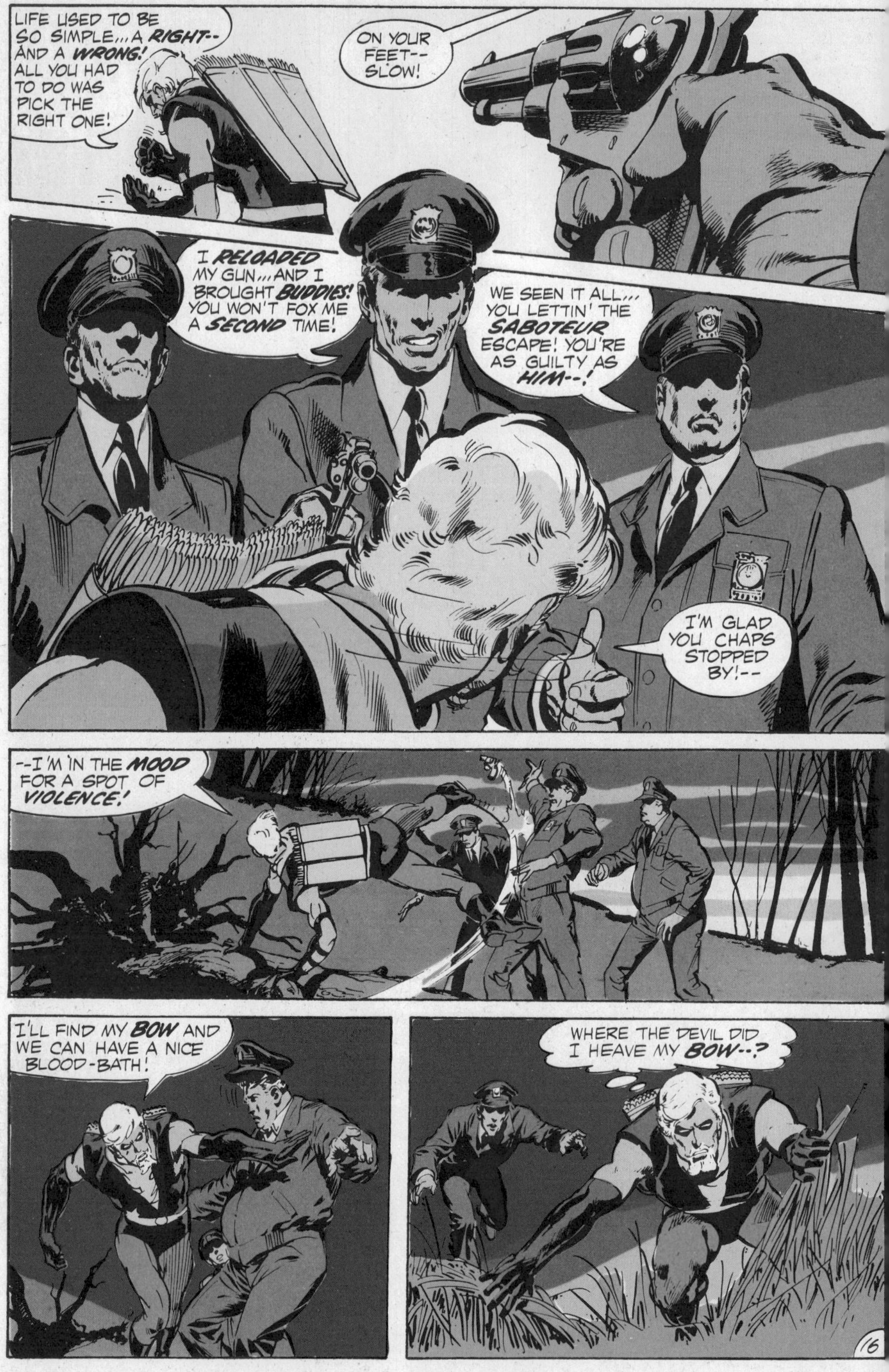
LIFE USED TO BE SO SIMPLE... A RIGHT-- AND A WRONG! ALL YOU HAD TO DO WAS PICK THE RIGHT ONE!
ON YOUR FEET-- SLOW!
I RELOADED MY GUN... AND I BROUGHT BUDDIES! YOU WON'T FOX ME A SECOND TIME!
WE SEEN IT ALL... YOU LETTIN' THE SABOTEUR ESCAPE! YOU'RE AS GUILTY AS HIM--!
I'M GLAD YOU CHAPS STOPPED BY!--
--I'M IN THE MOOD FOR A SPOT OF VIOLENCE!
I'LL FIND MY BOW AND WE CAN HAVE A NICE BLOOD-BATH!
WHERE THE DEVIL DID I HEAVE MY BOW--?
16

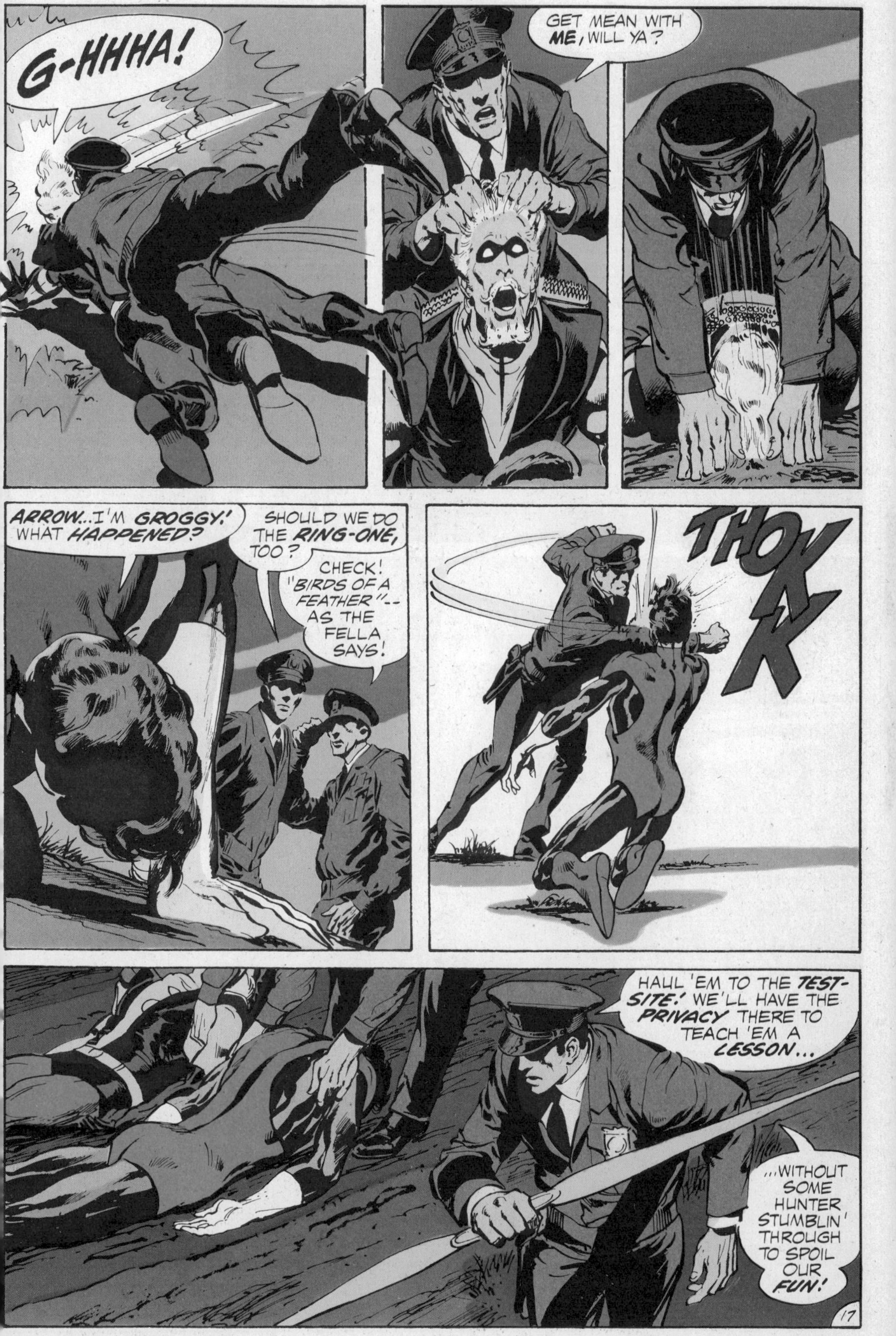
G-HHHA!
GET MEAN WITH ME, WILL YA?
ARROW...I'M GROGGY! WHAT HAPPENED?
SHOULD WE DO THE RING-ONE, TOO?
CHECK! "BIRDS OF A FEATHER"-- AS THE FELLA SAYS!
THOKK
HAUL 'EM TO THE TEST-SITE! WE'LL HAVE THE PRIVACY THERE TO TEACH 'EM A LESSON...
...WITHOUT SOME HUNTER STUMBLIN' THROUGH TO SPOIL OUR FUN!
17

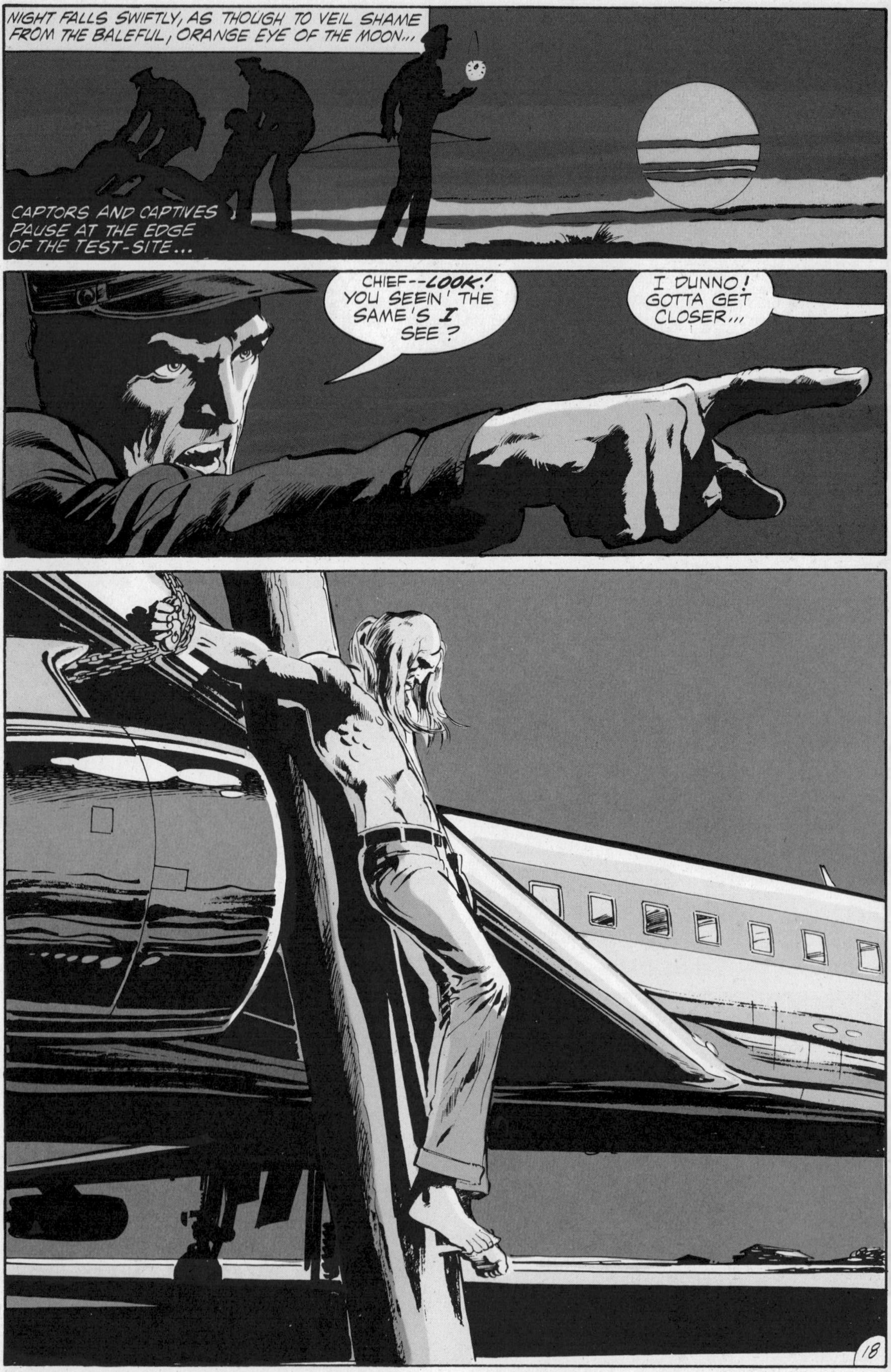
NIGHT FALLS SWIFTLY, AS THOUGH TO VEIL SHAME FROM THE BALEFUL, ORANGE EYE OF THE MOON...
CAPTORS AND CAPTIVES PAUSE AT THE EDGE OF THE TEST-SITE...
CHIEF--LOOK! YOU SEEIN' THE SAME'S I SEE?
I DUNNO! GOTTA GET CLOSER...
18

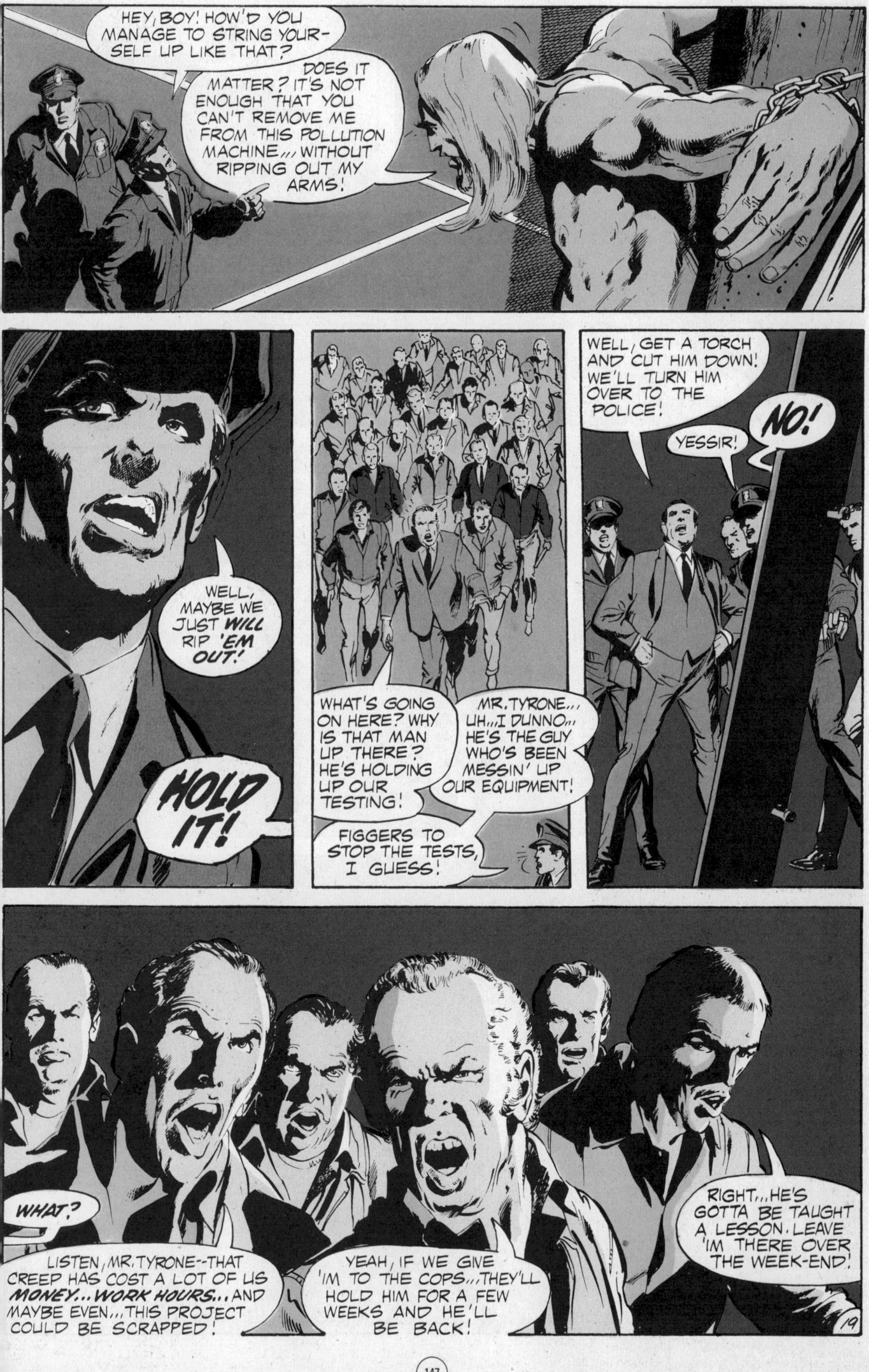
HEY, BOY! HOW'D YOU MANAGE TO STRING YOURSELF UP LIKE THAT?
DOES IT MATTER? IT'S NOT ENOUGH THAT YOU CAN'T REMOVE ME FROM THIS POLLUTION MACHINE... WITHOUT RIPPING OUT MY ARMS!
WELL, MAYBE WE JUST WILL RIP 'EM OUT!
HOLD IT!
WHAT'S GOING ON HERE? WHY IS THAT MAN UP THERE? HE'S HOLDING UP OUR TESTING!
MR. TYRONE... UH... I DUNNO... HE'S THE GUY WHO'S BEEN MESSIN' UP OUR EQUIPMENT!
FIGGERS TO STOP THE TESTS, I GUESS!
WELL, GET A TORCH AND CUT HIM DOWN! WE'LL TURN HIM OVER TO THE POLICE!
YESSIR!
NO!
WHAT?
LISTEN, MR. TYRONE--THAT CREEP HAS COST A LOT OF US MONEY... WORK HOURS... AND MAYBE EVEN... THIS PROJECT COULD BE SCRAPPED!
YEAH, IF WE GIVE 'IM TO THE COPS... THEY'LL HOLD HIM FOR A FEW WEEKS AND HE'LL BE BACK!
RIGHT... HE'S GOTTA BE TAUGHT A LESSON. LEAVE 'IM THERE OVER THE WEEK-END!
19

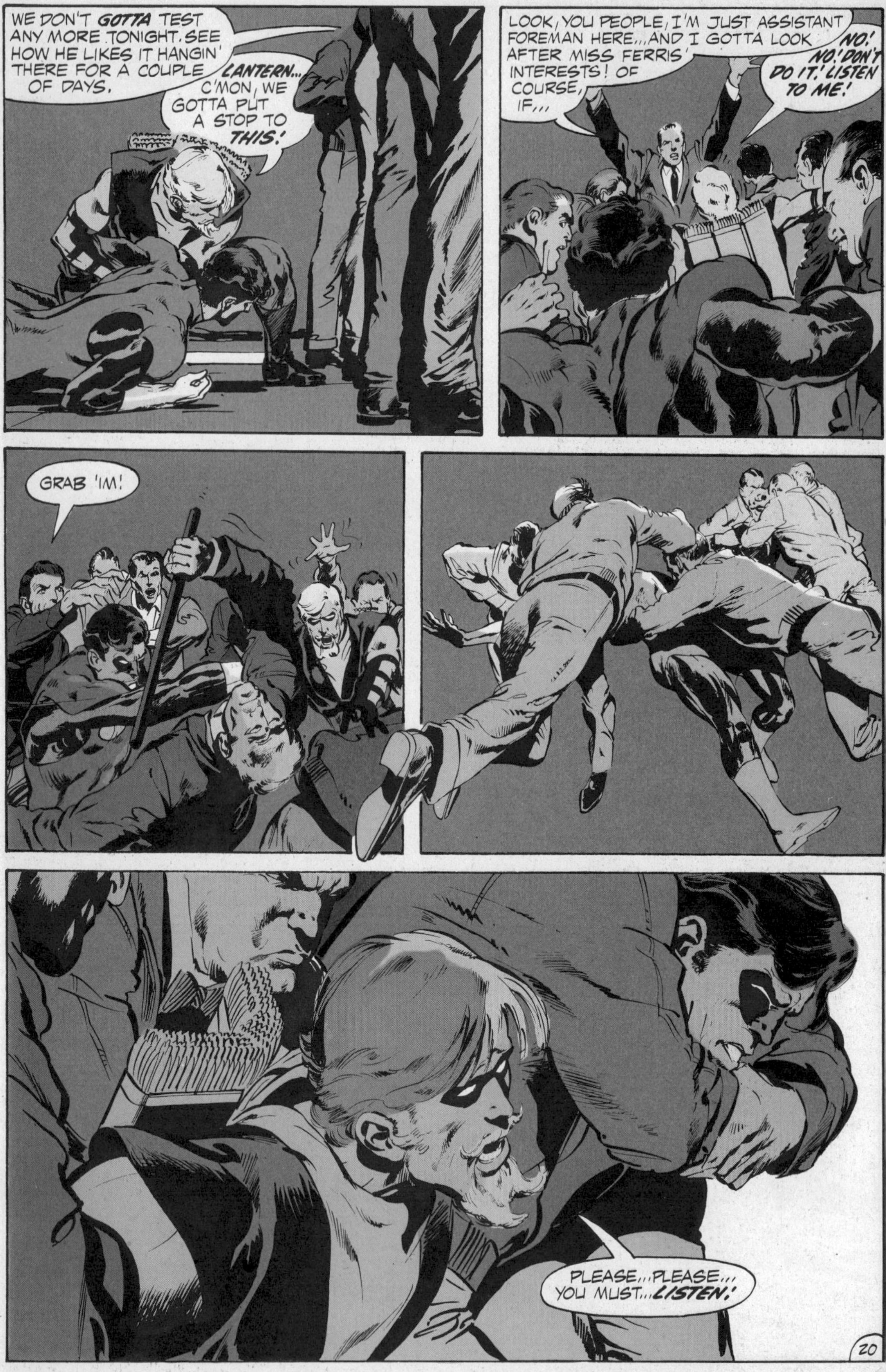
WE DON'T GOTTA TEST ANY MORE TONIGHT. SEE HOW HE LIKES IT HANGIN' THERE FOR A COUPLE OF DAYS.
LANTERN... C'MON, WE GOTTA PUT A STOP TO THIS!
LOOK, YOU PEOPLE, I'M JUST ASSISTANT FOREMAN HERE... AND I GOTTA LOOK AFTER MISS FERRIS' INTERESTS! OF COURSE, IF...
NO! NO! DON'T DO IT! LISTEN TO ME!
GRAB 'IM!
PLEASE... PLEASE... YOU MUST... LISTEN!
20

HE'S JUST TRYING TO HELP US ALL, DON'T YOU SEE? WHAT'S HAPPENING HERE IS **WRONG!**

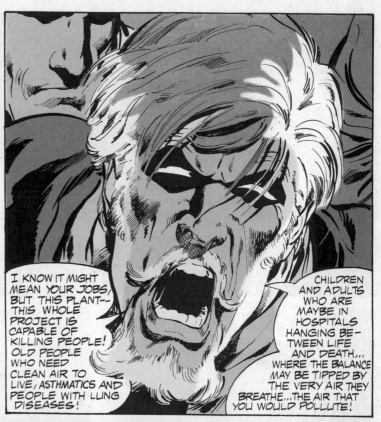

I KNOW IT MIGHT MEAN YOUR JOBS, BUT THIS PLANT-- THIS WHOLE PROJECT IS CAPABLE OF KILLING PEOPLE! OLD PEOPLE WHO NEED CLEAN AIR TO LIVE, ASTHMATICS AND PEOPLE WITH LUNG DISEASES!

CHILDREN AND ADULTS WHO ARE MAYBE IN HOSPITALS HANGING BE- TWEEN LIFE AND DEATH... WHERE THE BALANCE MAY BE TIPPED BY THE VERY AIR THEY BREATHE...THE AIR THAT YOU WOULD POLLUTE!

TAKE HIM DOWN, TALK TO HIM! MAYBE YOU CAN WORK OUT A *COMPROMISE...* A DEAL...

NEVER! NO DEALS!

HOW CAN I *COMPROMISE* WITH DEATH? SHALL WE HAVE *HALF- DEATH*--SHALL WE HAVE *HALF-DIS- EASE*--SHALL WE POLLUTE *HALF* THE POPULATION--SHALL WE HAVE *ONE* CHILD DIE INSTEAD OF *TWO?* NO, GREEN ARROW... YOU TOO ARE *GUILTY*...

ME? WHAT ABOUT *YOU?* YOU ALMOST KILLED A COUPLE PEOPLE TODAY BECAUSE OF YOUR ATTITUDE! DID YOU TELL THESE PEOPLE *THAT*... YOU POMPOUS...

ARROW!

21

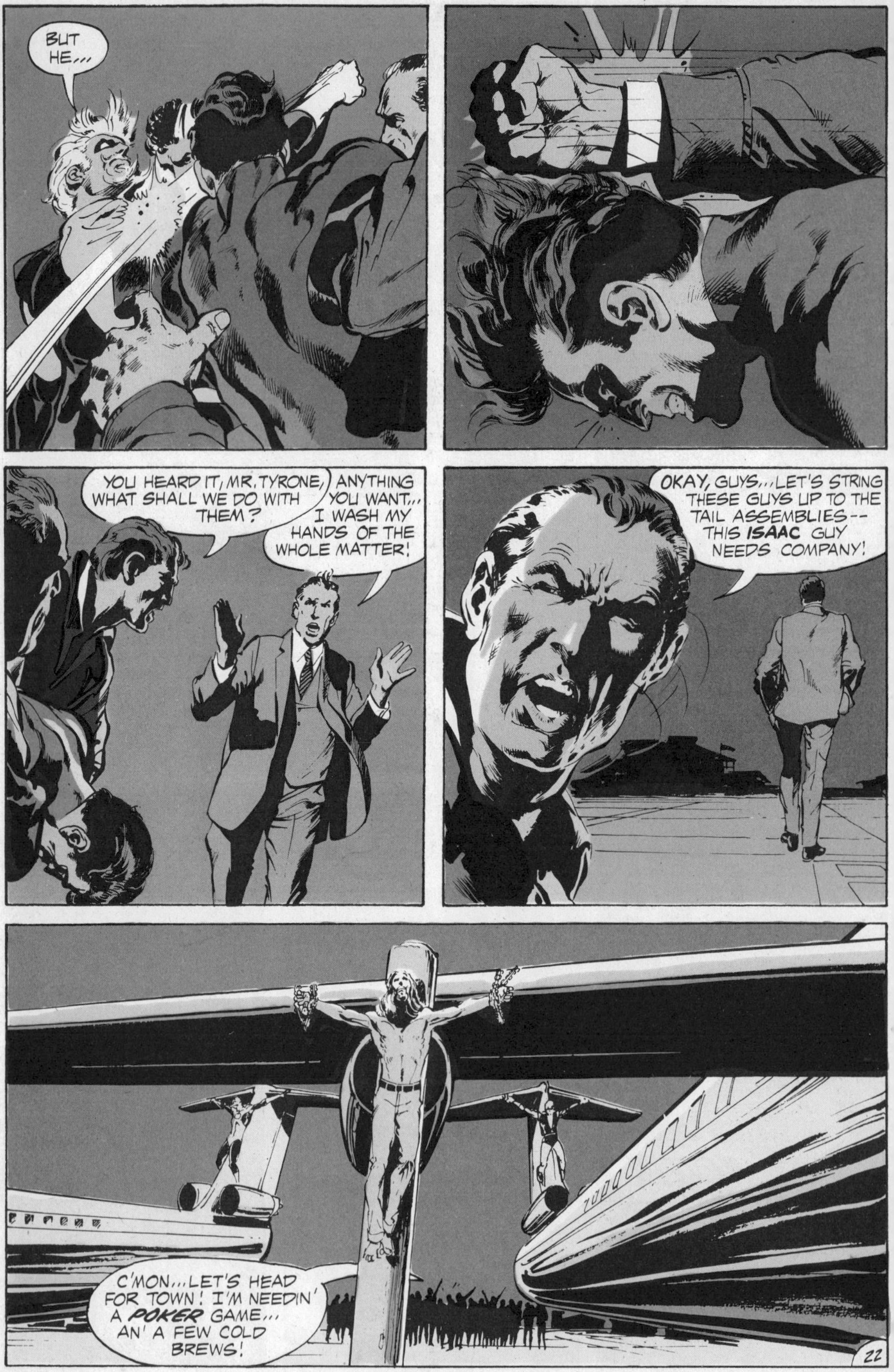
BUT HE...
YOU HEARD IT, MR. TYRONE, WHAT SHALL WE DO WITH THEM?
ANYTHING YOU WANT... I WASH MY HANDS OF THE WHOLE MATTER!
OKAY, GUYS... LET'S STRING THESE GUYS UP TO THE TAIL ASSEMBLIES-- THIS ISAAC GUY NEEDS COMPANY!
C'MON... LET'S HEAD FOR TOWN! I'M NEEDIN' A POKER GAME... AN' A FEW COLD BREWS!
22

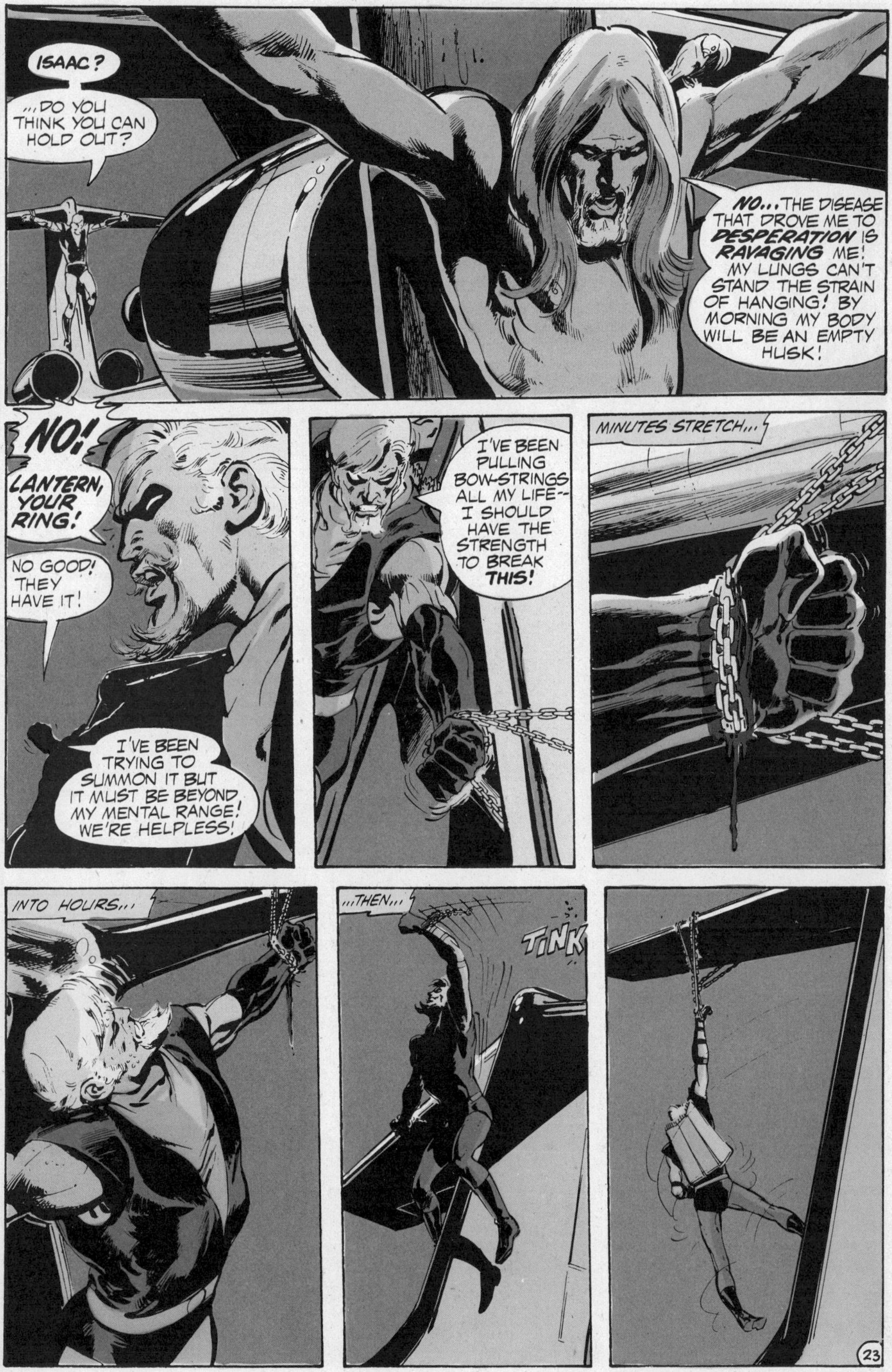
ISAAC?
...DO YOU THINK YOU CAN HOLD OUT?
NO...THE DISEASE THAT DROVE ME TO **DESPERATION** IS **RAVAGING** ME! MY LUNGS CAN'T STAND THE STRAIN OF HANGING! BY MORNING MY BODY WILL BE AN EMPTY HUSK!
NO! LANTERN, YOUR RING!
NO GOOD! THEY HAVE IT!
I'VE BEEN TRYING TO SUMMON IT BUT IT MUST BE BEYOND MY MENTAL RANGE! WE'RE HELPLESS!
I'VE BEEN PULLING BOW-STRINGS ALL MY LIFE-- I SHOULD HAVE THE STRENGTH TO BREAK **THIS!**
MINUTES STRETCH...
INTO HOURS...
...THEN...
TINK
23

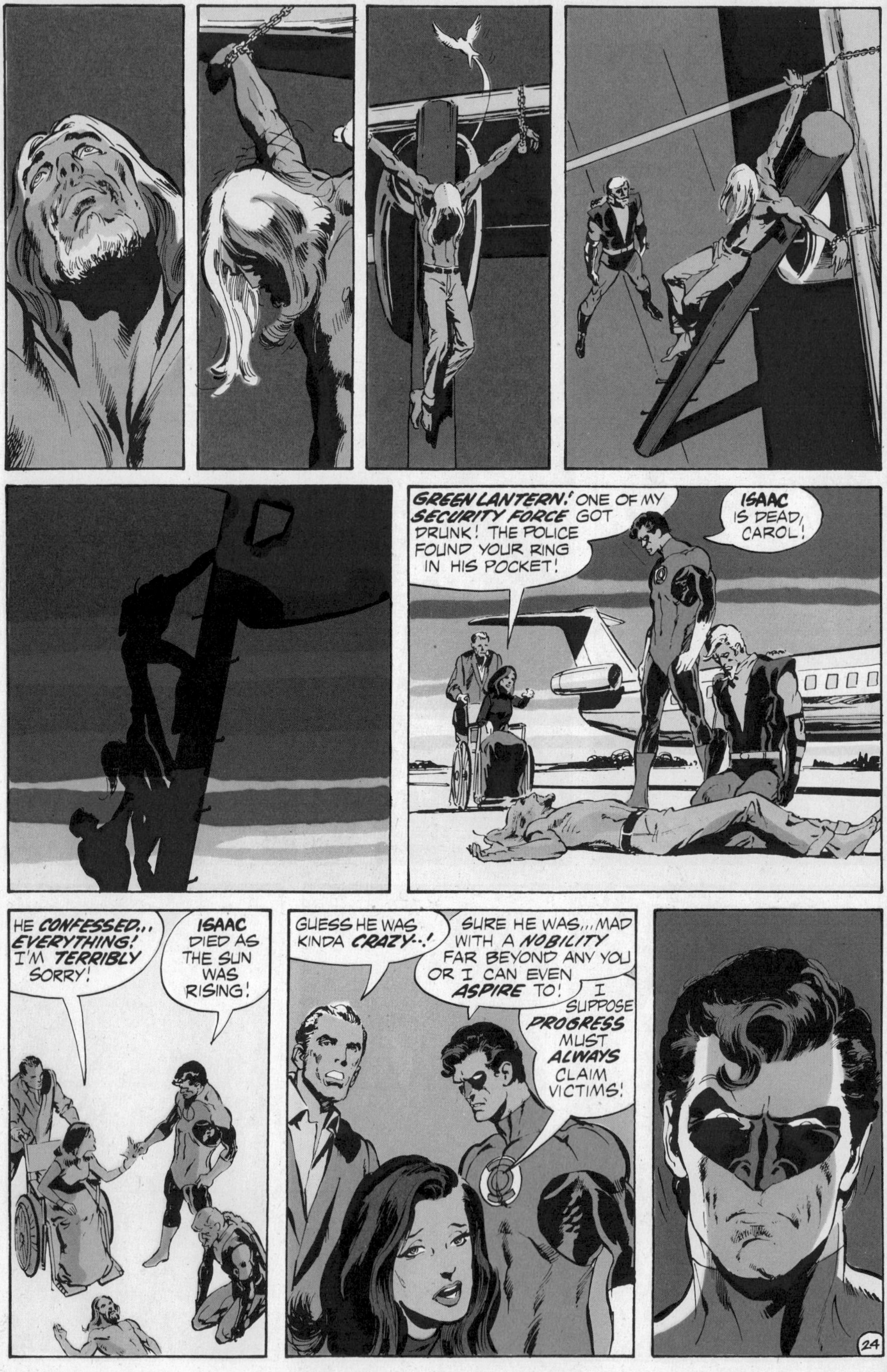
GREEN LANTERN! ONE OF MY SECURITY FORCE GOT DRUNK! THE POLICE FOUND YOUR RING IN HIS POCKET!
ISAAC IS DEAD, CAROL!
HE CONFESSED... EVERYTHING! I'M TERRIBLY SORRY!
ISAAC DIED AS THE SUN WAS RISING!
GUESS HE WAS KINDA CRAZY..!
SURE HE WAS,...MAD WITH A NOBILITY FAR BEYOND ANY YOU OR I CAN EVEN ASPIRE TO!
I SUPPOSE PROGRESS MUST ALWAYS CLAIM VICTIMS!
24

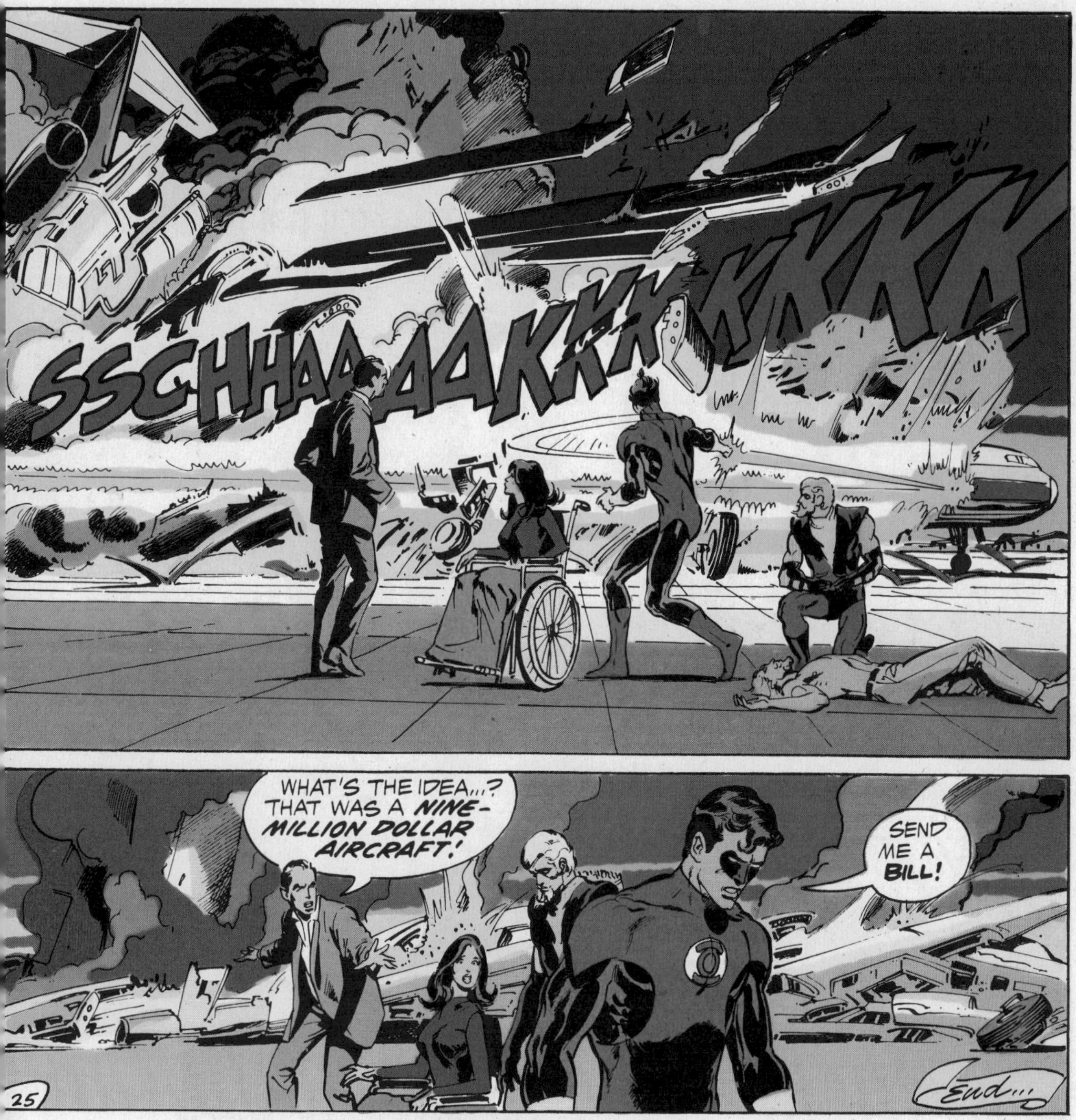
SSCHHAAAAKKKKKKKK
WHAT'S THE IDEA...? THAT WAS A NINE-MILLION DOLLAR AIRCRAFT!
SEND ME A BILL!
25
End...

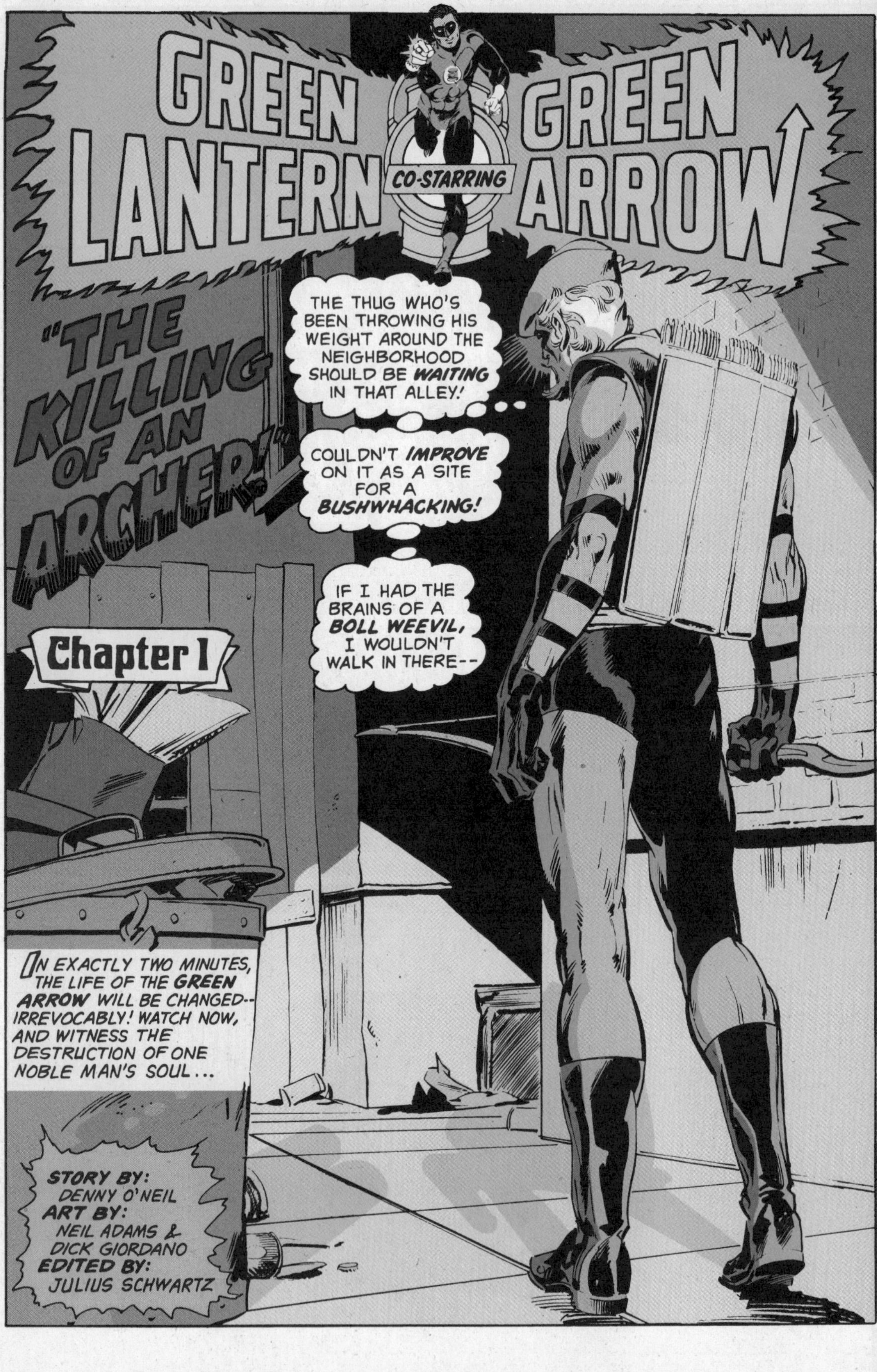
GREEN LANTERN
CO-STARRING
GREEN ARROW
"THE KILLING OF AN ARCHER!"
Chapter 1
THE THUG WHO'S BEEN THROWING HIS WEIGHT AROUND THE NEIGHBORHOOD SHOULD BE WAITING IN THAT ALLEY!
COULDN'T IMPROVE ON IT AS A SITE FOR A BUSHWHACKING!
IF I HAD THE BRAINS OF A BOLL WEEVIL, I WOULDN'T WALK IN THERE--
ON EXACTLY TWO MINUTES, THE LIFE OF THE GREEN ARROW WILL BE CHANGED--IRREVOCABLY! WATCH NOW, AND WITNESS THE DESTRUCTION OF ONE NOBLE MAN'S SOUL...
STORY BY: DENNY O'NEIL
ART BY: NEIL ADAMS & DICK GIORDANO
EDITED BY: JULIUS SCHWARTZ

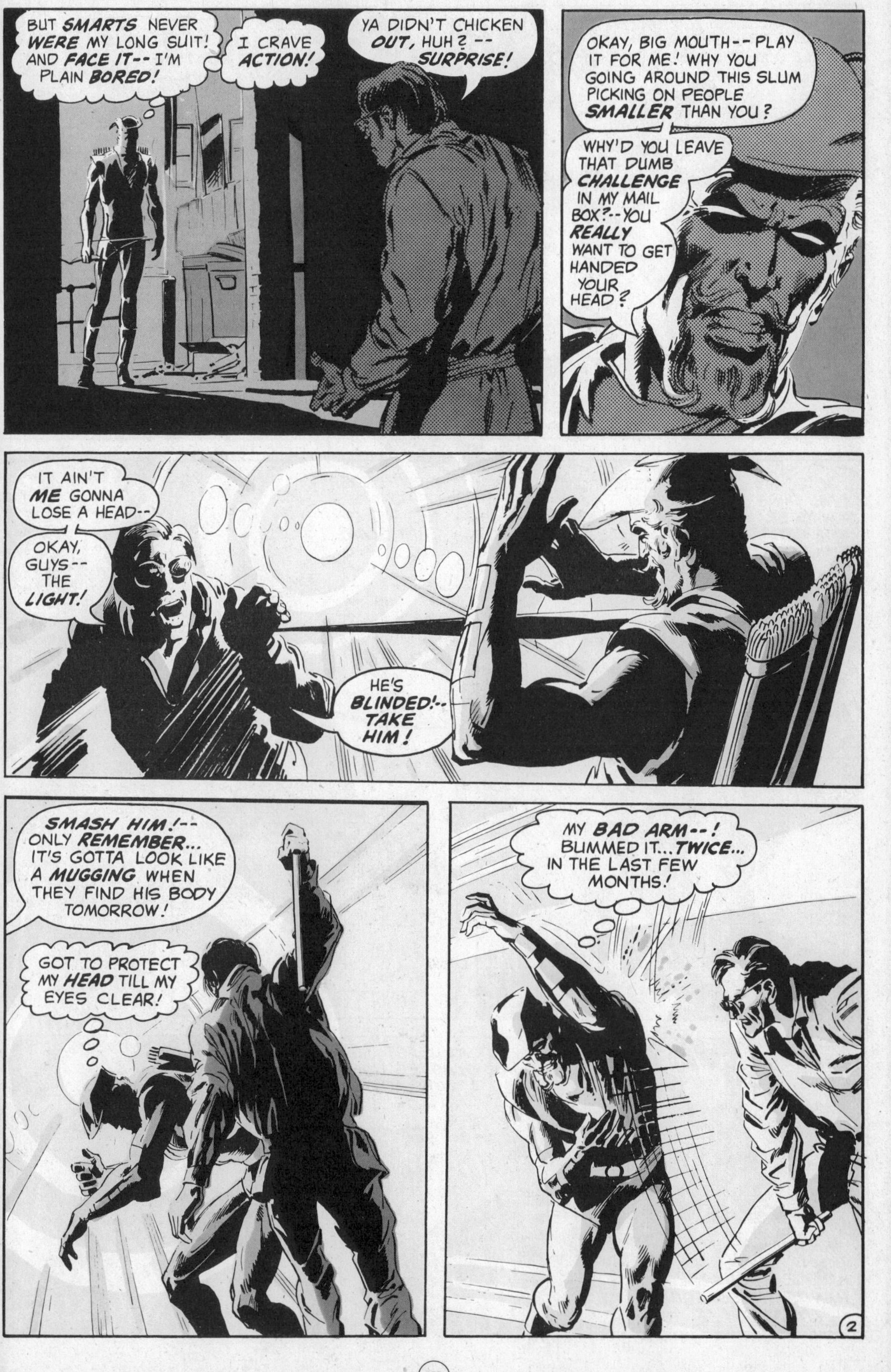
BUT SMARTS NEVER WERE MY LONG SUIT! AND FACE IT-- I'M PLAIN BORED!
I CRAVE ACTION!
YA DIDN'T CHICKEN OUT, HUH? -- SURPRISE!
OKAY, BIG MOUTH-- PLAY IT FOR ME! WHY YOU GOING AROUND THIS SLUM PICKING ON PEOPLE SMALLER THAN YOU?
WHY'D YOU LEAVE THAT DUMB CHALLENGE IN MY MAIL BOX?--YOU REALLY WANT TO GET HANDED YOUR HEAD?
IT AIN'T ME GONNA LOSE A HEAD--
OKAY, GUYS-- THE LIGHT!
HE'S BLINDED!-- TAKE HIM!
SMASH HIM!-- ONLY REMEMBER... IT'S GOTTA LOOK LIKE A MUGGING WHEN THEY FIND HIS BODY TOMORROW!
GOT TO PROTECT MY HEAD TILL MY EYES CLEAR!
MY BAD ARM--! BUMMED IT...TWICE... IN THE LAST FEW MONTHS!
2

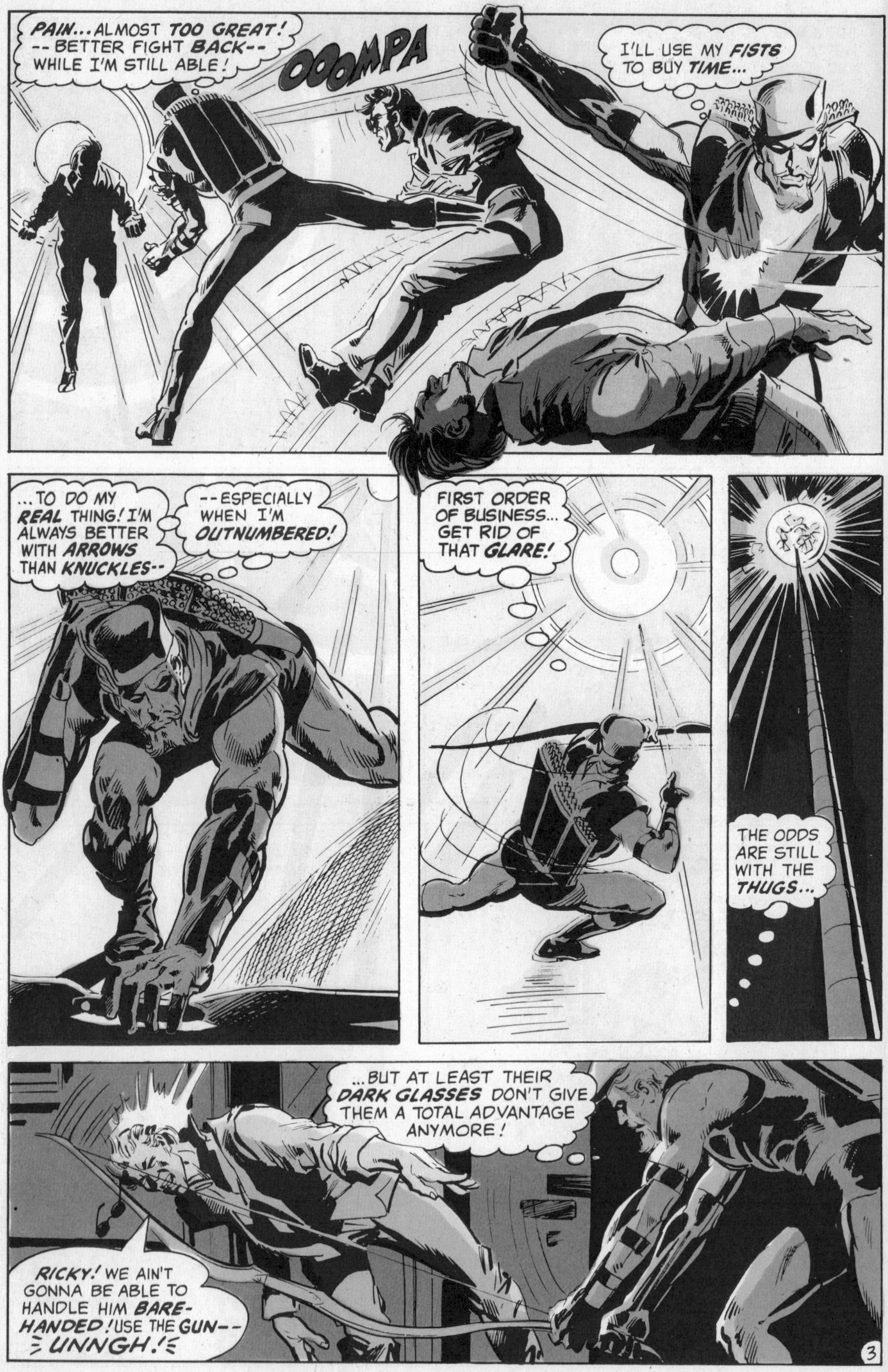
PAIN... ALMOST TOO GREAT! -- BETTER FIGHT BACK-- WHILE I'M STILL ABLE!
OOOMPA
I'LL USE MY FISTS TO BUY TIME...
...TO DO MY REAL THING! I'M ALWAYS BETTER WITH ARROWS THAN KNUCKLES--
--ESPECIALLY WHEN I'M OUTNUMBERED!
FIRST ORDER OF BUSINESS... GET RID OF THAT GLARE!
THE ODDS ARE STILL WITH THE THUGS...
...BUT AT LEAST THEIR DARK GLASSES DON'T GIVE THEM A TOTAL ADVANTAGE ANYMORE!
RICKY! WE AIN'T GONNA BE ABLE TO HANDLE HIM BARE-HANDED! USE THE GUN-- UNNGH!
3

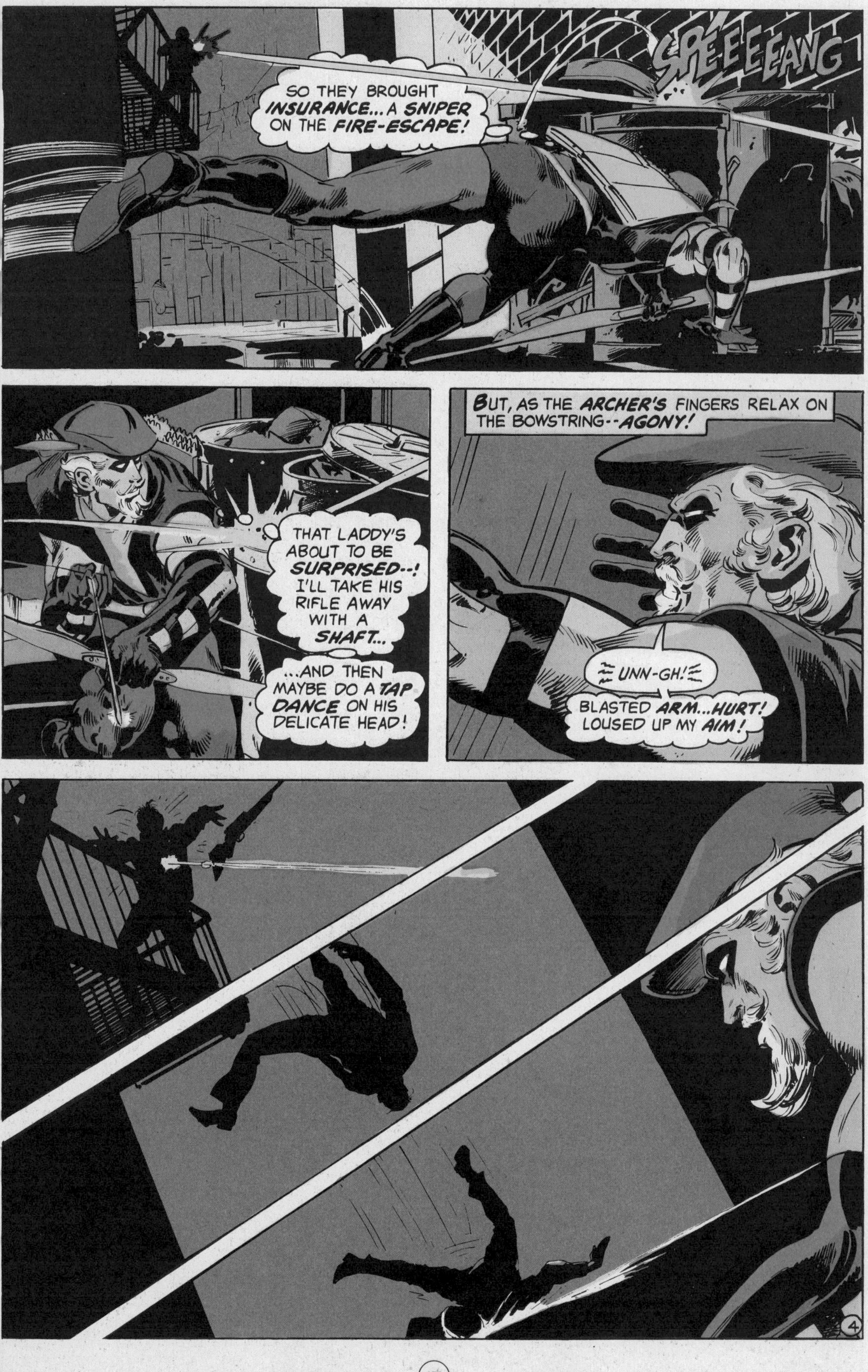
SPEEEEANG
SO THEY BROUGHT INSURANCE... A SNIPER ON THE FIRE-ESCAPE!
THAT LADDY'S ABOUT TO BE SURPRISED--! I'LL TAKE HIS RIFLE AWAY WITH A SHAFT...
...AND THEN MAYBE DO A TAP DANCE ON HIS DELICATE HEAD!
BUT, AS THE ARCHER'S FINGERS RELAX ON THE BOWSTRING--AGONY!
UNN-GH!
BLASTED ARM... HURT! LOUSED UP MY AIM!
4

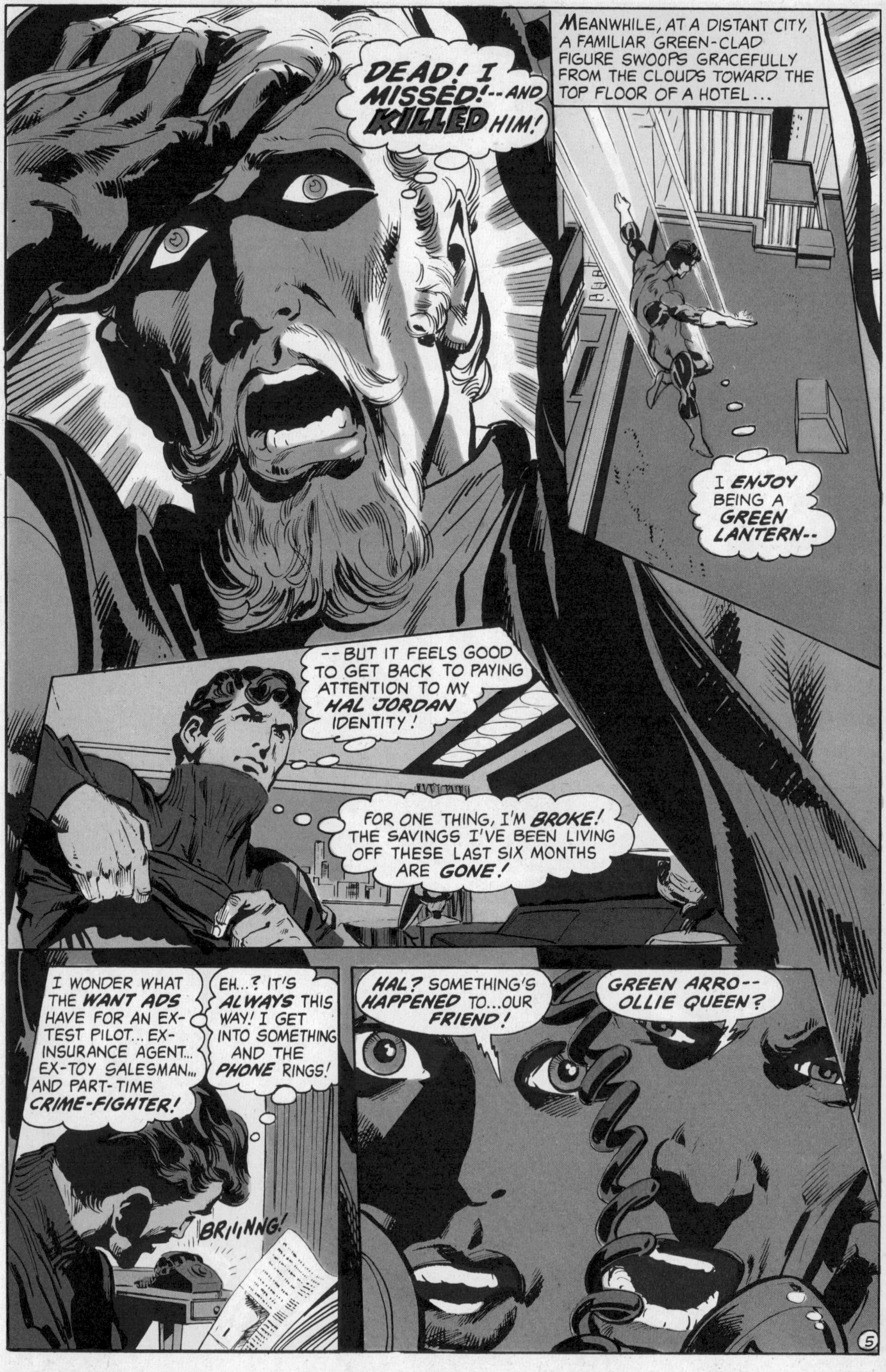
DEAD! I MISSED!--AND KILLED HIM!
MEANWHILE, AT A DISTANT CITY, A FAMILIAR GREEN-CLAD FIGURE SWOOPS GRACEFULLY FROM THE CLOUDS TOWARD THE TOP FLOOR OF A HOTEL...
I ENJOY BEING A GREEN LANTERN--
--BUT IT FEELS GOOD TO GET BACK TO PAYING ATTENTION TO MY HAL JORDAN IDENTITY!
FOR ONE THING, I'M BROKE! THE SAVINGS I'VE BEEN LIVING OFF THESE LAST SIX MONTHS ARE GONE!
I WONDER WHAT THE WANT ADS HAVE FOR AN EX-TEST PILOT... EX-INSURANCE AGENT... EX-TOY SALESMAN... AND PART-TIME CRIME-FIGHTER!
EH...? IT'S ALWAYS THIS WAY! I GET INTO SOMETHING AND THE PHONE RINGS!
BRIIINNG!
HAL? SOMETHING'S HAPPENED TO...OUR FRIEND!
GREEN ARRO-- OLLIE QUEEN?
5

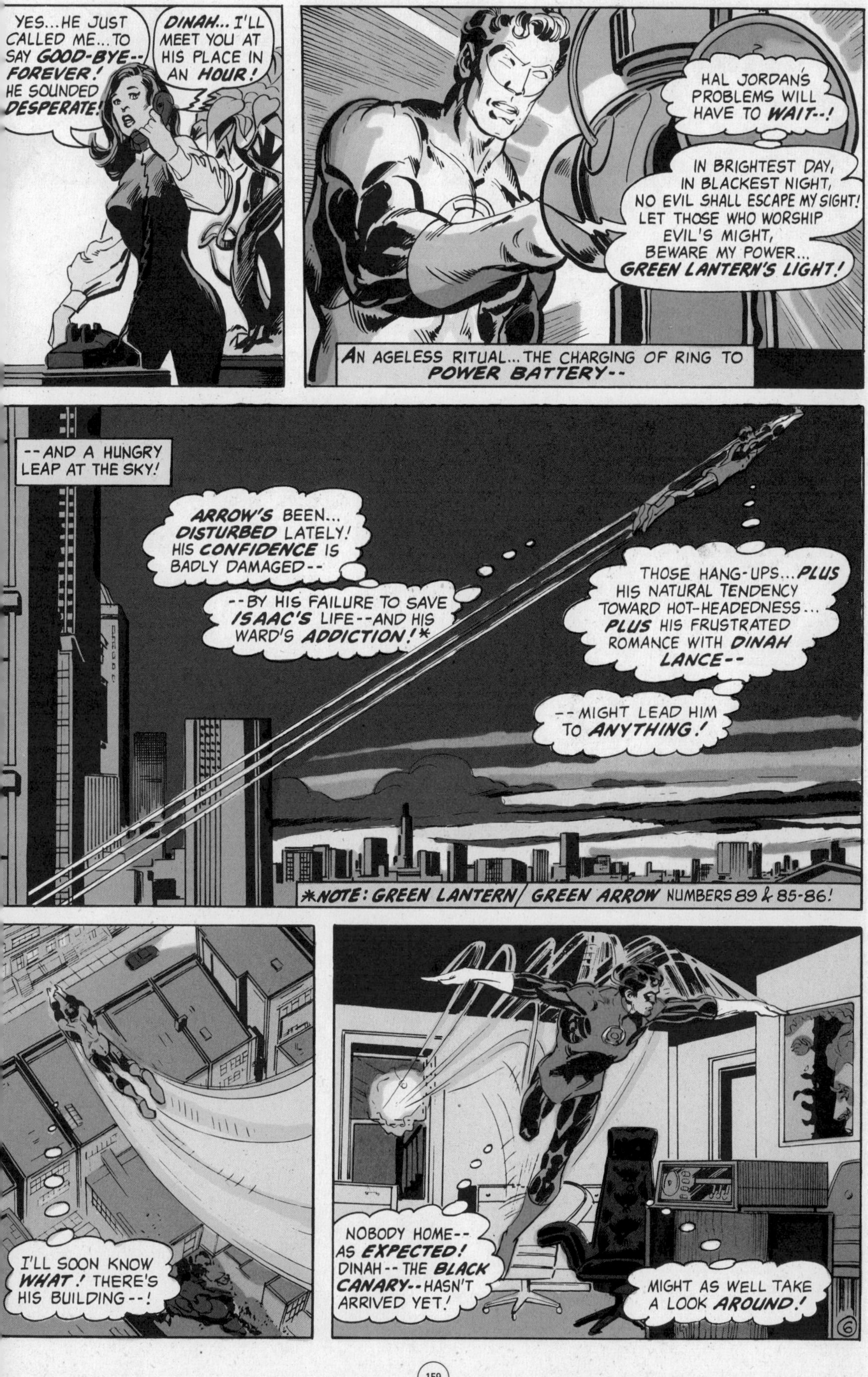

YES...HE JUST CALLED ME...TO SAY GOOD-BYE--FOREVER! HE SOUNDED DESPERATE!
DINAH... I'LL MEET YOU AT HIS PLACE IN AN HOUR!
HAL JORDAN'S PROBLEMS WILL HAVE TO WAIT--!
IN BRIGHTEST DAY, IN BLACKEST NIGHT, NO EVIL SHALL ESCAPE MY SIGHT! LET THOSE WHO WORSHIP EVIL'S MIGHT, BEWARE MY POWER... GREEN LANTERN'S LIGHT!
AN AGELESS RITUAL...THE CHARGING OF RING TO POWER BATTERY--
--AND A HUNGRY LEAP AT THE SKY!
ARROW'S BEEN... DISTURBED LATELY! HIS CONFIDENCE IS BADLY DAMAGED--
--BY HIS FAILURE TO SAVE ISAAC'S LIFE--AND HIS WARD'S ADDICTION!*
THOSE HANG-UPS...PLUS HIS NATURAL TENDENCY TOWARD HOT-HEADEDNESS... PLUS HIS FRUSTRATED ROMANCE WITH DINAH LANCE--
--MIGHT LEAD HIM TO ANYTHING!
*NOTE: GREEN LANTERN/GREEN ARROW NUMBERS 89 & 85-86!
I'LL SOON KNOW WHAT! THERE'S HIS BUILDING--!
NOBODY HOME--AS EXPECTED! DINAH--THE BLACK CANARY--HASN'T ARRIVED YET!
MIGHT AS WELL TAKE A LOOK AROUND!
6

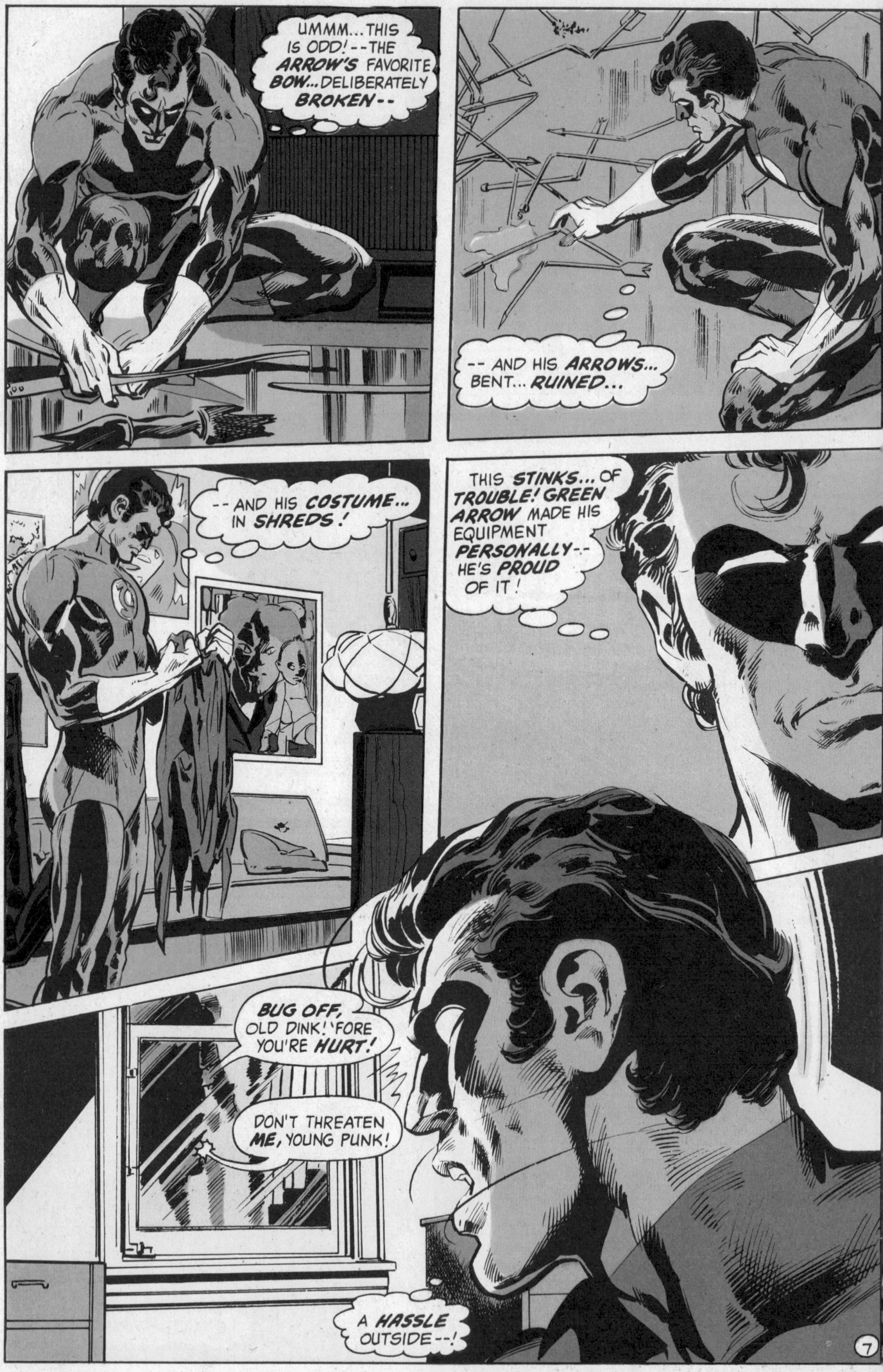

UMMM... THIS IS ODD!--THE ARROW'S FAVORITE BOW... DELIBERATELY BROKEN--
-- AND HIS ARROWS... BENT... RUINED...
--AND HIS COSTUME... IN SHREDS!
THIS STINKS... OF TROUBLE! GREEN ARROW MADE HIS EQUIPMENT PERSONALLY--HE'S PROUD OF IT!
BUG OFF, OLD DINK! 'FORE YOU'RE HURT!
DON'T THREATEN ME, YOUNG PUNK!
A HASSLE OUTSIDE--!
7

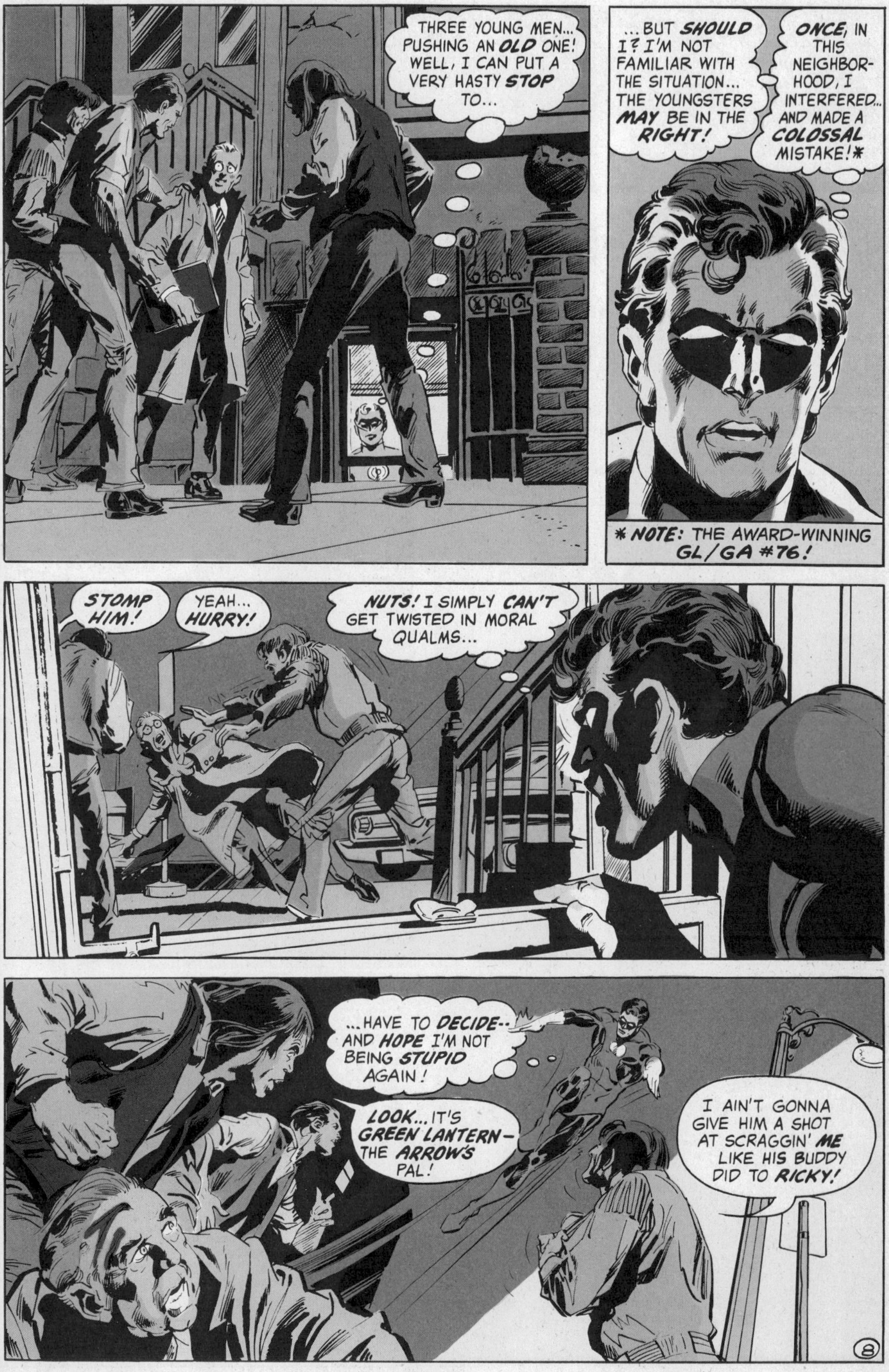
THREE YOUNG MEN... PUSHING AN OLD ONE! WELL, I CAN PUT A VERY HASTY STOP TO...
...BUT SHOULD I? I'M NOT FAMILIAR WITH THE SITUATION... THE YOUNGSTERS MAY BE IN THE RIGHT!
ONCE, IN THIS NEIGHBORHOOD, I INTERFERED... AND MADE A COLOSSAL MISTAKE!*
* NOTE: THE AWARD-WINNING GL/GA #76!
STOMP HIM!
YEAH... HURRY!
NUTS! I SIMPLY CAN'T GET TWISTED IN MORAL QUALMS...
...HAVE TO DECIDE-- AND HOPE I'M NOT BEING STUPID AGAIN!
LOOK... IT'S GREEN LANTERN— THE ARROW'S PAL!
I AIN'T GONNA GIVE HIM A SHOT AT SCRAGGIN' ME LIKE HIS BUDDY DID TO RICKY!
8

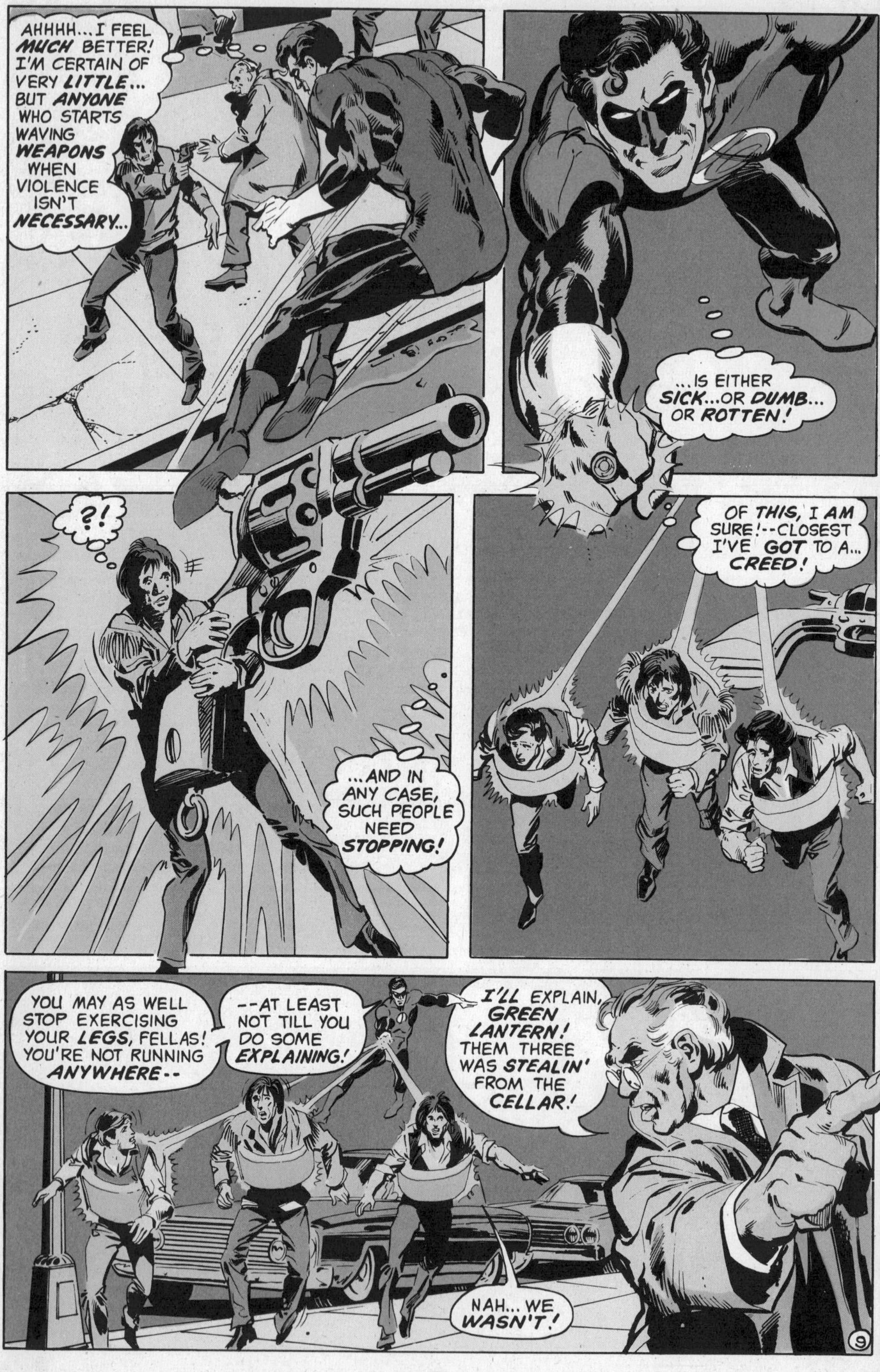
AHHHH...I FEEL MUCH BETTER! I'M CERTAIN OF VERY LITTLE... BUT ANYONE WHO STARTS WAVING WEAPONS WHEN VIOLENCE ISN'T NECESSARY...
...IS EITHER SICK...OR DUMB... OR ROTTEN!
?!
...AND IN ANY CASE, SUCH PEOPLE NEED STOPPING!
OF THIS, I AM SURE!--CLOSEST I'VE GOT TO A... CREED!
YOU MAY AS WELL STOP EXERCISING YOUR LEGS, FELLAS! YOU'RE NOT RUNNING ANYWHERE--
--AT LEAST NOT TILL YOU DO SOME EXPLAINING!
I'LL EXPLAIN, GREEN LANTERN! THEM THREE WAS STEALIN' FROM THE CELLAR!
NAH... WE WASN'T!
9

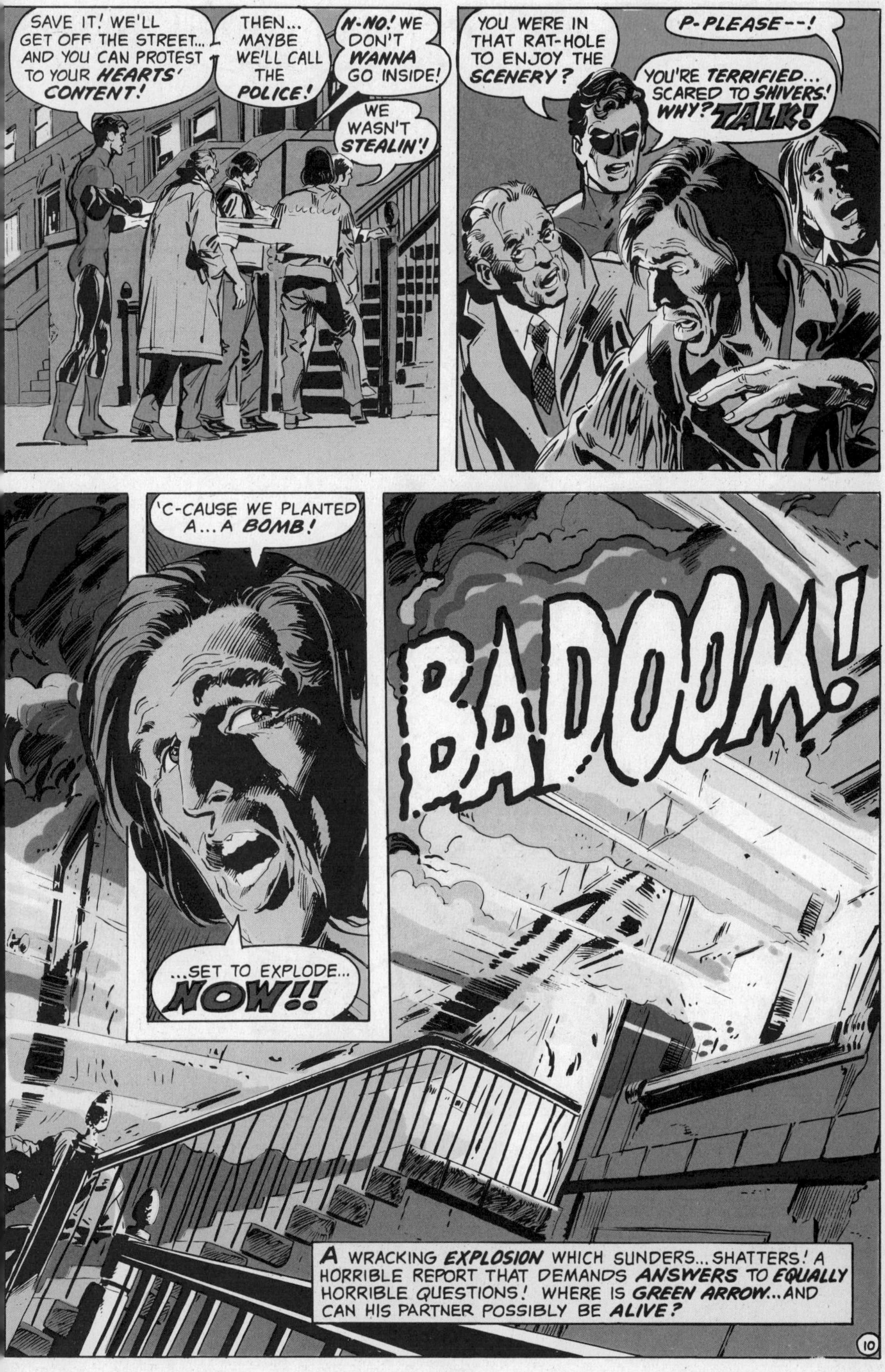
SAVE IT! WE'LL GET OFF THE STREET... AND YOU CAN PROTEST TO YOUR HEARTS' CONTENT!
THEN... MAYBE WE'LL CALL THE POLICE!
N-NO! WE DON'T WANNA GO INSIDE!
WE WASN'T STEALIN'!
YOU WERE IN THAT RAT-HOLE TO ENJOY THE SCENERY?
P-PLEASE--!
YOU'RE TERRIFIED... SCARED TO SHIVERS! WHY? TALK!
'C-CAUSE WE PLANTED A... A BOMB!
...SET TO EXPLODE... NOW!!
BADOOM!
A WRACKING EXPLOSION WHICH SUNDERS... SHATTERS! A HORRIBLE REPORT THAT DEMANDS ANSWERS TO EQUALLY HORRIBLE QUESTIONS! WHERE IS GREEN ARROW... AND CAN HIS PARTNER POSSIBLY BE ALIVE?
10

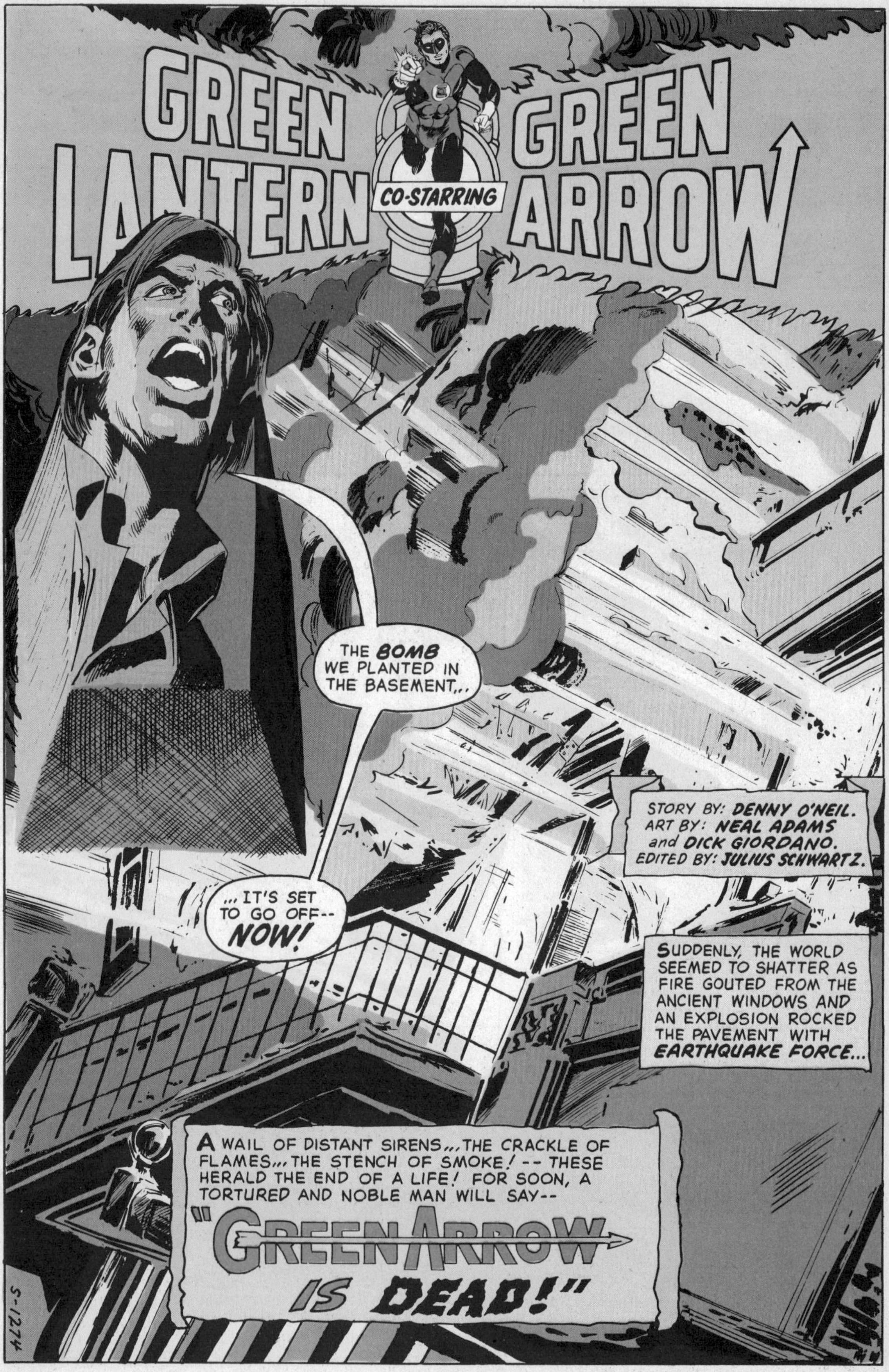
GREEN LANTERN
CO-STARRING
GREEN ARROW
THE BOMB WE PLANTED IN THE BASEMENT...
...IT'S SET TO GO OFF-- NOW!
STORY BY: DENNY O'NEIL. ART BY: NEAL ADAMS and DICK GIORDANO. EDITED BY: JULIUS SCHWARTZ.
SUDDENLY, THE WORLD SEEMED TO SHATTER AS FIRE GOUTED FROM THE ANCIENT WINDOWS AND AN EXPLOSION ROCKED THE PAVEMENT WITH EARTHQUAKE FORCE...
A WAIL OF DISTANT SIRENS... THE CRACKLE OF FLAMES... THE STENCH OF SMOKE! -- THESE HERALD THE END OF A LIFE! FOR SOON, A TORTURED AND NOBLE MAN WILL SAY--
"GREEN ARROW IS DEAD!"
S-1274

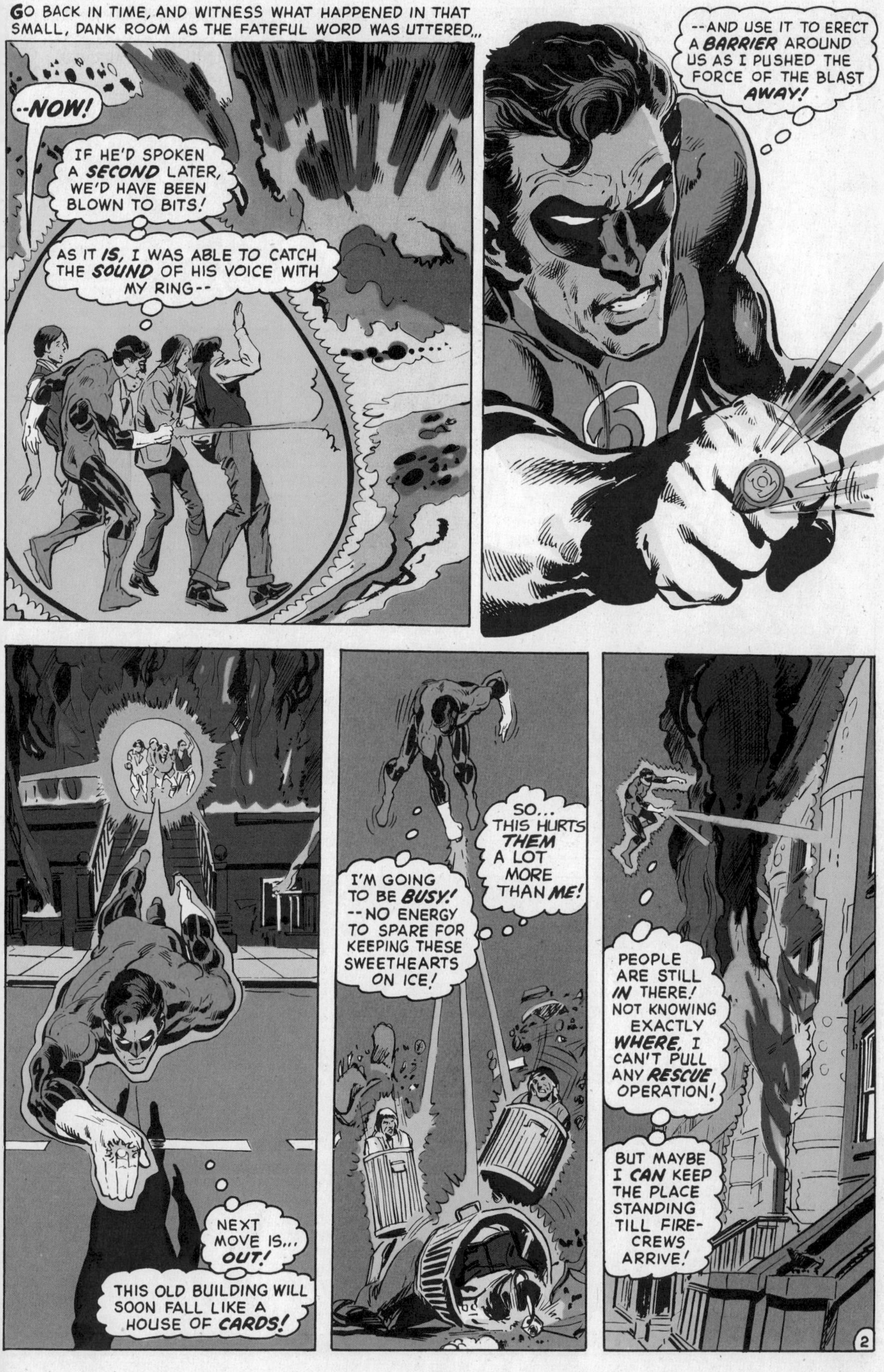

GO BACK IN TIME, AND WITNESS WHAT HAPPENED IN THAT SMALL, DANK ROOM AS THE FATEFUL WORD WAS UTTERED...
--NOW!
IF HE'D SPOKEN A SECOND LATER, WE'D HAVE BEEN BLOWN TO BITS!
AS IT IS, I WAS ABLE TO CATCH THE SOUND OF HIS VOICE WITH MY RING--
--AND USE IT TO ERECT A BARRIER AROUND US AS I PUSHED THE FORCE OF THE BLAST AWAY!
NEXT MOVE IS... OUT!
THIS OLD BUILDING WILL SOON FALL LIKE A HOUSE OF CARDS!
I'M GOING TO BE BUSY! --NO ENERGY TO SPARE FOR KEEPING THESE SWEETHEARTS ON ICE!
SO... THIS HURTS THEM A LOT MORE THAN ME!
PEOPLE ARE STILL IN THERE! NOT KNOWING EXACTLY WHERE, I CAN'T PULL ANY RESCUE OPERATION!
BUT MAYBE I CAN KEEP THE PLACE STANDING TILL FIRE-CREWS ARRIVE!
2

GOT TO **CONCENTRATE**... POUR EVERY **IOTA** OF **WILL-POWER** INTO THE **RING**--

--OR THE **TENEMENT** WILL **CRASH**... **LIVES** WILL BE LOST!

I'M ABOUT **FINISHED**! BUT HELP HAS ARRIVED... **FINALLY**!

I'VE **HAD** IT... TOO TIRED TO **MOVE**!

GOTTA GATHER MY **STRENGTH** BEFORE I DELIVER THE BOMBERS TO THE **AUTHORITIES**...

GREEN LANTERN! I SAW WHAT YOU DID! YOU WERE **MAGNIFICENT**!

THANKS, **BLACK CANARY**! I APPRECIATE A BIT OF EGO-BOO NOW AND **AGAIN**!

YOU DIDN'T COME TO START MY **FAN CLUB**, THOUGH-- DID YOU?

NOT **EXACTLY**! I WAS WONDERING IF YOU'VE HAD ANY WORD FROM **OLLIE**... GREEN **ARROW**!

I'VE BEEN TERRIBLY **WORRIED** ABOUT HIM... EVER SINCE HE CALLED TO TELL ME GOOD-BYE!

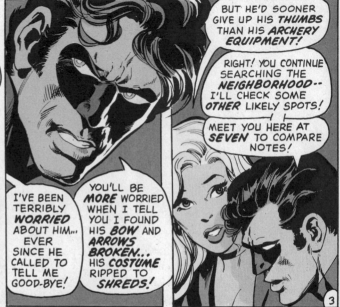

BUT HE'D SOONER GIVE UP HIS **THUMBS** THAN HIS **ARCHERY** EQUIPMENT!

RIGHT! YOU CONTINUE SEARCHING THE **NEIGHBORHOOD**-- I'LL CHECK SOME **OTHER** LIKELY SPOTS!

MEET YOU HERE AT **SEVEN** TO COMPARE NOTES!

YOU'LL BE **MORE** WORRIED WHEN I TELL YOU I FOUND HIS **BOW** AND **ARROWS BROKEN**... HIS **COSTUME** RIPPED TO **SHREDS**!

3

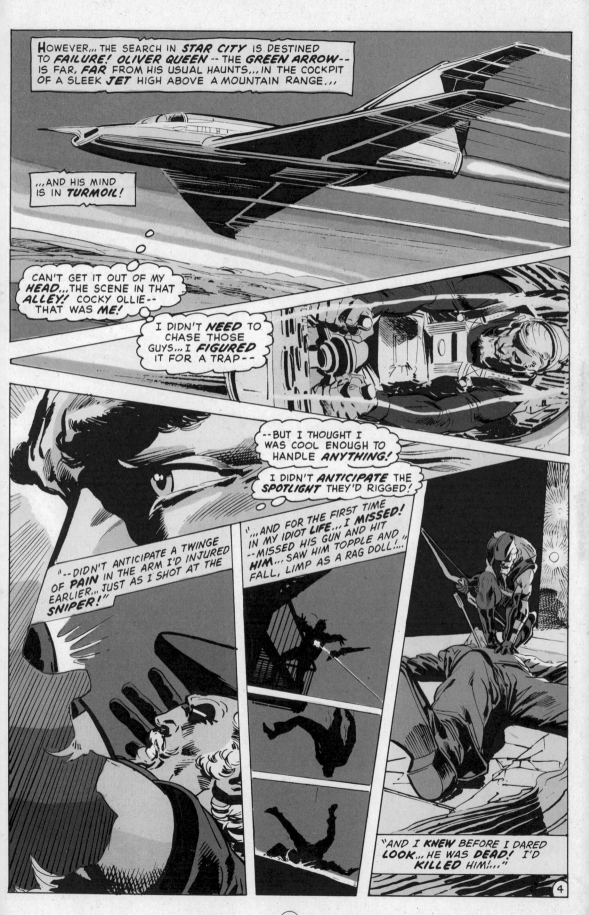

HOWEVER... THE SEARCH IN *STAR CITY* IS DESTINED TO *FAILURE!* OLIVER QUEEN -- THE *GREEN ARROW*-- IS FAR, *FAR* FROM HIS USUAL HAUNTS...IN THE COCKPIT OF A SLEEK *JET* HIGH ABOVE A MOUNTAIN RANGE...

...AND HIS MIND IS IN *TURMOIL!*

CAN'T GET IT OUT OF MY *HEAD*...THE SCENE IN THAT *ALLEY!* COCKY OLLIE-- THAT WAS *ME!*

I DIDN'T *NEED* TO CHASE THOSE GUYS... I *FIGURED* IT FOR A TRAP--

--BUT I THOUGHT I WAS COOL ENOUGH TO HANDLE *ANYTHING!*

I DIDN'T *ANTICIPATE* THE *SPOTLIGHT* THEY'D RIGGED!

"--DIDN'T ANTICIPATE A TWINGE OF *PAIN* IN THE ARM I'D INJURED EARLIER... JUST AS I SHOT AT THE *SNIPER!*"

"...AND FOR THE FIRST TIME IN MY IDIOT *LIFE*... I *MISSED!* --MISSED HIS GUN AND HIT *HIM*.... SAW HIM TOPPLE AND FALL, LIMP AS A RAG DOLL!..."

"AND I KNEW BEFORE I DARED *LOOK*...HE WAS *DEAD!* I'D *KILLED* HIM!...."

4

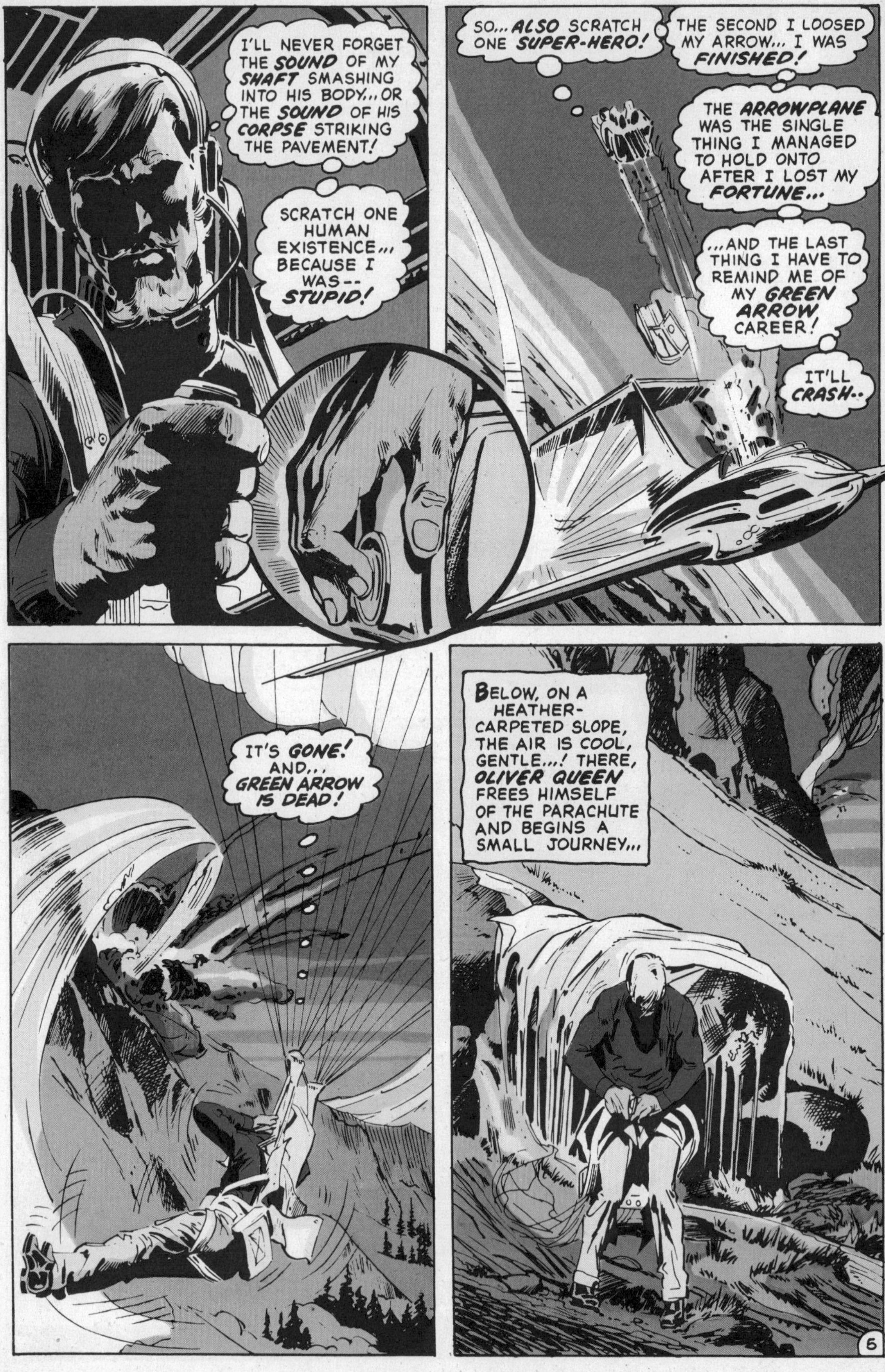
I'LL NEVER FORGET THE SOUND OF MY SHAFT SMASHING INTO HIS BODY...OR THE SOUND OF HIS CORPSE STRIKING THE PAVEMENT!
SCRATCH ONE HUMAN EXISTENCE... BECAUSE I WAS-- STUPID!
SO... ALSO SCRATCH ONE SUPER-HERO!
THE SECOND I LOOSED MY ARROW... I WAS FINISHED!
THE ARROWPLANE WAS THE SINGLE THING I MANAGED TO HOLD ONTO AFTER I LOST MY FORTUNE...
...AND THE LAST THING I HAVE TO REMIND ME OF MY GREEN ARROW CAREER!
IT'LL CRASH..
IT'S GONE! AND... GREEN ARROW IS DEAD!
BELOW, ON A HEATHER-CARPETED SLOPE, THE AIR IS COOL, GENTLE...! THERE, OLIVER QUEEN FREES HIMSELF OF THE PARACHUTE AND BEGINS A SMALL JOURNEY...
6

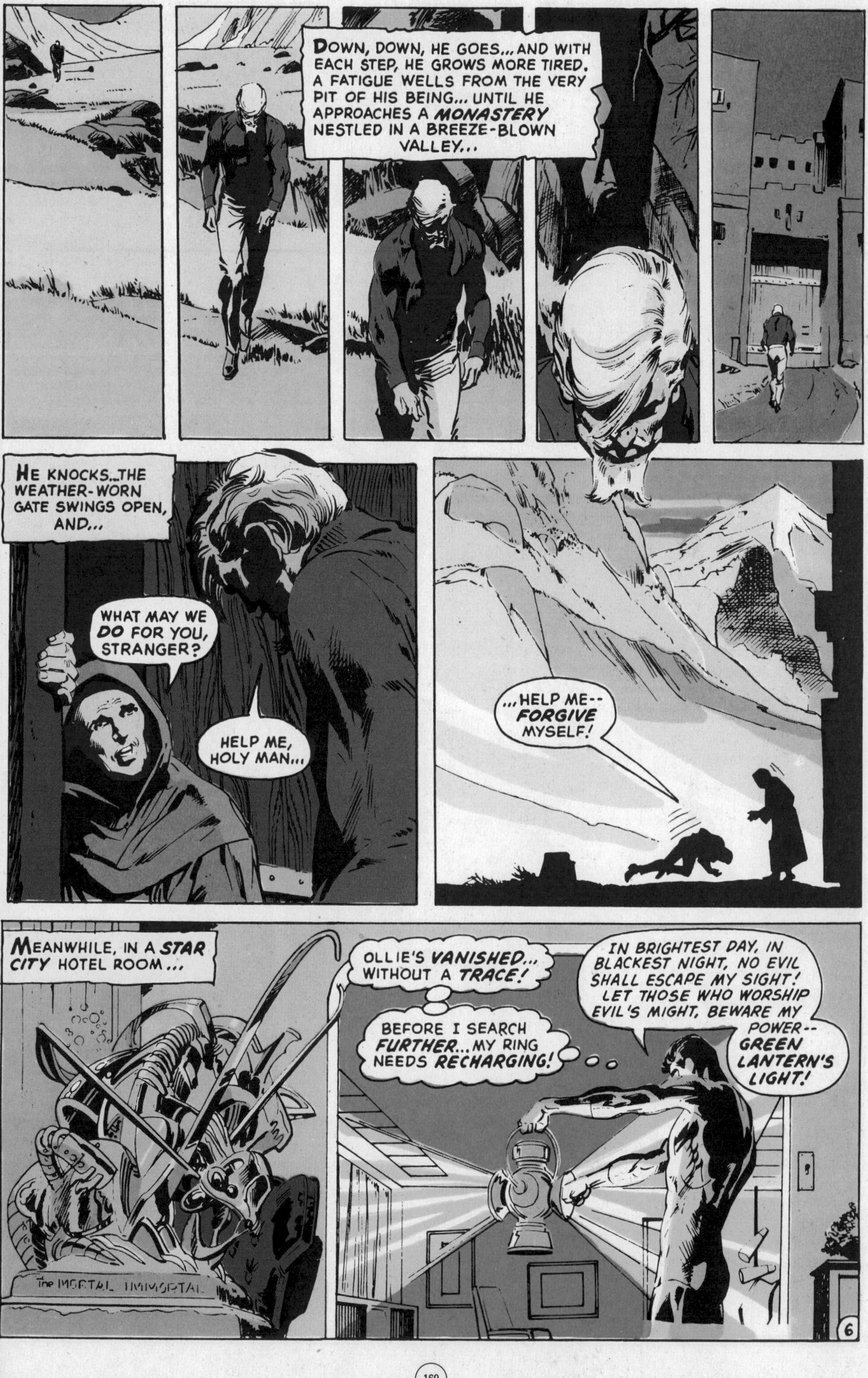
DOWN, DOWN, HE GOES... AND WITH EACH STEP, HE GROWS MORE TIRED. A FATIGUE WELLS FROM THE VERY PIT OF HIS BEING... UNTIL HE APPROACHES A MONASTERY NESTLED IN A BREEZE-BLOWN VALLEY...
HE KNOCKS...THE WEATHER-WORN GATE SWINGS OPEN, AND...
WHAT MAY WE DO FOR YOU, STRANGER?
HELP ME, HOLY MAN...
...HELP ME-- FORGIVE MYSELF!
MEANWHILE, IN A STAR CITY HOTEL ROOM...
OLLIE'S VANISHED... WITHOUT A TRACE!
BEFORE I SEARCH FURTHER... MY RING NEEDS RECHARGING!
IN BRIGHTEST DAY, IN BLACKEST NIGHT, NO EVIL SHALL ESCAPE MY SIGHT! LET THOSE WHO WORSHIP EVIL'S MIGHT, BEWARE MY POWER-- GREEN LANTERN'S LIGHT!
THE MORTAL IMMORTAL
6

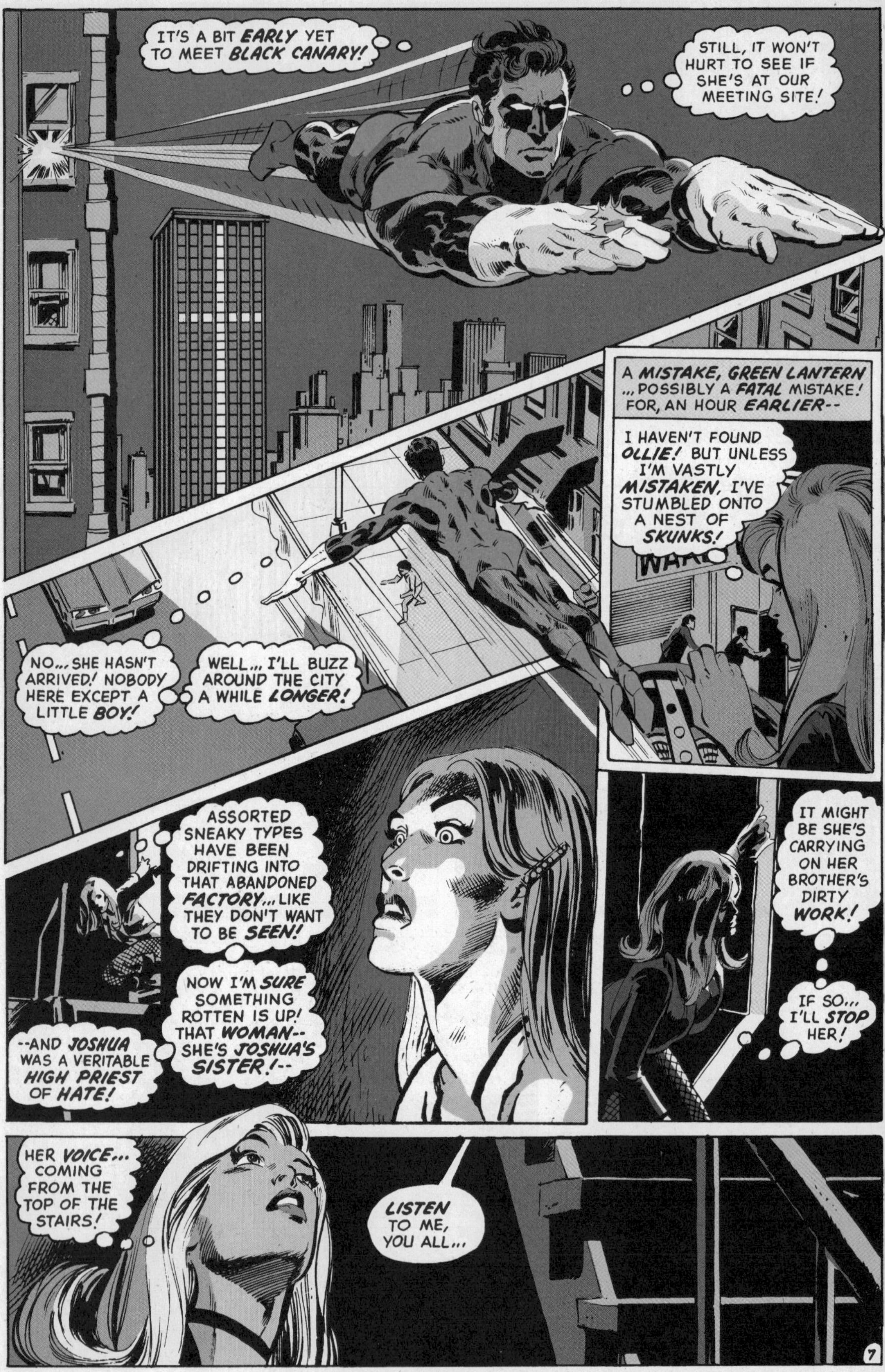
IT'S A BIT EARLY YET TO MEET BLACK CANARY!
STILL, IT WON'T HURT TO SEE IF SHE'S AT OUR MEETING SITE!
NO... SHE HASN'T ARRIVED! NOBODY HERE EXCEPT A LITTLE BOY!
WELL... I'LL BUZZ AROUND THE CITY A WHILE LONGER!
A MISTAKE, GREEN LANTERN ...POSSIBLY A FATAL MISTAKE! FOR, AN HOUR EARLIER--
I HAVEN'T FOUND OLLIE! BUT UNLESS I'M VASTLY MISTAKEN, I'VE STUMBLED ONTO A NEST OF SKUNKS!
ASSORTED SNEAKY TYPES HAVE BEEN DRIFTING INTO THAT ABANDONED FACTORY... LIKE THEY DON'T WANT TO BE SEEN!
NOW I'M SURE SOMETHING ROTTEN IS UP! THAT WOMAN-- SHE'S JOSHUA'S SISTER!--
--AND JOSHUA WAS A VERITABLE HIGH PRIEST OF HATE!
IT MIGHT BE SHE'S CARRYING ON HER BROTHER'S DIRTY WORK!
IF SO... I'LL STOP HER!
HER VOICE... COMING FROM THE TOP OF THE STAIRS!
LISTEN TO ME, YOU ALL...
7

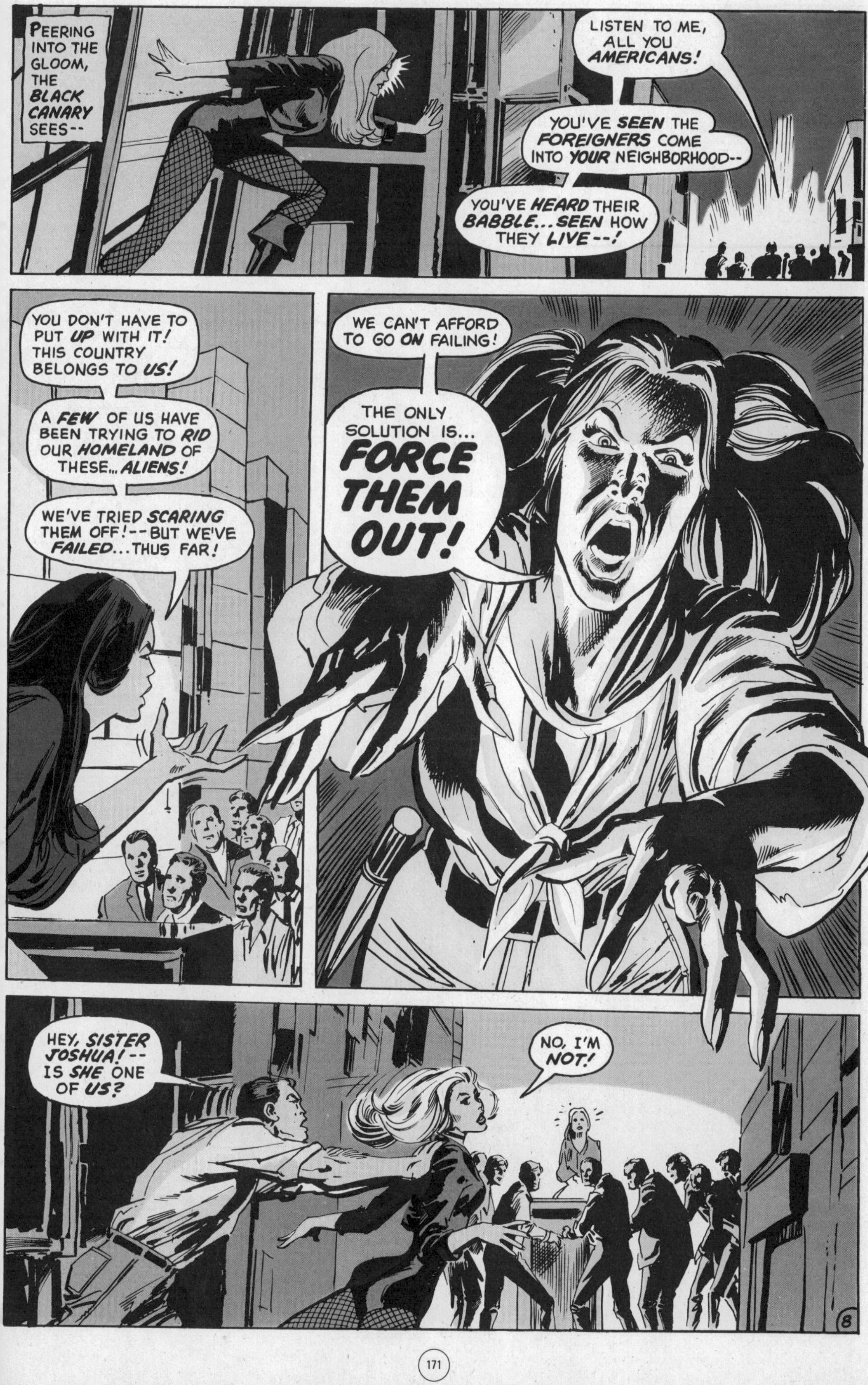
PEERING INTO THE GLOOM, THE BLACK CANARY SEES--
LISTEN TO ME, ALL YOU AMERICANS!
YOU'VE SEEN THE FOREIGNERS COME INTO YOUR NEIGHBORHOOD--
YOU'VE HEARD THEIR BABBLE... SEEN HOW THEY LIVE--!
YOU DON'T HAVE TO PUT UP WITH IT! THIS COUNTRY BELONGS TO US!
A FEW OF US HAVE BEEN TRYING TO RID OUR HOMELAND OF THESE... ALIENS!
WE'VE TRIED SCARING THEM OFF!--BUT WE'VE FAILED... THUS FAR!
WE CAN'T AFFORD TO GO ON FAILING!
THE ONLY SOLUTION IS... FORCE THEM OUT!
HEY, SISTER JOSHUA!--IS SHE ONE OF US?
NO, I'M NOT!
8

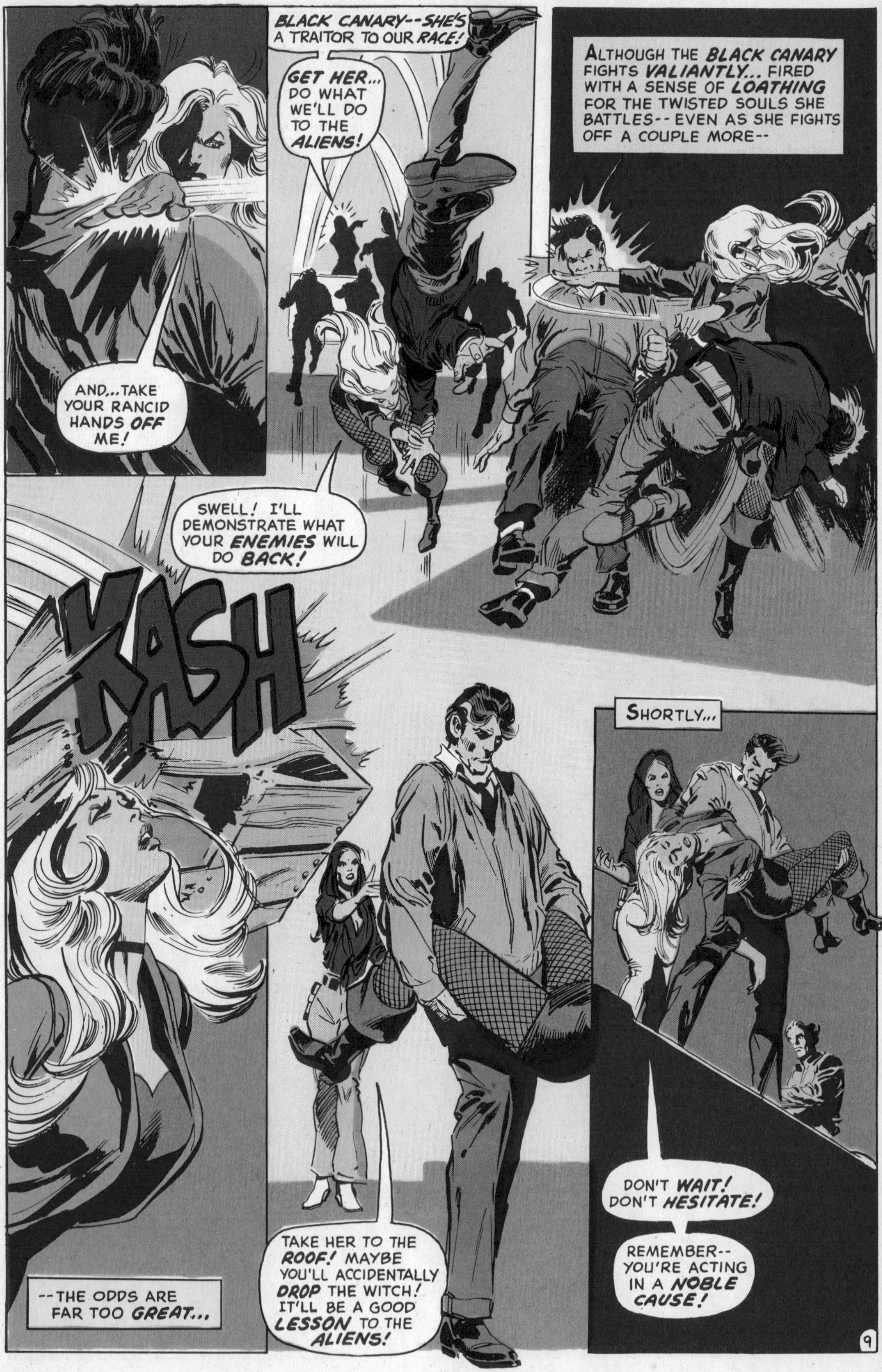
AND...TAKE YOUR RANCID HANDS OFF ME!
BLACK CANARY--SHE'S A TRAITOR TO OUR RACE!
GET HER... DO WHAT WE'LL DO TO THE ALIENS!
SWELL! I'LL DEMONSTRATE WHAT YOUR ENEMIES WILL DO BACK!
ALTHOUGH THE BLACK CANARY FIGHTS VALIANTLY... FIRED WITH A SENSE OF LOATHING FOR THE TWISTED SOULS SHE BATTLES-- EVEN AS SHE FIGHTS OFF A COUPLE MORE--
KASH
--THE ODDS ARE FAR TOO GREAT...
TAKE HER TO THE ROOF! MAYBE YOU'LL ACCIDENTALLY DROP THE WITCH! IT'LL BE A GOOD LESSON TO THE ALIENS!
SHORTLY...
DON'T WAIT! DON'T HESITATE!
REMEMBER-- YOU'RE ACTING IN A NOBLE CAUSE!
9

GREEN LANTERN! --RUN!

SURE,... STAMPEDE LIKE *ANIMALS!* BECAUSE THAT'S WHAT YOU *ARE!*

YOU'VE *ABANDONED* ANY CLAIM TO *HUMANITY!*

YOU MIGHT RECALL,... ANIMALS END THEIR DAYS ON-- *MEAT-HOOKS!*

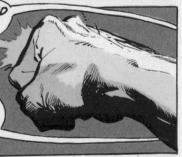

YOU OKAY, KID?

APART FROM A *HEADACHE*... YES!

THANKS FOR THE LAST-MINUTE *RESCUE,* GL!

YOU RESCUED *YOURSELF!* -- BY TELLING THE BOY ON THE STREET CORNER WHERE YOU'D *GONE!*

WHEN YOU DIDN'T *SHOW,* I LANDED AND GOT YOUR MESSAGE!

BETWEEN US, WE'VE DONE *EVERYTHING!*

EXCEPT -- FIND OUR,... FRIEND...

10

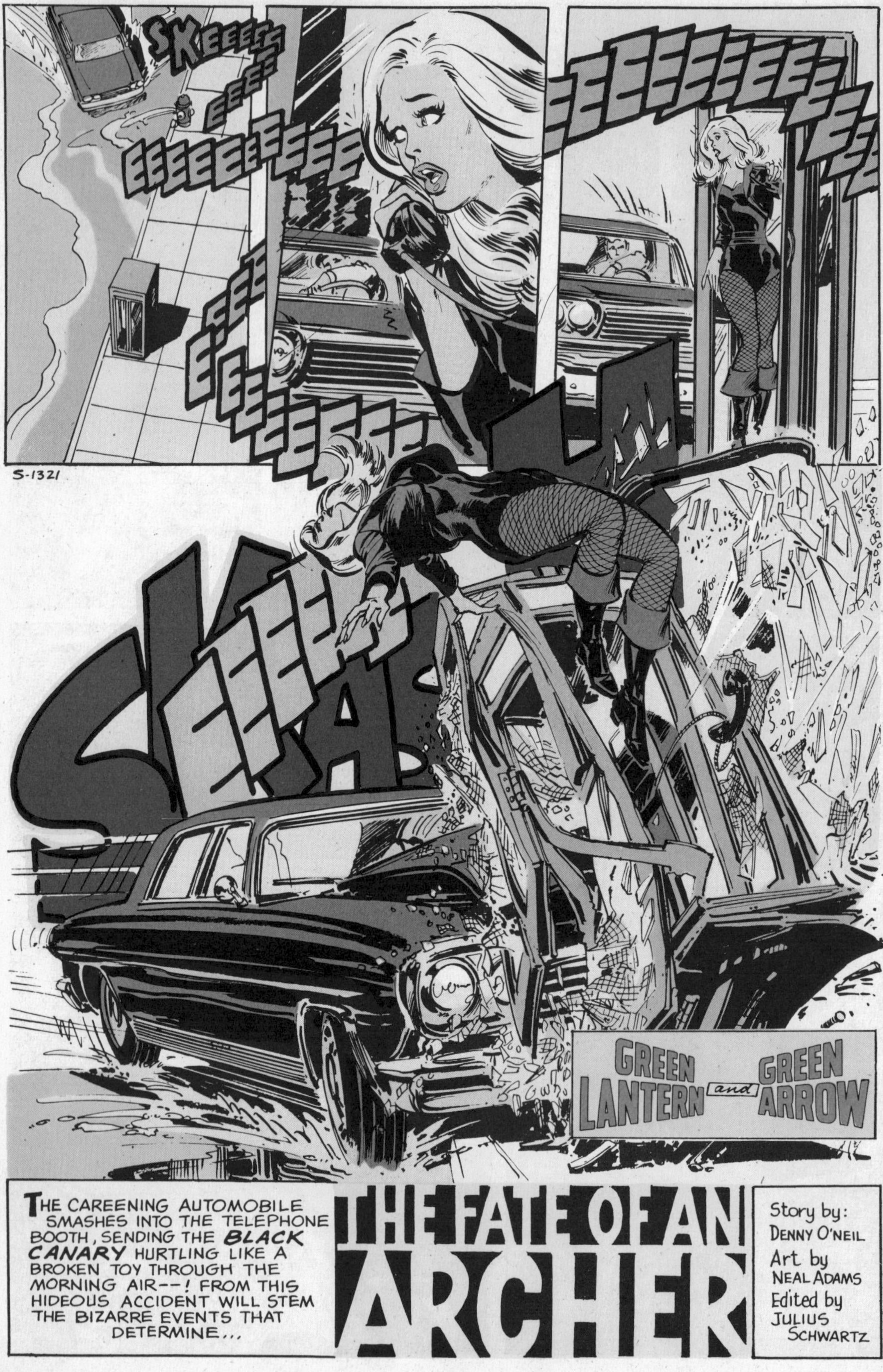
S-1321
GREEN LANTERN and GREEN ARROW
THE CAREENING AUTOMOBILE SMASHES INTO THE TELEPHONE BOOTH, SENDING THE BLACK CANARY HURTLING LIKE A BROKEN TOY THROUGH THE MORNING AIR--! FROM THIS HIDEOUS ACCIDENT WILL STEM THE BIZARRE EVENTS THAT DETERMINE...
THE FATE OF AN ARCHER
Story by: DENNY O'NEIL
Art by NEAL ADAMS
Edited by JULIUS SCHWARTZ

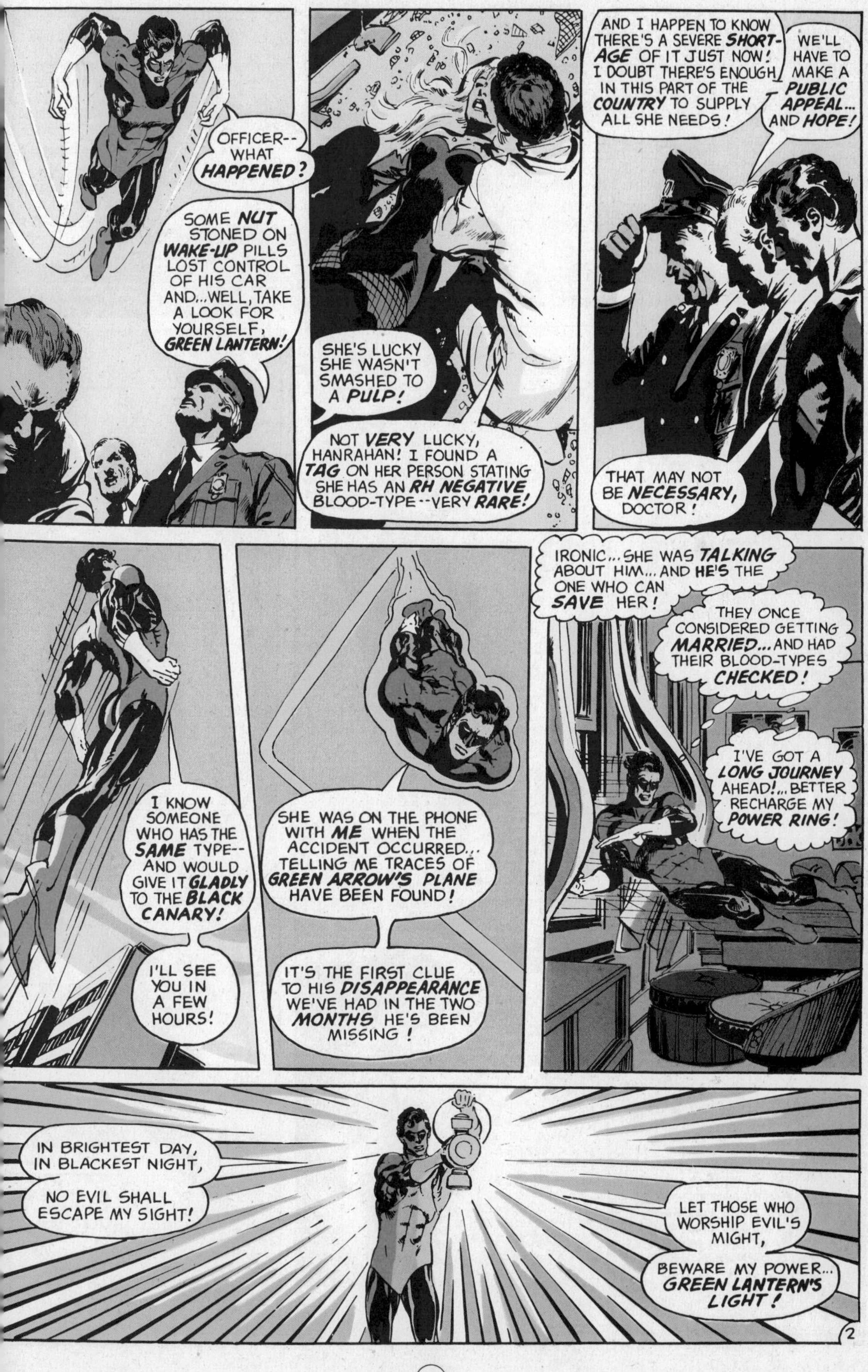

OFFICER-- WHAT HAPPENED?
SOME NUT STONED ON WAKE-UP PILLS LOST CONTROL OF HIS CAR AND...WELL, TAKE A LOOK FOR YOURSELF, GREEN LANTERN!
SHE'S LUCKY SHE WASN'T SMASHED TO A PULP!
NOT VERY LUCKY, HANRAHAN! I FOUND A TAG ON HER PERSON STATING SHE HAS AN RH NEGATIVE BLOOD-TYPE--VERY RARE!
AND I HAPPEN TO KNOW THERE'S A SEVERE SHORTAGE OF IT JUST NOW! I DOUBT THERE'S ENOUGH IN THIS PART OF THE COUNTRY TO SUPPLY ALL SHE NEEDS!
WE'LL HAVE TO MAKE A PUBLIC APPEAL... AND HOPE!
THAT MAY NOT BE NECESSARY, DOCTOR!
I KNOW SOMEONE WHO HAS THE SAME TYPE-- AND WOULD GIVE IT GLADLY TO THE BLACK CANARY!
I'LL SEE YOU IN A FEW HOURS!
SHE WAS ON THE PHONE WITH ME WHEN THE ACCIDENT OCCURRED... TELLING ME TRACES OF GREEN ARROW'S PLANE HAVE BEEN FOUND!
IT'S THE FIRST CLUE TO HIS DISAPPEARANCE WE'VE HAD IN THE TWO MONTHS HE'S BEEN MISSING!
IRONIC... SHE WAS TALKING ABOUT HIM... AND HE'S THE ONE WHO CAN SAVE HER!
THEY ONCE CONSIDERED GETTING MARRIED... AND HAD THEIR BLOOD-TYPES CHECKED!
I'VE GOT A LONG JOURNEY AHEAD!... BETTER RECHARGE MY POWER RING!
IN BRIGHTEST DAY, IN BLACKEST NIGHT,
NO EVIL SHALL ESCAPE MY SIGHT!
LET THOSE WHO WORSHIP EVIL'S MIGHT,
BEWARE MY POWER... GREEN LANTERN'S LIGHT!
2

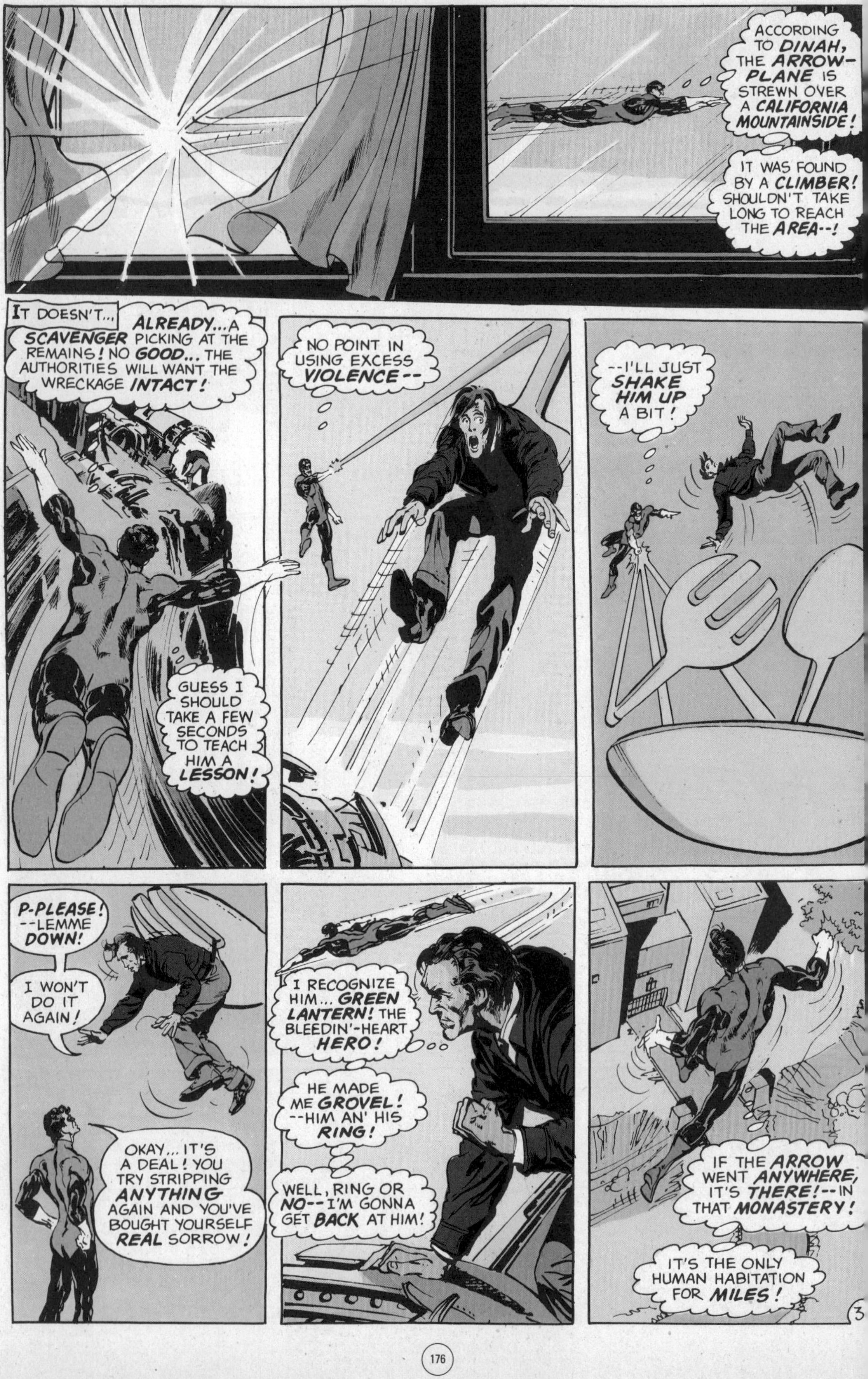
ACCORDING TO DINAH, THE ARROW-PLANE IS STREWN OVER A CALIFORNIA MOUNTAINSIDE!
IT WAS FOUND BY A CLIMBER! SHOULDN'T TAKE LONG TO REACH THE AREA--!
IT DOESN'T...
ALREADY...A SCAVENGER PICKING AT THE REMAINS! NO GOOD... THE AUTHORITIES WILL WANT THE WRECKAGE INTACT!
GUESS I SHOULD TAKE A FEW SECONDS TO TEACH HIM A LESSON!
NO POINT IN USING EXCESS VIOLENCE--
--I'LL JUST SHAKE HIM UP A BIT!
P-PLEASE! --LEMME DOWN!
I WON'T DO IT AGAIN!
OKAY,.. IT'S A DEAL! YOU TRY STRIPPING ANYTHING AGAIN AND YOU'VE BOUGHT YOURSELF REAL SORROW!
I RECOGNIZE HIM... GREEN LANTERN! THE BLEEDIN'-HEART HERO!
HE MADE ME GROVEL! --HIM AN' HIS RING!
WELL, RING OR NO-- I'M GONNA GET BACK AT HIM!
IF THE ARROW WENT ANYWHERE, IT'S THERE!--IN THAT MONASTERY!
IT'S THE ONLY HUMAN HABITATION FOR MILES!
3

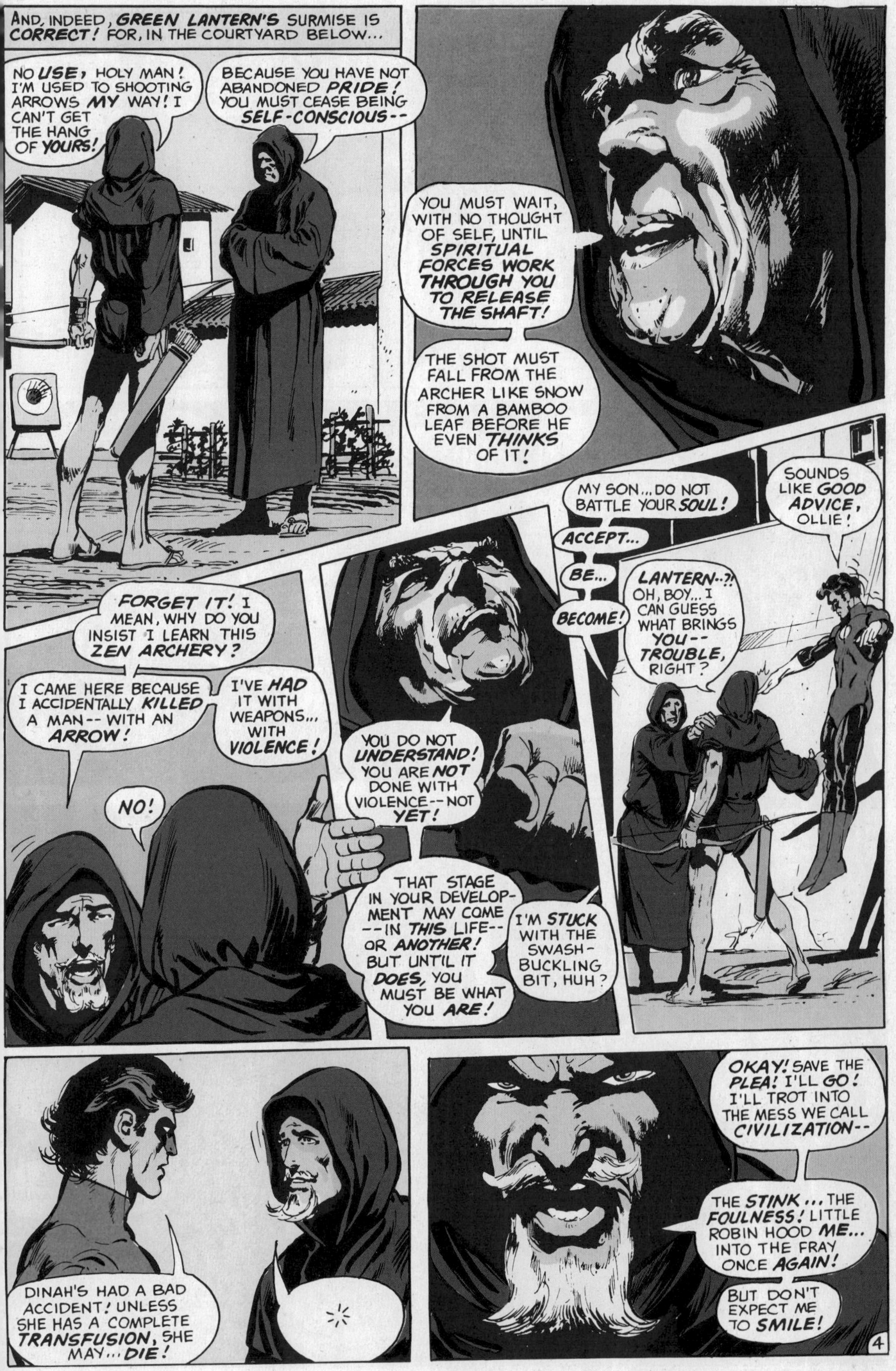

AND, INDEED, GREEN LANTERN'S SURMISE IS CORRECT! FOR, IN THE COURTYARD BELOW...
NO USE, HOLY MAN! I'M USED TO SHOOTING ARROWS MY WAY! I CAN'T GET THE HANG OF YOURS!
BECAUSE YOU HAVE NOT ABANDONED PRIDE! YOU MUST CEASE BEING SELF-CONSCIOUS--
YOU MUST WAIT, WITH NO THOUGHT OF SELF, UNTIL SPIRITUAL FORCES WORK THROUGH YOU TO RELEASE THE SHAFT!
THE SHOT MUST FALL FROM THE ARCHER LIKE SNOW FROM A BAMBOO LEAF BEFORE HE EVEN THINKS OF IT!
FORGET IT! I MEAN, WHY DO YOU INSIST I LEARN THIS ZEN ARCHERY?
I CAME HERE BECAUSE I ACCIDENTALLY KILLED A MAN-- WITH AN ARROW!
I'VE HAD IT WITH WEAPONS... WITH VIOLENCE!
NO!
YOU DO NOT UNDERSTAND! YOU ARE NOT DONE WITH VIOLENCE-- NOT YET!
THAT STAGE IN YOUR DEVELOPMENT MAY COME --IN THIS LIFE-- OR ANOTHER! BUT UNTIL IT DOES, YOU MUST BE WHAT YOU ARE!
I'M STUCK WITH THE SWASH-BUCKLING BIT, HUH?
MY SON... DO NOT BATTLE YOUR SOUL!
ACCEPT...
BE...
BECOME!
SOUNDS LIKE GOOD ADVICE, OLLIE!
LANTERN..?! OH, BOY... I CAN GUESS WHAT BRINGS YOU-- TROUBLE, RIGHT?
DINAH'S HAD A BAD ACCIDENT! UNLESS SHE HAS A COMPLETE TRANSFUSION, SHE MAY... DIE!
OKAY! SAVE THE PLEA! I'LL GO! I'LL TROT INTO THE MESS WE CALL CIVILIZATION--
THE STINK... THE FOULNESS! LITTLE ROBIN HOOD ME... INTO THE FRAY ONCE AGAIN!
BUT DON'T EXPECT ME TO SMILE!
4

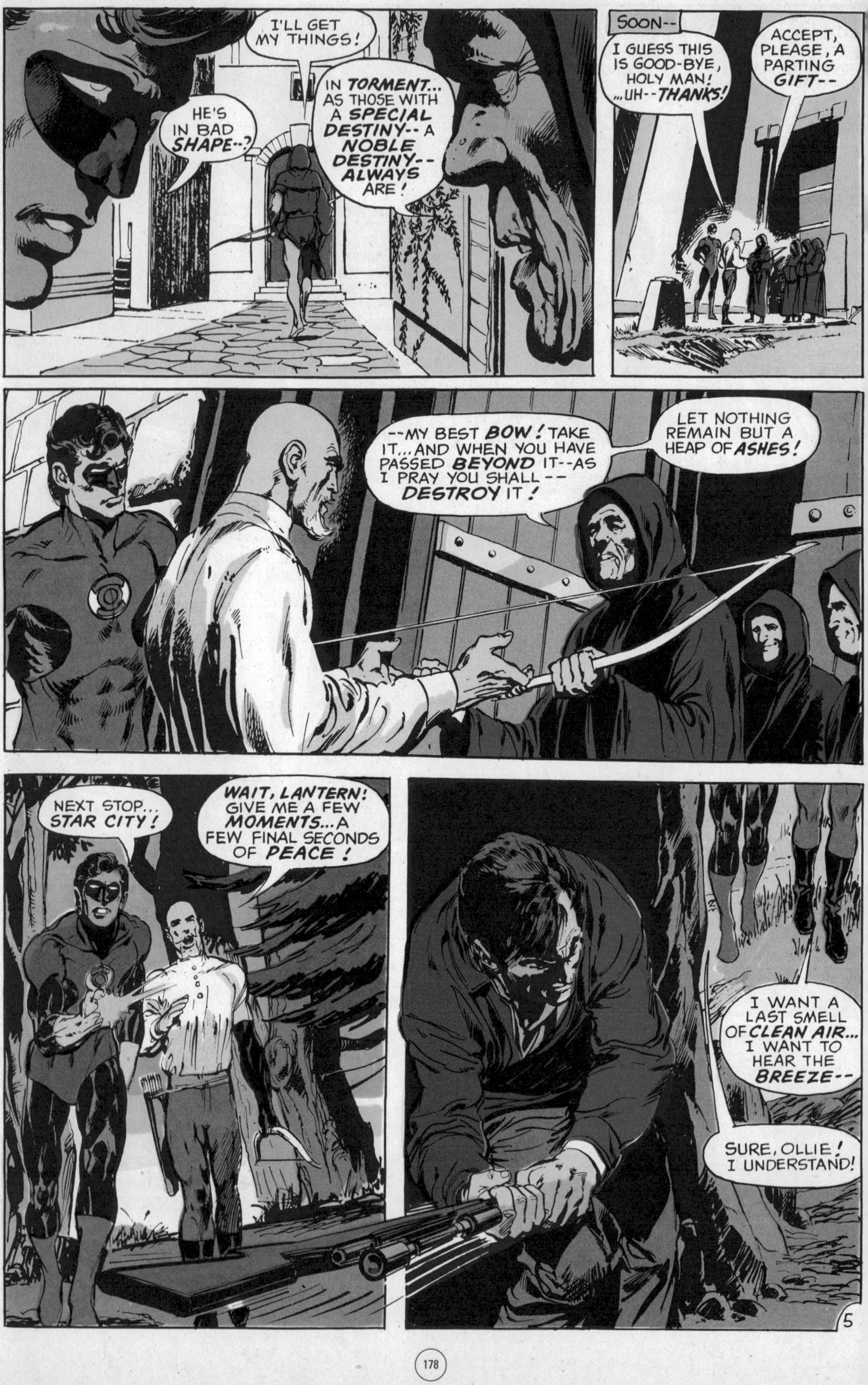
HE'S IN BAD SHAPE--?
I'LL GET MY THINGS!
IN TORMENT... AS THOSE WITH A SPECIAL DESTINY-- A NOBLE DESTINY-- ALWAYS ARE!
SOON--
I GUESS THIS IS GOOD-BYE, HOLY MAN! ...UH--THANKS!
ACCEPT, PLEASE, A PARTING GIFT--
--MY BEST BOW! TAKE IT... AND WHEN YOU HAVE PASSED BEYOND IT--AS I PRAY YOU SHALL-- DESTROY IT!
LET NOTHING REMAIN BUT A HEAP OF ASHES!
NEXT STOP... STAR CITY!
WAIT, LANTERN! GIVE ME A FEW MOMENTS... A FEW FINAL SECONDS OF PEACE!
I WANT A LAST SMELL OF CLEAN AIR... I WANT TO HEAR THE BREEZE--
SURE, OLLIE! I UNDERSTAND!
5

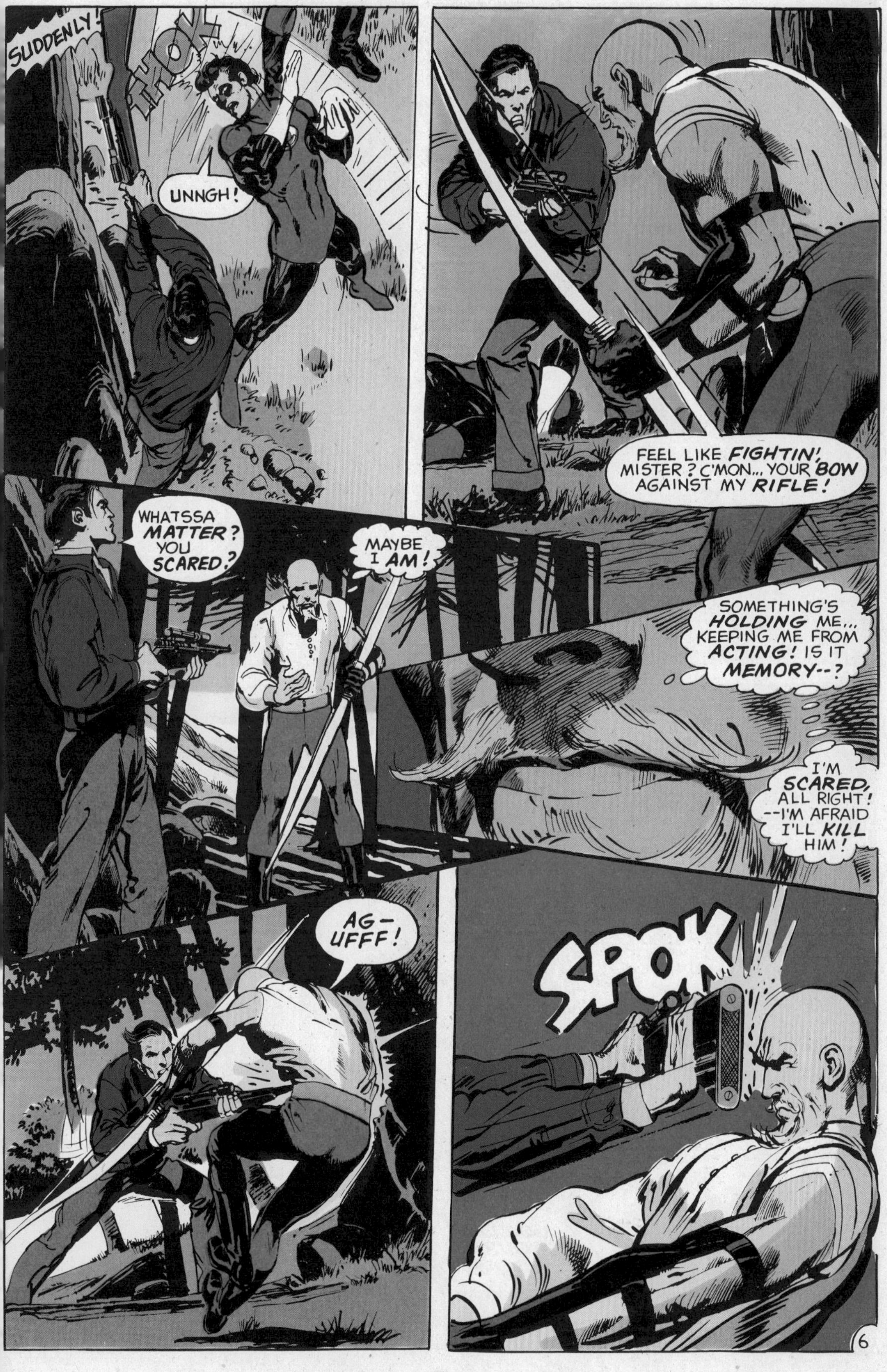
SUDDENLY!
THOK
UNNGH!
FEEL LIKE FIGHTIN', MISTER? C'MON... YOUR BOW AGAINST MY RIFLE!
WHATSSA MATTER? YOU SCARED?
MAYBE I AM!
SOMETHING'S HOLDING ME... KEEPING ME FROM ACTING! IS IT MEMORY--?
I'M SCARED, ALL RIGHT! --I'M AFRAID I'LL KILL HIM!
AG-UFFF!
SPOK
6

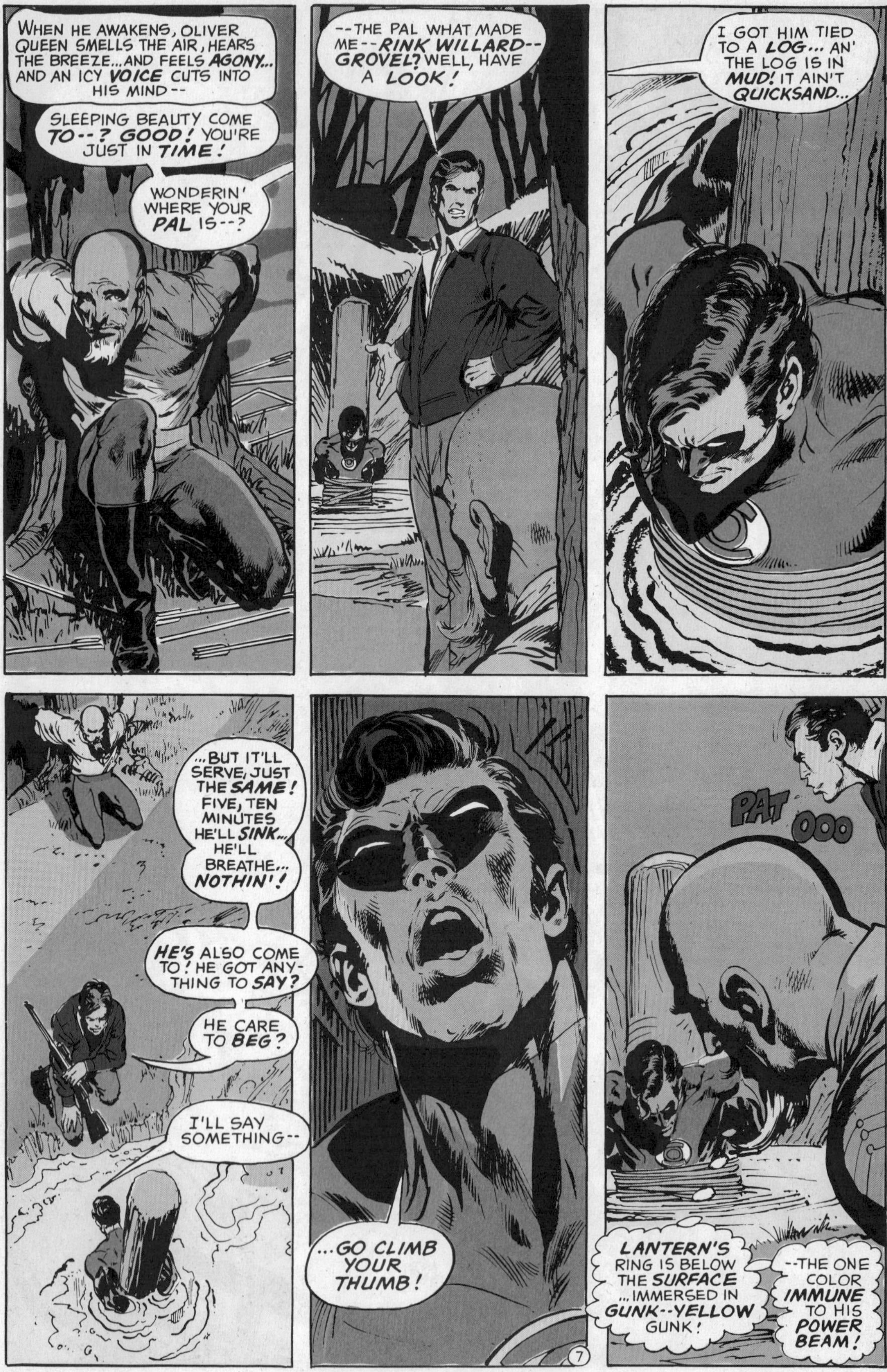
WHEN HE AWAKENS, OLIVER QUEEN SMELLS THE AIR, HEARS THE BREEZE...AND FEELS AGONY... AND AN ICY VOICE CUTS INTO HIS MIND--
SLEEPING BEAUTY COME TO--? GOOD! YOU'RE JUST IN TIME!
WONDERIN' WHERE YOUR PAL IS--?
--THE PAL WHAT MADE ME--RINK WILLARD--GROVEL? WELL, HAVE A LOOK!
I GOT HIM TIED TO A LOG... AN' THE LOG IS IN MUD! IT AIN'T QUICKSAND...
...BUT IT'LL SERVE, JUST THE SAME! FIVE, TEN MINUTES HE'LL SINK... HE'LL BREATHE... NOTHIN'!
HE'S ALSO COME TO! HE GOT ANYTHING TO SAY?
HE CARE TO BEG?
I'LL SAY SOMETHING--
...GO CLIMB YOUR THUMB!
PAT
OOO
LANTERN'S RING IS BELOW THE SURFACE ...IMMERSED IN GUNK--YELLOW GUNK!
--THE ONE COLOR IMMUNE TO HIS POWER BEAM!
7

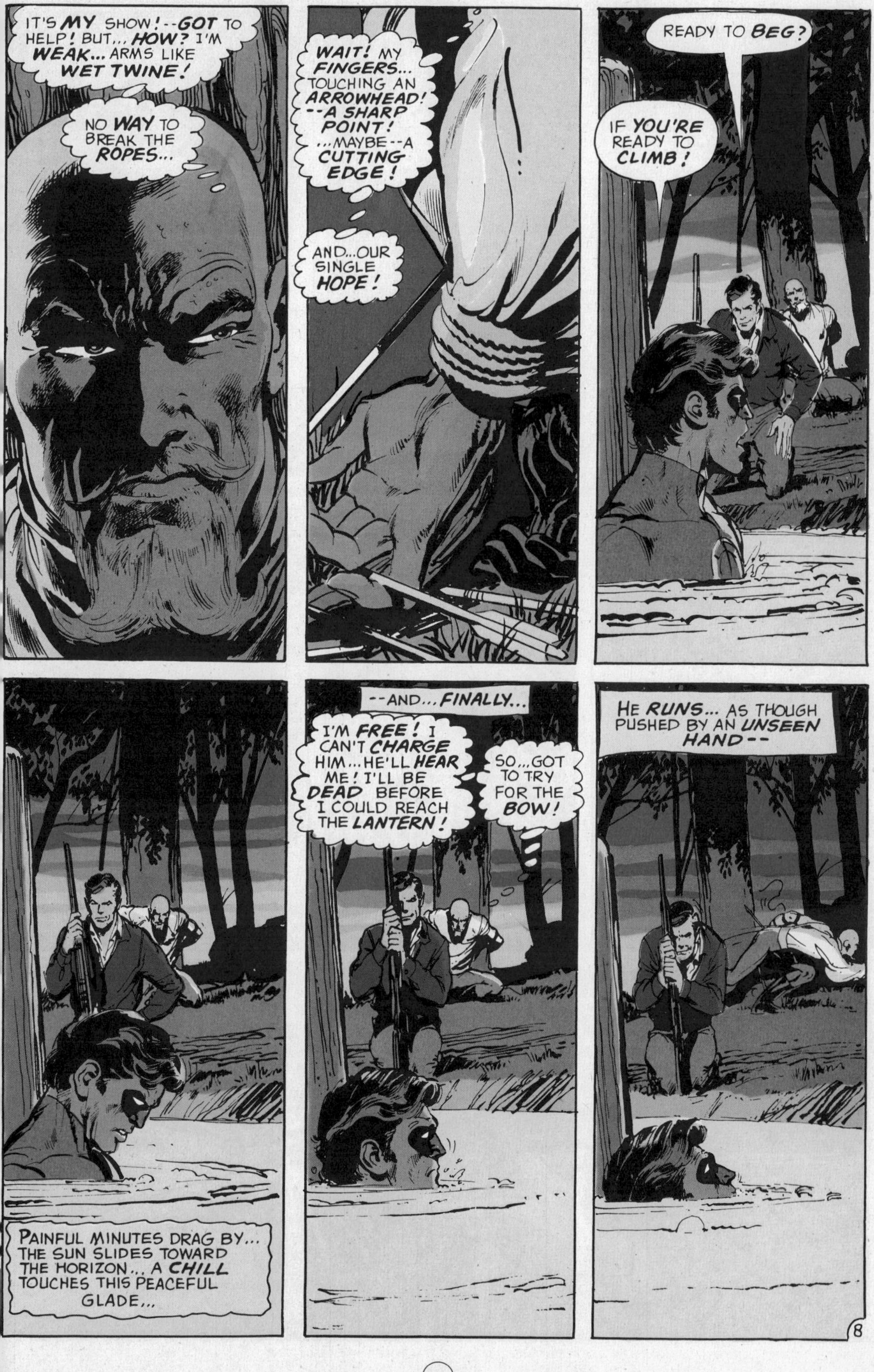
IT'S MY SHOW! --GOT TO HELP! BUT... HOW? I'M WEAK... ARMS LIKE WET TWINE!
NO WAY TO BREAK THE ROPES...
WAIT! MY FINGERS... TOUCHING AN ARROWHEAD! --A SHARP POINT! ...MAYBE--A CUTTING EDGE!
AND...OUR SINGLE HOPE!
READY TO BEG?
IF YOU'RE READY TO CLIMB!
PAINFUL MINUTES DRAG BY... THE SUN SLIDES TOWARD THE HORIZON... A CHILL TOUCHES THIS PEACEFUL GLADE...
--AND... FINALLY...
I'M FREE! I CAN'T CHARGE HIM...HE'LL HEAR ME! I'LL BE DEAD BEFORE I COULD REACH THE LANTERN!
SO...GOT TO TRY FOR THE BOW!
HE RUNS... AS THOUGH PUSHED BY AN UNSEEN HAND--
8

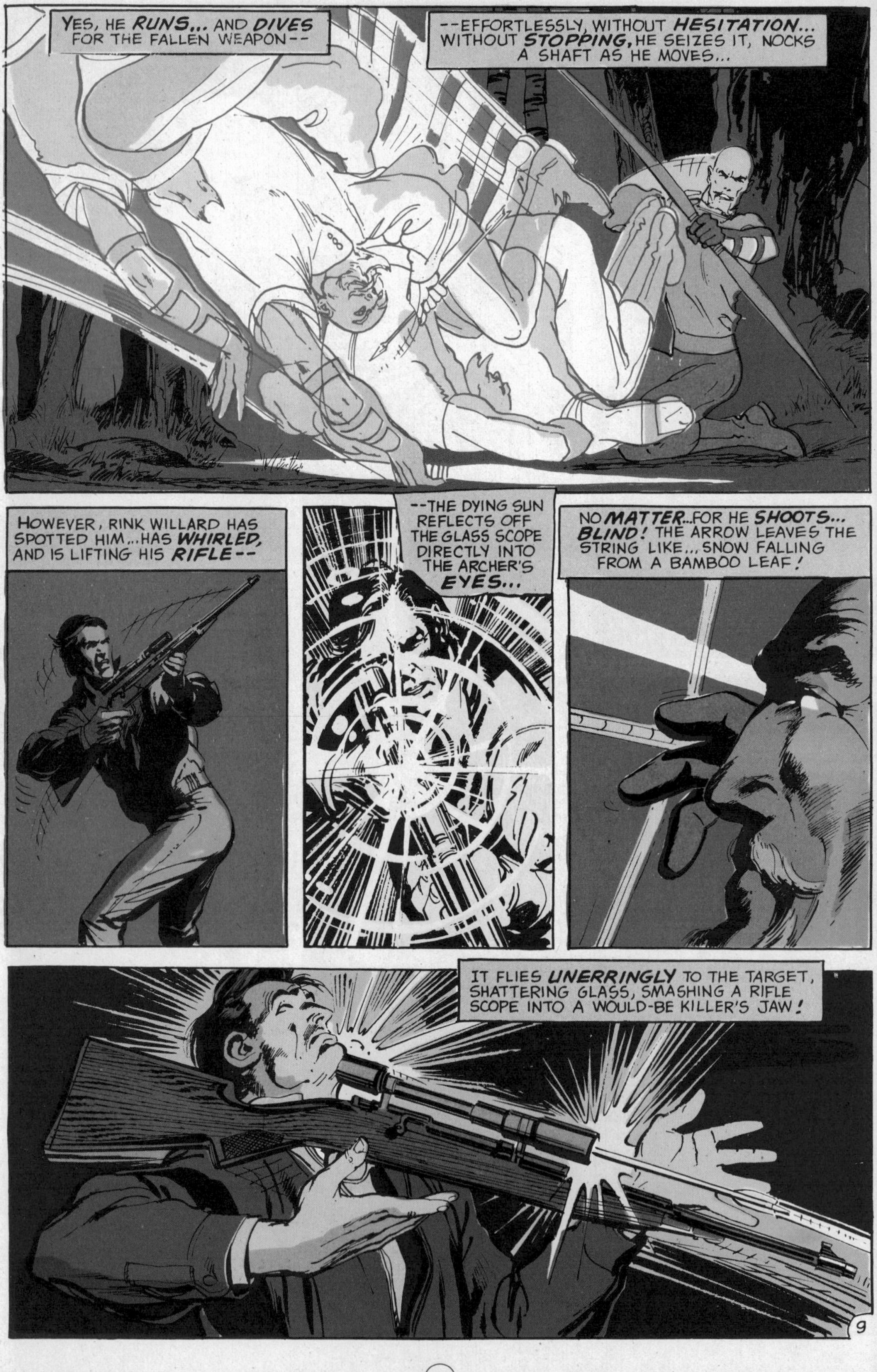
YES, HE RUNS... AND DIVES FOR THE FALLEN WEAPON--
--EFFORTLESSLY, WITHOUT HESITATION... WITHOUT STOPPING, HE SEIZES IT, NOCKS A SHAFT AS HE MOVES...
HOWEVER, RINK WILLARD HAS SPOTTED HIM...HAS WHIRLED, AND IS LIFTING HIS RIFLE--
--THE DYING SUN REFLECTS OFF THE GLASS SCOPE DIRECTLY INTO THE ARCHER'S EYES...
NO MATTER...FOR HE SHOOTS... BLIND! THE ARROW LEAVES THE STRING LIKE... SNOW FALLING FROM A BAMBOO LEAF!
IT FLIES UNERRINGLY TO THE TARGET, SHATTERING GLASS, SMASHING A RIFLE SCOPE INTO A WOULD-BE KILLER'S JAW!
9

WITHIN AN HOUR...
WE'VE BEEN SO BUSY GETTING HERE, I HAVEN'T HAD AN OPPORTUNITY TO TELL YOU...YOU DID GOOD!
YEAH...I FOUND MYSELF OUT THERE! AT LEAST TEMPORARILY, I KNOW WHO I AM!
SOMETIMES, LANTERN, I CAN ALMOST BELIEVE IN A HAPPY ENDING!
10

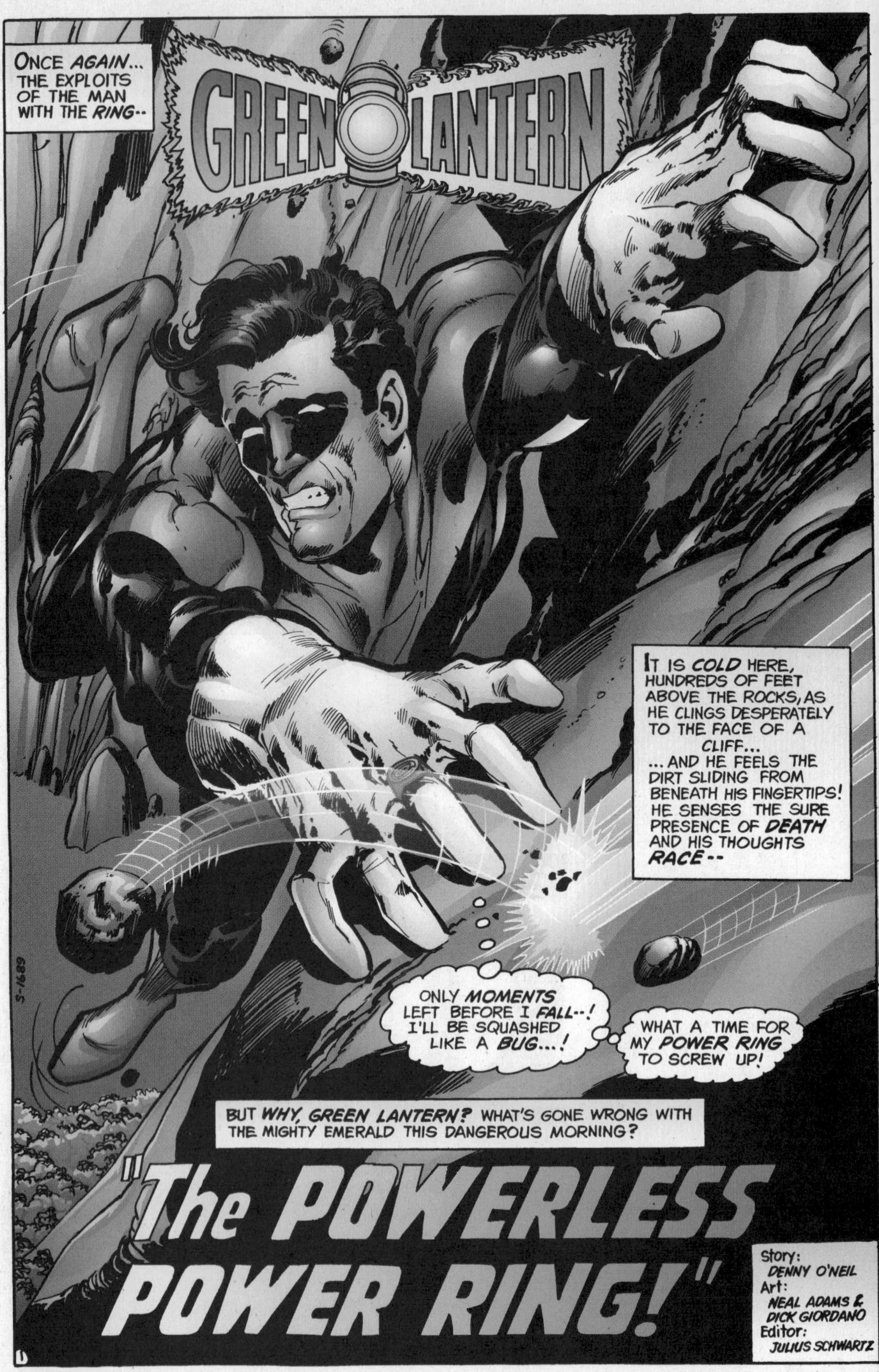
ONCE AGAIN... THE EXPLOITS OF THE MAN WITH THE RING--
GREEN LANTERN
IT IS COLD HERE, HUNDREDS OF FEET ABOVE THE ROCKS, AS HE CLINGS DESPERATELY TO THE FACE OF A CLIFF... ...AND HE FEELS THE DIRT SLIDING FROM BENEATH HIS FINGERTIPS! HE SENSES THE SURE PRESENCE OF DEATH AND HIS THOUGHTS RACE--
ONLY MOMENTS LEFT BEFORE I FALL--! I'LL BE SQUASHED LIKE A BUG...!
WHAT A TIME FOR MY POWER RING TO SCREW UP!
BUT WHY, GREEN LANTERN? WHAT'S GONE WRONG WITH THE MIGHTY EMERALD THIS DANGEROUS MORNING?
"The POWERLESS POWER RING!"
Story: DENNY O'NEIL
Art: NEAL ADAMS & DICK GIORDANO
Editor: JULIUS SCHWARTZ
S-1689
1

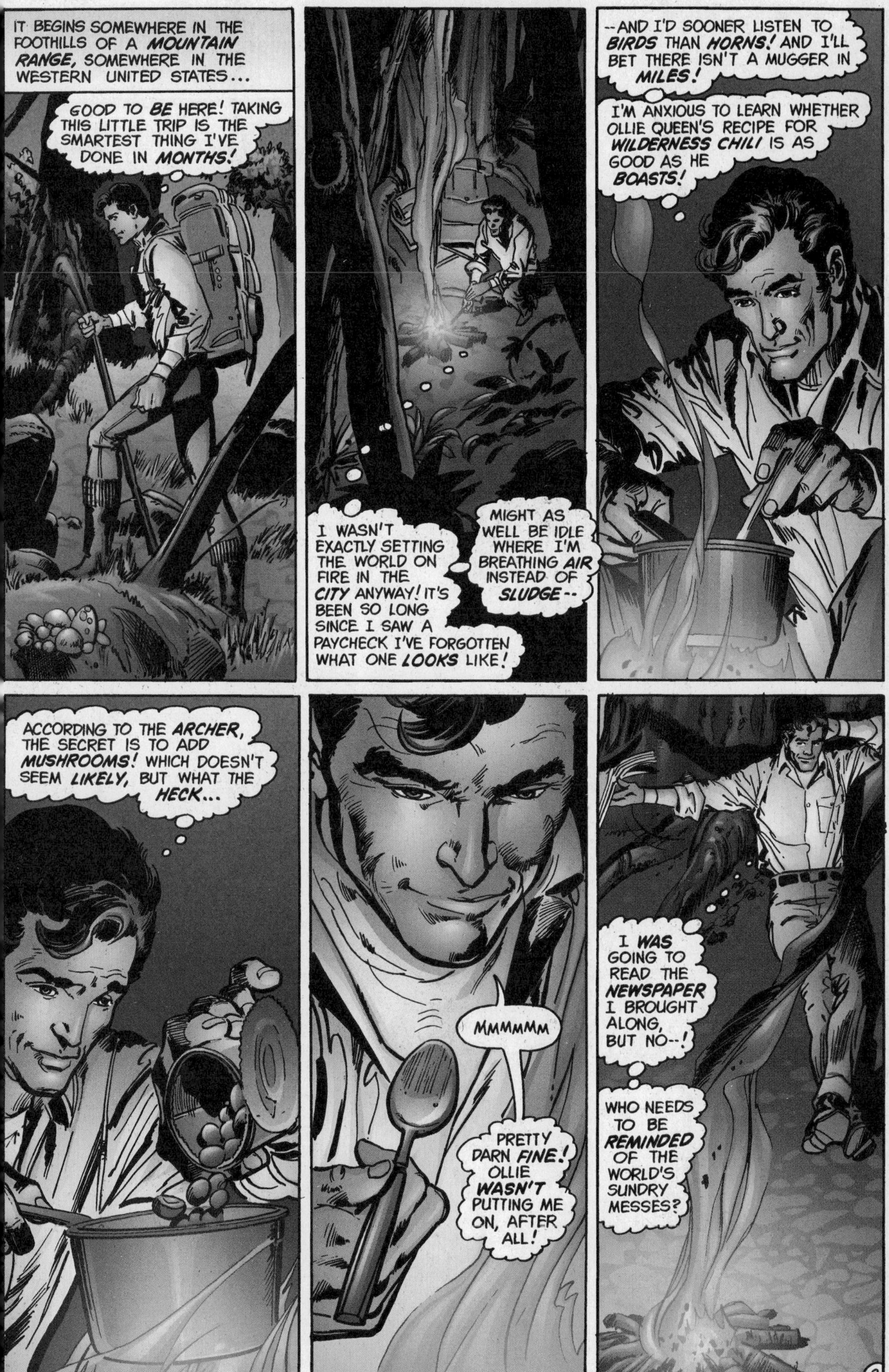
IT BEGINS SOMEWHERE IN THE FOOTHILLS OF A MOUNTAIN RANGE, SOMEWHERE IN THE WESTERN UNITED STATES...
GOOD TO BE HERE! TAKING THIS LITTLE TRIP IS THE SMARTEST THING I'VE DONE IN MONTHS!
I WASN'T EXACTLY SETTING THE WORLD ON FIRE IN THE CITY ANYWAY! IT'S BEEN SO LONG SINCE I SAW A PAYCHECK I'VE FORGOTTEN WHAT ONE LOOKS LIKE!
MIGHT AS WELL BE IDLE WHERE I'M BREATHING AIR INSTEAD OF SLUDGE--
--AND I'D SOONER LISTEN TO BIRDS THAN HORNS! AND I'LL BET THERE ISN'T A MUGGER IN MILES!
I'M ANXIOUS TO LEARN WHETHER OLLIE QUEEN'S RECIPE FOR WILDERNESS CHILI IS AS GOOD AS HE BOASTS!
ACCORDING TO THE ARCHER, THE SECRET IS TO ADD MUSHROOMS! WHICH DOESN'T SEEM LIKELY, BUT WHAT THE HECK...
MMMMMM
PRETTY DARN FINE! OLLIE WASN'T PUTTING ME ON, AFTER ALL!
I WAS GOING TO READ THE NEWSPAPER I BROUGHT ALONG, BUT NO--!
WHO NEEDS TO BE REMINDED OF THE WORLD'S SUNDRY MESSES?
2

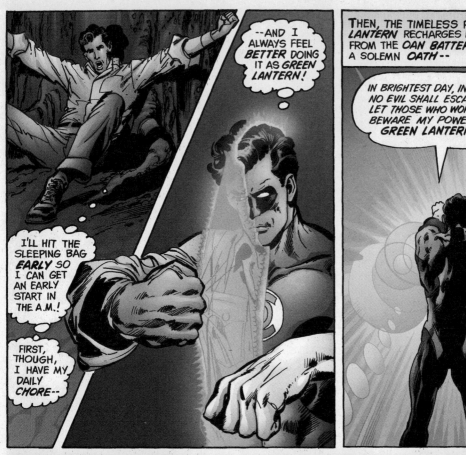

--AND I ALWAYS FEEL *BETTER* DOING IT AS *GREEN LANTERN!*

I'LL HIT THE SLEEPING BAG *EARLY* SO I CAN GET AN EARLY START IN THE A.M.!

FIRST, THOUGH, I HAVE MY DAILY *CHORE*--

THEN, THE TIMELESS RITUAL, AS *GREEN LANTERN* RECHARGES HIS *POWER RING* FROM THE *OAN BATTERY* AND RENEWS A SOLEMN *OATH*--

IN BRIGHTEST DAY, IN BLACKEST NIGHT, NO EVIL SHALL ESCAPE MY SIGHT! LET THOSE WHO WORSHIP EVIL'S MIGHT BEWARE MY POWER-- *GREEN LANTERN'S LIGHT!*

SUDDENLY, THE PURPLE SHADOWS *VANISH* AS A SUDDEN, FIERY *DISPLAY* SHATTERS THE NIGHT SKY--

WHAT'S *THAT?* A *BOLIDE*--AN *EXPLODING METEOR?* --OR MAYBE THE *AURORA BOREALIS?*

IT'S *FADING...* GUESS IT WASN'T *HARMFUL!*-- NOTHING TO LOSE *SLEEP* ABOUT!

3

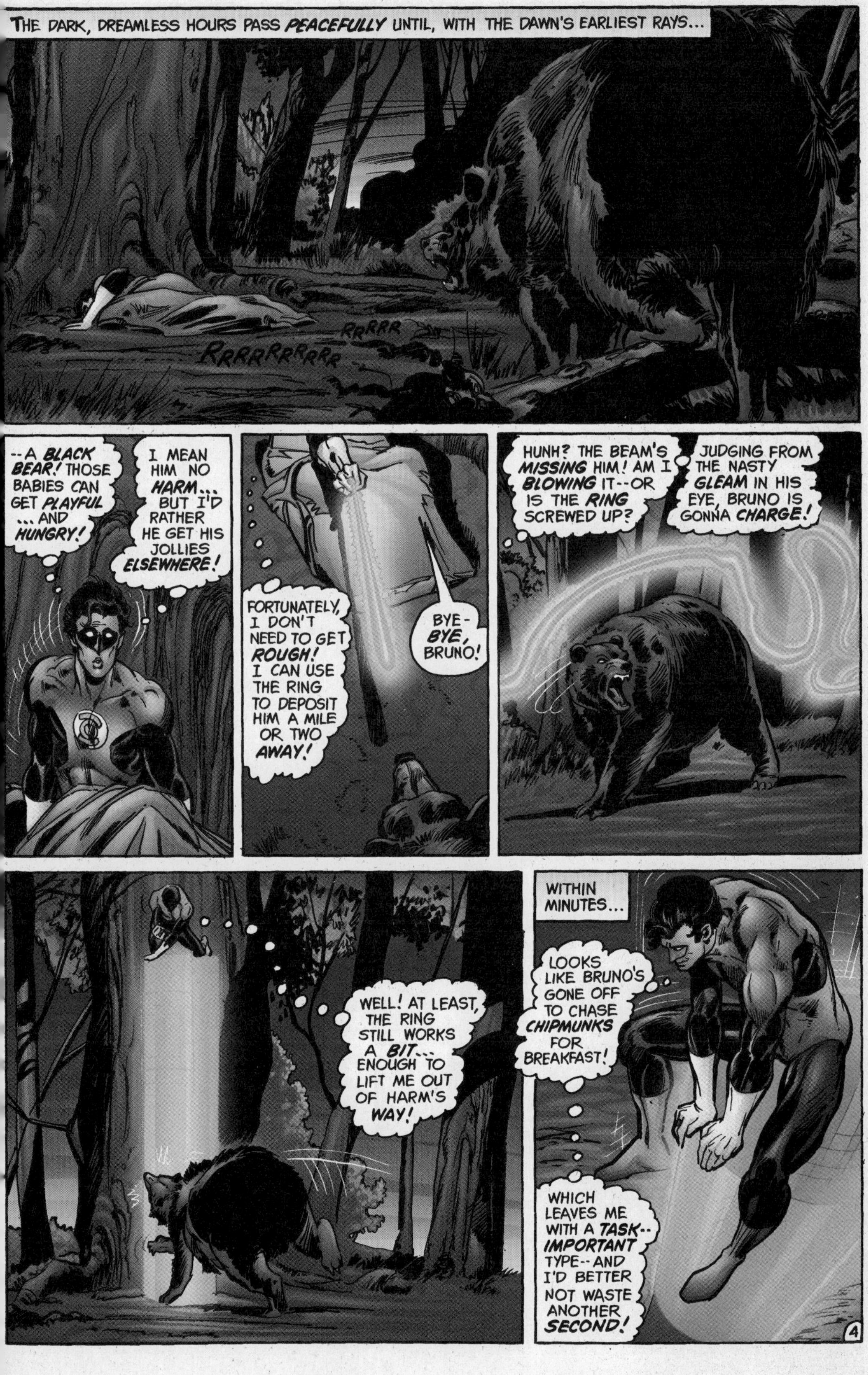

THE DARK, DREAMLESS HOURS PASS PEACEFULLY UNTIL, WITH THE DAWN'S EARLIEST RAYS...
RRRRR
RRRRRRRRRR
--A BLACK BEAR! THOSE BABIES CAN GET PLAYFUL ...AND HUNGRY!
I MEAN HIM NO HARM... BUT I'D RATHER HE GET HIS JOLLIES ELSEWHERE!
FORTUNATELY, I DON'T NEED TO GET ROUGH! I CAN USE THE RING TO DEPOSIT HIM A MILE OR TWO AWAY!
BYE-BYE, BRUNO!
HUNH? THE BEAM'S MISSING HIM! AM I BLOWING IT--OR IS THE RING SCREWED UP?
JUDGING FROM THE NASTY GLEAM IN HIS EYE, BRUNO IS GONNA CHARGE!
WELL! AT LEAST, THE RING STILL WORKS A BIT... ENOUGH TO LIFT ME OUT OF HARM'S WAY!
WITHIN MINUTES...
LOOKS LIKE BRUNO'S GONE OFF TO CHASE CHIPMUNKS FOR BREAKFAST!
WHICH LEAVES ME WITH A TASK-- IMPORTANT TYPE-- AND I'D BETTER NOT WASTE ANOTHER SECOND!
4

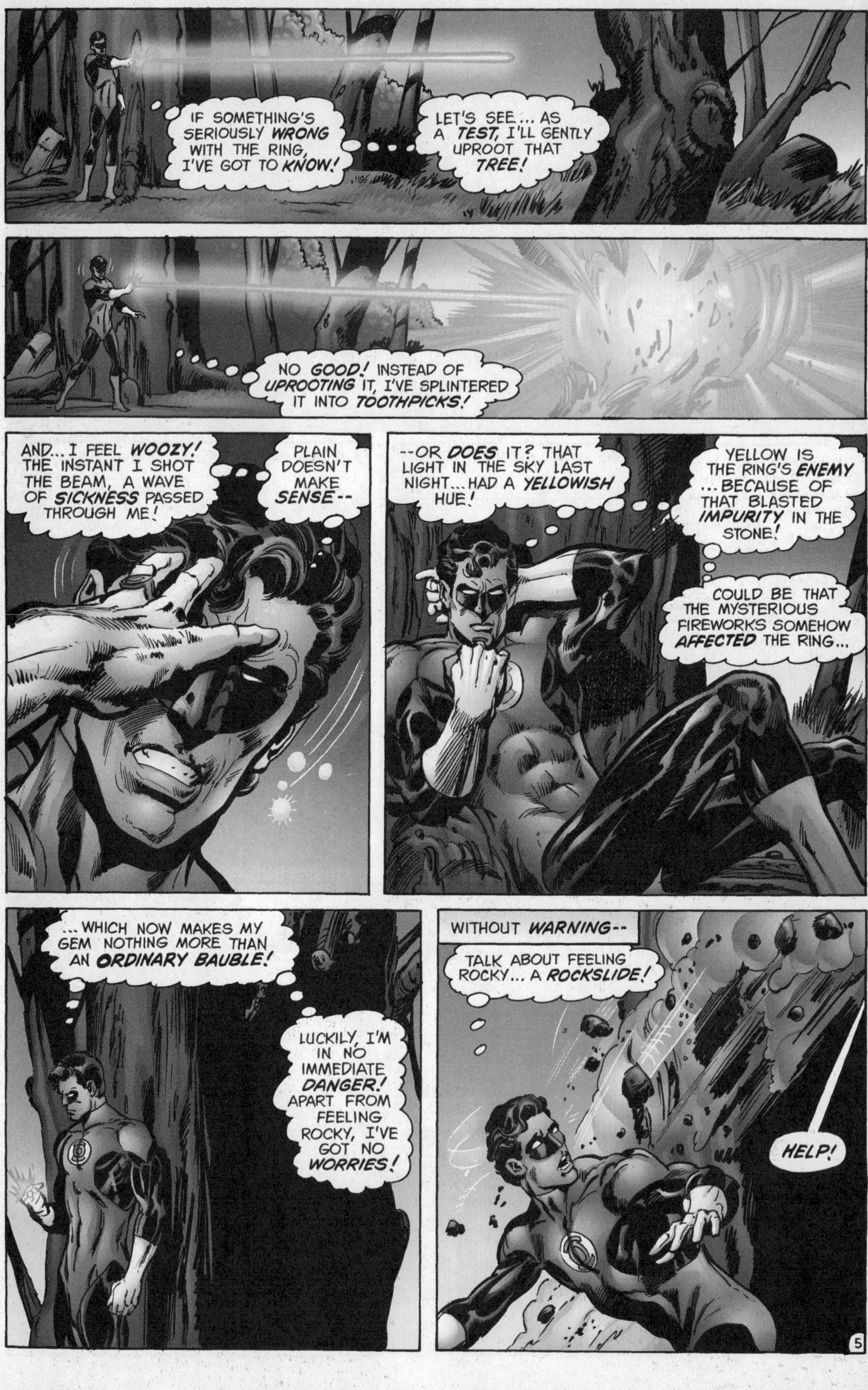
IF SOMETHING'S SERIOUSLY WRONG WITH THE RING, I'VE GOT TO KNOW!
LET'S SEE... AS A TEST, I'LL GENTLY UPROOT THAT TREE!
NO GOOD! INSTEAD OF UPROOTING IT, I'VE SPLINTERED IT INTO TOOTHPICKS!
AND... I FEEL WOOZY! THE INSTANT I SHOT THE BEAM, A WAVE OF SICKNESS PASSED THROUGH ME!
PLAIN DOESN'T MAKE SENSE--
--OR DOES IT? THAT LIGHT IN THE SKY LAST NIGHT... HAD A YELLOWISH HUE!
YELLOW IS THE RING'S ENEMY ... BECAUSE OF THAT BLASTED IMPURITY IN THE STONE!
COULD BE THAT THE MYSTERIOUS FIREWORKS SOMEHOW AFFECTED THE RING...
... WHICH NOW MAKES MY GEM NOTHING MORE THAN AN ORDINARY BAUBLE!
LUCKILY, I'M IN NO IMMEDIATE DANGER! APART FROM FEELING ROCKY, I'VE GOT NO WORRIES!
WITHOUT WARNING--
TALK ABOUT FEELING ROCKY... A ROCKSLIDE!
HELP!

A *CRY*... FROM THE DIRECTION OF THE *SLIDE!*

MAYBE THE *BINOCULARS* WILL SHOW ME WHO'S IN *TROUBLE*-- AND *WHY!*

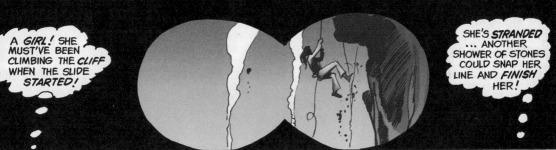

A *GIRL!* SHE MUST'VE BEEN CLIMBING THE *CLIFF* WHEN THE SLIDE STARTED!

SHE'S *STRANDED* ... ANOTHER SHOWER OF STONES COULD SNAP HER LINE AND *FINISH* HER!

NO TIME TO GO FOR *ASSISTANCE* ... I'VE GOT TO DO THE RESCUE-BIT *MYSELF!*

IT'D BE SO *EASY* TO USE THE *RING* ... AND SO *WRONG!*

I'D BE GAMBLING WITH HER *LIFE!* THE BEAM *MIGHT* SAVE HER--OR IT MIGHT SPLINTER HER ROPE LIKE THE *TREE!*

SO IT'S A RESCUE-- *IN PERSON!*

6

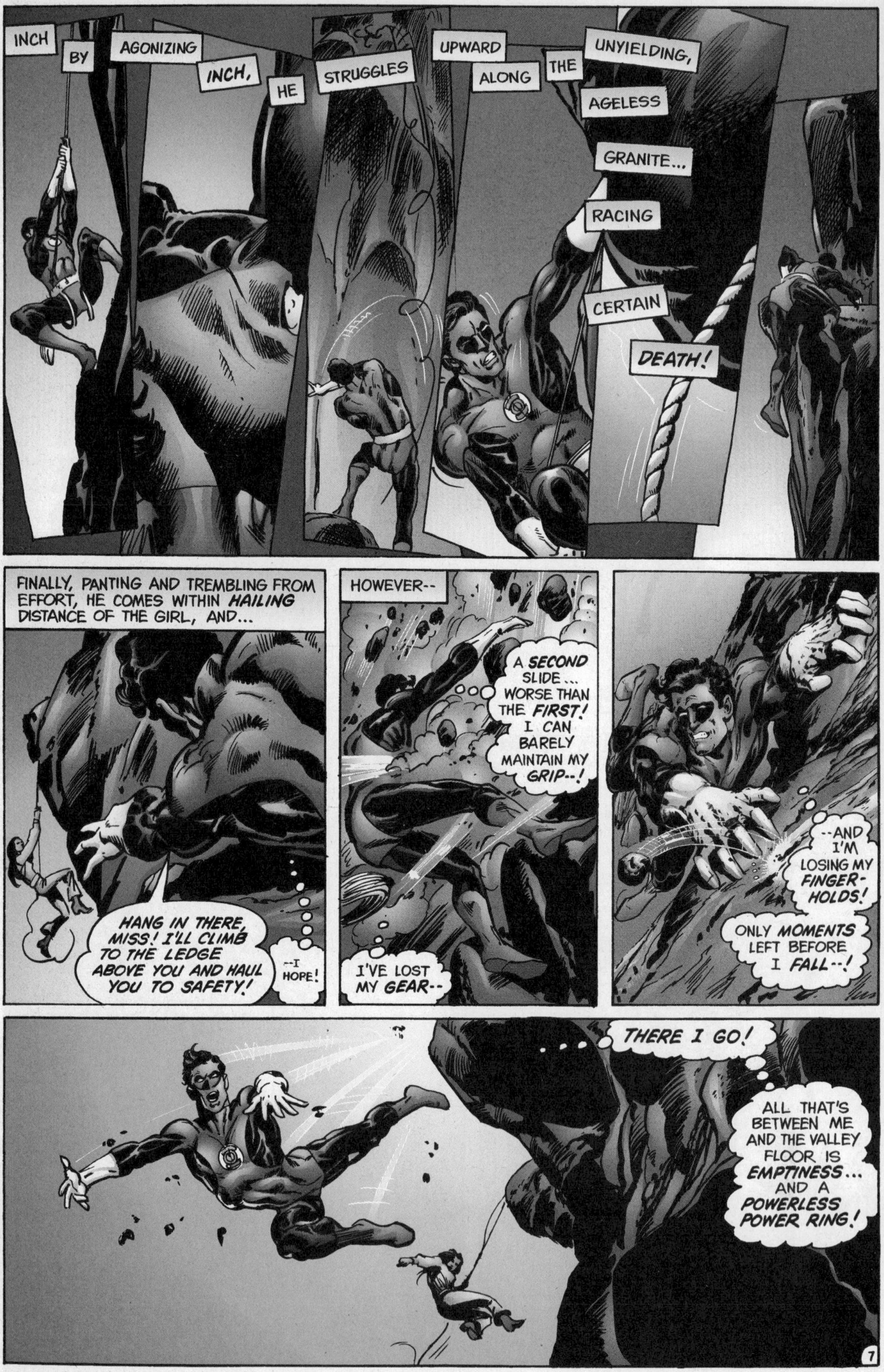
INCH
BY
AGONIZING
INCH,
HE
STRUGGLES
UPWARD
ALONG
THE
UNYIELDING,
AGELESS
GRANITE...
RACING
CERTAIN
DEATH!
FINALLY, PANTING AND TREMBLING FROM EFFORT, HE COMES WITHIN HAILING DISTANCE OF THE GIRL, AND...
HANG IN THERE, MISS! I'LL CLIMB TO THE LEDGE ABOVE YOU AND HAUL YOU TO SAFETY!
--I HOPE!
HOWEVER--
A SECOND SLIDE... WORSE THAN THE FIRST! I CAN BARELY MAINTAIN MY GRIP--!
I'VE LOST MY GEAR--
--AND I'M LOSING MY FINGER-HOLDS!
ONLY MOMENTS LEFT BEFORE I FALL--!
THERE I GO!
ALL THAT'S BETWEEN ME AND THE VALLEY FLOOR IS EMPTINESS... AND A POWERLESS POWER RING!
7

INSTINCT? DESPERATION? OR A SOUL-DEEP DETERMINATION TO *SURVIVE*... WHATEVER THE REASON, GREEN LANTERN SURGES HIS WILL THROUGH THE RING AND, TO HIS UTTER *ASTONISHMENT*--

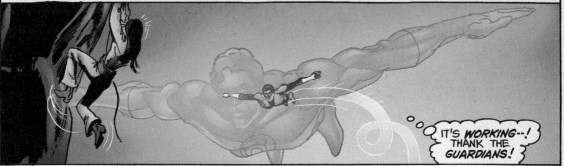

IT'S *WORKING*--! THANK THE *GUARDIANS*!

MISS, CONSIDER YOURSELF *RESCUED*-- IN *STYLE*!

LATER... *RELAX*, MISS --AND PREPARE FOR A *TREAT*! CHILI À LA *LANTERN*-- SPECIALTY OF THE *HOUSE*!... ER-- *CAMP*!

BY THE WAY... DID YOU SEE THE *FLAREUP* IN THE *SKY* LAST EVENING?

I SURE DID! THERE WAS A BIG DISCUSSION ABOUT IT ON THE *RADIO*--

--SOME KIND OF THINGY WITH THE *WEATHER*... OR A *COMET*... OR *BOTH*! I THOUGHT IT WAS *GORGEOUSEST*!

SAAYYY...YOU HAVEN'T BEEN EATING THESE *MUSHROOMS*? FOR DAYS THE NEWSPAPERS HAVE BEEN WARNING THIS BRAND IS *DANGEROUS* -- CAUSES *WEIRDS* TO HAPPEN TO PEOPLE!

FOR *HOURS* AFTER EATING THEM, PEOPLE CAN'T OPERATE A *CAR*... OR AN *AIRPLANE*... OR *ANYTHING*--!

OR... A *POWER RING*!

DAILY $1 NEWS
GREEN LANTERN RESCUES MAIV

The End

8

191

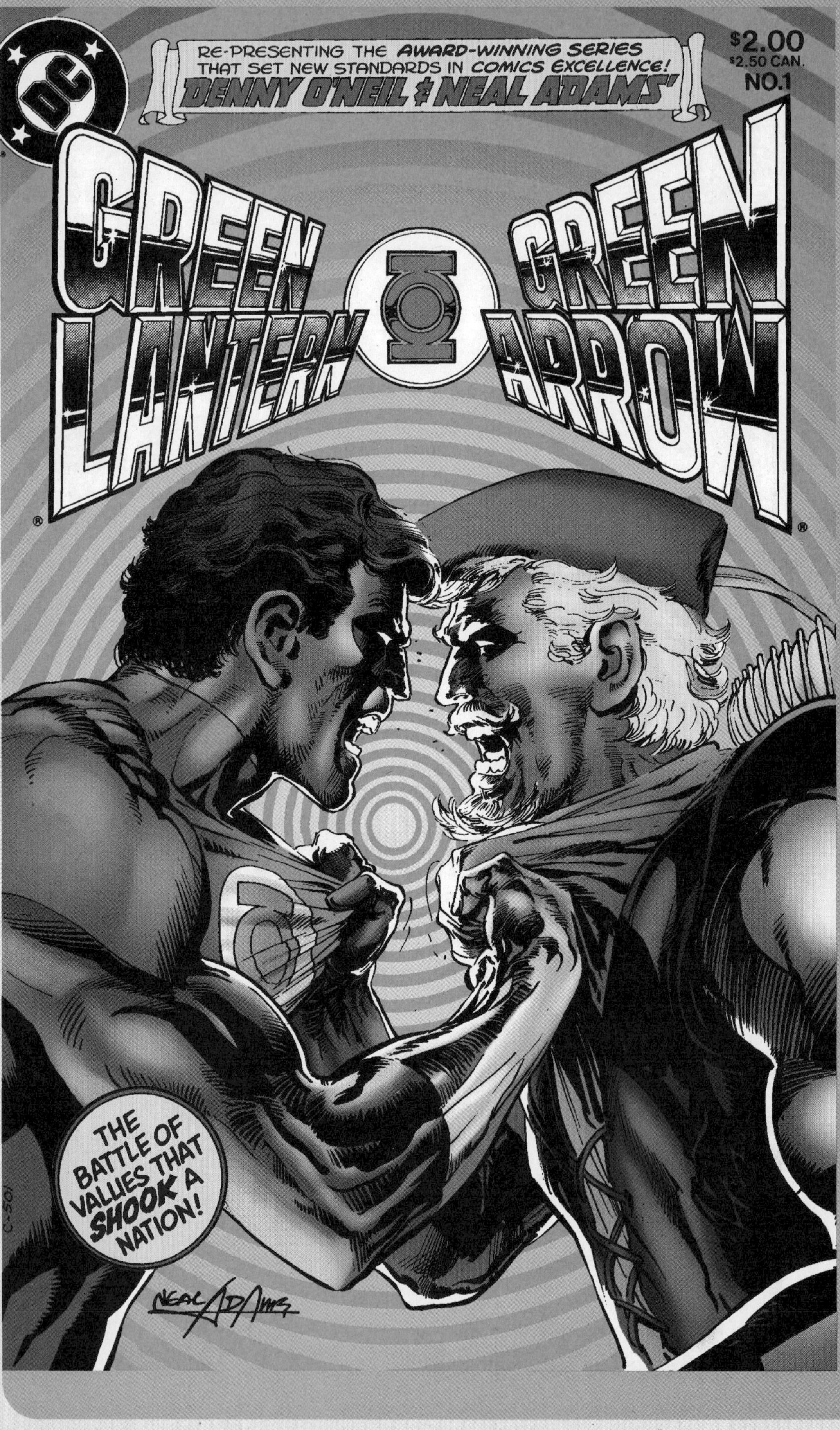
DC
RE-PRESENTING THE AWARD-WINNING SERIES
THAT SET NEW STANDARDS IN COMICS EXCELLENCE!
DENNY O'NEIL & NEAL ADAMS'
$2.00
$2.50 CAN.
NO.1
GREEN LANTERN
GREEN ARROW
THE BATTLE OF VALUES THAT SHOOK A NATION!
NEAL ADAMS

All covers by Neal Adams

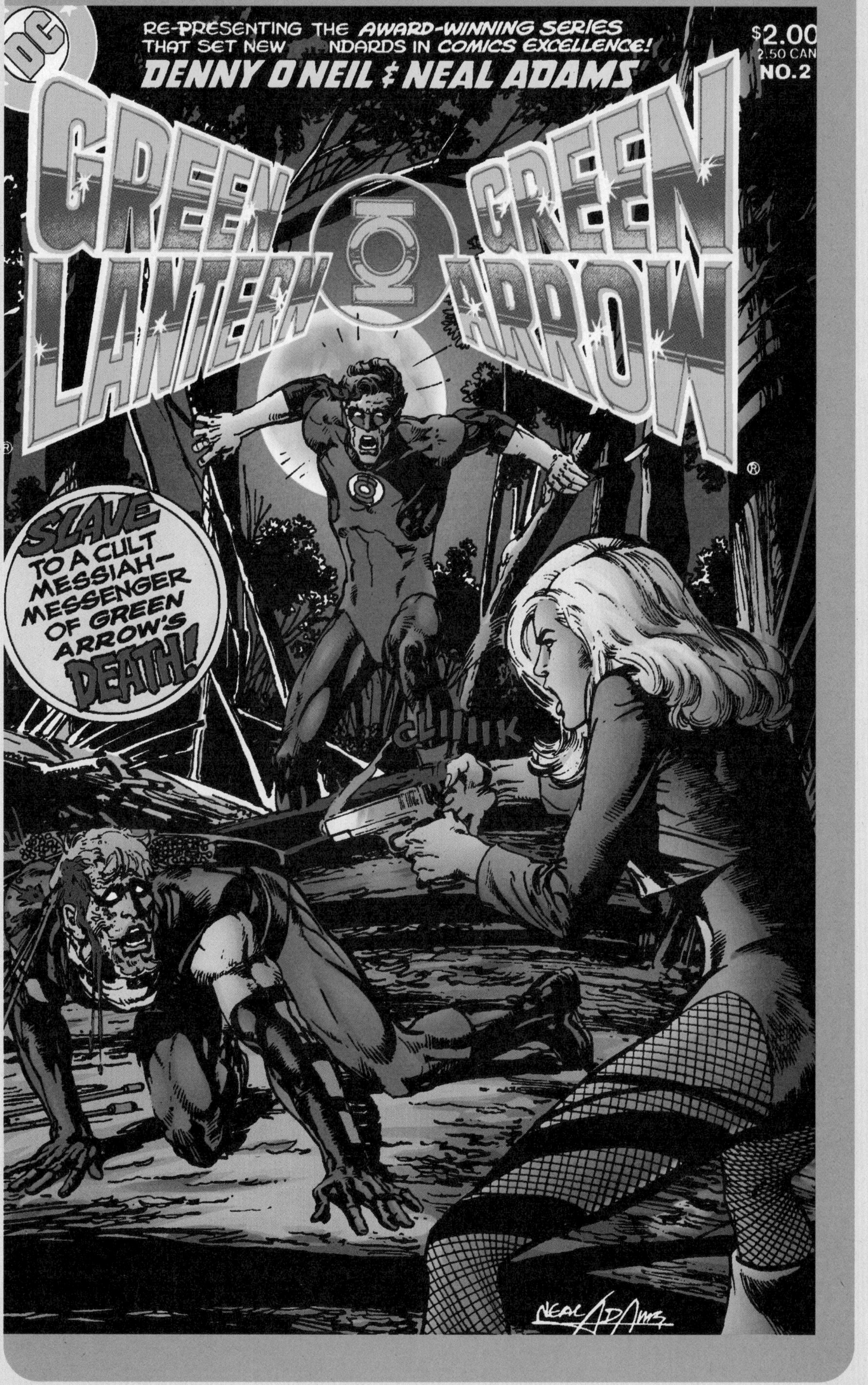

RE-PRESENTING THE AWARD-WINNING SERIES
THAT SET NEW NDARDS IN COMICS EXCELLENCE!
DENNY O'NEIL & NEAL ADAMS
$2.00
2.50 CAN
NO.2
GREEN LANTERN
GREEN ARROW
SLAVE TO A CULT MESSIAH— MESSENGER OF GREEN ARROW'S DEATH!
CLIIIIK
NEAL ADAMS

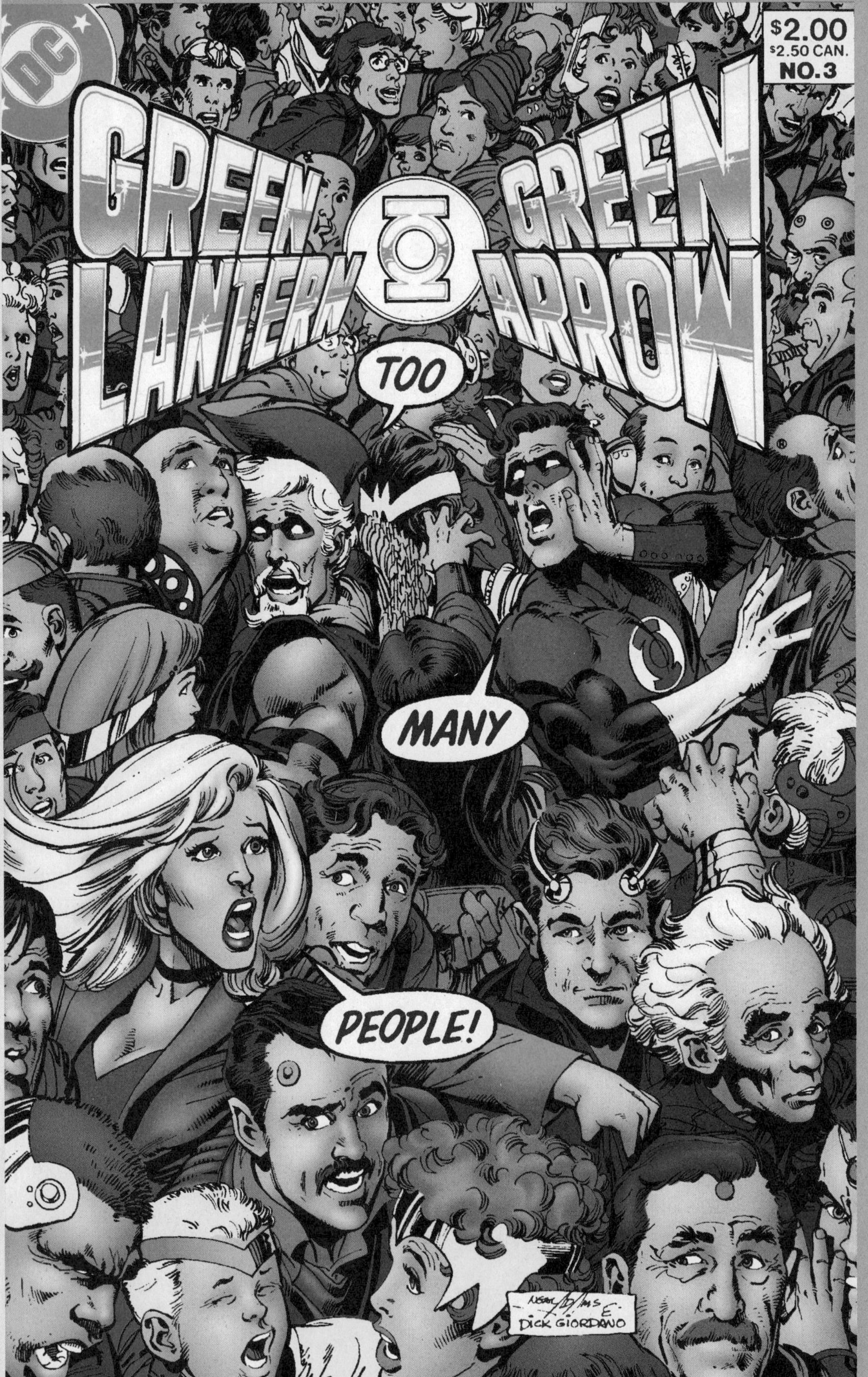

$2.00
$2.50 CAN.
NO.3
GREEN LANTERN
GREEN ARROW
TOO
MANY
PEOPLE!
DICK GIORDANO

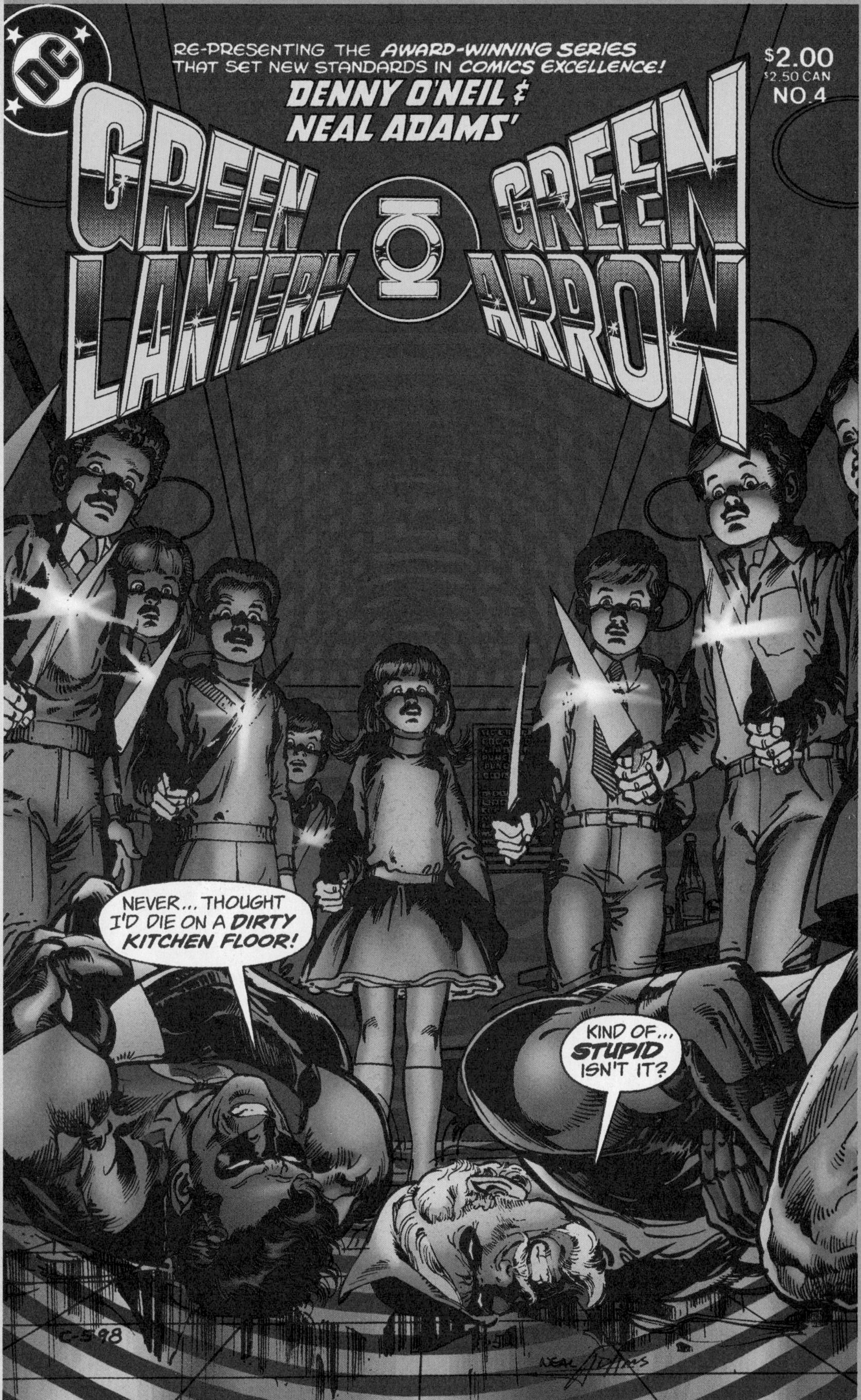
RE-PRESENTING THE AWARD-WINNING SERIES THAT SET NEW STANDARDS IN COMICS EXCELLENCE!
$2.00
$2.50 CAN
NO.4
DENNY O'NEIL & NEAL ADAMS'
GREEN LANTERN
GREEN ARROW
NEVER... THOUGHT I'D DIE ON A DIRTY KITCHEN FLOOR!
KIND OF... STUPID ISN'T IT?

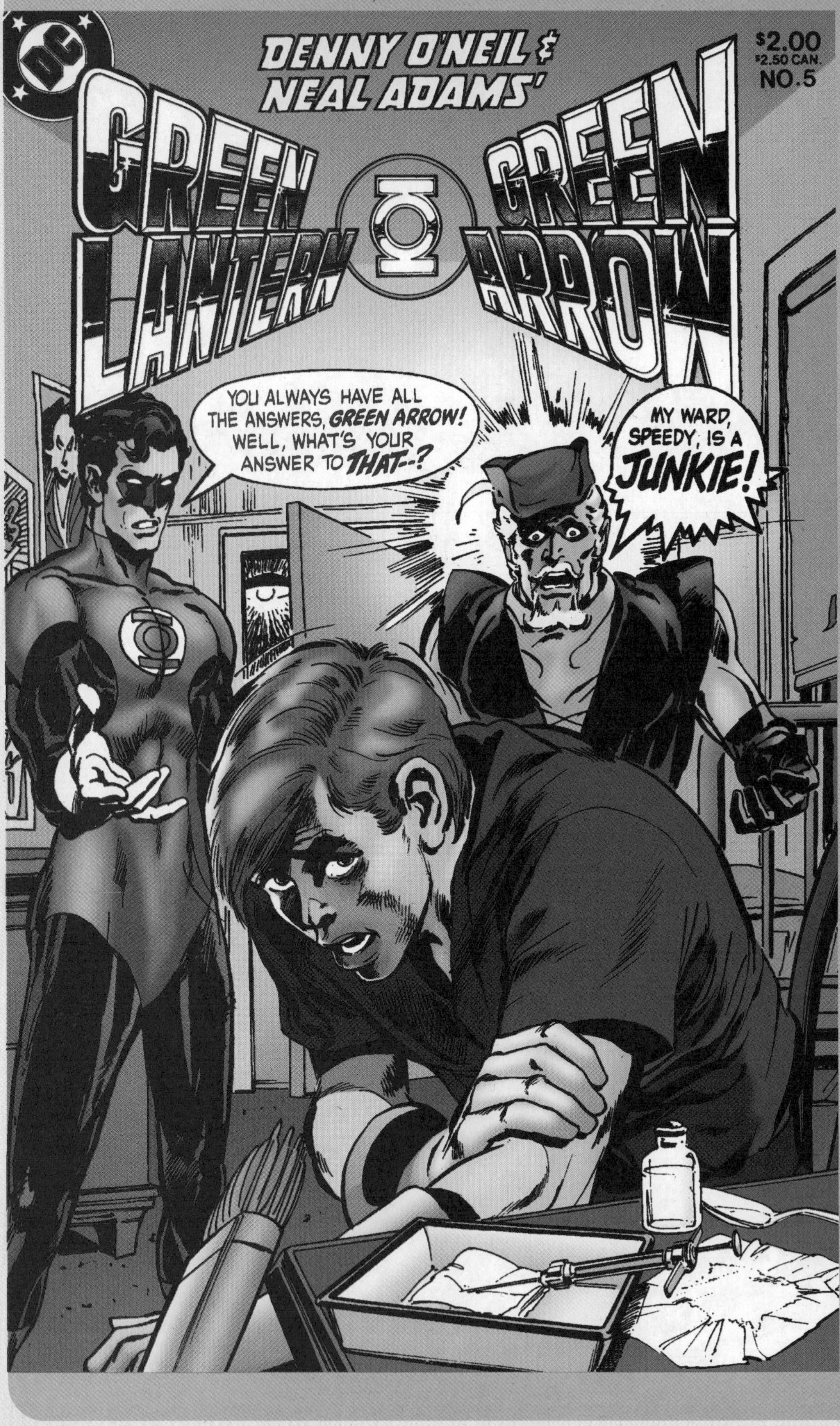
DENNY O'NEIL & NEAL ADAMS'
$2.00
$2.50 CAN.
NO.5
GREEN LANTERN
GREEN ARROW
YOU ALWAYS HAVE ALL THE ANSWERS, GREEN ARROW! WELL, WHAT'S YOUR ANSWER TO THAT--?
MY WARD, SPEEDY, IS A JUNKIE!

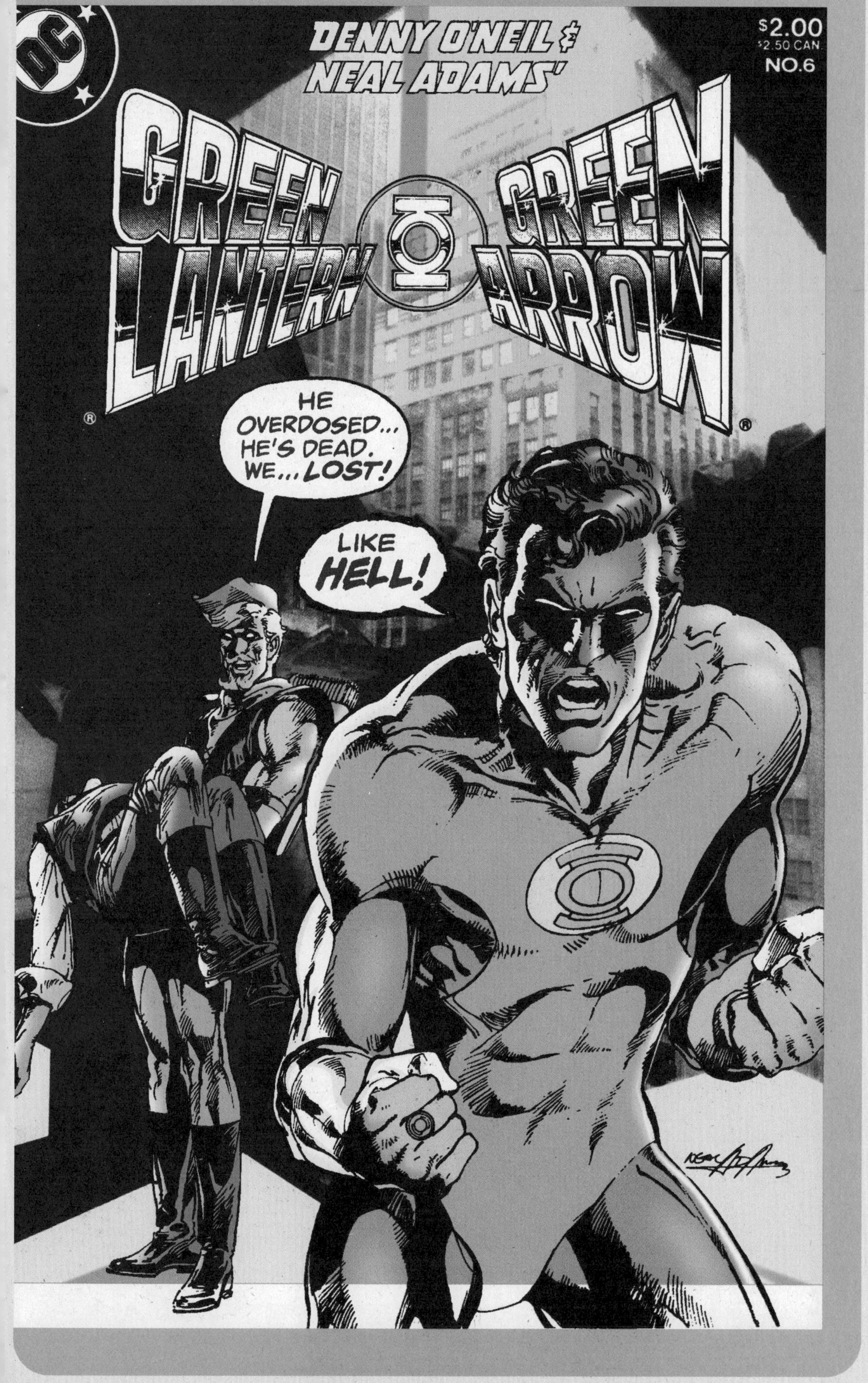

DENNY O'NEIL &
NEAL ADAMS'
$2.00
$2.50 CAN.
NO.6
GREEN LANTERN
GREEN ARROW
HE OVERDOSED... HE'S DEAD. WE... LOST!
LIKE HELL!

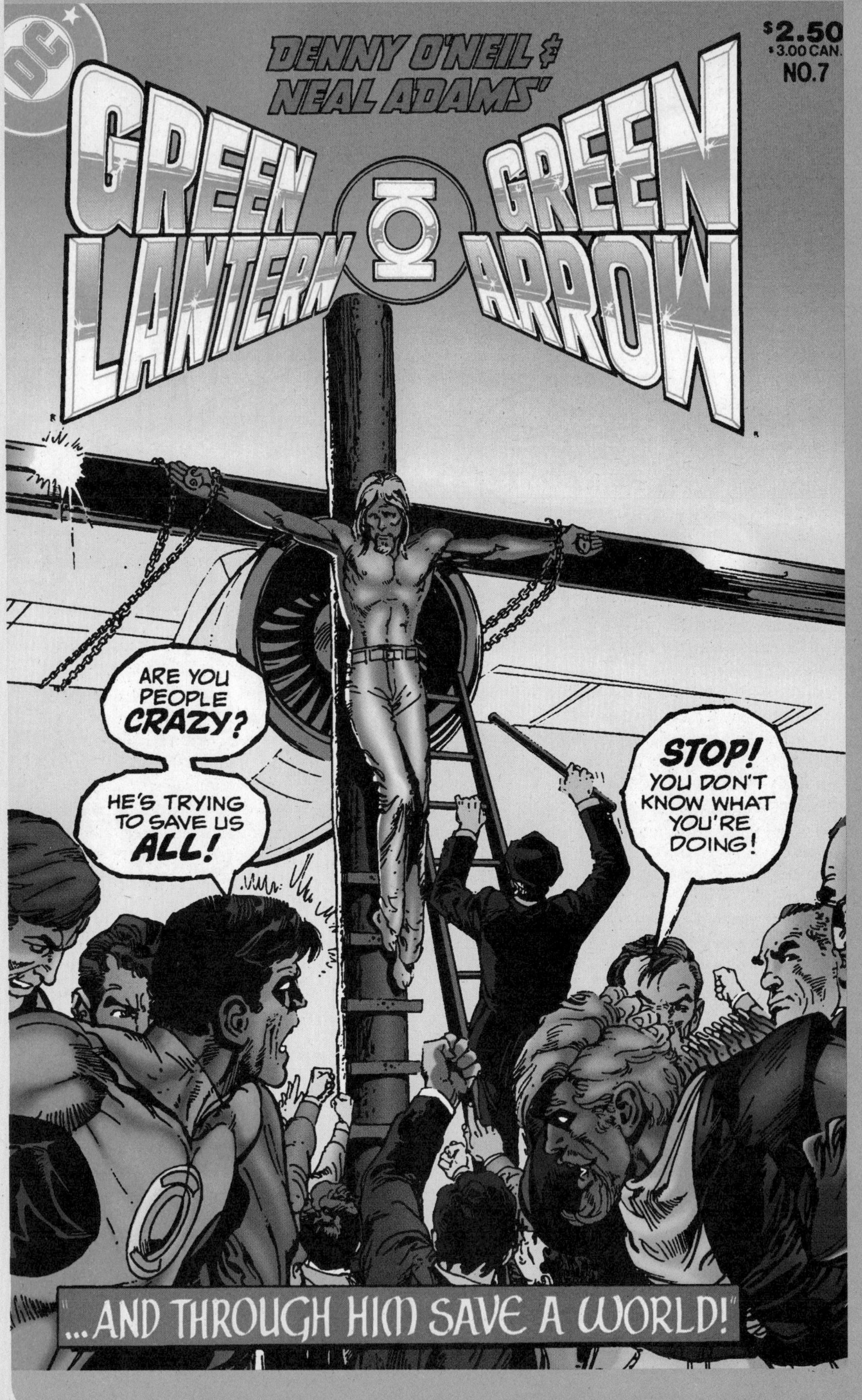

DC
DENNY O'NEIL & NEAL ADAMS'
GREEN LANTERN GREEN ARROW
$2.50
$3.00 CAN.
NO.7
ARE YOU PEOPLE CRAZY?
HE'S TRYING TO SAVE US ALL!
STOP! YOU DON'T KNOW WHAT YOU'RE DOING!
"...AND THROUGH HIM SAVE A WORLD!"

NEAL ADAMS

Born on June 6, 1941 in New York, Neal Adams began his career assisting on and occasionally pencilling the *Bat Masterson* syndicated comic strip. At the same time, Adams did advertising illustration, developing a realistic art style that would become his trademark. From there, Neal went on to a brief stint at Archie Comics and to his own newspaper strip, *Ben Casey*, based on the popular television series. Adams joined DC in 1967 and became an overnight sensation by infusing a new visual vitality into longtime characters. Working closely with Carmine Infantino, Adams quickly became DC's preeminent cover artist during this period, contributing radical and dynamic illustrations to virtually the company's entire line. His work on WORLD'S FINEST COMICS, SUPERMAN, THE SPECTRE, GREEN LANTERN and the Deadman feature made him an instant fan favorite. Adams became one of the most talked-about creator/writer/artist/publishers in the medium and continues to influence, directly and indirectly, today's young comics artists.

DICK GIORDANO

Dick Giordano was part of a creative team that helped change the face of comic books in the late 1960s and early 1970s. Along with writer Dennis O'Neil and penciller Neal Adams, Giordano helped bring Batman back to his roots as a dark, brooding "creature of the night," and brought relevance to comics in the pages of GREEN LANTERN/GREEN ARROW. Giordano began his career as an artist for Charlton Comics in 1952 and became the company's editor-in-chief in 1965. In that capacity, he revamped the Charlton line by adding an emphasis on such heroes as the Question, Captain Atom, and the Blue Beetle. In 1967, Giordano came over to DC for a three-year stint as editor, bringing with him many of the talents who would help shape the industry of the day, including Dennis O'Neil, Jim Aparo, and Steve Skeates. Winner of numerous industry awards, Giordano later returned to DC, rising to the position of Vice President-Executive Editor before "retiring" in 1993 to once again pursue a full-time career as penciller and inker.

ELLIOT S! MAGGIN

Elliot Maggin broke into comics in 1972 with a legendary Green Arrow story originally written as a college treatise. So impressed with Maggin's style was editor Julius Schwartz that Maggin quickly became a key writer in Schwartz's creative stable, penning years of Superman stories as well as the occasional Batman — or, more often, Robin — tale. Now living in California, Maggin continues to write comics as circumstances allow while enjoying a teaching career.

DENNIS O'NEIL

Dennis O'Neil began his career as a comic-book writer in 1965 at Charlton, where then-editor Dick Giordano assigned him to several features. When Giordano moved to DC, O'Neil soon followed. At DC, O'Neil scripted several series for Giordano and Julius Schwartz, quickly becoming one of the most respected writers in comics. O'Neil earned a reputation for being able to "revamp" such characters as Superman, Green Lantern, Captain Marvel — and the Batman, whom O'Neil (with the help of Neal Adams and Giordano) brought back to his roots as a dark, mysterious, gothic avenger. Besides being the most important Batman writer of the 1970s, O'Neil served as an editor at both Marvel and DC. After a long tenure as group editor of the Batman line of titles, he retired to write full-time. O'Neil, fittingly, wrote a Green Lantern novel for Pocket Books, to be published in 2005.

JULIUS SCHWARTZ

Perhaps more than any other editor, Julie Schwartz helped shape the face of the comic-book medium. Born in New York in 1915, Schwartz was one of the earliest and most vocal fans of the literary genre that became known as "science fiction," in time establishing himself as an agent for Ray Bradbury, Henry Kuttner, Robert Bloch and other giants of the SF and fantasy field. Hired as a DC editor in 1944, Schwartz brought an inventiveness and dedication to the craft of storytelling that soon made him a legend in his own right, a man known for employing only the finest and most talented writers and artists in the field. His true legacy, however, came to flower in the 1950s and early 1960s, at a time when the future of comics was at best dubious. Schwartz — together with John Broome, Robert Kanigher, Gardner Fox, and others — revived and revitalized the all but abandoned super-hero genre, transforming such nearly forgotten heroes as the Flash and Green Lantern into super-stars. Julie passed away on February 8, 2004, leaving behind an amazing legacy.

BERNI WRIGHTSON

Born in 1948, Berni Wrightson is best known as the co-creator of the Swamp Thing. He has disturbed impressionable readers for nearly two decades with his uncanny renderings of imaginary horrors. At present he resides in Los Angeles, creating book covers and movie production art. His most recent efforts include covers for Stephen King's *The Dark Tower* series. In Hollywood, he did designs for Lion's Gates' forthcoming *Ghost Rider* film.

THE STARS OF THE

DC UNIVERSE

CAN ALSO BE FOUND IN THESE BOOKS:

GRAPHIC NOVELS

ENEMY ACE: WAR IDYLL
George Pratt

THE FLASH: LIFE STORY OF THE FLASH
M. Waid/B. Augustyn/G. Kane/
J. Staton/T. Palmer

GREEN LANTERN: FEAR ITSELF
Ron Marz/Brad Parker

THE POWER OF SHAZAM!
Jerry Ordway

WONDER WOMAN: AMAZONIA
William Messner-Loebs/
Phil Winslade

COLLECTIONS

THE GREATEST 1950s STORIES EVER TOLD
Various writers and artists

THE GREATEST TEAM-UP STORIES EVER TOLD
Various writers and artists

AQUAMAN: TIME AND TIDE
Peter David/Kirk Jarvinen/
Brad Vancata

DC ONE MILLION
Various writers and artists

THE FINAL NIGHT
K. Kesel/S. Immonen/
J. Marzan/various

THE FLASH: BORN TO RUN
M. Waid/T. Peyer/G. LaRocque/
H. Ramos/various

GREEN LANTERN: A NEW DAWN
R. Marz/D. Banks/R. Tanghal/
various

GREEN LANTERN: BAPTISM OF FIRE
Ron Marz/Darryl Banks/
various

GREEN LANTERN: EMERALD KNIGHTS
Ron Marz/Darryl Banks/
various

HAWK & DOVE
Karl and Barbara Kesel/
Rob Liefeld

HITMAN
Garth Ennis/John McCrea

HITMAN: LOCAL HEROES
G. Ennis/J. McCrea/
C. Ezquerra/S. Pugh

HITMAN: TEN THOUSAND BULLETS
Garth Ennis/John McCrea

IMPULSE: RECKLESS YOUTH
Mark Waid/various

JACK KIRBY'S FOREVER PEOPLE
Jack Kirby/various

JACK KIRBY'S NEW GODS
Jack Kirby/various

JACK KIRBY'S MISTER MIRACLE
Jack Kirby/various

JUSTICE LEAGUE: A NEW BEGINNING
K. Giffen/J.M. DeMatteis/
K. Maguire/various

JUSTICE LEAGUE: A MIDSUMMER'S NIGHTMARE
M. Waid/F. Nicieza/J. Johnson/
D. Robertson/various

JLA: AMERICAN DREAMS
G. Morrison/H. Porter/J. Dell/
various

JLA: JUSTICE FOR ALL
G. Morrison/M. Waid/H. Porter/
J. Dell/various

JUSTICE LEAGUE OF AMERICA: THE NAIL
Alan Davis/Mark Farmer

JLA: NEW WORLD ORDER
Grant Morrison/
Howard Porter/John Dell

JLA: ROCK OF AGES
G. Morrison/H. Porter/J. Dell/
various

JLA: STRENGTH IN NUMBERS
G. Morrison/M. Waid/H. Porter/
J. Dell/various

JLA: WORLD WITHOUT GROWN-UPS
T. Dezago/T. Nauck/H. Ramos/
M. McKone/various

JLA/TITANS: THE TECHNIS IMPERATIVE
D. Grayson/P. Jimenez/
P. Pelletier/various

JLA: YEAR ONE
M. Waid/B. Augustyn/
B. Kitson/various

KINGDOM COME
Mark Waid/Alex Ross

LEGENDS: THE COLLECTED EDITION
J. Ostrander/L. Wein/J. Byrne/
K. Kesel

LOBO'S GREATEST HITS
Various writers and artists

LOBO: THE LAST CZARNIAN
Keith Giffen/Alan Grant/
Simon Bisley

LOBO'S BACK'S BACK
K. Giffen/A. Grant/S. Bisley/
C. Alamy

MANHUNTER: THE SPECIAL EDITION
Archie Goodwin/Walter Simonson

THE RAY: IN A BLAZE OF POWER
Jack C. Harris/Joe Quesada/
Art Nichols

THE SPECTRE: CRIMES AND PUNISHMENTS
John Ostrander/Tom Mandrake

STARMAN: SINS OF THE FATHER
James Robinson/Tony Harris/
Wade von Grawbadger

STARMAN: NIGHT AND DAY
James Robinson/Tony Harris/
Wade von Grawbadger

STARMAN: TIMES PAST
J. Robinson/O. Jimenez/
L. Weeks/various

STARMAN: A WICKED INCLINATION...
J. Robinson/T. Harris/
W. von Grawbadger/various

UNDERWORLD UNLEASHED
M. Waid/H. Porter/
P. Jimenez/various

WONDER WOMAN: THE CONTEST
William Messner-Loebs/
Mike Deodato, Jr.

WONDER WOMAN: SECOND GENESIS
John Byrne

WONDER WOMAN: LIFELINES
John Byrne

DC/MARVEL: CROSSOVER CLASSICS II
Various writers and artists

DC VERSUS MARVEL/ MARVEL VERSUS DC
R. Marz/P. David/D. Jurgens/
C. Castellini/various

THE AMALGAM AGE OF COMICS: THE DC COMICS COLLECTION
Various writers and artists

RETURN TO THE AMALGAM AGE OF COMICS: THE DC COMICS COLLECTION
Various writers and artists

OTHER COLLECTIONS OF INTEREST

CAMELOT 3000
Mike W. Barr/Brian Bolland/
various

RONIN
Frank Miller

WATCHMEN
Alan Moore/Dave Gibbons

ARCHIVE EDITIONS

THE FLASH ARCHIVES Volume 1
(FLASH COMICS 104, SHOWCASE 4, 8, 13, 14, THE FLASH 105-108)
J. Broome/C. Infantino/J. Giella/
various

THE FLASH ARCHIVES Volume 2
(THE FLASH 109-116)
J.Broome/C. Infantino/J. Giella/
various

GREEN LANTERN ARCHIVES Volume 1
(SHOWCASE 22-23, GREEN LANTERN 1-5)

GREEN LANTERN ARCHIVES Volume 2
(GREEN LANTERN 6-13)
All by J. Broome/G. Kane/
J. Giella/various

SHAZAM ARCHIVES Volume 1
(WHIZ COMICS 2-15)

SHAZAM ARCHIVES Volume 2
(SPECIAL EDITION COMICS 1, CAPTAIN MARVEL ADVENTURES 1, WHIZ COMICS 15-20)
All by B. Parker/C.C. Beck/
J. Simon/J. Kirby/various

THE NEW TEEN TITANS Volume 1
(DC COMICS PRESENTS 26, THE NEW TITANS 1-8)
Marv Wolfman/George Pérez/
various

TO FIND MORE COLLECTED EDITIONS AND MONTHLY COMIC BOOKS FROM DC COMICS,
CALL 1-888-COMIC BOOK FOR THE NEAREST COMICS SHOP OR GO TO YOUR LOCAL BOOK STORE.

Visit us at www.dccomics.com

DCU0011